f
TH
812
53
985

THE
SUPERINSULATED
HOME BOOK

THE SUPERINSULATED HOME BOOK

J. D. Ned Nisson
Gautam Dutt

illustrated by
Michael L. Webb

John Wiley & Sons

New York   Chichester   Brisbane   Toronto   Singapore

Library of Congress Cataloging in Publication Data:

Nisson, J. D. Ned.
  The superinsulated home book.

  Includes index.
  1. House construction.   2. Dwellings—Insulation.
3. Dwellings—Energy conservation.   I. Dutt, Gautam.
II. Title.

TH4812.N53   1985   693.8′32   84-21945
ISBN 0-471-88734-X
ISBN 0-471-81343-5

Printed in the United States of America

10 9 8 7 6 5 4 3 2 1

Preface

The energy crisis created a demand for houses that use less energy. Whereas the crisis has passed, the demand persists. For more than a decade, many of the best builders, designers, and researchers have applied their skills toward constructing energy-efficient houses. The result? A vast compendium of new resources and a new body of information about how to use them.

This research is an ongoing process, and superinsulation is its most recent development. Not merely an idea, superinsulation is a method of designing and constructing houses that draws from hundreds of innovative methods and products, *all tested in the field*. In a few short years, superinsulation has become a comprehensible and highly sensible building technology.

The Superinsulated Home Book brings together pertinent information about that technology, for the first time, into one resource volume. In writing this book, it has been our intention to make a usable and valuable construction approach accessible to the interested reader. This book can be used on many levels. It includes scientifically accurate explanations and formulas for researchers and students as well as simple descriptions and explanations for laypersons and homeowners. It is our hope that this book will find its way to field offices and construction sites where it can serve as a practical building guide.

We have endeavored to provide you not only with a description of the superinsulated house as a system, but also with the many details needed to assemble the components of that system into a functional superinsulated house. Part I, *Principles,* includes introductory material, history, and chapters on the fundamentals of insulation and airtightness, proper air quality, and ventilation. Part II, *Practice,* presents details of design and construction for walls, foundations, roofs, windows, and air-vapor barriers, as well as discussions of ventilation systems, heating systems, appliances, and methods of evaluating these. The appendices include useful information that is not readily available in other books. Appendix C, for example, contains degree day data for different base temperatures, and average solar radiation data—information crucial for energy calculations relating to superinsulated houses.

In preparing this book, we have relied heavily on the first-hand experience of hundreds of people to whom we wish to express our gratitude. We would like to express particular gratitude to Harold Orr of the Canadian National Research Council, who supplied much of the groundwork upon which the book is based. For their careful review and criticism of the manuscript, we would also like to express our gratitude to William Shurcliff of Harvard University, Howard Faulkner of the University of Southern Maine, Bob Corbett of Superinsulation Designs, and Edward Allen, A.I.A.

For their support and technical review, we would like to thank Robert Socolow, David Jacobson, and Kenneth Gadsby, all of Princeton University, Howard Geller of the American Council for an Energy-Efficient Economy, and Harvey Sachs of the National Indoor Environmental Institute. For a superlative job of organizing and editing the manuscript, we extend our appreciation to Diana Amsterdam. Also, of course, special thanks to Michael Webb, our illustrious illustrator, and to Cathy Ennis for her help in preparing the manuscript.

We would like to thank our reviewers for their constructive suggestions and comments: Jennifer R. Wang, Owens-Corning Fiberglass, Toledo, Ohio; Stewart Byrne, Owens-Corning Fiberglass, Toledo, Ohio; G. Z. Brown, University of Oregon, Eugene, Oregon; and Alan Meier, Lawrence Berkeley Laboratory, Berkeley, California. Finally, special thanks to David Eyre of the Saskatchewan Research Council for allowing us to excerpt information from "Air-Vapour Barriers;" and to the National Center for Appropriate Technology for letting us use text and illustrations from "Heat Recovery Ventilation for Houses." We hope their contributions and ours will help pave the way for superinsulation building technology to become standard practice.

J. D. Ned Nisson
Gautam Dutt
January, 1985

Contents

II PRACTICE

THE
SUPERINSULATED
HOME BOOK

PART I   PRINCIPLES

One

Superinsulation: background and benefits

Superinsulation—the word conjures up images of extraordinary insulating powers and magical levels of energy conservation. True, superinsulated houses can be superbly energy-efficient, with annual heating bills little more than the cost of one or two nights in a good hotel. However, the technology of superinsulation is common sense—not magic. Encompassing both a new design concept and a collection of construction details, superinsulation is the most recent—and the most widely applicable—development in the evolution of energy efficient house design.

Until the "energy crisis" of 1974, energy-efficient housing was not much of an issue in the United States. However, high energy bills in the seventies created a demand for houses that people could afford not only to buy, but to live in. Since then, despite fluctuations in the cost of conventional fuel, energy efficiency has consistently remained a prime factor in house selection, as evidenced by surveys both in the private and public sectors. Moreover, government figures and the opinions of experts suggest that average energy costs for all U.S. households will continue to rise.

These were some of the reasons for the birth—and continuing growth—of energy-efficient housing technology. The first developments involved solar energy. Early research demonstrated that enough solar energy falls on the roof of the average house to replace all or most of the fossil fuel burned in the furnace or boiler. The question was: how to harness that "free" energy for home heating? At first it was thought that all that was needed was to build solar collectors on the roof and to install a thermal storage device in the basement. This kind of heating, called "active solar," gave rise to a new industry and led to the development of many ingenious types of collectors. But unfortunately, active solar space heating proved too expensive and too complicated for widespread application.

The next step was the marriage of engineering and architecture called "passive solar" design, an innovative concept that asked a few simple questions: Why bother with all that solar hardware? Why not simply let the sun shine into the house through large south-facing windows? Passive solar design certainly makes sense, as evidenced by thousands of new houses that get much of their space-heating energy from the sun.

But there was one question that remained unasked throughout the evolution of solar design. It is a question that takes a step back, preceding common suppositions about space-heating energy requirements. *Is all that energy really necessary?* Whether it comes from the sun, from oil, from gas, or from electricity, energy is difficult and often expensive to provide. (Although solar energy itself is free, collecting and storing it in active or passive solar-heated houses increases the cost of the house.) How about designing a house that *needs less energy to stay warm* in the first place? Before we think about satisfying the heating demand, is there a practical way to first *reduce* that demand? The answer is yes.

The answer is *superinsulation*: a method of design and construction that can reduce energy demand so drastically that a house hardly needs any heating system at all. What's more, the method called superinsulation can be employed without sacrificing comfort, health, or aesthetics, and at relatively little extra cost.

Superinsulation represents the current evolutionary stage in energy-efficient design.

WHAT IS A SUPERINSULATED HOUSE?

In this chapter, we have included photographs of many superinsulated houses. As can be readily seen, they are all different. What, then, distinguishes a superinsulated house from any other?

One essential feature: superinsulated houses lose so little heat they need much less energy, solar or otherwise, for space heating and cooling. The houses pictured in this chapter, for example, consume remarkably small amounts of fuel annually, ranging from $30 for the Buffalo Homes house (Figure 1.6) to $300 for the Rideau River Residence (Figure 1.11).

If one did not know these houses' annual fuel consumption, it would be difficult, at first glance, to distinguish them from others. *Superinsulation is a design tool, not a design type.* Builders' favorite designs—from ranch to colonial, Victorian to contemporary split level—can be superinsulated. Single family houses, two-story houses, row houses, attached houses—*any kind of residential or light commercial construction can be and has been superinsulated, on sites as far south as Georgia and as far north as the Arctic Circle.*

Just looking at a house does not immediately reveal whether it is superinsulated. What about cutting a cross section from a wall and studying the thickness of the insulation? This isn't a gauge of superinsulation either. For while *amount* of insulation is important, it's only one part of a carefully thought-out *system* designed to minimize heat loss and energy waste.

Every feature of a house—walls, windows, attic, basement, framing, site orientation, heating system, ventilation system—is different in a superinsulated structure. Conventional building methods have not been discarded. Rather, they have been subtly but pervasively rethought to meet one goal: using energy efficiently.

If we all saw with the eyes of a builder of superinsulated houses, conventional houses would seem like sieves leaking preposterous amounts of heat and thus wasting energy and money. Using large amounts of fuel to heat relatively small areas is commonplace and has become accepted; but it *isn't* necessary. The investment value of a superinsulated house is its capacity to function at an efficient level that uses *every* dollar spent for energy to its maximum potential. The aesthetic value is found in heightened comfort, quiet, and coziness: the resident of a superinsulated house can stand, for instance, inches from his or her outer wall or even from a window on a cold, stormy day and feel not the slightest draft.

The Thermal Envelope

The first step in understanding a superinsulated house is to think of an artificially created (heated) environment separated from the larger (unheated) environment by a physical boundary, or shell. When discussing space heating and cooling, this boundary is referred to as the **thermal envelope**. In superinsulated houses, the thermal envelope is never regarded haphazardly: it is carefully defined, and once defined, every possible precaution is taken to make certain that the envelope is insulated and sealed.

Correctly defining the thermal envelope is one of the first steps in planning a superinsulated structure. Should the envelope enclose the living room, bedroom, kitchen, and bathroom, but leave out the attic, basement, crawl space, and garage? This is the conventional approach—thinking of the envelope as encompassing only the space actually intended to be heated (or cooled).

The superinsulation approach is somewhat different: the thermal envelope broadens in scope to include not only the primary heated/cooled spaces but, in some cases, secondary spaces as well. For instance, the basement, even though it doesn't have to be kept warm, is often included in the thermal envelope of superinsulated houses; therefore the boundary between the basement and the outside is carefully insulated and sealed. This alternate configuration creates a more effective thermal padding around the primary living area of a house.

Defining the thermal envelope is one of the decisions, based on economics, aesthetics and efficiency, that must be made when designing a superinsulated structure. Once defined, however, the thermal envelope in *every* superinsulated house is treated the same: *It is made airtight and insulated as effectively as possible.*

Airtightness

If quantities of warm air are allowed to escape from a house, energy will be wasted because the air leaking out is replaced by cold air that must be heated.

In conventional houses, **air leakage**, or what is called **exfiltration** and **infiltration**, occurs unintentionally through so many chinks, gaps, cracks, and imperfect closures that the air in an average conventional house "turns over"—is replaced by entirely new air—.5 to 3 times *per hour*! The heating or cooling system must work longer to maintain temperature.

Superinsulated houses are designed and built to guard against air leakage. Airtight construction—meaning careful attention to all potential leaks in the thermal envelope—is essential. Windows, doors, utility entrances, and every other penetration or seam in the building envelope are carefully sealed.

Controlled Ventilation

Uncontrolled air leakage, which is the norm in most houses, is sometimes thought necessary for adequate ventilation. This is a myth. Although air leakage does mean that fresh air can get into a house, the presence of that fresh air is erratic and problematic. Air that enters unintentionally can make a house too dry, cause moisture problems, and cause too much ventilation in some places and not enough in others; and it needs to be continuously heated or cooled.

Superinsulated houses are airtight, and residents of airtight houses must rely on controlled ventilation systems.

Figure 1.1 The Sklare House. That superinsulation does not preclude "curb appeal" is easily demonstrated by this house built by Bay Development Corporation, Indianapolis, Indiana. Annual heating costs are roughly $150 in this 6100 degree-day climate. (Photo by Bruce Sklare.)

This can be put another way. Residents of airtight houses are fortunate enough to reap the benefits of controlled ventilation, which include uniform temperatures throughout the house; freedom from drafts; freedom from humidity problems; and fresh air at all times. Ventilation is supplied by one of several types of systems, which generally includes an *air-to-air heat exchanger* which makes it possible to recover and reuse heat from the outgoing air.

By the way, windows in superinsulated houses can be and are often opened. Superinsulated houses are *not* sealed boxes: they are at least as well ventilated as most other houses. However, ventilation in a superinsulated house is intentional, not erratic.

Insulation

Every material has a certain degree of resistance to heat transmission. Those with high **thermal resistance** are useful as thermal insulation in buildings. A material's thermal resistance is measured by its **R-value**; the higher the R-value, the greater the resistance to heat transmission. The most popular insulation materials, such as fiberglass, cellulose and plastic foam, have R-values ranging from R-3.0 to R-7.0 per inch. In Chapter 2 we will show how R-value is related to heat loss in houses.

Superinsulated houses are generally characterized by a high R-value created by insulation and structural building materials. Walls are typically between R-25 and R-40; ceilings range from R-35 to R-65. Windows are at least R-2 and sometimes higher than R-4. Foundations are insulated below grade to nearly the same levels as above grade walls.

As we will emphasize again and again, *the key to superinsulation is not just the purchase of insulation with high R-value, but its installation in a way that makes it work to maximum efficacy.* A truly effective insulation system, for example, reduces or eliminates many or all *thermal defects* present in ordinary construction—defects such as insulation voids, thermal bridges, and convective loops. Techniques and details for designing and constructing a flawless insulation system constitute much of superinsulation building practice.

Passive Solar Features

Many superinsulated houses contain no space heating furnace or boiler at all. Where do they get heat? Some heat may come from small space heaters; more commonly, however, it comes from people, pets, light bulbs, appliances—and the sun.

On a sunny day, more than 200 Btu/hr (59 watts) shines in through a square foot of window glass during midday hours. If a house at 40° N latitude has 60 sq. ft. of glass facing east and 60 sq. ft. facing south, the solar heat input on a sunny day will be about 20,500 Btu/hr (6000 watts) from 9 A.M. till noon. The amount of solar energy gained depends on the area, type, and orientation of windows and the amount of shading. In superinsulated houses, windows are placed predominantly in the south and east walls to afford maximum solar heat input. Solar energy through windows is the simplest form of passive solar heating. Trombe walls, water walls, sunspaces, wall collectors, and other more sophisticated passive solar features *can* be integrated into superinsulated house design, but they are seldom necessary.

What, then, is a superinsulated house? It is a house whose thermal envelope is carefully designed and meticulously insulated and sealed; it is a house characterized by airtightness, high and efficient levels of insulation, controlled ventilation, and passive solar features.

HISTORY

The roots of superinsulation predate the energy crisis, extending back to the mid-1960s when two men, Harry Tschumi and Les Blades, were interested in promoting the use of heat pumps. Tschumi sold heat pumps and Blades worked for the Arkansas Power and Light Company. Around 1961, they "discovered" that by increasing insulation levels and improving window thermal performance, houses could be made to use much less energy and be better suited for heat pump applications. At that time, however, with low energy prices, few homeowners wanted to pay the extra construction costs.

It wasn't until 1974 that Frank Holtzclaw, a housing analyst working for the U.S. Department of Housing and Urban Development (HUD), brought Tschumi's ideas to fruition. Holtzclaw initiated what was to become known as the "Arkansas Project," a series of radically designed "superinsulated" houses that were not only very energy efficient, but also inexpensive! Between 1974 and 1975, thirty-five homes were built and their energy consumption monitored. Annual heating and cooling costs were about $130—low, even at 1975 energy prices. The Arkansas houses had 6-inch walls with R-19 fiberglass insulation and a special "raised heel" roof truss, now commonly referred to as the "Arkansas Truss."

The man usually credited with coining the term "superinsulation" is Wayne Schick, an architect with the Small Homes Council at the University of Ilinois at Urbana-Champaign. Together with several other faculty members, he had been working since the 1940s on methods of increasing the thermal performance of houses. Legend has it that while lecturing about energy savings from increased levels of insulation, Schick made reference to a maximum practical level and called it "super" insulation. In 1976, Schick's team developed a design known as the "Lo-Cal" house. It included double 2 × 4 walls with R-30 insulation, ceilings insulated to R-40, and double glazed windows with most of the glass on the south side of the house. Computer simulations indicated that a house built to the Lo-Cal design would need one-third as much heating energy as specified in the newly created HUD standards. Schick's team never built a Lo-Cal house, but many of the details of that design are incorporated into present-day superinsulation techniques.

If it's a good idea, it's worth patenting. That must have been Richard Bentley's thought when he applied for U.S. Patent #3,969,860, issued on July 20, 1976, for a "Thermal Efficiency Structure." Working independently, Bentley developed and patented a design for a double-wall house, using an innovative truss sytem. His patent stresses the need for airtightness and also includes a site-built heat recovery ventilation system (air-to-air heat exchanger). Bentley and his family built a few houses to his design, and although he hasn't gained much publicity, he is definitely one of the originators of the concept of superinsulation.

That superinsulation could really perform incredibly well was first demonstrated to the American public by two well-publicized houses in distant parts of the continent—the Saskatchewan Conservation Home (Figure 1.2), built by the Canadian government, and the Leger House (Figure 1.3), built by Eugene Leger. The Saskatchewan Conservation Home was built in 1977 by a Canadian team headed by David Eyre of the Saskatchewan Research Council. It is surely one of the most energy-efficient houses ever constructed—probably the first superinsulated house to demonstrate that airtight construction is practical and can drastically reduce energy consumption. The 12-inch thick walls are filled with R-44 insulation; the ceiling is insulated to over R-60. But the most distinctive feature is its airtightness. A continuous airtight membrane

Figure 1.2 The Saskatchewan Conservation House. Located in Saskatoon, Saskatchewan (12,000 degree days), this experimental house was originally built to demonstrate 100-percent solar heating. But the solar collector array on the roof was removed after the first year. Annual heating costs without the solar collectors are about $35 per year. (Photo by Harold Orr.)

was carefully installed under the supervision of Harold Orr of the Canadian National Research Council. The end result was an air leakage rate far below that of conventional houses. To ensure adequate fresh air and indoor air quality, a ventilation system with air-to-air heat exchanger was incorporated into the design.

Of course, the most fantastic aspect of this house is its energy performance. When the outdoor temperature is −10°F, the total heat demand is about 3000 watts (10,640 Btu per hour), or less than the average output of a clothes dryer. With the shutters closed, no people in the house, and no heat sources inside, the house cools down at a rate of less than 1°F per hour. Originally, an expensive array of evacuated tube solar collectors were in-

Figure 1.3 The Leger House. Built by Gene Leger in 1979, this was one of the first houses that proved that superinsulation was practical for U.S. climates. A domestic water heater is the main heating system, and annual heating costs are well under $100. It is located in eastern Massachusetts.

Figure 1.4 The Johnston House. Located in Gorham Maine (7700 degree days). This 1540 square foot cape has an annual heating bill of about $150. It was designed and built by Roki Associates, Standish, Maine. (Photo by Howard Faulkner.)

Figure 1.5 Interior view of the Johnston House. Just about the only way to tell a superinsulated house is by the extra wide window sills which, as this photo illustrates, provide an attractive and functional feature to the house interior. (Photo by Howard Faulkner.)

stalled on the roof. According to Harold Orr, the total annual heating cost would be about $35 (Canadian, at 1978 energy costs), even without the solar heating system. The project managers were quick to realize that it would be very hard to justify a $10,000 solar heating system to displace $35 worth of fuel per year. The solar collectors were removed.

The Saskatchewan Conservation Home is an example of extreme applications of superinsulation technology. Neither its enormously thick insulation systems nor its general design is likely to be widely acceptable to the housing market. But the experience gained in building it has affected superinsulation more than any other project. *It proved an important principle: it is possible to design and build a comfortable house that needs almost no heat.*

At about the same time that the Saskatchewan Home was constructed, a builder named Eugene Leger was inventing a superinsulated house design in eastern Massachusetts. Leger's design also included double walls and extremely airtight construction, although many of his framing details were quite different from those of the Lo-Cal design or the Saskatchewan Conservation Home. His first house, the Leger House, required so little space heat

that the requirements could be met by using a regular-size domestic water heater with no need for a furnace or boiler. The annual heating bill was $40. Unlike the Saskatchewan house, Leger's house looks like millions of conventional American houses and costs only slightly more to build. Leger and his house were widely publicized. Needless to say the public was impressed by the Leger House, which proved that superinsulation was practical and economical.

With the technical feasibility of superinsulation established, the next natural step was to hand it over to the professional building industry and observe the results. Three projects in the United States and Canada did just that with surprising outcomes.

The first was the Energy Showcase Project. In 1979 and 1980, fourteen superinsulated houses were built by private builders with technical assistance from researchers at the Canadian NRC and Saskatchewan Research Council, some of whom had been involved in building the original Saskatchewan Conservation Home. The results were outstanding. Many of the homes had annual fuel bills under $100 and all were less than $200. Although mistakes were made, those houses still serve as models for much of the superinsulation construction done today.

A similar project was sponsored in the United States by the State of Minnesota's Housing Finance Agency. They initiated a demonstration program in which builders put up 140 houses designed to meet a set of minimum performance standards. The builders were given complete flexibility, except for the single requirement that calculated energy use meet the mandatory standards. The houses included a variety of passive solar and superinsulated designs. Completed in 1981 and monitored the following year, most of the houses performed better than predicted.

SHURCLIFF'S RECOGNITION OF SUPERINSULATION

Leger described his house in a letter to William Shurcliff, a Harvard physicist and noted author of books on solar-heated houses. Shurcliff was so impressed by Leger's design that within a few days of getting the letter, he put out the following press release.

PRESS RELEASE
FROM WILLIAM A. SHURCLIFF
     19 APPLETON ST.
     CAMBRIDGE, MASSACHUSETTS
     02138

JUNE 29, 1979

ARRIVAL OF A FIFTH KIND OF SOLAR HEATING SYSTEM FOR A HOUSE

Everyone knows that a solar heated house may employ
    an active system
    a direct-gain passive system
    an indirect-gain passive system, and
    a hybrid system.
But is there not a fifth kind—just now being born?

I think so. Consider the Saskatchewan Energy Conserving Demonstration House. Or consider the Leger House in Pepperell Mass. They fit none of the four listed categories.

The essence of the new category is:

1. Truly superb insulation. Not just thick, but clever and thorough. Excellent insulation is provided even at the most difficult places: sills, headers, foundation walls, windows, electric outlet boxes, etc.
2. Envelope of house is practically airtight. Even on the windiest days the rate of air change is very low.
3. No provision of extra-large thermal mass. (Down with Trombe walls! Down with water-filled drums and thick concrete floors!)
4. No provision of extra-large south windows. Use normal number and size of south windows—say 100 square feet.
5. No conventional furnace. Merely steal a little heat, when and if needed, from the domestic hot water system. Or use a miniscule amount of electrical heating.
6. No conventional distribution system for such auxiliary heat. Inject the heat at one spot and let it diffuse throughout the house.
7. No weird shape of house, no weird architecture.
8. No big added expense. The costs of the extra insulation and extra care in construction are largely offset by the savings realized from not having huge areas of expensive Thermopane, not having huge well-sealed insulating shutters for huge south windows, not having a furnace or a big heat distribution system.
9. The passive solar heating is very modest—almost incidental.
10. Room humidity remains near 50 percent all winter. No need for humidifiers.
11. In summer the house stays cool automatically. There is no tendency for the south side to become too hot—because the south window area is small and the windows are shaded by eaves.

What name should be given to this new system? Superinsulated passive? Super-save passive? Mini-need passive? Micro-load passive? I lean toward "micro-load passive."

Whatever it is called, it has (I predict) a big future.

(Shurcliff didn't stop with his press release. He continued investigating on his own and wrote a book, completed that same year, called *Superinsulated and Double-Envelope Houses,* published privately by the author and later by Brick House Publishing Co.)

HOW MUCH MORE DOES IT COST TO BUILD A SUPERINSULATED HOUSE?

Given the extraordinary attractiveness and benefits of superinsulated houses, one must naturally ask: "OK, great! But how much extra will I have to pay for all those features?" Unfortunately, the answer to that question is very difficult to pin down. Obviously there are extra costs for materials: insulation, plastic air/vapor barrier, extra framing lumber, more expensive windows, a ventilation system, and possibly an air-to-air heat exchanger. Labor costs also increase: air/vapor barrier installation, possibly some extra framing, and more careful construction in general. Balanced against extra costs are savings from downsizing and the possible elimination of central heating system and chimney.

The actual cost of superinsulation is elusive for the following reasons:

1. There is no accepted "base case" with which to compare a superinsulated house. Does superinsulation cost more . . . than what? When compared with a pre-1970 house with minimum insulation and high air leakage, a superinsulated house costs considerably more. But when compared with many of the conventional houses built today with 6-inch walls and foam sheathing, a superinsulated house costs only marginally more.

2. Superinsulation covers a broad spectrum of design types. Some require significant "retooling" and modification of construction sequence; others entail mostly extra materials with little change in the construction process. The extra cost for any specific superinsulation design depends in part on the builder. Some custom builders, with one or two framing crews, find it easy to adapt to the changes in framing patterns or construction sequence because their framing crews are used to lots of variation from house to house. To them, switching to superinsulation is less expensive than for the tract builder, with twenty or thirty framing crews, who can frame a conventional house in two days with their eyes closed, but might get slowed down considerably when confronted with some of the modifications involved in superinsulation construction.

While researching this book, we interviewed many builders and designers of superinsulated houses. Despite the variables mentioned above, we found a certain range of agreement about the extra cost. Surprisingly, the extra cost does not seem to be proportional to house size. For example, a case study presented as part of the Canadian R2000 Program showed that the extra cost for superinsulating a 700-square-foot house was $4350. But a similar case study, performed by Superinsulation Ltd., a design and consulting firm in Minnesota, examined case studies for six different types of superinsulated houses and found that the extra cost ranged from $4500 to $5500 for a 2000-square-foot house. With few exceptions, most builders interviewed agreed that superinsulation added between $4000 and $8000 to the selling price of their houses.

One surprising and paradoxical result was that houses with intentionally expanded areas of south-facing glass for passive solar heating tended to use *more* heating energy than those with average amounts of south glass. Thus it was proven possible to achieve as much or more energy efficiency without resorting to extra-large south-facing glass. The project created a great deal of interest.

Several of the builders continued building superinsulated houses.

The superinsulated housing industry was born in the United States.

Canada sponsored a third program for builders in 1982–83, called the R2000 Program. Designed to encourage superinsulated construction in Canada, the project offered free training and a small subsidy to offset extra costs. Each design had to meet certain energy performance standards and each house had to pass a test for airtightness after construction. Design and construction assistance were based on experience gained during the Saskatchewan Energy Showcase Project. Over 1000 homes were built through this project.

The subsequent story is difficult to trace. Nobody knows how many superinsulated houses have been built, and any attempt to catalog them would surely be frustrated by the lack of generally accepted criteria for defining superinsulation. A conservative estimate puts the number at 10,000 in the United States and Canada; 20,000 is more likely. At the time of this writing, the word "superinsulation" is beginning to crop up in popular magazines and newspapers all across the country, and more and more builders are making superinsulation an option for their customers. Without the urgent impetus created by an energy crisis, however, superinsulation is likely to be accepted slowly and soberly by the public and the building community.

THE SUPERB FUNCTIONING OF SUPERINSULATED STRUCTURES

When enough superinsulation features are incorporated into a house, the overall *heat loss is reduced to the point where the house behaves differently from ordinary houses*. It can be kept warm, even during cold, cloudy weather, with tiny space heaters. The homeowner may happily discover his or her space heating cost is lower than the water heating cost.

At this point, the house can be considered "superinsulated."

Reduced Heat Loss and Lowered Fuel Bills

The heat loss of a superinsulated house is 60 to 80 percent lower than that of conventional houses, and at the same time annual fuel costs are reduced by 80 to 90 percent or more. Why does this happen?

There are three main sources of heat in a house: intrinsic, solar, and auxiliary. **Intrinsic heat** is produced by people, animals, lights, and appliances. **Solar heat** comes mainly through windows. **Auxiliary heat** is supplied by a furnace or another heating system.

A conventional house loses so much heat that to replace it, the auxiliary heating system must keep pumping away. In fact, most residents of conventional houses never even consider the heating potential of light bulbs, German shepherds, and picture windows because, in conventional houses, intrinsic and solar heat constitute only a small fraction of the overall heat produced.

Let's start adding hypothetical superinsulation features to a conventional house. Fill up the gaps and cracks; now

less heat is lost, and the furnace needs to run less often. Add insulation in the right places; even less heat is lost, and the furnace needs to run *even* less. Triple glaze the windows; even *less* heat escapes, and the furnace's "on" time is further reduced. Shore up those last air leaks and add more insulation; now, so little heat escapes that the furnace doesn't need to come on at all. The house, at this point, can be kept warm solely by intrinsic and solar heat.

Because of their low heat loss, superinsulated houses can often be heated *solely* by intrinsic and solar heat even when outdoor temperatures are extremely low. For example, the Saskatchewan Conservation Home often stays warm without auxiliary heat even when the outdoor temperature falls as low as 10°F! If we define heating season as the period during which a house needs auxiliary heat to maintain a comfortable indoor temperature, then one consequence of superinsulation is to effectively *shorten the heating season*. While conventional houses in cold climates often need auxiliary heat from October to April, a superinsulated house may need it only for one or two months during the dead of winter. The heating season is shortened from seven months to two or three months.

That's why a superinsulated house costs only 10 to 20 percent as much to keep 100 percent as warm as a conventional house.

Energy-Sensitive Inside, Weather-Impervious Outside

Because of their remarkably low rate of heat loss, superinsulated houses are highly sensitive to relatively small energy flows within the thermal envelope. A seemingly insignificant addition of heat—say, a clothes dryer running all afternoon—will significantly help to maintain acceptable indoor temperatures. The homeowner who said, "I heat with cats" *was* exaggerating; but nonetheless his words are not without truth.

This indoor "energy sensitivity" makes it possible to get away with a very small heating system—in fact, finding small enough furnaces or boilers is often a problem. Superinsulated houses are typically so sensitive that even moderate amounts of incidental sunshine coming through regular size windows can supply 50 to 80 percent of home heating requirements. Along these lines, while conventional solar structures require specially rigged areas of *thermal mass*, such as concrete or water tanks, to absorb and store excess solar heat, superinsulated structures are so sensitive that the *intrinsic thermal mass* of walls, furniture, etc., is sufficient for everyday heat storage.

While the superinsulated house is so sensitive on the inside, the combination of intrinsic thermal mass and high insulation levels makes it nearly impervious to shifts in outdoor temperature and wind conditions. Sudden outdoor drops in temperature are not felt indoors for many

Figure 1.6 Modular superinsulated house. Located in Butte, Montana (8000 degree days), this 2000-square-foot modular house has an annual heating cost of less than $30. It was designed and built by Buffalo Homes, Butte, Montana. (Photo by Brian Curran.)

hours, if at all. Often an entire cold night, even during a winter storm, will pass without indoor temperature having been affected, and without the homeowner having to turn on the furnace.

THE BENEFITS OF SUPERINSULATION

The Most Obvious Benefit: Savings in Energy and Dollars

The superinsulated house in Figure 1.6 uses about $30 worth of energy per year for space heating. While not all superinsulated houses perform quite this well, savings consistently range from 60 to 99 percent of the heating costs of conventional pre-1980 housing.

In other words, a homeowner living in a conventional house pays $1700 annually for heat, while a homeowner in a similarly sized superinsulated house pays $200. Not

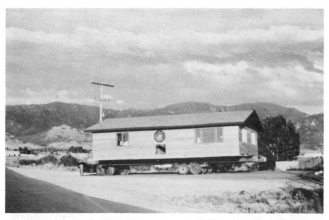

Figure 1.7 A Buffalo Homes superinsulated house on the road. These houses are all pressure tested for airtightness before leaving the yard and after installation. (Photo by Brian Curran.)

only is the second homeowner saving money, but he or she may also enjoy conserving energy and enjoy the security of being protected by a hedge against energy prices, which, though not skyrocketing as they were in the mid-seventies, are projected to rise steadily over the next ten years.

Anything could happen. What if some overseas political upheaval doubles energy prices in 1990? Fuel bills may rise 100 percent. An owner of a conventional home with, for example, a $1000 annual fuel bill will have to pay $2000 per year. But the owner of a superinsulated house with, for example, a $100 fuel bill will have to pay only $200—a much more manageable increase. Protection from energy price fluctuations is attractive to many prospective homeowners, particularly those in the low income bracket and people on fixed incomes.

Almost No Architectural Constraints

One distinctive feature of superinsulated houses is their lack of distinctive features! Although walls are usually thicker, this extra thickness is not visible from the outside and usually not noticeable even from the inside. Few energy-related features need to be designed into, or hidden in, the architecture of a superinsulated house, and many so-called energy design dictums fall by the wayside.

For example, to reduce wall heat loss, designers have sometimes reduced the amount of exposed wall area of a house. This is not necessary in a superinsulated house, where wall heat loss is small compared to losses via windows and ventilation. Thus, the designer is free to vary the shape of the house without compromising energy efficiency.

Even more important, the designer does not have to compromise other considerations to make sure that there is adequate glass on the south side of the house. South-facing windows are helpful in any house, superinsulated or not; but in a superinsulated house, broad expanses of south-facing glass can be foregone without dire consequences. *They are not the main element of energy efficiency.* Window placement can, therefore, be guided by homeowner and/or designer preference.

Microclimate Is Not Significant

Because superinsulated houses are thermally isolated from the outdoors, they are less sensitive to microclimate, that is, factors of wind and solar availability. In conventional houses, wind increases air leakage, a major component of heat loss. It is therefore important to protect conventional houses from wind by building on the leeward side of the hill, planting trees as windbreaks, etc. Superinsulated houses are hardly affected by wind; they leak only minimally even under high wind conditions. The designer is free to site the house as he/she pleases without particular concern for sheltering or construction of windbreaks.

Figure 1.8 That superinsulation does not impose any design restraints is well illustrated by this beautiful double-wall house located in Cape Elizabeth, Maine (7,500 degree days). Built by Roki Associates, Standish, Maine, this approximately 3000-square-foot house has an estimated annual heating bill of $375 using electric heat at $.07 per kWh. (Photo by Howard Faulkner.)

Figure 1.9 Interior of the Roki Cape Elizabeth House. (Photo by Howard Faulkner.)

Solar availability is also less critical. At one time, fears arose that sunless north-sloping land would become worthless because solar heating was thought to be the only way to limit heating costs. Superinsulation changed that. While a south-facing site is still desirable, it is much less crucial. The loss of free solar heat becomes relatively minor compared with other home operating costs.

Even the Macroclimate Is Less Important

In the cold but sunny regions of Colorado, large windows may be an attractive option because window heat loss can be easily offset by solar energy input. In the cold but cloudy regions of Oregon, on the other hand, expansive windows are more likely to be an energy liability, since sunshine is less available to offset window heat loss. In this respect, window design and placement are significant even in superinsulated houses. But the *predominant* features of superinsulation—effective insulation, airtightness, and quality construction—do not vary drastically with climate. Nearly *identical* wall construction, for instance, is used in Virginia and Montana. Only in *extreme* climates are wall and ceilings distinctly tailored to likely weather patterns.

The Housing Industry Does Not Have to Retool To Use Superinsulation

Superinsulation is not a new technology; rather, it is a refinement of existing technology. Constructing superinsulated houses does not require a whole new set of skills. The same basic materials and tools are used. There are some exceptions, but they are just that—exceptions. Double-framed walls, for instance, are often identified

Figure 1.10 The Magar Zero Heat™ house. Located near Rochester, New York (7000 degree days), this 1276-square-foot house has no installed heating system. During its first winter, it was completely heated by people, lights, and appliances (except for one period of a few hours when a small portable electric heater was used). It was designed and built by Magar Construction Company, Livonia, New York. (Photo by John Magar.)

Figure 1.11 The Rideau River Residence. With 2900 square feet of heated floor area, this superinsulated house costs only $300 per year to heat in Manotick, Ontario (8700 degree days). It was designed and built by Allen-Drerup-White, Toronto. (Photo by Allen-Drerup-White.)

SUPERINSULATION FOR HOT CLIMATES

In North America, we spend more money on heating than on cooling. For this reason, most of the development work for superinsulation has been in cold climate housing. However, that is starting to change. The first superinsulated house in the southeastern United States was built in Georgia during the summer of 1983.

Superinsulation is well suited to hot climates. But although many superinsulation principles and techniques are the same for hot and cold climates, there are some differences. For example, intrinsic heat from people, lights, and appliances is an asset in cold climates but a liability in warm climates; reflective insulation (radiation barriers) seem to work better in warm climates than in cold climates; heat recovery ventilation must be designed differently for warm climates.

Unfortunately, the technology of warm weather superinsulation is not fully developed. What about superinsulation in really hot climates? What R-value is needed, and where does the vapor barrier go? The answers to these questions will have to wait for the next book.

with superinsulation because they are so noticeable. But several superinsulation designs use single-stud walls. Many superinsulation techniques require only slight departures from conventional construction methods.

There *is* one new and important demand that superinsulation places on the building industry—strict attention to quality. Not new *levels* of quality, but new *areas* of quality: maintaining quality control where it hasn't previously been considered very important. Insulation, for example, must be installed perfectly, with *zero* gaps. Sound too rigorous? It shouldn't. After all, how many leaks do we allow in the average plumbing system? Zero. And insulation is *easier* to install than plumbing. Perfection may be new but certainly not beyond present capabilities.

Superinsulation Does Not Require Sacrifices

To some people, the concept of superinsulation suggests dimly lit caves, styrene igloos, foam pillboxes. While there may be a few houses that warrant those descriptions, they are the victims of poor design, not energy efficiency. "Nothing is foolproof because fools are so ingenious," says Harold Orr of the Canadian National Research Council. If improperly designed, superinsulated houses may overheat in spring and fall; indoor air quality may be poor; condensation may be a problem on windows and even on walls; and moisture may cause structural damage. But when approached in an intelligent manner,

Figure 1.12   Another example of the versatility of superinsulation design is the Toller/Tener house, designed and built by Allen-Drerup-White, Toronto. Located in Ottawa, Ontario, this 2900-square-foot house has an annual heating bill of $100!

Figure 1.13   The Robinson House. With over 4000 square feet of heated floor area and vaulted ceilings, this superinsulated house, owned by Brad Robinson, is one of the most closely monitored superinsulated houses in North America. Located in Excelsior, Minnesota (8000 degree days), it is heated by about 8000 pounds of wood per year. (Photo by Brad Robinson.)

Figure 1.14 Interior view of the Robinson house. The open floor plan allows even distribution of heat and light throughout the main living area. (Photo by Brad Robinson.)

Figure 1.15 The first superinsulated house in Georgia. To test and demonstrate the merits of superinsulation in warm, humid climates, this superinsulated house was built using truss frame construction (see Chapter 7). Located in Macon, Georgia, it was built by the Greater Macon Housing Corporation.

Figure 1.16 The Styro House. Designed and built by Buffalo Homes, Riegelsville, Pennsylvania. This superinsulated house uses an innovative wall construction system consisting of $5\frac{1}{4}$ inches of polystyrene foam over conventional 2×4 frame construction (see cross section, Chapter 7). Located in central Pennsylvania, this 1600-square-foot house is heated by about 1 cord of wood per year. (Photo by Bill Brodhead.)

superinsulation design and construction can result in a house that is airy, well lit, comfortable, and superbly energy efficient.

Superinsulated Houses Can Have Better Air Quality Than Ordinary Houses Hundreds of substances are released into indoor air by manufactured products, building materials, and even the earth beneath the house and water from the tap. Many of these may be unhealthy or dangerous if not removed.

Ordinarily we rely on air leakage through cracks and openings to refresh home air. But superinsulated houses are airtight; they must have controlled ventilation. For every discernible purpose, controlled ventilation is preferable to haphazard ventilation. Fresh air can be supplied to all parts of the house, in any proportion and at any time. Furthermore, since all the exhaust air is discharged through a duct, it is easy to extract the waste heat from the outgoing air. Thus an airtight house can have better ventilation with less energy use.

Superinsulated Houses Can Have Plenty of Natural Light Many remarkably efficient superinsulated houses have as many windows as conventional houses.

Figure 1.17 The Markham Residence. Demonstrating that superinsulation is applicable to any size house, this house, designed by Allen-Drerup-White, Toronto, has an annual fuel cost of $275 with 6500 square feet of heated floor area. It is located in Markham, Ontario (6800 degree days). It was built by Rick Romain, Nobelton, Ontario.

Figure 1.18 Superinsulated house in Edmonton, Alberta. With 12,000 degree-day winters, northern Canada has served as the proving ground for superinsulation. This 3600-square-foot house, designed by Passive Solar Designs, Ltd., Edmonton, Alberta, has an annual space heating cost of about $200. It was built by Branford Construction Company, Edmonton. (Photo by John Hughes.)

Figure 1.19 The Riverbank house. Located in Bracebridge, Ontario (8800 degree days), this simple 1450-square-foot house, designed by Allen-Drerup-White, has an annual heating cost of $80. It was built by William Cairns Construction, Bracebridge, Ontario.

Typically, total window area ranges between 12 and 15 percent of the floor area—a sufficient amount to provide adequate light, ventilation, and emergency egress. There are no rigid restrictions; if larger windows are desired, then the design may be adjusted to accommodate them. Nor is there any magic: a homebuyer wanting an all-glass house must be prepared to provide more heat from a heating system.

Superinsulated Houses Are More Comfortable What makes people thermally uncomfortable? Temperature change, drafts, cold surfaces, low humidity—all of which are reduced in a superinsulated house.

Temperatures Are Even Because there are no large expanses of glass and because heavy insulation lengthens the response time to outdoor temperature changes, indoor temperatures in a superinsulated house do not alter abruptly. Moreover, the temperature is uniform throughout a room, not colder near the floor or walls.

No Drafts These houses are "wind-tight." Sitting next to a window during a winter storm, a resident remains cozy and comfortable.

No Cold Surfaces Recent research shows that people feel particularly uncomfortable when one side of the body faces a warm surface and the other a cool surface, like a cold wall or a large cold window. In superinsulated houses, the exterior walls are about as warm as the interior walls and do not contribute to radiant cooling. The windows are only slightly cooler, so the discomfort is minimized.

Controlled Humidity Dry winter air adds to body cooling and thermal discomfort and increases the rate of moisture evaporation from the skin. In a superinsulated house, low humidity is rarely a problem because of air-tight construction. Humidity is maintained at comfortable levels by the ventilation system.

Superinsulated Houses Are Quiet Many superinsulation techniques—double walls, thick insulation, and multiple pane windows—are like those used in acoustic construction, serving to reduce sound transmission into and out of the house. To some people, this may be a drawback, cutting off the bird songs of dawn. For the poor soul living next to the highway, on the other hand, the din of rush hour traffic will probably not be missed.

SUPERINSULATED HOUSES MAY WELL BE THE ORDINARY HOUSES OF TOMORROW

When Tschumi, Schick, and others began experimenting with super-energy-efficient design, they were simply trying to improve the technology of housing. The technology they helped develop is now being implemented in thousands of American homes, prompted by the driving force of energy prices. But even without that economic whip, don't superinsulated houses simply make sense? They preserve the best features of traditional design and construction, while adding new dimensions in comfort, air quality, and efficiency. They are well within the reach of most homeowners; and within the scope of most builders. Any other type of house, when compared to one that is superinsulated, can only seem disadvantageous.

Communications, transportation, medicine, and entertainment—all these fields have benefitted from dramatic technological advances in recent years. But housing has remained comparatively stagnant. Superinsulation is certainly not the only available improvement, but it *is* the most widely applicable. If, in the long run, better ideas do gain popular acceptance, what is considered "super" today may be quite ordinary tomorrow.

Two

Insulation and superinsulation

INSULATION IS A MATERIAL, SUPERINSULATION IS A SYSTEM

Insulation—or "thermal insulation," as it is sometimes called—is a building material used to retard heat flow through the thermal envelope of a house. Fiberglass, cellulose, and plastic foams are a few of the common types of insulation in use today. Each has its advantages and disadvantages. None is "super" compared to the others. Merely installing 18 inches of *any* kind of insulation will not make a superinsulated house. When we talk about superinsulation, we are talking about something quite different from the insulating materials alone.

Superinsulation is a system. A plumbing system is more than just pipes, an electrical system is more than just wires, and an insulation system is more than just fiberglass, cellulose, or foam insulation. It consists of thermal insulation plus several other components which, when designed and installed properly in concert with each other, produce superb thermal performance. The value of proper installation and design is paramount. A superinsulated wall is "super" because it is thicker *and it is better.*

Historically, the building industry has not considered thermal insulation a system. As a result, conventionally built houses may have loads of thermal insulation, but they still perform poorly because they are full of thermal defects. Throwing more insulation at problems will not always solve them. First eliminate defects in design and installation, then add more insulation. By doing *both* we create a superinsulated house.

HEAT FLOWS IN COMPLEX WAYS

Heat transfer through the thermal envelope of a house, with or without insulation, is a very complex process. There are three basic mechanisms of heat transfer—conduction, convection, and radiation.

Conduction

Conduction is the transfer of heat energy through a solid by particle interaction. Heat will always conduct toward cold.

If you heat one end of a metal rod, the heat energy will be conducted along the rod toward the cooler end, raising the temperature as it goes (Figure 2.1). Heat will be continuously conducted as long as there is a temperature difference between the two ends. The same phenomenon is at work in all the solid components of a building envelope. With a solid brick wall, for example, if the interior of the wall is warmer than the exterior, then heat energy will be conducted through the brick.

The rate of heat conduction through a material depends on its "thermal conductivity," thickness, and the temperature difference between one side and the other.

The **thermal conductivity** of a material is a measure of its ability to conduct heat. Materials with low thermal

Figure 2.1 Heat transfer by conduction.

conductivity are good insulators; materials with high thermal conductivity are poor insulators. Aluminum has a very high thermal conductivity, that is, it conducts heat rapidly. Wood has a lower thermal conductivity. Air has a very low conductivity and can be a good insulator if it is prevented from moving. Glass has a very high thermal conductivity, which is why windows are such a troublesome source of heat loss in a house.

The conductivity of most common building materials has been determined experimentally in laboratories over the years. Samples are tested according to methods prescribed by the American Society for Testing and Materials (ASTM). Typically, a 1.5-inch thick sample is used, although recently much thicker samples and even whole wall sections have been tested. The results are translated into a conductivity or "k" value, which is the number of Btu transmitted in one hour through one square foot of the material, one inch thick, when there is a one degree Fahrenheit difference in temperature across the sample. Table 2.1 lists k-values for several common materials.

Another term related to conductivity is "conductance." **Conductance** is similar to conductivity except it refers to a particular thickness of material. Conductance values (C) for several common building materials are included in Table 2.1.

The heat conduction rate through a material depends on thickness as well as on thermal conductivity. The thicker the section of the same material, the slower the conduction. For all practical purposes, the rate of conduction through a material is inversely proportional to thickness, that is, when the thickness is doubled, the rate of conduction is halved.

Most building elements are, of course, made of several materials with varying degrees of thickness and conductivity. This makes the heat flow by conduction more complex to estimate with important implications for energy-efficient design.

Convection

Convection is the transport of heat energy by a moving fluid. The two fluids that concern us most are water and air.

There are two types of convection—natural and forced. **Natural convection** is fluid movement resulting from temperature differences—warm fluids are less dense and rise within cooler fluids. A room radiator or baseboard heater (Figure 2.2) functions through natural convection. The air around the heater is warmed by contact with the heater and becomes lighter than the surrounding cooler air. The warm air rises and transfers its heat to other room surfaces, while cooler air replaces it and is warmed in turn. Natural convection causes about half of the heat loss through a hollow, uninsulated wall.

Forced convection happens when an external force acts to move the fluid and promote heat transfer. Blowing

TABLE 2.1 Conductivities and Conductances for Several Common Materials

All values are expressed in units of Btu per hour per square foot per degree Fahrenheit temperature difference. Conductivities (k) are for 1-inch thickness; conductances (C) are for thickness listed. Values are for 70 degrees Fahrenheit.

Material	k	C
Air	0.18	
Aluminum	1536.	
Cellulose insulation	0.27–0.32	
Concrete (140 lb/cubic foot)	9.00	
Glass (soda—lime)	7.08	
Gold	2064.	
Gypsum board—3/8″		3.10
Gypsum board—5/8″		1.78
Marble	18.0	
Mineral wool insulation		
3–3.5″		0.09
6–7″		0.04
Paper	0.9	
Plaster	5.16	
Plywood—1/4″		3.20
Plywood—5/8″		1.29
Polystyrene (expanded)		
1 pound per cubic foot		
density	0.26	
2 pound per cubic foot		
density	0.23	
Polystyrene (extruded)	0.20	
Polyurethane	0.16	
Rubber	0.96	
Sand	2.28	
Sawdust	0.36	
Snow (fresh)	4.08	
Steel	314.4	
Wood (softwood)	0.80	

Source: *ASHRAE Handbook of Fundamentals, 1977 and 1981.*

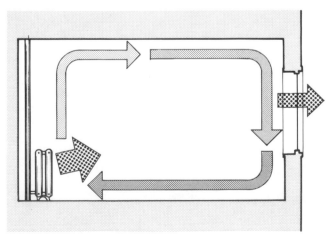

Figure 2.2 Heat transfer by natural convection.

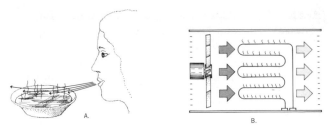

Figure 2.3 Heat transfer by forced convection.

to cool a hot bowl of soup is an example of forced convection (Figure 2.3a). The cooling effect of a cold breeze on the outside wall of a house is another example of forced convection. Here, although wind is a natural force, the convection it induces is not a result of temperature difference—hence it is forced convection. Forced convection can also be created by a fan; the fan in a forced-air heating system causes convection which transfers heat from the furnace heat exchanger to the circulating air (Figure 2.3b).

Radiation

All surfaces radiate heat. The amount and type of radiation emitted depend on the temperature and properties of the surface. Warm surfaces radiate more heat than cool surfaces do; dull surfaces radiate more heat than shiny surfaces do. Technically, it is not "heat" that is radiated, but electromagnetic energy. With conduction and convection, the transfer of heat takes place through matter. For radiant heat transfer, there is a change in energy form, from heat energy at the source to electromagnetic energy for transmission and then back to heat energy at the receiver.

Electromagnetic radiation includes a wide range of types, which are defined by their wavelength. The electromagnetic spectrum is divided into sections (Figure 2.4). At one end are the short wavelengths, including gamma rays and X-rays; at the other end are longer wavelengths, including infrared, microwaves, and radio waves. The most familiar form of electromagnetic radiation is visible light, which includes wavelengths between the ultraviolet and infrared regions of the spectrum. The different wavelengths within the visible region appear to us as different colors. The sun's surface, at 10,000°F, gives off radiation in the ultraviolet, visible, and infrared regions of the spectrum. The earth is much cooler than the sun, and most of its radiation is given off as long-wave infrared radiation referred to as "far-infrared" or, sometimes, "heat radiation."

Most objects around us, and for that matter we ourselves, radiate in the far-infrared wavelengths, and it is this radiation that is most important in superinsulated building design. When you feel heat from a hot wood-burning stove, you are sensing radiant heat transfer. The air between you and the stove is not affected; the transfer is directly from the stove to your skin. When you feel cold sitting next to a large window during the winter, that sensation is due in part to radiant heat transfer from your skin to the cold surface of the window (Figure 2.5).

Thermal comfort is influenced by radiant heat transfer. The "averaged" temperature of all the exposed surfaces in a room is called the **mean radiant temperature** (MRT). The MRT can affect thermal comfort just as much as air temperature does. If the walls of a room are warm, people in that room feel warmer than they do if the walls are cooler, even though the room air temperature in both cases is the same. This is due to radiant heat transfer and is independent of the temperature of the air. One reason superinsulated houses work well is because the warm walls allow people to turn down their thermostats, yet still feel thermally comfortable.

Some radiant heating systems work by raising the surface temperature of the floor or ceiling just a few degrees, increasing the room MRT enough to make the occupants feel warm. Again, the occupants may feel warm even though the room air temperature may be quite low.

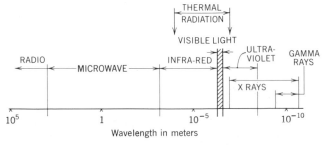

Figure 2.4 The electromagnetic spectrum.

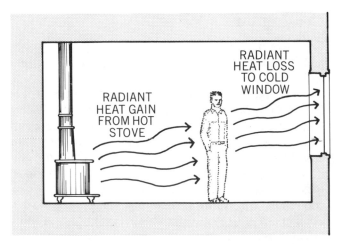

Figure 2.5 Heat transfer by radiation.

One problem with many passive solar designs is the uncomfortable feeling created by large expanses of cold glass at night. The glass absorbs radiation given off by the occupants' bodies, creating a sensation of coolness. To compensate, people may turn up the room thermostats to raise the air temperature.

Radiant Heat Transfer Depends on Surface Properties In addition to temperature, the amount of radiation given off or absorbed by a surface depends on two surface properties, called emissivity and absorptivity.

Emissivity is a measure of the amount of radiation of a specific wavelength given off by a surface when compared to the amount given off by a perfect "black body" at the same temperature. It is expressed as a fraction between 0 and 1. Most building materials and common room surfaces have high emissivities (0.9 or greater). Shiny surfaces, such as aluminum foil, have low emissivities (0.1 or less) and will transfer less heat by radiation.

Suppose you have two cans filled with hot water. One has a polished aluminum surface (low emissivity) and the other has a flat black surface (high emissivity). Both cans are set at room temperature to cool. What happens? The black can will cool faster than the shiny can since its surface emits more long-wave radiation, causing it to lose heat faster.

Absorptivity is a measure of the amount of radiation of a specific wavelength absorbed by a surface, when compared to a perfect "black body" at the same temperature. For any particular surface, the absorptivity is always equal to the emissivity for a particular wavelength radiation. Thus shiny foils, which tend to emit very little far-infrared radiation, also tend to absorb very little of the same wavelength radiation. The radiation that is not absorbed is reflected. (A third surface property, called **reflectivity**, is the complement of absorptivity, that is, reflectivity = 1 − absorptivity.) Suppose you take the cans from the above experiment, fill them both with water at room temperature, and place them in front of a hot wood-burning stove which is emitting lots of infrared radiation. This time the black can will heat up much faster due to the high absorptivity of its surface. The shiny can will warm up much more slowly since its surface reflects most of the radiant energy back to the stove.

Low emissivity foils, called **radiation barriers**, are sometimes used in walls and roofs to retard heat flow. Recently, special low emissivity coatings have been developed for windows to improve their thermal performance (see Chapter 10). Special selective surfaces, which selectively absorb or emit radiation of various wavelengths, have been used in solar heating applications for quite some time. Table 2.2 lists the emissivities and absorptivities of several types of surfaces.

TABLE 2.2 Long-Wave Emissivity of Common Surfaces

Surface	Emissivity
Silver, polished	0.02
Aluminum foil	0.05
Iron, cast	0.44
Brick, building	0.93
Concrete, rough	0.88
Glass, soda—lime	0.94
Paint	
White enamel	0.91
Flat black	0.96
Paper	0.92

Note: The long-wave absorptivity of any surface is the same as its long-wave emissivity.

AN UNINSULATED WALL PROVIDES ALMOST NO RESISTANCE TO HEAT TRANSFER

In a hollow wall, all three heat flow mechanisms—conduction, convection, and radiation—are present. Let's look at an uninsulated 2 × 4 stud wall with gypsum board on the interior surface and with plywood sheathing and lap siding on the exterior surface (Figure 2.6a). Let's assume that the air in contact with the interior surface is at room temperature, and that the air in contact with the exterior surface is at 30°F. There is no air movement at either surface. Here is what happens:

1. First heat is transferred through the gypsum board by conduction.
2. The gypsum board radiates heat through the air space (without interacting with the air in the space) to the inner surface of the sheathing.
3. The gypsum board also warms the air directly in contact with it. The warm air becomes buoyant and rises to the top of the cavity until it comes in contact with the cool inner surface of the sheathing, where it loses some of its heat (by conduction), becomes less buoyant and flows down the surface of the sheathing.
4. Some heat is also conducted by the air itself across the stud cavity. This occurs independently of the transfer by convection.
5. Finally, heat is conducted through the sheathing to the siding and then through the siding to the outside air.

Note: The above description ignores the presence of thin films of air that cling to the inner and outer surfaces of the wall. Before heat is conducted into or out of the wall, it

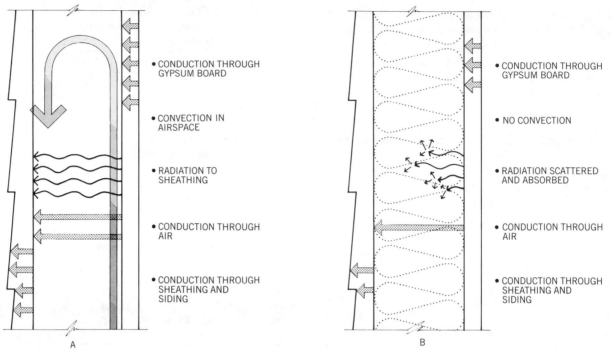

Figure 2.6 Heat flow through walls. a. Uninsulated wall. b. Insulated wall.

must first travel through these air films. Any air movement at the inner or outer surface of the wall will increase the overall heat transfer.

A great deal of heat is transferred through a hollow wall by all three mechanisms of heat transfer. This transfer can be slowed by insulation and almost stopped with superinsulation techniques.

The Insulation Material

The purpose of the insulation material is to retard heat flow through the thermal envelope. Insulation is obviously the heart of any insulation system. A superinsulated house should have at least enough insulation to attain an *actual effective* R-value of R-25 in all walls, ceilings, and exposed floors. In a "perfect" insulation system, you would simply install insulation with an R-value of R-25. In a "less than perfect" system, however, you need to compensate for thermal bridges and other defects by installing insulation with a somewhat higher R-value.

Besides thickness, the most characteristic feature of the insulation in a superinsulated house is the quality of its installation. The material is always installed properly. There are no voids, no partially filled cavities. Typically, the installation is inspected before the interior sheathing goes on.

There is a wide variety of insulation materials on the market, each with specific advantages and disadvantages for various applications. Appendix A includes a list of the most common insulation materials together with a summary of their most important characteristics. Part II of this

book includes specific recommendations for selecting insulation materials for walls (Chapter 7), foundations (Chapter 8), and roofs/ceilings (Chapter 9).

INSULATION MATERIALS RETARD THE TRANSFER OF HEAT BY SUPPRESSING CONVECTION AND RADIATION

Except for foil insulation (radiation barriers), all insulation works basically the same way: the large single space of a hollow wall cavity is divided up by insulation material into thousands of tiny air pockets (Figure 2.6b). Convective heat transfer is virtually eliminated because the air is trapped and prevented from moving; radiant transfer is also greatly reduced because the long-wave infrared radiation is absorbed and/or scattered by the insulation material. The primary remaining mechanism of heat transfer is conduction through still air. From Table 2.1, you can see that still air has a very low thermal conductivity (k = 0.18 Btu/hr-ft²-°F). In most insulation materials, it is the air entrapped within the insulation which provides the thermal resistance, not the insulation material. Batts, loose fill, and some plastic foams all work by virtue of this cellular division.

R-Value Is Measured Thermal Resistance

The labeled R-value of an insulation material is based on its measured conductivity (k) as determined by laboratory tests (see the above section on conductivity). The R-value for a 1-inch thickness of a material is simply the reciprocal of the k value. If a material has a k of 0.5, the R-value would be 1/0.5 or R-2.0 per inch. R-value has units of ft^2-°F-hr/Btu and is usually expressed as R *per inch*. The R-value for thicker materials is simply the R per inch multiplied by the thickness of the material. For example, the R-value of 8-inch thick lightweight concrete is 8 × 0.19, or 1.62.

Technically, any air-based insulation material cannot exceed a theoretical maximum R-value of R-5.5 per inch—the R-value of still air. Plastic foams such as urethane and polystyrene sometimes exceed that value by using a fluorocarbon gas instead of air within the insulation cells. Other exceptions to the above maximum are special experimental air-based insulation materials that contain very fine powders. These materials increase R-value by virtue of extremely small powder particles that interfere with conduction through air. Although they are not commercially available now, they may appear on the market some time in the future.

Appendix A lists the R-values and other important properties of most of the common insulation materials used in residential construction.

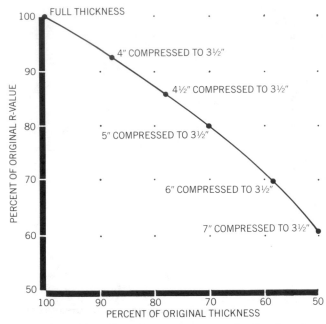

Figure 2.7 The effect of compression on the R-value of fiberglass batts.

R-Values Are Not Always Constant

The R-value per inch of a specific material is not necessarily always the same. It can be affected by several factors including temperature, density, and thickness.

Temperature The R-values listed in Appendix A and in most construction guides are usually based on tests performed at 75°F. But most insulation materials have a higher R-value at lower temperatures. The variation is caused by changes in the conductivity of air within the insulation and by changes in radiant heat transfer. In some cases, this variation can be significant.

For example, in winter, the outside temperature may be 0°F and the inside temperature 70°F, resulting in a mean temperature of 35°F. Alternatively, for summer conditions, particularly in southern climates, mean temperatures of 90° to 110°F can be experienced. The variation in R-value between these two extremes can be as much as 27 percent.

Density The R-value of certain insulation materials can vary considerably with density. This has important implications in the use of blown-in insulation, the installed density of which is under the direct control of the contractor. For example, blown-in fiberglass is usually listed as having an R-value of about R-2.2 per inch. But that is measured at its "settled" density of about 0.7 pounds per cubic foot. If that same material is forced into walls at a density of 2.0 pounds per cubic foot, the R-value jumps to almost R-4.0 per inch! The same effect does not hold for cellulose, which decreases in R-value as its density increases. In Chapter 9 (Roofs and Ceilings), the implica-

tions of insulation settling and density will be discussed further.

With batt insulation, stuffing a thick batt into a narrow stud cavity will result in a more densely installed material. For example, if you stuff a 6-inch (R-19) fiberglass batt into a 3.5-inch stud cavity, the insulation will have a higher *R per inch* than the original 6-inch batt. However, since the new thickness is now only 3.5 inches, the *total* R-value of the batt will be less than R-19. Figure 2.7 shows the effects of compression on fiberglass batts of various sizes. At least one American fiberglass insulation manufacturer produces two types of 3.5-inch thick fiberglass batts; one is R-11 and the other R-13. The difference is caused by density (and to some extent by fiber diameter).

Figure 2.8 shows the change in R-value with density for several common insulation materials. As can be seen, the fibrous insulations are much more sensitive than the rigid foam materials.

Thickness Generally, R-value increases linearly with thickness. That is, a 2-inch thickness of a material will have twice the R-value of a 1-inch thickness of the same material. Recent advances in thermal insulation technology, however, have shown a phenomenon known as the "thickness effect" in low-density materials. Simply stated, the "thickness effect" is an apparent decrease in R-value per inch with increased thickness. A material with R-3.0 for a 1-inch thickness may be less than R-30 for a 10-inch thickness. Why? Evidently the first inch or two of a fibrous

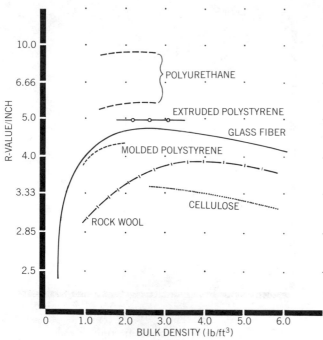

Figure 2.8 Variation of R-value with density for several common types of insulation materials.

insulation is the most effective because it absorbs or scatters most of the infrared radiation. Successive inches of insulation absorb less radiation and therefore have lower effective R-values per inch.

This phenomenon has caused something of a hubbub in the insulation industry and has promoted ASTM to issue new "Standard Test Methods" which impose the requirement that the insulation material be tested at "full thickness," defined as that thickness for which the R-value of the material does not change by more than 2 percent with further increases in thickness.

Despite the discovery of this phenomenon and the institutional adjustment to adapt test methods to include it, the actual variation caused by the "thickness effect" is usually less than 5 percent and not of serious practical concern to the building professional.

SUPERINSULATION AVOIDS THERMAL DEFECTS

A wall has a calculated R-value of 20. Does that mean it performs as an R-20 wall? No. The true R-value of a conventional wall is less than its total calculated R-value. This is a key to understanding superinsulation. Numerous environmental factors adversely affect thermal performance. In conventional construction, these factors are typically not addressed. The result? Conventional walls are full of "defects" which allow heat to flow around and through the insulation. In a superinsulated wall, each of these defects is addressed and substantially reduced or

eliminated. Some of the troublemakers are insulation voids, thermal bridges, air leaks, air intrusion, convective loops, and moisture.

Insulation Voids

An area where insulation has been left out because of improper installation is referred to as a **void**. The extent to which a void degrades the thermal performance of an insulated wall or ceiling increases with the level of insulation installed. For a superinsulated house with high levels of insulation, this defect cannot be underestimated. Consider the following example (Figure 2.9): 1500 square feet of wall has been insulated with 5.5 inches of blown cellulose insulation. The total R-value of the wall is about R-23. Now suppose that just 3 percent of the wall area was missed. How much will the thermal resistance be degraded? The 3 percent with no insulation will have an R-value of about R-3.0. This will degrade the overall wall R-value to 19.2—a reduction of over 17 percent. If 5 percent of the wall is missed, the wall will be degraded by 25 percent!

For another, even more astonishing example, take a 25 × 40-foot attic to be insulated to R-60 with some type of loose-fill insulation. And suppose the roof rafters are very low at the eaves, making it difficult to get good insulation coverage in that area. The contractor is not all that conscientious so he/she misses a 6-inch wide band of floor under the eaves. After all, how much difference could a little 6-inch band make over 1000 square feet of attic floor area? Some simple arithmetic shows that a 6-inch wide band under the eaves (40 feet long each) is equal to 40 square feet, or about 4 percent of the attic floor. The effect of that 4 percent insulation void is to reduce the overall attic thermal resistance from R-60 to R-34—a 43 percent reduction! In other words, missing that 6-inch wide band would be like throwing away about half of the attic insulation.

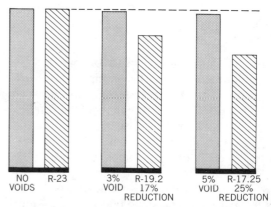

Figure 2.9 R-value degradation caused by insulation voids. Six-inch wall (5.5-inch nominal thickness) filled with cellulose insulation.

A superinsulated house should have as many insulation voids as roof leaks—*none*.

Thermal Bridges

Thermal bridges are points or components that have relatively low thermal resistance and that intrude or "bridge" through the insulation layer of the thermal envelope. To the extent that they are present, these bridges reduce the overall thermal resistance of the thermal envelope. In a wood-framed wall, as much as 18 to 20 percent of the wall area is taken up by the studs. Wood is not a very good insulating material (R-1.25 per inch). Even a 6-inch stud has an R-value of only R-6.9 (5.5 inches × R-1.25 per inch). Each stud acts as a thermal bridge, conducting heat around the insulation and through the wall.

In addition to the studs, there are top plates, bottom plates, corner framing, and window and door headers and frames—all of which act as thermal bridges (see Figure 2.10). An 8- × 24-foot stud wall with 6-inch studs, 16 inches on center, has about 35 square feet of thermal bridging. If the wall is insulated with R-19 fiberglass insulation, the effect of the thermal bridges is to reduce the overall R-value by 24 percent to R-14.4!

As with insulation voids, the extent of degradation in thermal performance caused by thermal bridging increases with the level of insulation. However, unlike insulation voids, which may be eliminated by careful installation, thermal bridging must be eliminated during the design phase. In the design of a superinsulated house, the framing system is seen as part of the insulation system (in addition to being part of the structural support system), and is designed for maximum energy efficiency. Sometimes the framing is modified with, for example, two-stud corners, strapped walls, or box headers over windows. In other cases, the thermal bridges are isolated with, for example, insulative sheathing or balloon framing (see Chapter 7). In every case, thermal bridges are identified and eliminated wherever possible.

Air Intrusion

Air leakage *through* the thermal envelope past the insulation is a large component of heat loss which can be treated separately from insulation performance; this is discussed in Chapter 3. But even if air is not allowed to flow all the way through an insulation system, it can degrade thermal performance by merely penetrating the insulation from one side. This phenomenon is called **air intrusion**. It can occur in attics (Figure 2.11), where ventilation air is allowed to pass over the insulation and penetrate into the upper surface of the insulation. Another place where it may occur is around leaky siding, where outdoor air can pass into and out of the insulation at the exterior surface.

Recent research has produced conflicting information about the severity of the effects of air intrusion on insula-

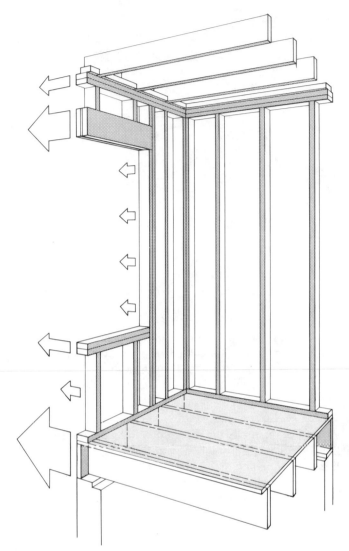

Figure 2.10   Thermal bridges in conventional 2 × 4 frame construction.

tion performance. Air intrusion is definitely not a problem with relatively impermeable insulation materials such as rigid foams. The most current research suggests that it may not even be a serious problem with low-density fibrous insulation. European studies, however, have shown considerable thermal degradation in attics and walls due to air intrusion. Until the issue is resolved, we recommend that insulation be protected from unnecessary exposure to air currents.

Convective Loops

Whenever there are hollow spaces around the insulation in a wall or ceiling, heat can be transmitted through the system by convection, even if the insulation is completely sealed against air leakage or air intrusion and no indoor or outdoor air penetrates the system. These thermal short circuits are called **convective loops**.

Conventional houses are often full of convective

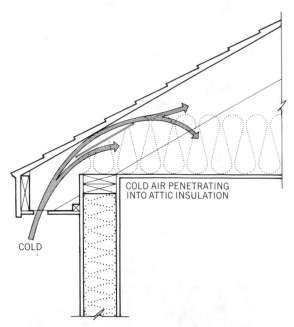

Figure 2.11 Air intrusion into attic insulation. Although this has not been proven to be a serious problem, it is probably good practice to protect the perimeter sections of attic insulation with an air barrier.

loops. For example, the recommended way to install foil-backed fiberglass insulation is to staple it to the sides of the studs, creating an air space between the foil and the inner wall surface (Figure 2.12). While the intent of this practice is to create a radiation barrier and to reduce radiant heat flow, an overriding side effect is the creation

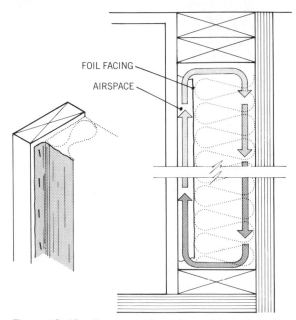

Figure 2.12 Convective loop formed by stapling foil-faced fiberglass batts to the inner face of studs, forming an air space between the insulation and interior sheathing.

of a channel through which air can flow up and circulate around the insulation, carrying heat with it.

Another type of convective loop is often seen in row housing where living units are separated by hollow masonry block walls that extend from the living space up into the attic. Heat is conducted from the living space into the wall cavity. Warm air in the hollow wall rises up into the cold upper section where heat is conducted out through the upper wall into the cold attic. The cooled air then drops down, picks up more heat, and the process repeats itself. Even if the party wall is completely sealed off from the attic air, house heat is continuously pumped out through the convective loop.

Some convective loops combine with air leaks to worsen the problem. An example is the clearance space around chimneys. Often there is a 2-inch space that runs from the basement to the attic—an uninterrupted pathway for warm air to flow out of the interior space into the attic, as well as for cooler attic air to go down into the living space. Another example is the cornices above kitchen cabinets (Figure 2.13). If the insulation is not well protected, warm buoyant air from above the cabinets rises up through the insulation into the cooler attic and is replaced by attic air. This air movement short circuits heat flow through the insulation and is sometimes referred to as a "bypass."

MOISTURE IS A DOUBLE PROBLEM

The first problem with moisture is that when any insulation gets wet, its thermal performance is degraded. The second problem is that water can damage the physical structure of the insulation system; wood members may rot and some insulation materials may be ruined by water, even after they dry out.

The sources of water in an insulation system are rain, leaking pipes, and water vapor condensation. Rain protection and plumbing are not within the scope of this book, but we will look in some detail at the causes and effects of condensation and how it may be minimized.

Water vapor itself is not "wet"; it is one of the gases that constitute the gas mixture of air. Depending on its temperature, air can "hold" a certain amount of water vapor. Warm air can hold more water vapor than cooler air can. When air contains the maximum amount of water vapor it can hold at a certain temperature, it is said to be "saturated." For example, a cubic foot of air at 70°F can hold about 0.00118 pounds of moisture at saturation. **Relative humidity** (rh) is a term used to describe the degree of saturation of an air/water vapor mixture at a certain temperature. If air at 70°F has a relative humidity of 40 percent, then it is holding 40 percent of the saturated amount of water vapor (i.e., 0.40×0.00118, or 0.00047 pounds of moisture per cubic foot of air in this case).

As air cools, it gradually loses some of its ability to hold water vapor. When 70°F air with 40 percent relative hu-

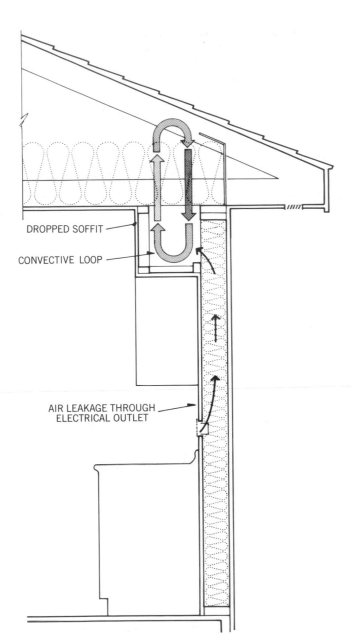

Figure 2.13 Combination of a convective loop and air leakage in a soffited ceiling. The dropped soffit provides a pathway for air to pass into and out of the attic. In some cases, it may also allow air to flow from the exterior (or interior) wall into the soffit and then into the attic.

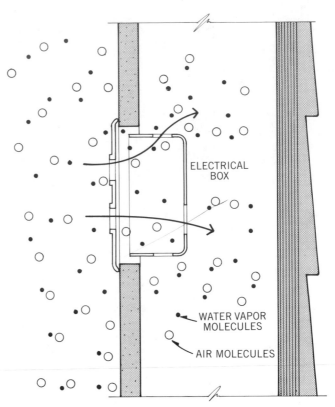

Figure 2.14 Moisture transport into a wall by convection.

midity is cooled to 50°F, the relative humidity goes up to 80 percent. (The amount of water vapor in the air does not change; the relative humidity is higher because the amount of water vapor that air at 50°F can hold is less than the amount that 70°F air can hold.) If it is further cooled to 43°F, the relative humidity reaches 100 percent, or saturation. Below that temperature, the air will not be able to hold all its moisture and the water vapor will begin to condense into liquid water. The temperature at which condensation begins to occur is called the **dew point** temperature. On a humid summer day, the outside of a glass of cold lemonade becomes wet because the humid air in contact with the glass gets cooled below the dew point, causing water vapor from the air to condense into water on the glass surface. The dew point temperature is an important value for designing superinsulation systems.

Moisture Transport Into Insulation Systems

Household air is continuously supplied with water vapor by evaporation from showering, cooking, metabolic activities, and plants. The average family of four generates about 25 pounds of water vapor per day. Water vapor from indoor air can be transported into an insulation system by two mechanisms: convection and diffusion.

Convection Causes Most Condensation Problems
Convection is the movement of air. Air (and the water vapor in it) passes into and out of walls and ceilings through cracks, holes, and building seams whenever there is a greater air pressure on one side than the other (see Figure 2.14). During cold weather, as warm interior air leaks through the thermal envelope, it cools down below the dew point and condenses.

A simple calculation will illustrate the potential magnitude of the problem of moisture transport by convection. Let's look at a 2000-square-foot house containing 16,000 cubic feet of air at 70°F and 40 percent relative

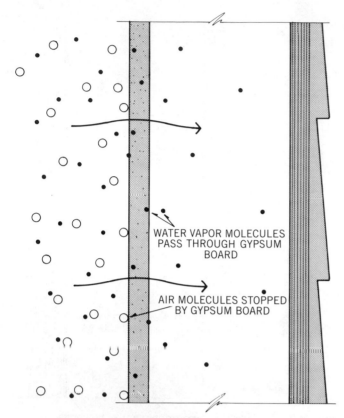

WATER VAPOR MOLECULES
PASS THROUGH GYPSUM
BOARD

AIR MOLECULES STOPPED
BY GYPSUM BOARD

Figure 2.15 Moisture transport into a wall by diffusion.

TABLE 2.3 Water Vapor Pressure of Saturated Air at Various Temperatures

Air Temperature (degrees Fahrenheit)	Vapor Pressure (inches mercury)
−60	.00101
−55	.00143
−50	.00199
−45	.00259
−40	.00379
−35	.00486
−30	.00700
−25	.00940
−20	.01259
−15	.01670
−10	.02203
−5	.02888
0	.03764
5	.04878
10	.06286
15	.08056
20	.05045
25	.06400
30	16450
35	.20342
40	.24767
45	.30023
50	.36240
55	.43564
60	.52160
65	.62209
70	.73916
75	.87506
80	1.0323
85	1.2136
90	1.4219
95	1.6607
100	1.9334

humidity. The total amount of water vapor in the air will be about 7.6 pounds (16,000 cubic feet × 0.00047 pounds of water per cubic foot of air). Conventional houses of this size might leak about 8000 cubic feet of air per hour, carrying about 3.8 pounds (a little less than half a gallon) of water per hour through the thermal envelope. If that air reaches a point in the thermal envelope where the temperature is below the dew point, some of the water vapor will condense. Of course, not all the water vapor in the leaking air condenses in the insulation system, and the house doesn't always leak air at a rate of 8000 cubic feet per hour. But this example clearly illustrates the potentially huge amount of water that can be transported into and through the thermal envelope by convection.

Moisture transport by convection is reduced or eliminated in a superinsulated house by installing an air/vapor barrier within the insulation system. Air/vapor barriers are described more fully below.

Diffusion Is a Second, Less Important Transport Mechanism Diffusion is the transport of water vapor through a material. The water vapor moves independently of air (Figure 2.15) and can pass through some materials that are impervious to air. In a house, water vapor diffuses through the solid components of the building envelope, such as gypsum board, plaster, wood pan-

eling, etc. The amount of vapor that diffuses through the thermal envelope depends on the vapor pressure difference across the thermal envelope and the permeance of the envelope.

Vapor Pressure Is the Driving Force of Vapor Diffusion Water vapor in air creates its own pressure, called **vapor pressure**. When a difference in vapor pressure exists across a wall, water vapor tends to diffuse from the higher pressure side to the lower. The greater the difference, the higher the rate of diffusion. Vapor pressure depends on relative humidity and temperature. Under most typical winter conditions, vapor pressure is higher indoors than outdoors, so that diffusion is therefore outward. During warm humid weather, on the other hand, when a house is air conditioned, diffusion may be inward from outdoors.

Table 2.3 lists the vapor pressure for saturated air at various temperatures. To find the vapor pressure of any air/water-vapor mixture, simply multiply the saturated vapor pressure by the relative humidity. For example, for air at 70°F and 40 percent relative humidity, the vapor pressure will be 0.7392 inches mercury (the saturated vapor pressure for 70°F air) times 0.40 (the relative humidity), which equals 0.2957 inches mercury.

The Permeance of the Thermal Envelope Also Controls Vapor Diffusion **Permeance** is to vapor diffusion as conductance is to heat conduction. Expressed in "perm" units, permeance is a measure of the tendency of a material to transmit water vapor by diffusion. A permeance of 1.0 perm means that under a vapor pressure differential of 1.0 inch of mercury, 1.0 grain per hour of water vapor will diffuse through each square foot of surface. (What's a grain? Just another of those obscure measurement units that almost nobody uses. One grain is equal to 1/7000 pound.) Materials with high permeance allow water vapor to diffuse relatively freely. Gypsum board, for example, has a relatively high permeance (50 perms for 3/8-inch thickness). Polyethlyene sheeting, on the other hand, has a very low permeance (0.06 for 6-mil thickness). Materials with a permeance of less than 0.1 perms are considered **vapor retarders** or **vapor barriers**. Table 2.4 lists permeance values for several common building materials.

Note: Permeance can be measured several different ways, and different tests of the same material may produce different results. It is beyond the scope of this book to discuss the differences between the methods.

TABLE 2.4 Permeance and Permeability of Materials to Water Vapor

Units are grains per hour per square foot per inch mercury vapor pressure differential. Values for permeance are for thickness listed; values for permeability are for 1-inch thickness.

Material	Permeance	Permeability
Concrete block, 8''	2.4	
Plaster on metal lath, 3/4''	15	
Gypsum wall board, 3/8''	50	
Hardboard, 1/8''		
standard	11	
tempered	5	
Plywood, exterior	0.7	
Plywood, interior	1.9	
Mineral wool, unfaced		116
Polyurethane board stock		0.4–1.6
Polystyrene, expanded		2.0–5.8
Polystyrene, extruded		1.2
Phenolic foam		26
Aluminum foil, 1-mil	0.0	
Polyethylene		
4-mil	0.08	
6-mil	0.06	
8-mil	0.04	
Paint, latex		
Primer-sealer		6.28
"vapor-retarder" paint		0.45
Primer plus 1 coat flat oil		
paint on plaster		1.6–3.0
Enamel paint on smooth		
plaster		0.5–1.5

Water Vapor Is Not a Problem Unless It Condenses into Liquid Water

In an insulated wall, there is a temperature gradient across the wall ranging from indoor temperature at one side to outdoor temperature at the other side. If the coldest section inside the wall is above the dew point of the air within the wall, no condensation will occur. If more moisture enters the wall by convection or diffusion, or if the temperature of the wall decreases so that the dew point is reached, condensation can occur. If the dew point occurs somewhere in the middle of the insulation, water or ice will form first at that point.

A second process occurs simultaneously with the first. The water or ice formed also gives off water vapor, which continues to move outward or upward through the building skin until it recondenses farther out. Thus what usually happens in a wall is that all or most of the condensation eventually migrates out to the cold outer surface. The effect of the condensed water is usually confined to the sheathing and outer layers of insulation.

Once moisture condenses in an insulation system, three things can happen:

1. It can get absorbed by the insulation material and wooden components of the wall.
2. It can be expelled to the outside either by diffusion or by convection.
3. It can be expelled back to the inside of the house either by diffusion or air leakage through the inside surface of the wall.

Historically, building design guidelines for dealing with moisture problems have only addressed the control of diffusive transport. (Convective transport, rather than diffusive transport, has only recently been recognized as the dominant mechanism by which water vapor gets into walls.) In the past, builders were advised to make sure that the outside surface of the building skin had five to ten times the permeance of the inside surface, to ensure that water vapor could diffuse out through the outer skin faster than it would diffuse in through the inner skin.

For the past ten to twenty years, however, walls have commonly been built with extremely *low* exterior permeability. Exterior-grade plywood, aluminum and vinyl siding, and rigid foam sheathing, usually installed on the outside of a house, all have low permeance. They should, in theory, cause problems from moisture condensation

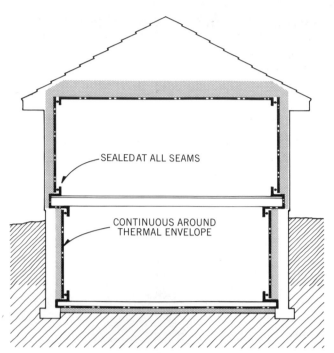

SEALED AT ALL SEAMS

CONTINUOUS AROUND
THERMAL ENVELOPE

Figure 2.16 The air/vapor barrier.

(unless a good air/vapor barrier is installed on the inside). However, recent field studies have shown surprisingly few moisture problems in houses with exterior vapor barriers. More research is necessary before we completely understand the complexities of moisture transport and condensation in buildings.

The Insulation System Should Be Protected from Water Vapor Intrusion

Despite the research findings mentioned above, the best design philosophy for a superinsulated house is "better safe than sorry." Insulation systems should therefore be completely protected from water vapor through the installation of an *effective interior air/vapor barrier*, which retards *both* diffusive and convective flow of water vapor. The foil facing on some fiberglass batts has a very low permeability and can be an *effective vapor* barrier, but not a good *air* barrier; installing foil-faced fiberglass batts will *not* effectively stop moisture transport into a wall if there is air leakage through, for instance, electrical outlets, or around poorly fitted molding.

SUPERINSULATION IS A SYSTEM

Insulation alone is not enough. As described above, the effectiveness of thermal insulation depends on many factors other than published R-values and installed thicknesses. In a perfect insulation system, problems and defects that reduce effective R-value would be entirely eliminated; thermal performance would depend solely on the R-value of installed insulation. In practice this is impossible, but through careful systematic design and construction, one can build an insulation system that approaches optimal performance.

Every superinsulated wall, floor, or ceiling has three separate components: the air/vapor barrier, the support structure, and the insulation material. A fourth component—an additional air barrier—is sometimes also used.

The Air/Vapor Barrier

The **air/vapor barrier** is a tightly sealed membrane which surrounds the thermal envelope to prevent air from leaking into or through the insulation system (Figure 2.16). The air/vapor barrier is the most important and most often underestimated component of a superinsulation system. It prevents infiltration into the house and prevents moisture transport into the insulation system. Given the choice of either a properly installed air/vapor barrier or thick insulation, one would be better off choosing the former.

The most common air/vapor barrier material is 6-mil polyethylene, which has a permeability of only 0.06 perm (see Table 2.4). (Please note that the most current terminology is "vapor retarder" instead of "vapor barrier," since no material is a complete and perfect barrier. However, we will continue to use the more familiar term, barrier, despite its technical imperfection.)

Any material with a permeability of less than 0.10 is considered a good air/vapor barrier. Some new "cross-laminated" polyethylene products are available (see Appendix D) that provide even lower permeability plus greater strength in only 3-mil or 4-mil thicknesses. Materials that are available in large sheets have the advantage of fewer seams to seal.

Water vapor from interior air diffuses through the thermal envelope until it reaches the air/vapor barrier. If the air/vapor barrier is installed properly, the water vapor stops there. As long as the air/vapor barrier is warm, the water vapor will not condense and there will be no problem. If, however, the temperature of the air/vapor barrier is below the dew point, condensation will occur. This happens if the barrier is installed on the outside of the wall in cold climates. (Sometimes this is done inadvertently around floor joists, as we shall see in Chapter 8.) For this reason, the air/vapor barrier must be placed on the inside (winter warm) side of the insulation, where it will stay warm.

The air/vapor barrier must be meticulously sealed at all seams and at every penetration, including windows, doors, electrical outlets, plumbing stacks, vent fans, etc. It must essentially form a bubble corresponding to the thermal envelope of the house. Subcontractors must not remove any sections of it; if they tear the plastic, it must be patched. Before the interior sheathing is installed, the house should be tested for airtightness by using a blower

THE CEILING AIR/VAPOR BARRIER QUESTION

A common practice in the building industry is to leave out the ceiling air/vapor barrier because it "causes moisture condensation problems." This belief was bolstered by the experiences of some builders who put in continuous air/vapor barriers on both the walls and ceilings of houses. One consequence was that the houses became more airtight and interior humidity rose to high levels. Their solution to the problem was to eliminate the ceiling air/vapor barrier, let the excess interior humidity escape into the attic, and vent the attic with large openings. This is not the best way to control humidity. A better way is with controlled ventilation, which is necessary anyway for good indoor air quality in an airtight house.

door (see Chapter 3 and 14). Any imperfections in the air/vapor barrier can be identified and repaired at that time.

The Optional Air Barrier

Sometimes, in addition to the air/vapor barrier on the warm side of the insulation, an **air barrier** is added to the outside of the insulation. Like the air/vapor barrier, the air barrier blocks air flow, but unlike the air/vapor barrier, it allows water vapor to pass through.

The purposes of the air barrier are to prevent *air intrusion* into the insulation and to make the thermal envelope tighter by compensating for small imperfections in the air/vapor barrier.

The most common air barrier material is spun-bonded polyethylene, which is similar chemically to sheet polyethylene but is made of thin fibers spun into a mat and bonded together. One popular brand is DuPont's Tyvek[R] (see Appendix D). The important difference between sheet polyethylene and spun-bonded polyethylene is that the latter allows water vapor to diffuse through.

In order to work properly, the air barrier must completely cover the wall insulation and be tightly sealed at all windows, doors, and other penetrations (Figure 2.17). (Installation of an air barrier over attic insulation, however, is a questionable practice (see Chapter 9).) Installed on the outer surface of the insulation, the air barrier prevents any wind or outdoor pressure fluctuation from disturbing the thermal integrity of the insulation system. *It is important for the air barrier to allow water vapor to pass easily through.* Otherwise, any interior water vapor that manages to get through the air/vapor barrier could condense within the wall and damage the insulation system.

The Support Structure

The purposes of the support structure are 1) to provide adequate containment for the insulation material while minimizing thermal bridges and 2) to support the air/vapor barrier(s). This is the most noticeable component in a superinsulated house. Wide studs, strapped walls, double walls, SuperTruss™, raised roof trusses, and Larsen trusses are all types of support structures for the superinsulation system.

Most of the elements of the support structure, such as studs, joists, and rafters, are already present in a conventional house and form the main structural support for the house itself. In a superinsulated house, however, these elements are modified to serve their purpose as part of the insulation system. Sometimes, special new elements are added.

Look at Figures 2.18 and 2.19. Figure 2.18 shows a house with 2 × 6 walls and site-built rafters, framed in the conventional manner. The walls are insulated with 6-inch (R-19) fiberglass and the ceiling is insulated with 15 inches of blown cellulose (R-55). By R-value alone, many people would call this an energy-efficient house.

Figure 2.19 shows a "Saskatchewan"-type double wall house with a raised roof truss system. The walls are insulated with three layers of 3.5-inch fiberglass (R-33) and the ceiling is insulated with 15 inches of blown cellulose (R-55). This superinsulated wall will greatly outperform the 2 × 6 wall, not only because it has more insula-

Figure 2.17 Air barrier installed over the exterior sheathing of a house. (Photo by Howard Faulkner.)

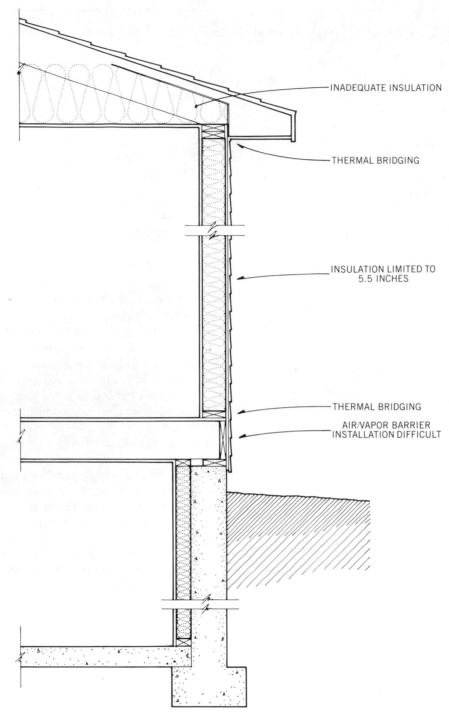

Figure 2.18   Wall section, conventional 2 × 6 construction.

tion, but also because the support structure is better designed.

How is the "Saskatchewan" support structure better?

1. It can accommodate the full thickness of attic insulation. Look at what happens to the insulation over and adjacent to the wall in the conventional house (Figure 2.18). The roof rafters don't provide enough clearance to install full thickness insulation. With the raised truss (Figure 2.19), the full 15 inches can be installed.

2. It can accomodate any thickness of wall insulation.

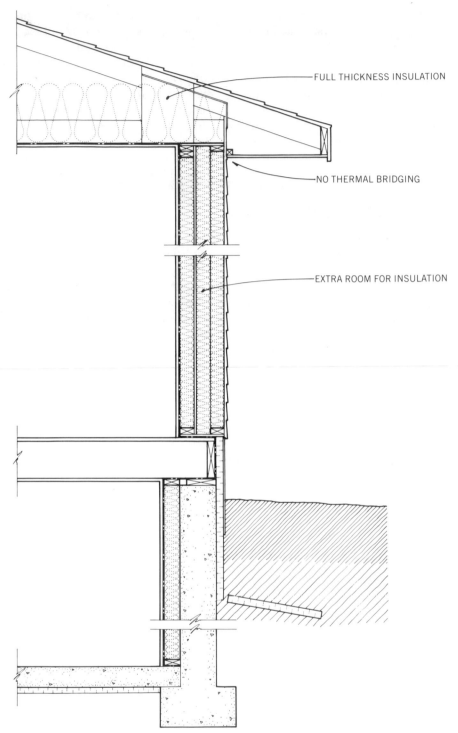

FULL THICKNESS INSULATION

NO THERMAL BRIDGING

EXTRA ROOM FOR INSULATION

Figure 2.19 Wall section, double-wall construction.

To add more insulation, you merely increase the space between the two walls. There is no need to use thicker studs.

3. It has much less thermal bridging. Again, look at the 2 × 6 wall. The studs, top plates, bottom plates, and window headers are all thermal bridges. In the su-

perinsulated wall, many of them are reduced or eliminated. There is a 3.5-inch layer of uninterrupted insulation between the two walls with no thermal bridges other than the thin plywood top and bottom plates. Several additional features of a superinsulated support structure, such as box headers over windows and doors and two-stud corner details, reduce thermal bridges. These will be presented in detail in Part II.

The Saskatchewan wall is only one example of improved support structure. To create a super-efficient support structure, double walls are not necessary. Single wall construction with exterior foam sheathing and other types of framing configurations can also achieve comparable performance. Part II of this book will show details for several other viable alternatives.

THE IMPORTANCE OF WORKMANSHIP

No amount of design sophistication will work if it is not supported by proper workmanship at the site. If the insulation contractor doesn't completely fill a wall cavity, or if the air/vapor barrier installer leaves out a couple of square feet because "such a little bit won't matter" then the system will not work as it should.

Superinsulation does not demand an extraordinary standard of work quality. As we pointed out in Chapter 1, it simply demands quality in an area where it has never before been stressed. *A plumbing system must not have even one leaky pipe; an electrical system must not have even one short circuit; a roofing system must not have even one leak; so an insulation system must not have even one square foot of missed insulation or one hole in the air/vapor barrier.*

Quality assurance begins during the design phase. Construction drawings must indicate important details such as sealing points for air/vapor barriers. The designer should also work out construction sequences in advance to anticipate as many problems as possible.

Of course, the best solution is the training of crews and subcontractors. Electricians never had to worry about air/vapor barriers in the past and cannot be expected to appreciate instantly the importance of maintaining the integrity of a plastic film around the house. Every builder of superinsulated houses has at least one horror story to tell about how a contractor or electrician inadvertently damaged the insulation system. Preventing those occurrences is a challenge to both the designer and general contractor.

Three

Air leakage and airtightness

The typical pre-1980 house is deplorably leaky, experiencing between 0.5 and 3 house volumes of air leaking in and out *every hour*!

Until the importance of energy conservation became apparent, this was not considered much of a problem or issue. Now that we have "discovered" the possibility of energy efficiency, we also discover that unintentional air leakage is not only wasteful, but also causes the homeowner all sorts of additional nuisances. Moreover, the "fresh air" usually associated with haphazard air leakage is highly undependable and often inadequate.

What *exactly* do we mean by *air leakage*? It is air that flows through the multiple layers of a thermal envelope, from the outside all the way to the inside (infiltration) or from the inside all the way to the outside (exfiltration). The total air infiltration rate is roughly equal to the total exfiltration rate; otherwise the house would blow up or cave in.

For our purposes here, both kinds of movement are called air leakage. Furthermore, air leakage implies the *unintentional* air flow found in most conventional homes. *Intentional* air flow is called *ventilation*.

The technology of building finally possesses the tools, the materials, the design details, and the initiative to measure air leakage and to prevent it. No longer must inordinately large amounts of energy be used for space conditioning—energy that is only compensating for unnecessary air leakage. A significant part of typical houses' energy use has been eliminated in superinsulated houses, which are virtually airtight.

People sometimes balk at the word "airtight." They think it means *sealed;* they envision slow suffocation. A superinsulated house is not a hermetically shut box. There's abundant ventilation in superinsulated houses, but it is *intentional and controlled,* expending the least possible amount of energy and causing the least damage to the building.

THE DYNAMICS OF AIR LEAKAGE

All houses contain openings. Some are intentional; some are not. *Intentional* openings include *open* windows, flues, fans, exhaust vents, and so on. *Unintentional* openings include windows and doors that leak even when shut; and gaps that occur wherever different parts of a building come together, for instance, where the wall meets the floor, where a pipe passes through the roof, around the window frame, etc. (Figure 3.1.) *One of the goals of superinsulated building design is to make sure that all openings are strictly intentional.*

A complicated pressure pattern generally exists around a house, both inside and outside. In order for leakage to occur, there must be not only openings or pathways, but also a driving force or pressure difference across the envelope where the openings exist. This pressure difference is caused by three factors: wind, the stack effect, and people's indoor activities.

Wind

The wind causes pressures that vary according to its speed and direction, the building shape, and the nature of nearby obstructions. Generally, surfaces on the windward side of a house are at a slightly higher pressure, while other surfaces are lower. The result? In the absence of other forces, air comes into a house through openings on the windward side and leaves through openings elsewhere (Figure 3.2). *The inside-outside pressure difference caused by wind is roughly proportional to square of the wind speed.*

The Stack Effect

Warm air rises because it is less dense than cooler air. In winter, when indoor air is heated, it rises to the top of a room or building, creating a positive pressure pushing

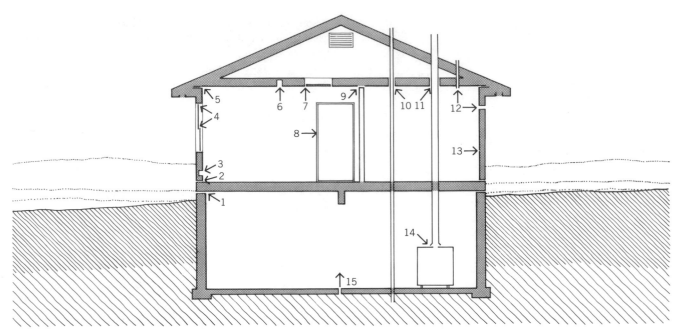

Figure 3.1 Some common air leakage paths in houses: 1) joints between joists and foundation; 2) joints between sill and floor; 3) electrical boxes; 4) joints at windows; 5) joints between wall and ceiling; 6) ceiling light fixtures; 7) joints at attic hatch; 8) cracks at doors; 9) joints at interior partitions; 10) plumbing-stack penetration of ceiling; 11) chimney penetration of ceiling; 12) bathroom and kitchen ventilation fans; 13) air/vapor barrier tears; 14) chimney draft air leaks; 15) floor drain (air enters through drain tile).

upward and outward; a negative pressure is created at the bottom, pulling air in. Somewhere in the middle, the two pressures are neutralized (Figure 3.3) and the air is placid. This is known as the **stack effect** or sometimes the **chimney effect**. The pressure differences created by the stack effect are directly proportional to the temperature difference between inside and outside, as well as to the height of the structure. The colder it is outside and the higher the building, the stronger the stack effect.

Because of the stack effect, winter air leaks in through openings near the bottom of a house and leaks out through higher openings. (At the neutral plane, openings don't leak at all.)

Combination of the Two

During cold periods, the stack effect tends to dominate, while during mild periods, the wind is the dominant effect. During much of the year, however, both are comparable, making the house subject to a combination of the two effects.

The wind and stack effect exert different pressure distributions over the building envelope. Sometimes these pressures reinforce each other to increase air leakage through a particular opening. In other situations, the pressures can oppose and partially cancel each other. What actually happens depends on the wind speed and direction, the inside-outside temperature difference, and the

distribution of openings over the building envelope. Recent research has shown that for all cases, the effects of wind and temperature difference on building air leakage are sub-additive. In other words, the air leakage under a combination of wind and stack effect will be less than or equal to the sum of the individual effects of the wind and temperature difference.

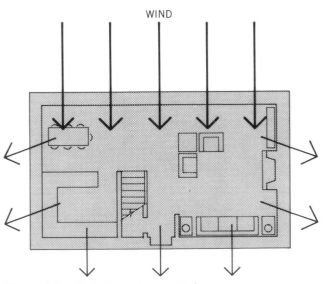

Figure 3.2 Air leakage due to wind.

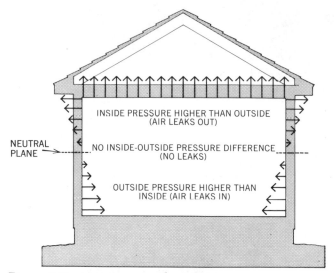

Figure 3.3 Air leakage due to stack effect.

Other Sources of Pressure Difference

People's activities also create pressure differences that affect air leakage. An exhaust fan in a bathroom or kitchen creates a pressure difference across the thermal envelope, and draws air out through its own opening. Flues of furnaces and water heaters create hot gases which are lighter than the air around them; these gases rise up and out of the house, to be replaced by outside air that leaks in. Forced air heating or air conditioning distribution systems can also induce air leakage; if part of the

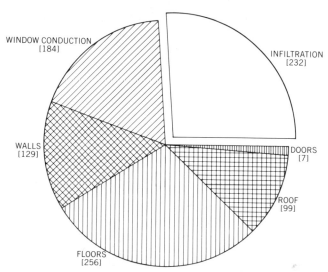

Figure 3.4 Heat losses in a typical house (therms). Data for a typical 1976 house in Chicago. (Source: Office of Technology Assessment, U.S. Congress, *Residential Energy Conservation*, 1979.)

system is outside the thermal envelope—for example, in an unheated attic—any leaks there will contribute to the house's overall air leakage.

Exhaust fans, chimneys, and flues all tend to depressurize the house; the pressure inside the house becomes lower than the pressure outside. Because of that, *infiltration through the thermal envelope often dominates over exfiltration.* Most of the outgoing air leaves through flues and fans.

UNINTENTIONAL AIR LEAKAGE CAUSES PROBLEMS

It is a myth that leakiness is good because it provides needed ventilation. Leakiness, when looked at more closely, provides nothing but headaches because it is haphazard, wasteful, and unpredictable. In superinsulated houses, ventilation is provided without these drawbacks.

Air Leakage Wastes Energy

Unintentional air leakage can account for as much as 40 percent of the total heat loss in ordinary houses (Figure 3.4); that's a great deal of energy and money vanishing into the air.

Air leakage is usually expressed in *air changes per hour (acph)*, where an air change is a house volume of air. For example, a 2000 square foot house with 8-foot ceilings has a house volume of 16,000 (8 × 2000) cubic feet. A leakage rate of 0.5 acph is equal to 8000 cubic feet per hour (0.5 × 16,000), or 133.3 cfm. The average air leakage rate for houses built in the United States since 1950 is 0.6 to 0.7 acph. A large survey carried out by the National Bureau of Standards measured natural air infiltration in some 200 houses eligible for the U.S. low-income weatherization program and found these houses averaged about 1 acph. Many of these, however, had broken windows and were unusually leaky. In Sweden, studies show that the average air infiltration rate ranges from 0.2 to 0.4 acph. Princeton University measured New Jersey houses of comparable vintage and found values around 0.4.

The amount of energy required to *warm the air* that leaks into a house can be easily calculated if the air leakage rate is known (see Chapter 5). Consider a 2000-square-foot house with a leakage rate of 0.5 acph. When the outdoor temperature is 40°F, the energy required to warm the leaking air to 70° indoor temperature is 4320 Btu/hr. When the outdoor temperature is 10°F, the energy requirement jumps to 8640 Btu/hr!

Air leakage increases energy consumption in another way. In winter, outside air is cold and dry. When it infiltrates into the house, its *humidity must be raised* as it is heated.

Where will that humidity come from? In a house, water

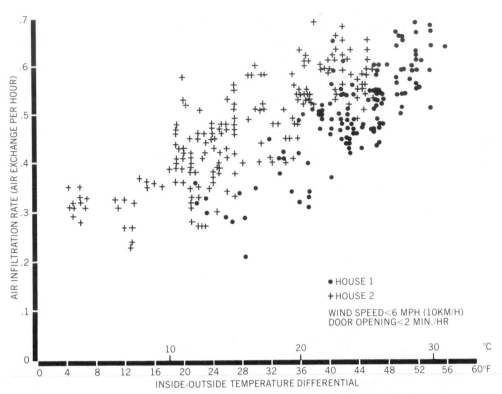

Figure 3.5 Air infiltration rate vs inside/outside temperature difference. Infiltration rates were measured using the tracer gas technique. The data shown correspond to situations in which the wind speed was low, below 6 mph, and where the occupant-induced leakage through door openings were minimal. (Source: Adapted from N. Malik, *Air Infiltration in Homes*, Princeton University Center for Energy and Environment Studies, Report 58-1977.)

vapor is generated by occupants' activities, plants, exposed soil under the house, and, in a relatively new house, by the drying of building materials like wood and concrete. However, when a great deal of cold, dry air is leaking in, these sources are inadequate, and unless a humidifier is used, air seems stale and dry.

Humidifiers break water into small particles which are easily evaporated. But humidifiers don't provide the heat to evaporate water (latent heat of evaporation)—1060 Btu per pound evaporated. That heat is drawn from the room air or directly from the heating system. This is an additional requirement, increasing a house's heat loss.

In summer, outdoor air is often hotter and more humid than indoor air. When it enters a house, it must be *cooled and dehumidified* for comfort. Air conditioners are used for this purpose. Obviously, the sensible and latent cooling requirements of air conditioners are increased when large amounts of air leak into the house.

Air Leakage Can Cause Moisture Problems

In ordinary houses, air leaks out through many openings. In winter, it cools as it passes through the building's ther-

mal envelope; if it comes into contact with a cold enough surface—one below its dew point temperature—it will condense on that surface, often building up a significant amount of liquid water or ice. Sometimes this is not too much of a problem: if the surface on which condensation occurs is well vented with outside air, condensed moisture can reevaporate easily. In other cases, however, moisture and ice continue to build up over the winter and cause significant structural damage to building materials.

In superinsulated airtight houses, on the other hand, proper sealing techniques and a continuous air/vapor barrier prevent warm moist air from leaking into areas where it may condense and cause moisture problems.

Unintentional Air Leakage Does Not Ensure Adequate Ventilation

Air leakage provides ventilation, but inconsistently. Figure 3.5 shows a distribution of air leakage rates for two conventional houses under varying inside/outside temperature differences. Figure 3.6 shows the distribution of air leakage rates for two houses: an average leaky house and a moderately airtight (but not superinsulated) house.

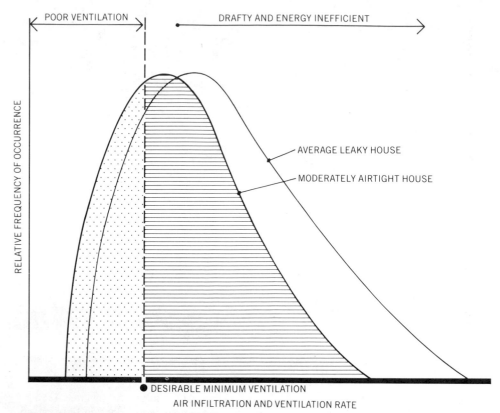

Figure 3.6 Typical variation in air leakage rate under natural conditions in an average leaky house and in a moderately airtight house.

Much of the time, ventilation is excessive and energy wasteful; for short periods of time, however, it's adequate. Despite the popular assumption that leaky houses get abundant amounts of fresh air, *both houses show poor ventilation much of the time*. If the houses were made somewhat more airtight, there would be less waste but prolonged periods of stuffiness. Thus a trade-off arises between energy conservation and air quality.

No such choice need be made in superinsulated houses, which are extremely airtight—but adequately ventilated (Figure 3.7). Unintentional air leakage is negligible, but ventilation is controlled within strict predetermined limits which consistently ensure residents' comfort.

Unintentional Air Leakage Ventilates Unevenly

Just as the ventilation resulting from uncontrolled air leakage is sporadic, it is also uneven—entire parts of the house may be consistently drafty, and other parts stuffy. Some adjustments can be made using bathroom and kitchen exhaust fans for short periods to remove moisture, odors, etc., but the amount of fresh air delivered to rooms such as bedrooms and family rooms, which are frequently occupied, cannot be ensured.

Controlled ventilation in a superinsulated house can be designed to deliver the correct ventilation to the various parts of the house as necessary.

THE ADVANTAGES OF CONTROLLED, INTENTIONAL VENTILATION

We have already noted several significant advantages of the controlled ventilation possible in airtight houses. Energy conservation is the most obvious. Other formidable advantages are comfortable and controllable indoor air temperature and humidity; adequate ventilation; and evenly distributed ventilation.

Controlled ventilation makes drafts obsolete: rooms are not colder near the edges, and in winter, people don't have to bundle up in sweaters to enter one part of a room, or one or two rooms that are particularly leaky.

During warm months, there are times when, because of solar and incidental heat gain indoors, outside air is cooler and dryer than inside air, so that ventilation is desirable. Remember that *it is always easier to bring air in than to keep it out*. A controlled ventilation system in an airtight house allows you to bring in summer air when it is cool, yet keep it out when it is too hot.

Another important advantage of controlled ventilation is that it permits heat recovery from outgoing air. Instead

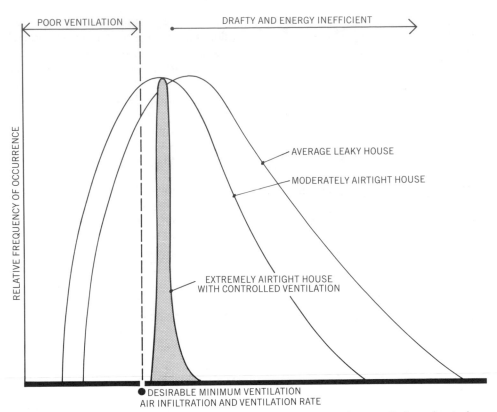

Figure 3.7 Variation in ventilation rate in an airtight house with controlled mechanical ventilation (shaded area), compared to natural air leakage in leaky and moderately tight houses with no mechanical ventilation.

of exfiltrating through scattered locations, air in superinsulated houses leaves through specific openings in which heat recovery devices—for instance, air-to-air exchangers—can recapture much of the heat that would otherwise be lost, and recycle it to the house interior.

AIRTIGHTNESS BY DESIGN

Superinsulated houses are designed to avoid air leakage. This is accomplished mainly by reducing the number and size of openings in the thermal envelope. Air leakage can also be cut down by reducing the pressure difference across the thermal envelope, that is, by careful site selection and house configuration. But these added precautions are not essential in superinsulated houses.

Seal Openings

Most openings through which air leaks into and out of a house are not only unintentional, but they are also not readily noticeable. For example, windows are commonly thought to be a prime source of air leakage. Yet various studies show that windows and doors account for less than 25 percent of the total area of openings in a house (Figure 3.8)! That means that 75 percent of openings are unintentional openings in the thermal envelope. To make

a house superinsulated, all unintentional openings where the walls meet the floors, where pipes pass through the roof, around the window frames, etc., must be sealed.

Other guidelines for superinsulation include the following. Because their leakage varies widely depending on the style and the materials used, windows should be chosen on the basis of airtightness. Many of the usual penetrations through the thermal envelope—for instance electrical, telephone, and antennae connections—should be brought in through a single, well-sealed opening. The air circulation system, which in houses with central air conditioning or warm air distribution can be a major source of leakage, should be placed entirely within the confines of the thermal envelope so that any leakage in the ducts is not an air leak from the house but merely a division of air within the house. Where the ducts *must* pass outside the thermal envelope, they should be tightly sealed at the joints and at the points where they penetrate the envelope.

Another common and significant air leakage site is the flue for a combustion appliance such as a furnace or water heater. For combustion, the device draws air from the space around it, that is, from inside the thermal envelope, venting combustion exhaust gases through the flue so that the flue is considered a large air leak. The problem

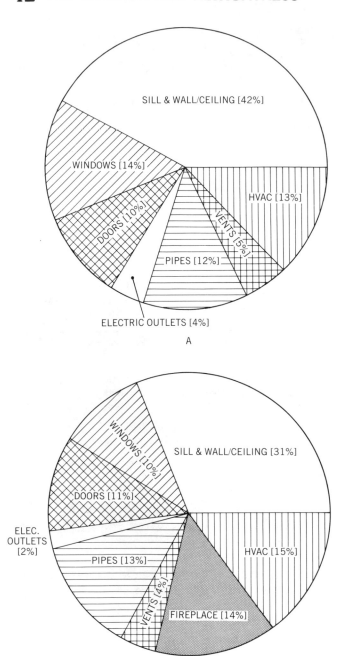

Figure 3.8 Air leakage through the various components in typical houses. a. Houses without fireplaces. b. Houses with fireplaces. (Source: Lawrence Berkeley Laboratory, University of California.)

can be avoided by using either electrical appliances, or direct-vented, sealed-combustion appliances, which draw air directly from outside the house; and vent combustion products directly to the outside as well.

Wood/coal stoves and fireplaces are extremely inefficient. Nonetheless, people may want them for aesthetic reasons, and if so, they present special difficulties for superinsulated houses. It is difficult to seal the house interior

from the combustion area, which must be accessible for adding wood or coal. This creates the double problem of a large, difficult-to-seal source of air leakage (the flue) and the need to provide combustion air. If a fireplace or wood/coal stove *must* be installed, a separate insulated and sealed duct should also be installed to provide combustion air, and the fire area should be sealed from the house as best as possible.

The Air/Vapor Barrier

Apart from the few specific openings that can be eliminated by design changes, most houses have countless other leakage sites which must be sealed in order to make the house airtight. The principal way for taking care of these miscellaneous leaks is through the use of an air/vapor barrier. The proper installation of the air/vapor barrier is essential to a superinsulated house; installation errors not only increase energy use but also increase the risk of moisture damage to the house. The details essential to proper installation are not difficult to understand, but need to be well-communicated to construction crews. The role of the subcontractors for plumbing, wiring, insulation, and drywall installation is also important because any one of these crews can unwittingly damage the air/vapor barrier.

Air/vapor barriers are discussed in greater detail throughout Part II of this book and specifically in Chapter 11.

Site Selection and Design

In conventional houses, air leakage can be reduced by decreasing the indoor-outdoor air pressure difference, the driving force for air leakage. This can be accomplished by building an underground or earth-sheltered structure or by planting a row of evergreens on the side of the house facing the prevailing wind. The pressure differences arising from the stack effect may be reduced by building a structure of low height.

A superinsulated house, however, does not need trees or other buildings to shield it from the wind, nor does it need to be short to minimize the stack effect. Air flow into superinsulated houses is controlled by the ventilation system and is little affected by wind or stack effects, a fact borne out by experience in both Canada and Sweden. Therefore, we do not suggest taking any significant steps to reduce indoor-outdoor pressure differences in airtight houses; this freedom adds considerable flexibility to site selection and design.

AIRTIGHT HOUSES SHOULD BE PRESSURE TESTED

Airtightness is an elusive quality—it cannot be seen. Most crews accustomed to building conventional houses neither appreciate the importance of proper sealing nor know how to tell if the job is well done. After the house is finished, many leakage sites may remain concealed and pass unnoticed.

When building a superinsulated house, it is highly advisable to test for airtightness. Not only do such tests reveal if the system is as flawless as possible; they also serve as a useful learning tool for workmen, who can note leakage sites and potential problem areas and avoid those problems in the future.

Tests for Airtightness

In the "early" days of energy-conserving construction and retrofit, several crude techniques were developed for measuring and evaluating the amount of air leakage into a house. Early energy auditing techniques, for example, used a test in which a dollar bill was inserted between the window sashes of double hung windows. If it went in easily, the infiltration rate was assumed to be 2 to 3 air changes per hour; if it stuck, then the rate was 1 air change per hour. The most common calculation method was the "crack method," in which the total length of window and door cracks was measured so that the infiltration rate could be calculated from leakage values published in engineering handbooks.

Fortunately, we now have more reliable methods for measuring actual leakage rates in both existing houses and new houses under construction. These techniques have allowed us not only to evaluate the relative significance of air leakage on overall energy consumption, but also, more importantly, to test houses before completion to check the quality of the work in progress.

The two most common techniques are the **pressurization method** and the **tracer gas method**. The first is commonly used by builders, while the second is primarily a research tool. The following section briefly describes the pressurization technique. For a more complete discussion and a description of the tracer gas technique, see Chapter 14.

The Pressurization/Depressurization or Blower Door Method A powerful fan is installed in an exterior doorway or window of a house (Figure 3.9). All *intentional* ventilation sources are closed off—windows are closed and the house ventilation system is sealed. The fan is turned on either to blow air into the house (pressurization) or out of the house (depressurization). The fan induces pressure differences that are much larger than those normally created by wind and temperature—an imposed pressure of 50 pascals (0.2 inches of water), or the rough equivalent of a 20 mph wind acting on all surfaces of the house at once.

Then the air flow past the fan is measured. This flow rate is divided by the interior volume of the house to calculate the **50 pascal leakage rate,** expressed in air changes per hour (acph).

The 50 pascal leakage rate is, at present, the most

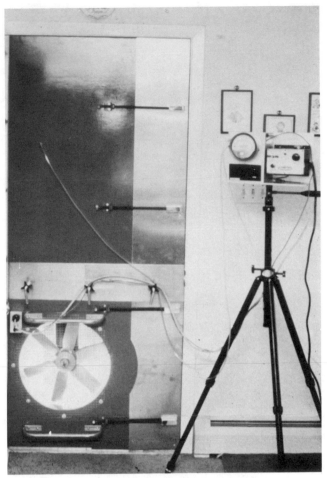

Figure 3.9 Blower door installed for testing a house using pressurization/depressurization technique.

practical way to express the airtightness of a superinsulated house and allows us to set up benchmarks and goals for airtightness. *A properly built superinsulated house should have a tested 50 pascal leakage rate between 1 and 3 acph.* A leakage rate of 3 acph is certainly an attainable standard; it is a specified part of the building code in Sweden. To build a house with a 50 pascal leakage rate less than 1 acph, although it is definitely possible and often achieved, is not worth the trouble; the effect on house performance will be negligible.

Note that the 50 pascal leakage rate is obtained according to the *exaggerated interior-exterior pressure difference* created by a blower door. By available methods of calculation, a 50 pascal leakage rate of 3.0 acph translates into about 0.15 acph average leakage rate under *natural, everyday air pressure differences*. A leakage rate of 0.15 acph means that air leakage is very low. A 50 pascal leakage rate of 1.0 acph translates into about 0.05 acph leakage rate under natural conditions. The relationship between the 50 pascal leakage rate and air leakage under natural conditions is discussed further in Chapter 14.

Four

Indoor air quality
and ventilation

All houses need ventilation for two purposes—to dilute indoor contaminants, and to bring in sufficient oxygen for residents (and for combustion in furnaces, boilers, fireplaces, and stoves).

There are five basic ways to ventilate houses:

1. Entirely by "natural," haphazard air leakage.
2. By natural leakage with intermittent exhaust fan use.
3. By exhaust fan(s) plus *intentional* fresh air intakes.
4. By balanced exhaust *and* supply fans.
5. By controlled passive ventilation schemes.

The first two methods, which depend greatly on the house's air leaks, open windows, operating exhaust fans, etc., are common in conventional houses: the first, completely haphazard air flow, is not really a "method" at all but merely a side effect of leaky construction. While it is, of course, the simplest and lowest in cost, requiring no moving parts or electricity, ventilation by method 1 is drafty, undependable, and energy-wasteful, costing a great deal more in the long run. Recently built houses are often equipped with exhaust fans (method 2) to ventilate kitchens and bathrooms and to remove excess moisture. Exhaust fans, however, do not ensure adequate ventilation, which still depends on outside air leaking in through random openings. Moreover, exhaust fans are only effective *if used;* many people disconnect them because of noise.

The third and fourth methods suit superinsulated houses and are discussed at greater length later in this chapter and in Chapter 12. The last method (5), while potentially ideal for energy-efficient structures in that it allows adequate ventilation with no machinery or moving parts, is still in the early developmental stages. Interesting ideas for controlled passive ventilation schemes exist, but they have never been field tested.

Advantages and disadvantages of the five methods are listed in Table 4.1.

WHY IS INDOOR AIR QUALITY IMPORTANT?

Clean, crisp air, which is not too hot or too cool and not too dry or too humid, is a pleasure to breathe, and contributes not only to a sense of well-being but also to long-term health.

What is healthy air? The normal oxygen level is 21 percent of total air volume; it can drop to a value as low as 15 percent without causing even a sense of fatigue. As for carbon dioxide, permissible concentrations vary depending on the circumstances, but an accepted standard, recommended by the American Society of Heating, Refrigerating, and Air-Conditioning Engineers (ASHRAE), sets levels at a concentration of not more than 0.25 percent in indoor air.

What outdoor-to-indoor ventilation rate maintains these standards? A minimum of about 5 cfm per person is acceptable; with this ventilation rate, indoor oxygen concentration drops from the outdoor level of 21 percent by only 0.26 of a percentage point, while carbon dioxide concentrations are kept within acceptable limits.

However, there's more to healthy air than just acceptable levels of oxygen and carbon dioxide. Air is a conglomeration of numerous substances; those inside a house include water vapor, various products of combustion, chemicals used in the house, as well as substances released by building materials, furnishings, and the soil and water below the house. Some of these substances are potentially unhealthy if present in sufficient quantities. Air containing greater-than-normal concentrations of these substances is considered *contaminated*. Air containing concentrations that may adversely affect health is considered *polluted*.

TABLE 4.1   Comparison of Alternative Ventilation Strategies*

Ventilation System	Advantages	Disadvantages
1) Natural air infiltration only	Low-cost installation. No moving parts. No electricity. No cost for operation.	Ventilation depends on many factors: —wind and temperature difference —behavior in opening windows —airtightness of house —distribution of leakage, and sheltering house from wind. Leaky houses have drafts and energy waste from excessive ventilation. In airtight houses, there is a risk of insufficient ventilation leading to moisture and indoor air quality problems. No known way of ventilation energy recovery.
2) Natural ventilation with intermittent exhaust fan use for baths and kitchen	Relatively low-cost installation. Little electricity cost for operation.	Same as above (1), except exhaust permits selective removal of moisture, cooking odors, and any pollution generated in the cooking process. Ventilation energy recovery is not practical.
3) Exhaust fans with designed fresh air inlet	Ventilation depends mostly on fan design and speed. Depressurization of house reduces risk of moisture penetration into building shell. An airtight envelope with properly sized and placed air inlets can provide well distributed and controlled ventilation. Ventilation heat recovery is possible with exhaust air heat pump for heating water.	Air inlets must be properly sized and located to reduce speed of air flow into conditioned space. Air flow can cause drafts during cold weather. Fan noise. A risk of insufficient ventilation in parts of the house if there are large leaks close to the exhaust.
4) Balanced exhaust and supply fans	In airtight houses, excellent control of ventilation in whole house. Incoming fresh air is conditioned by exhaust air. Much less draft than in other ventilation schemes. Supply air can be taken from outside location with lower air pollution. Easy to recover energy from ventilation air.	Relatively expensive ducting is required. Needs a very airtight building to function as intended. Ventilation balance is very sensitive to variations in pressure. Fan noise. Supply air devices must be located properly to avoid dirt on surfaces caused by airstream. Ducts may need to be cleaned frequently.
5) Controlled passive ventilation	No electricity cost for operation. Potential low-cost installation.	Has not yet been demonstrated in a house. Potential problem with long-term durability and ventilation control. Heat recovery may be difficult.

* Adapted from Elmroth, A. and Levin, P., *Air Infiltration Control in Housing—A Guide to International Practice*, Swedish Council for Building Research, Stockholm, Sweden, 1983.

Because people spend 80 to 90 percent of their time indoors, and because modern life is producing an ever-growing number of potential pollutants, indoor air quality is a serious issue which *every* homebuilder must consider.

It is worth mentioning that sources of indoor air pollution may come not only from indoors, but also from outdoors. However, pollutants generated indoors tend to remain more highly concentrated indoors than out; while indoor levels of exterior-produced pollutants are the same or lower than outdoor levels (Figure 4.1). Besides, since we cannot directly control outdoor levels of pollution, we will concern ourselves primarily with indoor sources.

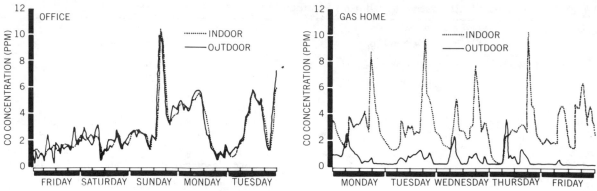

Figure 4.1 Carbon monoxide levels from indoor and outdoor sources. The high exchange rate in office environments where mechanical air-handling systems are used cuts indoor carbon monoxide (CO) concentration to about the same levels recorded outdoors (left graph); indoor CO concentrations in all-electric residences are slightly higher, although they still track the outdoor changes very closely. In contrast, the significantly higher CO levels in a residence with gas facilities (right graph) do not closely follow changes in outdoor concentrations, being more dependent on indoor activities, such a cooking and heating. Note the sharp peaks around the dinner hour. (Source: *Electric Power Research Institute Journal,* March 1982, p. 10.)

A Multitude of Indoor Air Pollution Sources

Some construction materials emit pollutants. Among them are urea-formaldehyde foam insulation, certain tiles, some concrete and masonry, tar paper used on exterior walls and roofs, solvents in paints, and types of plywood and particle board made with a formaldehyde-containing resin.

Furnishings and household appliances are additional sources of indoor air pollution. Fabrics, plastics, rubber, and furniture made with particle board or plywood may emit contaminants, while rugs, carpets, and other surfaces may harbor airborne particles and microorganisms. Gas stoves emit carbon monoxide, nitrogen oxides, and organic compounds. Some draperies emit formaldehyde, and clothes dryers that are not vented to the outside can contaminate the air with particles and with chemicals from fabric softeners.

Human activities contribute significantly to indoor air pollution. Cigarette smoking is a major source of respirable particles, even to nearby nonsmokers. Other less recognized polluting activities include vacuuming, cleaning the oven, cleaning with ammonia-containing solutions, polishing furniture, and working with all sorts of chemicals in the pursuit of hobbies and crafts.

The very presence of people and pets can pollute indoor air with by-products of metabolic activities, particles brought in from outside, and airborne infectious agents, such as bacteria, viruses, and fungi.

Indoor Air Pollution Affects Health Contaminants in the air may exist either as gases or particles and may enter the body through direct contact with skin or eyes, through the respiratory tract, or through the gastro-intestinal tract. Some contaminants are toxic, adversely affecting the health of all people, while others are allergens, affecting only hypersensitive people. Some contaminants are allergens at low concentrations but toxic at high concentrations. Physical reactions to these contaminants range from mild irritation of the eyes or mucous membranes to headaches, nausea, asthma, skin rashes, and cancer.

Radon Radon is a radioactive gas created by the decay of radium, a substance found in most soil, rocks, and mineral deposits. Its concentration varies greatly in different regions of the United States, being greater in areas having uranium and phosphate deposits. In many areas, water contains radon.

Radon gas is colorless, odorless, and undetectable by the senses. When radon decays, its radioactive products, or "radon progeny," attach themselves to tiny dust particles in the air. These particles, when inhaled, may become lodged in the lungs, where subsequent radioactive decay can damage tissue and cause lung cancer.

The average winter radon level in U.S. houses exposes the inhabitants to a lung cancer risk roughly equivalent to that of smoking one or two cigarettes a day. A significant number of houses have radon levels exposing their inhabitants to the equivalent risk of smoking forty to sixty cigarettes a day.

Carbon Monoxide Carbon monoxide is a colorless, odorless gas produced by the incomplete combustion of natural gas, oil, wood, coal, tobacco, and other materials.

High indoor levels of carbon monoxide may be caused by an inadequate supply of air for combustion, which may occur with wood-burning stoves and improperly maintained heating systems. Cracks in chimneys can allow carbon monoxide to leak back inside the house, and attached garages may permit auto exhaust to enter the house.

Because it combines with hemoglobin in the blood far more readily than oxygen, carbon monoxide can prevent normal oxygen uptake and distribution in the body. Mild oxygen deficiencies can impair vision and brain function, while more severe deficiencies can cause irregular heart function, headaches, nausea, weakness, mental confusion, and death.

Nitrogen Oxides Nitrogen dioxide and nitric oxide are formed by the reaction of oxygen and nitrogen when air is heated to high temperatures, as when something is burned. Common sources are gas-burning appliances (gas ovens, stoves, and furnaces) and unvented space heaters that burn natural gas, kerosene, fuel oil, and charcoal. Polluted outdoor air, particularly in highly industrialized areas, may contain high concentrations of nitrogen oxides.

Little is understood about the health effects of chronic exposure to low concentrations, but nitrogen dioxide is known to cause respiratory irritation and lung damage. There is also some evidence that it increases the occurrence of respiratory disease and reduces respiratory function in children.

Formaldehyde and Other Aldehydes Aldehydes are a group of colorless organic compounds which vaporize at room temperature; the simplest type is formaldehyde, whose most well-publicized source is urea-formaldehyde foam insulation (UFFI), (although many houses with UFFI do not have high formaldehyde levels). Many common household objects contain urea-formaldehyde adhesives and resins that may emit formaldehyde as they cure and age. These products include furniture made with plywood and particle board (such as shelves, kitchen cabinets, desks, and stereo speaker housings), carpets and carpet glues, wallpaper, and protective coatings for wooden floors. Burning of natural gas, tobacco, and other combustibles also produces formaldehyde.

Formaldehyde has a pungent odor and is highly irritating to the skin, eyes, mucous membranes, and respiratory tract. In high concentrations, it may cause headaches, nausea, dizziness, vomiting, skin rash, and coughing. It is a suspected carcinogen.

Chlordane Chlordane is an odorless and nearly colorless liquid insecticide that was once sprayed on lawns and gardens. In the mid-1970s the Environmental Protection Agency (EPA) banned chlordane for all uses other than termite control, because animal experiments revealed that it could cause cancer. However, to control termites,

chlordane was still allowed to be injected into the soil around and under houses.

Researchers believe that chlordane gets into houses by seeping through cracks in the foundations. In some cases, it may then get into the ventilation system and spread throughout the house. Houses most likely to be affected are those built on concrete slabs, with ventilation ducts in or below the slabs; those with half-basements or half-crawl spaces; and those with a plenum, or space, beneath the house.

Chlordane remains active for fifteen to twenty years and is readily absorbed by many household objects, including floor surfaces, fabrics, clothing, draperies, carpets, and fabric-covered furniture.

Although there is no absolute proof that breathing chlordane vapor causes health problems, the residents of contaminated houses have complained of headaches, dizziness, flulike symptoms, irritability, short-term memory loss, and hyperactivity in children. Chlordane has also been implicated in the development of liver cancer.

Other Organic Compounds More than 250 organic compounds, existing as gases or particles, have been found in the air in U.S. houses. They come from a variety of sources: the aging and deterioration of synthetic materials, such as those used in carpets, wall coverings, linoleum, fabrics, rubber, and plastics; evaporated solvents from paints, waxes, cleaning aides, personal hygiene products, and adhesives; vapors from aerosol can propellants and pesticides; gases and particles from the incomplete combustion of tobacco, natural gas, and other materials; and the metabolic processes of humans, animals, plants, and bacteria.

The health effects of these compounds vary greatly. Some cause cancer, while others affect the central nervous system or the body's metabolic processes, and still others are merely irritating.

Inhalable and Respirable Particles The degree to which particles suspended in the air affect our health depends largely on their size. The human nose filters out large particles but lets smaller *inhalable* particles enter the windpipe and be deposited. Smaller particles (10 microns or less) can penetrate deep into the lungs, and are therefore called *respirable* particles; these include allergens, asbestos, heavy metals, infectious agents, organic compounds, and smoke. (A micron is a millionth of a meter, or about 0.000039 inch.) Respirable particles are more dangerous than inhalable particles because they remain in the lungs for hundreds of days, contacting the lung tissue and being absorbed by blood or lymph and carried throughout the body. Inhalable particles usually leave the body within days.

Allergens include fungal spores, or mold, which are respirable and flourish at high relative humidities. Pollens are inhalable allergens that come from outdoors and some indoor plants. House dust is a significant allergen that may cause allergic rhinitis and asthma. It consists of animal danders, insect debris, bacteria, human skin, food remnants, inorganic substances, and mites. House dust is resuspended in the air by such activities as walking on carpets and vacuuming.

Asbestos is a source of respirable particles that can cause lung cancer and other respiratory disease. Historically, sources of asbestos included spackling compounds, cements, papier-mâché, wallboard, automobile brakes, hair dryers, and furnace and pipe insulation. Substitute materials have been developed for most of these applications, and asbestos need not be a concern in a newly built house.

Heavy metals in inhalable and respirable particles may endanger health, although their effects at concentrations usually found in the air are not known. These metals (lead, mercury, cadmium, etc.) are found in various compounds, most of which are highly toxic. Cigarette smoke contains cadmium and radioactive polonium.

The concentration of total suspended particles, inhalable and respirable, is two to four times greater in houses where smokers live. Wood and coal burning also increase their concentration.

Smoke   A product of incomplete combustion, smoke is a mixture of gases and particles including carbon monoxide, nitrogen oxides, organic compounds, water vapor, and heavy metals. Common indoor sources are tobacco, coal, and wood.

Tobacco smoke is probably the major source of respirable particles in indoor environments. It is associated with lung cancer and numerous ill effects among nonsmokers as well as smokers. Passive smoking (inhalation of sidestream and exhaled smoke by nonsmokers) may increase a person's heart rate, blood pressure, and carboxyhemoglobin level in the blood, may reduce respiratory capacity, and, in some cases, cause allergic reactions.

IN SUPERINSULATED HOUSES, AIR QUALITY IS PROTECTED IN TWO WAYS

As we have just seen, there are many sources of indoor air pollution. Pollutants may come from objects and activities inside the house, from the house itself, or from outside the house. Such diverse factors as surrounding soil, water supply, the presence or absence of nearby buildings or trees, the house's orientation to the prevailing wind, and weather conditions can affect indoor air quality. Indoor temperature and humidity also play an important role in the chemical and physiological processes related to indoor air pollution and health effects.

We can't do much about some of these sources and processes; others *can* be largely controlled.

Properly designed superinsulated houses are well ventilated. In addition, during the design and construction phases, certain precautions are taken to minimize the risk of indoor air pollution from contaminants in building materials and soil. If both ways of ensuring optimum air quality—proper ventilation *and* contaminant source control—are carefully considered, superinsulated houses can and do provide better air quality than is available in conventional houses.

Controlling Air Pollution at the Source

Wherever air quality, airtightness, energy efficiency, and ventilation are concerned, superinsulation building practices endeavor to eliminate potential problems *before* they arise. With this in mind, we now turn our attention to methods of preventing pollution by minimizing contamination at the source. While it may not be possible to eliminate the sources of contamination entirely, it is often practical to decrease their rate of generation to sub-pollution levels. If the rate of generation of a contaminant is very high, source control is not only helpful but *essential,* since no reasonable amount of ventilation alone can keep the concentration of the contaminant below an acceptable level.

The following strategies for designing and building houses with minimal indoor air pollutants are based on our present understanding of indoor air quality. Many of the strategies are applicable not only to superinsulated houses, but to *all* types of new houses.

Avoiding and Controlling Radon   Consider the soil on which the house is to be built: if it contains enough radium, the house above it could be polluted by a buildup of radon. Extreme cases have been found in houses built on phosphate slag or uranium mill tailings; cases in Florida and Grand Junction, Colorado are well documented. The builder who suspects that anything has been added to soil should have it analyzed for radium. However, even if no high-radium material has been added, levels can be high from natural sources, depending on the geology. At present no "radon-risk" map exists, but high risk areas have been found in eastern Pennsylvania and in Maine. No geographical area has yet been shown to be entirely free of radon.

Fortunately, even on relatively high radium soil, we can design and build houses to ensure that very little radon ever gets into the living space. Most radon enters through cracks and pores in concrete floor slabs and foundation walls (Figure 4.2). It can also diffuse from the soil into a crawl space and then pass into the rest of the house. Sometimes radon is picked up by sub-slab ventilating and air conditioning ducts, sumps, and rock bed heat storage systems and then vented into houses. In most high-radon houses, one or more of these pathways explain how the radon enters the living space.

Unless one is absolutely certain that the soil emits very little radon, no pathway should be left open for radon to enter the living space. Follow these simple rules:

1. *There should be no exposed soil in the basement or crawl space.* A concrete slab is an effective barrier against radon. There should be no paths or other openings, like an open sump, in the slab. Drainage problems should be taken care of outside the foundation wall.

2. *There should be no ducts built into a slab floor.* Hidden from our eyes, these ducts may be in contact with soil. The air circulation and the pressure differences in these ducts may actually help to suck radon out of the ground and distribute it around the house.

3. *Soil should not be exposed to air in interior wall cavities.* Sometimes there is no exposed soil in a basement, but there may be a bathtub or interior partition below which the soil is not covered by the slab. The soil is then connected to the rest of the house through interior wall cavities, and eventually any radon in the soil will leak into the living space.

4. *Living space air should be kept from coming into contact with exposed soil.* Some houses such as "double envelope" houses circulate air over soil underneath the house. Elsewhere, air is circulated through a rock bin storage located on exposed soil. In some houses, fresh air is drawn in through an underground pipe. In all these cases, the air would pick up any radon that might be present in the soil.

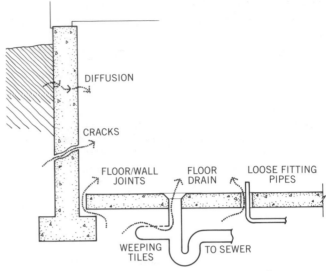

Figure 4.2 Some pathways for radon entry into houses. The ground below the house is often a major source of radon, which gets into the house through cracks and openings in the floor or walls of a basement. (Source: Lawrence Berkeley Laboratory, University of California.)

Controlling Carbon Monoxide and Nitrogen Oxides Indoor sources of carbon monoxide and nitrogen oxides include gas stoves, unvented gas or other combustion space heaters, cars in attached garages, and smoking. The space above gas stoves should be vented to the outside. When cars are started up in attached garages, not only should the garage door be wide open, but any door between the garage and the rest of the house should be closed to keep exhaust fumes out of the house. We do not recommend the use of unvented combustion-type space heaters, whether gas or kerosene, primarily because of the nitrogen oxides generated in the combustion process.

Controlling Formaldehyde As described above, formaldehyde is used in a plethora of household products and building materials. Fortunately, even with untreated materials, the emission rate decreases with time, reducing formaldehyde exposure within a few years. For building materials such as plywood or particle board, emission rates can be reduced by sealing exposed surfaces with a nonporous paint. However, the best way to guard against formaldehyde is to choose building materials carefully in the first place. In response to concern about health effects, the wood products industry has developed specially treated materials—for example LOFT, a kind of plywood manufactured by Weyerhauser—which emit much less formaldehyde.

Chlordane Chlordane injected into the soil around the house appears to enter the house in much the same way as radon. Thus the radon control strategies outlined above should be applicable to chlordane as well. However, this remains to be proven in the field. We are not aware of any experiments in controlling chlordane.

Improving Air Quality with Ventilation

The design goal for a ventilation system in a superinsulated house may be simply stated as follows: to provide adequate fresh outside air in an energy-efficient manner. This raises the following questions. What is an adequate amount of ventilation? What ventilation system can best provide it? Will it provide adequate ventilation to all parts of the house, and at all times? Will energy be wasted because ventilation is higher than it needs to be? The design and functioning of a ventilation system cannot be left to chance. These questions must be answered and the answers used as a basis for appropriate construction.

How Much Ventilation Is Necessary? How much ventilation is needed to ensure acceptable air quality? One of the most commonly accepted standards was developed by the American Society of Heating, Refrigerating and Air-Conditioning Engineers (ASHRAE) (Table 4.2). For typical house size and configuration, the ASHRAE ventilation guideline amounts to an average inflow of about 0.3 air changes per hour (Table 4.3). These standards were developed with a few specific contaminants in mind. In particular, the rate recommended for general living areas—10 cfm/room—is intended to

TABLE 4.2 Outdoor Air Requirements for Ventilation in Residences

(Based on ASHRAE Standard 62-1981)

	cfm/room (independent of room size)	
General living areas	10	
Bedrooms	10	
All other rooms	10	
Kitchens	100	Installed capacity for
Baths, toilets	50	intermittent use
Garages (separate for each dwelling unit)	100 cfm/car space	
Garages (common for several units)	1.5 cfm/ft^2 floor	

Comments: Operable windows or mechanical ventilation systems shall be provided for use when occupancy is greater than usual or when unusual contaminant levels are generated within the space.

Reprinted with permission from the American Society of Heating, Refrigerating, and Air-Conditioning Engineers (ASHRAE), Standard 62-1981.

keep carbon dioxide concentrations within acceptable limits when two sedentary persons are in the room. The rate recommended for kitchens and bathrooms is based on intermittent use, presumably intended to keep moisture levels and odors under control. Because each house is different, these guidelines will have varying implications and impact, depending on the circumstances.

ASHRAE is not the only organization that has proposed ventilation standards. Another set of standards, part of the U.S. Department of Housing and Urban Development's Minimum Property Standards, requires kitchens and bathrooms to be equipped with exhausts

TABLE 4.3 Ventilation Requirements for Typical Houses

(Based on ASHRAE Standard 62-1981)

Cases	1	2	3
Living space floor area (ft^2)	1000	1800	3000
No. of rooms excluding kitchens and bathrooms	3	5	8
No. of bathrooms	1	2	3
Typical ventilation requirement (1000 ft^3/day	58	90	136
or			
air change/hour)	0.30	0.26	0.29
Installed ventilation requirement (air change/hour)	1.35	1.04	0.88
Minimum ventilation requirement (air change/hour)	0.22	0.21	0.20

capable of ventilating at the rate of 15 and 8 air changes per hour respectively, and calls for natural air infiltration of 0.5 air changes per hour. In some parts of California, state laws require houses to have a minimum ventilation rate of 0.75 air changes per hour, apparently the highest minimum in the United States at this time.

Although researchers at Sweden's Chalmers University of Technology have found that a rate as low as 0.2 to 0.3 air changes per hour is sufficient *provided ventilation is well distributed and efficient,* we recommend a ventilation rate of 0.3 to 0.4 air changes per hour.

Controlled Ventilation Systems in Superinsulated Houses By a controlled ventilation system, we mean one that is purposely designed and installed and that contains *some* of the following components: ducts for air flow; a fan or fans, either for exhaust only or exhaust and supply; an air-to-air heat exchanger; and an exhaust-air heat pump.

Effective ventilation systems, suitable for superinsulated houses, fall into two categories: exhaust-only systems and exhaust-and-supply systems. Each category is described briefly below; design details are presented in Chapter 12.

Exhaust-Only Systems In a house with an exhaust-only ventilation system, fresh air comes in through a number of well-defined openings and is drawn out through a single exhaust opening by a fan. With this system, ventilation is fixed, well controlled, and inexpensive. Although the fan uses electricity, that expense is more than made up for by energy savings from avoiding excessive ventilation. Also, since exhaust air leaves the house *only* at a single location, it is easy to recover heat energy from the outgoing air—another savings. Moreover, exhaust ventilation tends to lower indoor air pressure relative to outdoor pressure, so that in wintertime, warm moist indoor air will not tend to leak out through openings in the thermal envelope. Thus the danger of moisture damage is reduced.

Are there disadvantages? Yes, a few. The most prominent is that the air flowing *into* the house is cold and can cause uncomfortable drafts. However, air inlets can be placed and sized to minimize this. Some people object to relying on a fan for health and comfort. What if the fan stops? This should happen rarely. Wiring an "on light" or even a buzzer to the fan circuit will notify occupants if and when the fan goes off. As for the fan noise itself, it is minimal since the fan is moving much less air at much lower velocities than an air conditioner or furnace.

Exhaust-and-Supply Systems In these systems, air is extracted from certain house locations and replaced by outside air brought in to other locations. These systems require two fans, one each for supply and exhaust. Generally, the two fans are balanced to make incoming and outgoing air streams comparable.

USING THE ASHRAE STANDARDS

Consider a three-bedroom house with a living room, a den, a kitchen, and two baths. The living-space floor area is 1800 sq. ft. and the interior ceiling height is 8 ft. According to the ASHRAE ventilation standard, the five rooms other than the bathrooms and the kitchen require a total of 50 cfm of outside air. The kitchen needs 100 cfm when used—let's say for two hours each day. Each of the two bathrooms are used an hour each day and need 50 cfm during this period. The daily total of the ventilation rate amounts to:

Five larger rooms —50 cfm × 60 min./hour × 24 hours/day
Kitchen   —100 cfm × 60 min./hour × 2 hours/day
Two bathrooms   —2 × 50 cfm × 60 min./hour × 1 hour/day
Total   —90,000 cubic ft/day or 3750 cu. ft./hour.

Since the living space volume is 1800 × 8 or 14,400 cu. ft., the daily average ventilation rate amounts to 0.26 air changes per hour. The minimum ventilation rate when bath and kitchen ventilation is off is 0.21 air changes per hour. The maximum ventilation rate when both baths and kitchen are being ventilated amounts to 1.04 air changes per hour.

The minimum ventilation rate for three houses of different size are shown in Table 4.3.

These systems share most of the advantages and disadvantages of exhaust-only systems discussed above. However, the potential problem of drafts is eliminated because the ducted incoming air can be preheated. Another advantage is that outside air can be purposely brought in from a location deemed less polluted than other locations.

Exhaust and supply systems are likely to be more expensive than exhaust-only ventilation because they require both supply and exhaust air ducting.

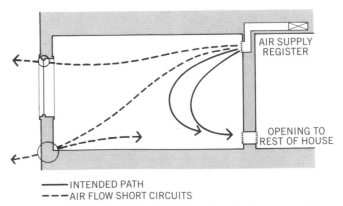

——— INTENDED PATH
- - - AIR FLOW SHORT CIRCUITS

Figure 4.3 Ventilation short circuits in a leaky house with mechanical ventilation. In an airtight house, these short circuits don't occur, making the ventilation system more efficient.

The Effectiveness of Intentional Ventilation Systems

How well pollutants will be removed from indoor air depends not only on the total ventilation rate but also on the mechanical ventilation system's effectiveness, which depends in turn on two things: the variation of ventilation over time, and the distribution of ventilation within the house. The long-term average ventilation rate doesn't tell how well the system counters the effects of pollutants with short-term effects. Ventilation must be consistent and continuous in time.

The effectiveness of spatial distribution has been studied in recent years by the researchers Skaret and Mathisen of Norway and Sandberg of Sweden. Sandberg's principal findings are not surprising: ventilation is best in rooms where outside air is introduced. *Uniform mixing of indoor air is not the best strategy.* It is better to exhaust air from the rooms where pollutants are generated.

It is most important that the house be as airtight as possible, because unintentional leakage sites sabotage the *effectiveness* of mechanical ventilation by providing short circuits for air flow as shown in Figure 4.3. In measurements of room ventilation rates in Sweden, Blomsterberg found that when some windows were opened slightly, the house ventilation rate increased but the rate *in certain rooms* decreased. Other Swedish studies confirm these findings: well-distributed and controlled ventilation is possible *only* in airtight houses in which air inlets are properly sized and located.

The practical aspects of designing and installing a house's ventilation system are discussed in Chapter 12.

Five

Heat loss and energy consumption

In previous chapters, we have seen how superinsulation leads to significant reduction in heat loss from a house. In this chapter, we will look at the relationship between heat loss and annual energy consumption and present some simple calculation methods for estimating both. We will take a closer quantitative look at heat loss, heat gain, balance point temperature, and the concept of degree days.

HEAT LOSS

The three main components of heat loss—*conduction, infiltration, and ventilation*—depend on the insulation and airtightness of the thermal envelope and on the house ventilation rate. All three components can be easily calculated.

Conduction

As explained in Chapter 2, heat is transferred by conduction through all the solid components of the thermal envelope whenever there is a temperature difference between inside and outside. The rate of heat transfer depends on R-value, area of the component, and temperature difference. The general conduction equation is:

$$Q = (A/R) \times (Ti - To) \qquad [5.1]$$

where Q is heat loss rate in Btu/hr, A is the area in square feet, R is R-value, Ti is indoor temperature, and To is outdoor temperature (both in °F).

For example, if a house has 240 square feet of windows which have an R-value of R-2.0, and the indoor temperature is 70°F and the outdoor temperature is 20°F, the rate of heat conduction through those windows is:

$$Q = (240/2.0) \times (70 - 20)$$
$$= 6000 \text{ Btu/hr}$$

For design purposes and energy calculations, one needs to calculate the conduction heat loss through each of the solid components of the thermal envelope—walls, ceiling, windows, doors, floors, and foundation. For each component, we calculate a component *heat loss coefficient* (HLC), defined as the heat loss rate for a *1°F temperature differential*. The equation for conduction HLC is:

$$q = A/R \qquad [5.2]$$

where q is the component HLC, expressed in units of Btu/hr-F.

Infiltration

In Chapter 3, we discussed that infiltration is very low in superinsulated houses. The basic equation for calculating infiltration heat loss is:

$$Q = 0.018 \times V \times AI \times (Ti - To) \qquad [5.3]$$

where V is the house volume in cubic feet; AI is the air leakage rate under natural conditions, in air change per hour (acph); Ti is indoor temperature; and To is outdoor temperature. The constant 0.018 is the heat capacity of air. (Heat capacity is a measure of the amount of energy necessary to raise the temperature of 1 cubic foot of a substance 1°F. Air has a heat capacity of 0.018 Btu per cubic foot per °F. To heat 1 cubic foot of air 1° requires 0.018 Btu. To heat 25 cubic feet of air 8° requires 3.6 Btu (25 × 8 × 0.018).)

For example, the infiltration heat loss rate for a 12,000-cubic-foot house with a natural air infiltration rate of 0.05 air changes per hour when the indoor temperature is 70°F and the outdoor temperature is 0°F is:

$$Q = 0.018 \times 12,000 \times 0.05 \times (70 - 0)$$
$$= 756 \text{ Btu/hr}$$

To calculate the infiltration heat loss coefficient (HLC), the equation is:

$$q = 0.018 \times V \times AI \qquad [5.4]$$

where q is heat loss in Btu/hr-F.

As explained in Chapter 3, air infiltration rates under natural conditions are very difficult to determine. So also is infiltration heat loss. However, in tightly built houses, infiltration heat loss is such a minor part of the total house heat loss that even a 50 percent uncertainty will not result in significant absolute error.

Ventilation

Ventilation is a significant source of heat loss: warm exhaust air carries heat out of the house, and cold intake air must be heated. However, some of the heat from ventilation exhaust air can be recovered and used to preheat the incoming fresh air or to heat domestic water. Usually this is accomplished with an air-to-air heat exchanger or air-to-water heat pump (see Chapter 12).

The equation for calculating ventilation heat loss is the same as that for calculating infiltration heat loss except for the addition of an extra term that accounts for heat recovery:

$$Q = 0.018 \times V \times Z \times (Ti - To) \times (1 - e) \qquad [5.5]$$

where Z is the ventilation rate in air changes per hour (acph), and e is the heat recovery efficiency of the air-to-air heat exchanger or other heat recovery device.

In the above case, the ventilation rate is expressed in air changes per hour (Z). If the ventilation rate is expressed in cubic feet per minute (cfm), the equation becomes:

$$Q = 1.08 \times ZF \times (Ti - To) \times (1 - e) \qquad [5.6]$$

where ZF is the ventilation rate in cfm.

To calculate the ventilation heating load coefficient (HLC) (for a 1° temperature differential), the equations are:

$$q = 0.018 \times V \times Z \times (1 - e) \qquad [5.7]$$

when the ventilation rate is expressed in air changes per hour, and

$$q = 1.08 \times ZF \times (1 - e) \qquad [5.8]$$

when the ventilation rate is expressed in cubic feet per minute.

Note: The ventilation heat loss equation presented above is simplified and ignores certain factors, such as latent heat loss and recovery.

THE TOTAL HOUSE HEAT LOSS COEFFICIENT

The total house HLC is the total house *heat loss rate for each degree of temperature difference between indoors and outdoors.* Expressed in units of Btu per hour per °F (Btu/hr-F), the house HLC is the sum of all the individual component HLC's—conduction, infiltration, and ventilation. The total house HLC, when multiplied by the indoor-outdoor temperature difference at any time, gives the total house heat loss rate.

The HLC is necessary for annual energy use calculations as well as design heat load calculations for sizing heating systems (see Chapter 12). It is also a useful term for characterizing the thermal envelope of a house (see Chapter 6).

Sample HLC Calculation for a Superinsulated House

The HLC is easy to calculate using the heat loss equations presented above.

Example: Calculate the house HLC for a superinsulated house that is a single story, 40 × 50-foot rectangle with 8-foot ceilings and no basement. The walls are insulated to R-30; the ceiling is R-60. The total window area is 12 percent of the floor area and the windows have an R-value of R-2.8. Two doors, with a total area of 42 square feet, have an R-value of R-10.0. The infiltration rate is 0.05 air changes per hour. A ventilation system with an air-to-air heat exchanger supplies an additional 0.45 air changes per hour with 70 percent heat recovery.

Conduction

Walls
Area = 1158 square feet (gross wall area minus windows and doors)
R-value = 30
q = 1158/30
 = 38.6 Btu/hr-F

Windows
Area = 240 square feet
R-value = 2.8
q = 240/2.8
 = 85.7 Btu/hr-F

Doors
Area = 42 square feet
R-value = 10.0
q = 42/10.0
 = 4.2 Btu/hr-F

Ceiling
Area = 2000 square feet
R-value = 60
q = 2000/60
 = 33.3 Btu/hr-F

Infiltration

House volume = 2000 × 8
 = 16,000 cubic feet
Infiltration rate = 0.05 acph
q = 0.018 × 16,000 × 0.05
 = 14.4 Btu/hr-F

Ventilation

Ventilation rate	= 0.45 acph
Heat recovery eff.	= 0.70
q	= $0.018 \times 16{,}000 \times 0.45 \times (1 - .70)$
	= 38.9 Btu/hr-F

The ventilation component of the house HLC is different from the other components in that it can be quite variable. At times, the ventilation rate might be reduced, lowering the house HLC. On the other hand, during a party with twenty-five smokers in the house, the ventilation might be increased, raising the house HLC.

Foundation   The foundation HLC is much more complex to calculate than the other house HLC's. The reasons are discussed in detail in Chapter 8. For this example, we will assume the slab to be very well insulated, so that q = 15 Btu/hr-F.

Summary   The total house HLC is summarized as follows:

Walls	38.6 Btu/hr-F	16.7%
Windows	85.7	37.3
Doors	4.2	1.8
Ceiling	33.3	14.5
Infiltration	14.4	6.3
Ventilation	38.9	16.9
Foundation	15.0	6.5
TOTAL HLC	230 Btu/hr-F	100%
	67 watts/F	

The Total Heat-Loss Rate at Any Time Depends on HLC and Indoor-Outdoor Temperature Difference

The HLC of 230 Btu/hr-F in the above example means that the house loses 230 Btu per hour for every degree it has to be heated above outdoor temperature. If the house is to be heated 30° above outdoor temperature—for example, to 70° inside when it is 40° outside—the total heat loss rate will be 230×30 or 6900 Btu/hr. The HLC is listed in watts/F as well as Btu/hr-F to provide some perspective on the relationship between the heating needs of the house and the electric power being used for lights and appliances inside the house. The HLC of 67 watts per °F is quite low for this size house. When it is 40° outside, it will only require 40 times 67, or 2680 watts to keep the house warm. That's the amount of power put out by two average hair dryers!

Note about heat loss calculations: These heat loss calculations are "steady-state" calculations. "Steady-state" means that indoor and outdoor temperatures do not change. In reality, that condition doesn't often exist, so that actual heat loss may be somewhat different.

HEAT GAIN

Of the three sources of heat gain into a house—intrinsic heat, solar heat, and auxiliary heat—the first two are difficult to quantify accurately. Intrinsic heat depends on occupancy and appliances; solar input depends on various factors, such as house location, window size and orientation, and shading.

Intrinsic Heat

Intrinsic heat is waste heat from processes or activities within a house. Lighting, cooking, hair drying, metabolism, television watching, and refrigeration—all occur in a typical house; all give off heat. A 100-watt light bulb produces about 10 watts of light and about 90 watts of heat; but even the 10 watts of light eventually becomes heat when it stops bouncing around the room (unless it bounces out of the house through the window glass). Each 100-watt light bulb is just like a small electric heater with an output of 100 watts or 341.3 Btu/hr. All the other appliances in a house are also heaters; each puts out just as much heat as an electric heater of equal wattage. A color television, for example, with a nameplate rating of 150 watts, puts out 150 watts of heat (512 Btu/hr)—the same as a 150-watt electric heater. Of course, the distribution is different, for while the electric heater puts out 150 watts of pure heat (except for maybe a little light from the glowing core), the television puts out heat, light, and sound; but all of it eventually ends up as heat. If a house needs 1500 watts of power to satisfy its heating demands, then ten 150-watt color televisions would work pretty much as well as one 1500-watt electric heater. (While it would seem rather eccentric to use televisions to heat a house, there is a chain of superinsulated convenience stores in Montana that are heated largely by the waste heat from video games.)

People and animals also give off heat. The average adult male gives off about 265 Btu/hr (78 watts) when at rest, and about 685 Btu/hr (201 watts) during heavy exertion.

The following are a few representative values of the amount of intrinsic heat in a house.

refrigerators	600 Btu/hr (average over a year)
freezers	500 Btu/hr (average over a year)
25-in. color television	1,000 Btu/hr (average over a year)
12-in. B&W television	350 Btu/hr (average over a year)
100-watt light	341 Btu/hr (average over a year)
person*	
at rest	225 Btu/hr (average over a year)
dancing	850 Btu/hr (average over a year)

* Adjusted for the average percentage of men, women, and children in population. Includes sensible heat dissipation only.

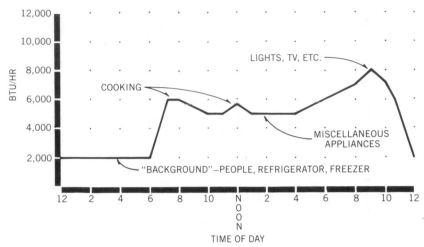

Figure 5.1 Intrinsic heat over a day in a "typical" house.

Intrinsic Heat over a "Typical" Day in the Average" Home Let's take a look at one scenario for intrinsic heat generation in a "typical" house over the course of one full winter day (Figure 5.1). The minimum intrinsic heat gain will most likely occur between midnight and 6 A.M., when the only heat sources are four sleeping people (900 Btu/hr), the refrigerator (600 Btu/hr), and maybe a freezer (500 Btu/hr). At around 7 A.M., the house comes to life and the intrinsic heat starts to flow: 500 watts of lights go on in the kitchen and bathrooms (1700 Btu/hr), hair dryer (4000 Btu/hr), toaster (4000 Btu/hr), and stove (5000 Btu/hr) all go on and off for the first hour of the day. After breakfast, the intrinsic heat is lower but a minimum "background" of appliance use persists as the day progresses—perhaps a couple of lights (700 Btu/hr) and about 200 watts of miscellaneous appliances. Another peak may occur around lunch when everyone heads for the stove, but the highest steady intrinsic gains occur during the evening when the 25-inch color television goes on (1000 Btu/hr) and perhaps the small television in the children's room (350 Btu/hr) as well. The teenagers may put on the stereo (300 Btu/hr) and maybe dance a little (1200 Btu per hour extra.) The intrinsic heat probably peaks at 9 or 10 P.M. in the range of 6000 to 8000 Btu/hr. Around midnight, everything gets shut off, and the intrinsic heat gain settles back to the 2000 Btu/hr nighttime minimum (people, refrigerator, and freezer).

According to an extensive survey performed by the U.S. Energy Information Agency (Residential Energy Consumption Survey), the average American household uses 5900 kWh of electricity per year for purposes other than heating or cooling. That translates into about 20 million Btu per year, or about 2300 Btu per hour. Of course, the actual amount of intrinsic heat produced will vary tremendously among households and with the seasons. But for energy calculations, *a reasonable estimate for intrinsic heat input is between 2000 and 3000 Btu per hour.*

Solar Heat

The amount of solar heat input entering through windows depends on (1) latitide of the house site, (2) time of year, (3) cloud cover, (4) orientation of the windows, (5) size of the windows, and (6) amount of shading. Appendix C lists the *average* amount of sunshine falling on vertical surfaces facing in each of the eight main compass directions. The data are presented for 85 U.S. and Canadian cities and for each month of the year. One can use these data to calculate the average amount of solar heat input into a house during any particular month simply by measuring the area of glass facing in each compass direction and multiplying that value by the amount of solar energy per square foot incident on a surface facing in that direction (from Appendix C).

For example, suppose a house located in New York City has 60 square feet of glass facing in each of the four cardinal compass directions. What will be the solar heat input on an average January day?

From Appendix C, we find the following values for average daily solar gain:

North	132	Btu/square foot-day
South	848	Btu/square foot-day
East	329	Btu/square foot-day
West	326	Btu/square foot-day

Our sample house has 60 square feet of windows facing in each of the four cardinal directions. The total daily solar heat input is therefore:

North	132 × 60 =	7,920 Btu/day
South	848 × 60 =	50,880 Btu/day

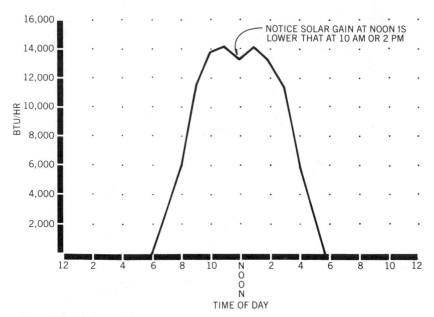

Figure 5.2 Total solar heat gain over a day for house with 240 square feet of glass facing north, south, east, and west (60 square feet in each direction). Data is for average conditions, including cloud cover, for New York City in January.

East   329 × 60 = 19,740 Btu/day
West   326 × 60 = 19,560 Btu/day
Total daily   98,100 Btu/day
Average hourly   = 98,100/24
                            =   4,088 Btu/hr

Keep in mind that in January, most of the solar energy comes during the midday hours between 10 A.M. and 2 P.M. (Figure 5.2). When the windows are distributed as in the above example, the highest input is at 10 A.M. and 2 P.M. Also, the values in Appendix C are *average* values taking into account cloud cover. On clear days, the solar intensity is much higher. (Because tables of "Clear Day Insolation" are published in almost *every* book on solar design, they are not included in this book.)

Auxiliary Heat

Auxiliary heat comes from a heating system. It is the one input that is completely controllable. The amount of auxiliary heat required is the difference between the total heat loss and the sum of intrinsic and solar heat:

Auxiliary heat = total heat loss − (Intrinsic heat + solar heat)

THE BALANCE-POINT TEMPERATURE

The concept of **balance-point temperature** is crucial to understanding and calculating annual energy consumption of a superinsulated house. It is also one of the most commonly misunderstood terms.

The balance-point temperature is the outdoor temperature at which the total house heat loss equals intrinsic plus solar heat. When the outdoor temperature is at or above the balance-point temperature, no auxiliary heat is needed. Conversely, auxiliary heat will be needed whenever the outdoor temperature falls below the balance point.

A common misunderstanding is that a specific house has a fixed balance-point temperature. You *cannot* say that a house has a balance-point temperature of, say, 50°F. Although partly dependent on the house heat loss coefficient (HLC), the balance-point temperature also depends on indoor temperature, the amount of intrinsic heat, and the amount of solar heat, *all of which vary constantly.*

For any *one* set of conditions at *one* specific time, the balance point-temperature can be calculated using the following equation:

BP = Ti − [(intrinsic heat input + solar heat input) / HLC]

$$[5.9]$$

where BP is balance-point temperature, Ti is the indoor temperature, and HLC is the total house heat-loss coefficient.

For example, let's take the superinsulated house for which we calculated the HLC to be 230 Btu/hr-F. Suppose the house is unoccupied late at night, all appliances are shut off, and the thermostat is set at 70°F. What is the balance-point temperature?

Ti   = 70°F
Intrinsic heat = 0 Btu/hr
Solar heat   = 0 Btu/hr
HLC   = 230 Btu/hr-F

Using Equation 5.9,

$$BP = 70 - [(0 + 0) / 230]$$
$$= 70°F$$

In other words, the house will need auxiliary heat whenever the outdoor temperature falls below 70°F.

Now suppose the homeowner comes home, plugs in the refrigerator, turns on seven 100-watt light bulbs and the color television, and puts a cake in the oven to bake. Now what is the balance point?

Ti = 70°F
Intrinsic heat
  1 person   250 Btu/hr
  refrigerator   600 Btu/hr
  7 lights   2389 Btu/hr
  color TV   1000 Btu/hr
  oven   4000 Btu/hr
Total   8239 Btu/hr
Solar heat   0 Btu/hr
HLC   230 Btu/hr-F

Again using equation 5.9,

$$BP = 70 - [(8239 + 0) / 230]$$
$$34.2°F$$

The balance-point temperature is now 34.2°F. If all those lights and appliances were left running, no auxiliary heat would be needed until the outdoor temperature falls below 34.2°F.

If the house were not superinsulated, that is, if it had a much higher HLC, the balance-point temperature would be considerably higher. Let's examine this because it is the key reason why superinsulated houses have such low annual energy consumption.

Suppose the house were a conventional house with an HLC of 900 Btu/hr-F:

$$BP = 70 - [(8239 + 0) / 900]$$
$$= 60.8°F$$

With the intrinsic heat gains described above, this house would need auxiliary heat whenever the outdoor temperature falls below about 61°F.

Because intrinsic heat, solar heat, and possibly indoor temperature change throughout the day, so does the balance point temperature. Figure 5.3 shows how the balance-point temperature might change over the course of a day, as affected by intrinsic heat only—*no solar heat*. Notice that on this relatively mild day, the outdoor temperature is above the balance-point temperature for a good part of the day. Heat is only needed during the early morning hours. Figure 5.4 shows how the balance point temperature changes when solar heat input is in-

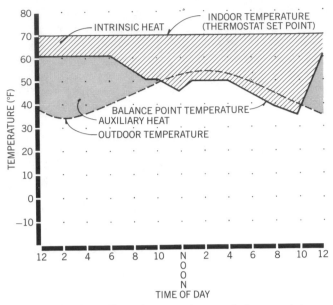

Figure 5.3 The effect of intrinsic heat on balance point temperature, assuming a total house HLC of 230 Btu/hr-F and using intrinsic heat data from Figure 5.1.

cluded. Notice that around noon, the balance-point temperature is below 0°F! (The values for intrinsic and solar heat inputs in Figures 5.3 and 5.4 are taken from the data in Figures 5.1 and 5.2.)

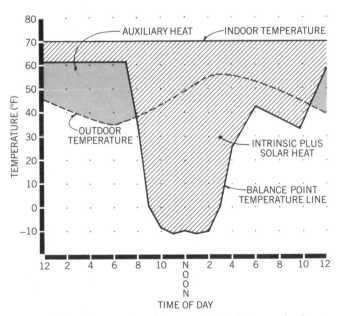

Figure 5.4 The combined effect of intrinsic plus solar heat on balance-point temperature during one day, assuming a total house HLC of 230 Btu/hr and using average solar data for New York City in January.

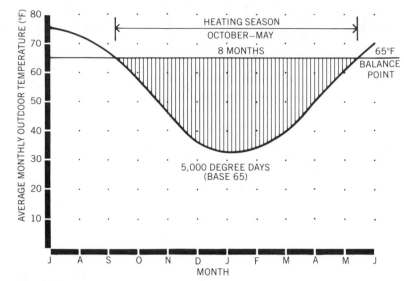

Figure 5.5 Average monthly temperatures and base-65 heating season for New York City.

ANNUAL AUXILIARY HEAT REQUIREMENTS

This is clearly the bottom line for this chapter. As stated above, auxiliary heat must fill the gap between total heat loss and the energy supplied by intrinsic and solar heat. Intrinsic and solar heat will supply enough heat to keep the house warm down to the balance-point temperature. Auxiliary heat is required when the outdoor temperature is below the balance point. *The amount of auxiliary heat required is proportional to how much and how long the outdoor temperature is below the balance point.* The amount of auxiliary heat needed *at any instant* is given by:

$$AH = HLC \times (BPT - T_o)$$

where AH is the auxiliary heat in Btu/hr, and BPT is the balance-point temperature.

To calculate the *total annual* auxiliary heat requirements, one could calculate the requirements for each hour of the heating season, using hourly weather data, and sum the results. This type of "hourly simulation" is obviously very tedious. Even with a computer, it is a relatively lengthy task. A more simple and common approach is to employ the concept of "degree days."

Degree days are a measure of the difference between the *average* daily outdoor temperature and a specified *base-temperature.* Traditionally, degree days were measured to a 65°F base-temperature. If, for example, the average daily outdoor temperature is 35°F, then 65 − 35, or 30 base-65 degree days accumulate during that day. The annual heating degree days for a specific location is simply the sum of the daily degree days over the winter.

Degree days have conventionally been measured to a base of 65°F because heating engineers assumed that 65°

F was the average balance point of most typical houses, i.e., the outdoor temperature below which houses need auxiliary heat was 65°F. As we have clearly seen, the balance-point temperature of superinsulated houses is often well below 65°F. If degree days are to be used as a measure of the need for auxiliary heat, then they must be measured to a base corresponding to the average balance point of the house. *Base-65 degree days won't work for energy calculations for superinsulated houses.* Figure 5.5 shows a plot of monthly average outdoor temperature for New York City over a year. The shaded area below the horizontal 65°F line represents the total base-65 degree days—5000. Notice that the heating season, defined as that period when the average outdoor temperature is below the balance-point temperature, extends from October to May.

Figure 5.6 shows the same weather data plotted against a 42°F balance point. The heating season is only four months long, and the total number of base-42 degree days is only 800.

Appendix C includes average degree-day data for several different base temperatures for 85 U.S. and Canadian cities.

Calculating Annual Energy Consumption and Cost by the Degree-Day Method

The *degree-day method* is a simple way to calculate the annual auxiliary heat requirements of a house. To be accurate, this method must use degree days calculated to a base temperature equal to the average balance-point temperature of the house. But as we have seen, balance-point temperature is variable. Selecting an average balance-point temperature entails a bit of guesswork, and

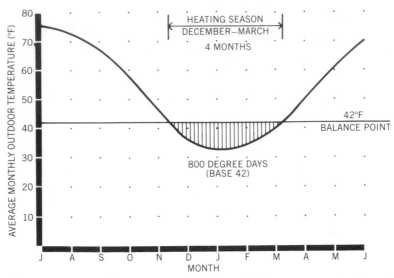

Figure 5.6 Average monthly temperatures and base-42 heating season for New York City.

the accuracy of degree-day energy calculations will only be as good as this guess. Despite its inaccuracy, the degree-day method is still useful. After all, if the total annual heating cost is, for instance, only $100, then even if the calculations are off by 100 percent, the difference would be only $100 per year.

Procedure

1. From Appendix C, find the number of degree days at the city nearest your site. Record the degree-day values for several different bases, say base-40, base-45, and base-50.
2. Calculate the total house Heating Load Coefficient (HLC).
3. Calculate annual auxiliary heat requirements using the following equation:

$$AAH = HLC \times 24 \times HDD \qquad [5.11]$$

where AAH is annual auxiliary heat requirements in Btu, and HDD is heating degree days. This calculation is done separately with each degree day value selected.
4. Calculate annual heating energy costs using the following equation:

$$AHC = [AAH/(F \times e)] \times P \qquad [5.12]$$

where AHC is the annual heating cost in dollars, F is the energy content per purchased unit of fuel in Btu (see Appendix F), e is the efficiency of the heating system, and P is the price per unit of purchased fuel.

Example. What is the annual heating energy cost for a house with an HLC of 260 Btu/hr-F, located in Boston? The heating system operates at 70 percent efficiency and uses oil costing $1.10 per gallon.

From Appendix C, we see that degree days for Boston are:

Base 40—1138
Base 45—1794
Base 50—2574

From Appendix F, we find that the energy content of heating oil is 138,000 Btu/gallon. For an assumed 40°F average balance point (degree day base of 40):

$$AAH = 260 \times 24 \times 1138$$
$$= 7.1 \text{ million Btu}$$
$$AHC = [7,100,000 / (138,000 \times 0.7)] \times 1.10$$
$$= \$81 \text{ per year}$$

For a 45°F average balance point:

$$AAH = 11.2 \text{ million Btu}$$
$$AHC = \$128 \text{ per year}$$

For a 50°F average balance point:

$$AAH = 16.1 \text{ million Btu}$$
$$AHC = \$183 \text{ per year}$$

Thus the annual energy costs for this house are somewhere between $81 and $183 per year. The average of the three calculated costs is $131, and we can expect the heating bill of this house to be within about $50 of this amount.

Six

Designing the superinsulated house

DESIGN IS A PROCESS— A PATH TOWARD A GOAL

The design of a superinsulated house is a relatively straightforward process. Beginning with specified goals, the designer proceeds through a logical sequence of five steps (Figure 6.1). A preliminary design is roughed out (step 1). Next, the basic energy-related specifications— R-values, window systems, and airtightness—are selected (step 2), and a preliminary energy analysis is performed (step 3). At that point, the designer knows whether or not the proposed design will lead to the specified goals. If not, he/she returns to the beginning, modifying the basic structure until the design is acceptable. Once the basic design is approved from both aesthetic and energy standpoints, the "energy systems"—insulation, passive solar, air management, heating, cooling, water heating, appliances, and lighting—are carefully selected to optimize cost and energy efficiency (step 4). Finally, the design is translated into detailed construction drawings and specifications (step 5).

Most of the superinsulation techniques described in this book are part of step 4, "energy systems design." While the general specifications for *what* is to be done are written in step 2 (energy specifications), the details on *how* it will be accomplished are designed in step 4. For example, during the second step, it may be decided that insulating the house walls to R-30 would be adequate to achieve design goals. But the important decisions with respect to superinsulation are yet to come. What type of support structure? 6-inch studs plus foam sheathing? interior strapping? double studs? How will thermal bridging and other thermal defects be minimized? Where will the air/vapor barrier go and how will it be carried continuously from basement to attic? What type of special accommodations need to be made for electrical and plumbing in-

stallations? These and scores of other details are addressed during step 4.

This chapter deals with basic design and analysis— steps 1 through 3. We present some important criteria concerning house geometry and floor plan, sizing and placement of windows, and selecting R-values for the various components of the thermal envelope. We then present methods for evaluating the thermal performance of the proposed design. Design steps 4 and 5—energy systems design and construction documents—are also briefly described.

PREDESIGN—SETTING GOALS

Before drawing anything, three basic design goals must be defined: size, cost, and energy efficiency.

Size

Size naturally depends on personal preference. Some homebuyers tend to request a larger house if it is superinsulated, since the bigger space will cost proportionately less to heat. Although that's true, keep in mind that there is no magic to superinsulation and, unfortunately, no "free lunch" in energy efficient housing. In fact, since intrinsic heat does not change proportionately with house size, a 4000-square-foot superinsulated house will generally require *more* than twice the heating energy of a 2000-square-foot house with equivalent insulation and occupancy.

Cost

As with any house design, the prospective homebuyer should have a firm budget. When designing a superinsulated house, an extra $5000 to $10,000 should be included for energy-related features.

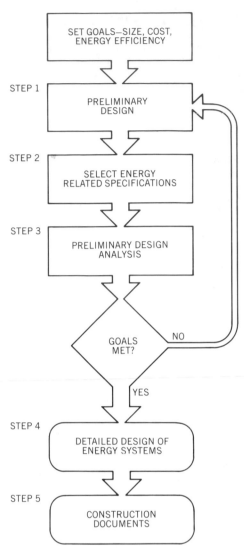

STEP 1

STEP 2

STEP 3

STEP 4

STEP 5

SET GOALS—SIZE, COST, ENERGY EFFICIENCY

PRELIMINARY DESIGN

SELECT ENERGY RELATED SPECIFICATIONS

PRELIMINARY DESIGN ANALYSIS

GOALS MET?

NO

YES

DETAILED DESIGN OF ENERGY SYSTEMS

CONSTRUCTION DOCUMENTS

Figure 6.1 The design process.

Energy Efficiency

There are two possible approaches for thinking about goals for energy efficiency. Consider the following two scenarios in which a prospective homebuyer discusses energy needs with a builder.

Scenario 1:

Homebuyer: *"I am interested in building a house I saw featured in this month's* Good Homes *magazine. It's a beautiful 2000-square-foot ranch. The only problem is this: it isn't very energy-efficient. The estimated annual cost for heat is $1200. What energy-conserving features or modifications can you add to this house? I'm willing to pay more for those features as long as they will pay for themselves through reduced energy costs after a reasonable amount of time—say five to ten years."*

Scenario 2:

Homebuyer: *"I want a 2000-square-foot house for which the annual heating costs are minimal—say about $150 per year at current fuel prices. I don't want heating costs ever to be a major part of my total operating costs. This is an important feature to me and I'm willing to pay for it as long as the extra cost isn't exorbitant. There are also several other features I would like and for which I am also willing to pay extra: I'd like wide pine floors, marble sinks in the bathroom. . . ."*

In the first scenario, the builder is asked to identify each individual energy saving feature, assign a cost for that feature, and determine its effect on the overall energy consumption of the house. Each component is individually justified based on cost effectiveness. The result is a "package" of cost-effective features.

In the second scenario, the designer can take a much different design approach. Here the client is only concerned with end product and final price, not individual components. Although the designer is still likely to analyze some discrete options, such as the air-to-air heat exchanger, for their individual cost-effectiveness, he is relieved of the burden of identifying and cost-justifying each energy-saving feature. The design will be acceptable as long as the final product meets the combined requirements of energy efficiency and construction costs.

While the component analysis approach of the first scenario is more traditional, the second scenario is more appropriate to superinsulation design. *For most of the thousands of superinsulated houses standing today, an economic analysis of the last inch of wall insulation will show it not to be cost effective.* But that analysis does not take into account savings on heating system cost or other factors related to house heat load. Interestingly, most successful builders of superinsulated houses tend to build *only* superinsulated houses and therefore cannot or will not quote an "extra" cost for the superinsulation package. If you ask them for a bid on a proposed 1500-square-foot house, they will give you a price for a 1500-square-foot superinsulated house, not two separate prices for a house with and without superinsulation.

An Energy Efficiency Rating How does one express energy efficiency goals? The homebuyer in the second scenario asked for a 1500-square-foot house with a $150 annual fuel bill. He/she is using the best terms. To eliminate house size as a factor, the best way to express energy efficiency is in terms of dollars (or Btu) per year per square foot of floor space. At 1985 energy prices, a realistic figure for superinsulated houses in North America is between $.05 and $.20 per square foot per year for total heating and cooling costs. Small houses (1200 square feet or less) often can be heated for $.05 per square foot per year. For larger houses, however, the $.20 figure is

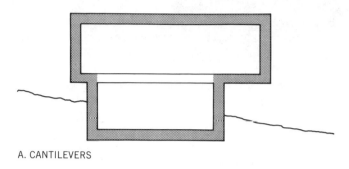

A. CANTILEVERS

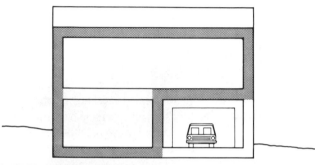

B. TUCK-UNDER GARAGE

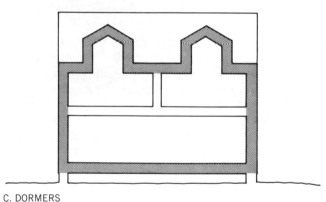

C. DORMERS

Figure 6.2 Examples of complex geometries that tend to be more difficult for superinsulation.

more realistic because intrinsic heat and solar energy input will usually supply a relatively smaller proportion of the total heat load.

Obviously, climate has a huge bearing on energy costs per square foot. To correct for climate, some people express energy performance in terms of "Btu per square foot per degree day" (Btu/ft^2/DD). Unfortunately, this climate correction is not very useful for superinsulated houses, since identical houses located in different climates will not have the same value of Btu/ft^2/DD. For a more detailed explanation, see Chapter 14.

STEP 1: PRELIMINARY DESIGN

Superinsulation offers the designer a great deal of latitude with few constraints. However, several basic design elements, particularly window size and placement, have considerable impact on energy efficiency. The following sections discuss those elements and offer guidelines for consideration during preliminary design.

Dwelling Form

Ideally, the shape of the "thermal envelope" should be as simple as possible. Since every corner and protrusion must be thoroughly insulated and sealed at all joints, complex geometries such as dormers, "tuck-under" garages, and cantilevered floors (Figure 6.2) all make superinsulation somewhat more difficult. Although a neat rectangle or cube is the best shape for the thermal envelope, it needn't be the final shape of the house. Unheated elements and climate modifiers such as porches, unheated garages, storage sheds, and sunspaces can be added on to the outside of a house to embellish the exterior design without complicating the thermal envelope (Figure 6.3).

Surface-to-Volume Ratio In theory, the greater the ratio of exterior surface area to enclosed volume of living space, the greater the heat loss for a house of a given size. According to this criterion, the ideal floor plan is a square. However, on occasion, the importance of surface-to-volume ratio is overemphasized and oversimplified. First of all, in a very well insulated house, increasing the surface area by 10 or 15 percent may add only an insignificant amount to the total heat load. Second, since some exterior surfaces are typically better insulated than others—ceilings, for example, compared to walls—simple surface-to-volume ratio is not always the main determinant of energy efficiency. For example, consider the two houses in Figure 6.4—a 30- × 60-foot single-story ranch, and a 30- × 30-foot two story colonial, each with 1800 square feet of floor area. Enclosing an equal volume, the single-story ranch has about 10 percent more surface area. But which is more energy efficient? Probably the single story ranch. Even though the two-story house more closely approaches the shape of a cube, it has much more wall area than the single story house. Assuming both houses have R-30 walls and R-60 ceilings, the Heat Loss Coefficient (HLC) for just walls and ceiling is about 6 percent less for the single story house, despite its higher surface-to-volume ratio.

Of course, the extra heat loss through the larger foundation of the single story house may even things out. The point here is not that single-story houses are more energy efficient, but that *with superinsulated houses, relative surface-to-volume ratio is not necessarily a prime determinant of energy efficiency.* Other factors, such as window size and placement, are much more important.

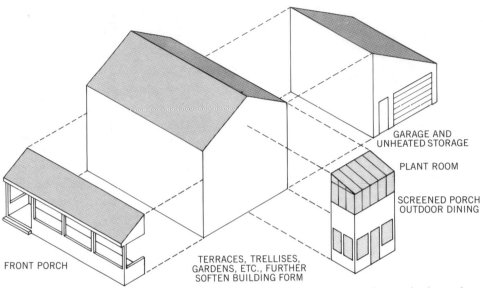

Figure 6.3 Unheated architectural elements attached to a geometrically simple thermal envelope.

GARAGE AND
UNHEATED STORAGE

PLANT ROOM

SCREENED PORCH
OUTDOOR DINING

FRONT PORCH

TERRACES, TRELLISES,
GARDENS, ETC., FURTHER
SOFTEN BUILDING FORM

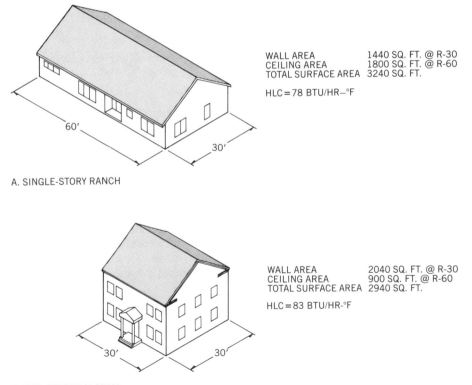

WALL AREA   1440 SQ. FT. @ R-30
CEILING AREA   1800 SQ. FT. @ R-60
TOTAL SURFACE AREA 3240 SQ. FT.

HLC = 78 BTU/HR—°F

60'

30'

A. SINGLE-STORY RANCH

WALL AREA   2040 SQ. FT. @ R-30
CEILING AREA   900 SQ. FT. @ R-60
TOTAL SURFACE AREA 2940 SQ. FT.

HLC = 83 BTU/HR-°F

30'

30'

B. TWO-STORY COLONIAL

Figure 6.4 Comparison of heat loss coefficient (HLC) between single-story ranch and two-story colonial of equal floor area. The two-story house has a higher HLC despite less exterior surface area. Basement heat loss is ignored in this example.

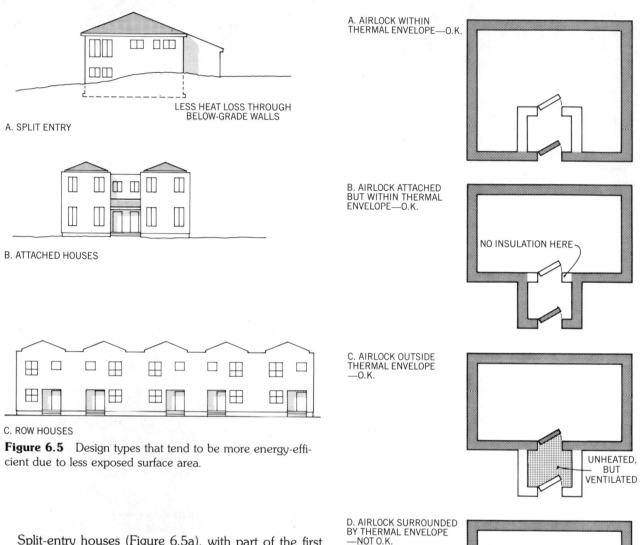

A. SPLIT ENTRY

LESS HEAT LOSS THROUGH
BELOW-GRADE WALLS

B. ATTACHED HOUSES

C. ROW HOUSES

Figure 6.5 Design types that tend to be more energy-efficient due to less exposed surface area.

A. AIRLOCK WITHIN
THERMAL ENVELOPE—O.K.

B. AIRLOCK ATTACHED
BUT WITHIN THERMAL
ENVELOPE—O.K.

NO INSULATION HERE

C. AIRLOCK OUTSIDE
THERMAL ENVELOPE
—O.K.

UNHEATED,
BUT
VENTILATED

D. AIRLOCK SURROUNDED
BY THERMAL ENVELOPE
—NOT O.K.

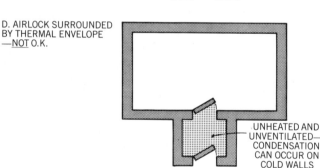

UNHEATED AND
UNVENTILATED—
CONDENSATION
CAN OCCUR ON
COLD WALLS

Split-entry houses (Figure 6.5a), with part of the first floor below grade, lose less heat than standard two-story buildings because of the lower heat loss through below-grade walls.

The most energy efficient dwelling forms are, of course, attached houses and row houses (Figure 6.5b and c), where one or two boundary walls are shared with another living unit. Here the exterior surface-to-volume ratio is drastically less than that of any other design type.

Basement, Crawl Space, or Slab

Any type of foundation is fine for a superinsulated house. If a basement is planned, it should be considered to be inside the thermal envelope and heated. Reasons are explained fully in Chapter 8.

Unheated Attics and Cathedral Ceilings

Unheated attics are well suited for superinsulation because they allow for easy installation of large amounts of insulation. Cathedral ceilings are slightly more difficult and expensive to insulate. Chapter 9 explains the specific advantages and disadvantages of these two ceiling types.

Figure 6.6 Airlock entries. A. Airlock within the house—OK. B. Airlock attached to house but within the thermal envelope—OK. C. Airlock outside the thermal envelope—unheated and vented to the outdoors—OK. D. Airlock surrounded by thermal envelope—NO GOOD (see text).

Airlock Entries

That airlock entries are not cost effective has been discovered over and over again in the energy design community. Although they may provide ancillary benefits such as "mud room" space or protection from uncomfortable wind gusts, airlock vestibules can never be justified on energy savings alone. If an airlock entry or any type of

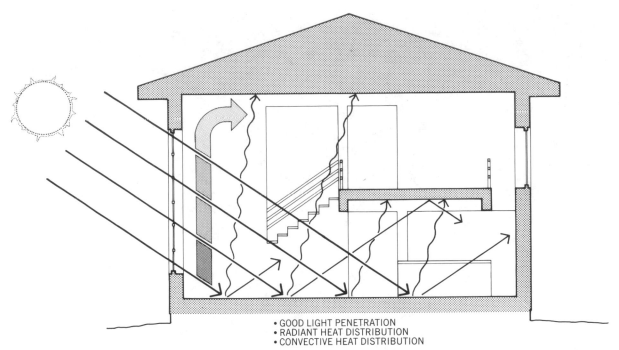

Figure 6.7 Open floor plan showing good distribution of heat and light.

• GOOD LIGHT PENETRATION
• RADIANT HEAT DISTRIBUTION
• CONVECTIVE HEAT DISTRIBUTION

"buffer space" is incorporated in a house design, it must be *clearly* either inside the thermal envelope or outside the thermal envelope—not somewhere in between. Figures 6.6a and 6.6b show two acceptable examples of airlocks *inside* the thermal envelope. Notice that in Figure 6.6b there is no insulation between the airlock and the house. Figure 6.6c shows an airlock *outside* the thermal envelope—unheated and ventilated to the outdoor air.

The design in Figure 6.6d is a mistake; the airlock is in the *middle* of the thermal envelope, inside the air barrier, with most of the insulation (at least half) on the inside of the airlock. The result? Moisture from indoor air may condense on the cold vestibule walls. In some cases, the outer door can freeze shut.

Floor Plan and Layout

For natural distribution of heat, light, and air, an open floor plan is best. An open plan allows sunlight to penetrate deep into the house, providing natural lighting and also increasing solar utilization efficiency. An open plan also allows good heat circulation and distribution (Figure 6.7). Warmed air circulates naturally and solar heated surfaces can radiate heat to opposite cooler surfaces. By comparison, small enclosed spaces are subject to overheating because of their limited thermal storage capacity.

To take advantage of the sun's movement, locate morning activity spaces, such as kitchen and breakfast areas, in the southeast corner where the morning sun will supply some instant heat. Living room, den, or great room are best situated on the west side for sunset and

evening views (Figure 6.8). Kitchens and bathrooms should be located to minimize heat losses from hot water pipes. This is discussed further in Chapter 13.

Ideally, unused rooms and unheated spaces are put on the north and west sides of the house to provide a buffer between the living space and the winter weather, but this is a relatively minor design requirement in superinsulated houses because the walls themselves are so "weathertight."

Window Sizing and Placement— Heat Loss and Solar Gain

Windows are the "thinnest" part of the thermal envelope, the place where the outside environment can most easily affect indoor conditions. *A square foot of double-glazed window loses heat fifteen times faster than a square foot of an average superinsulated wall.* Large windows not only cause increased energy usage, but may also necessitate a higher capacity heating system. While it's true that each square foot of south-facing glass can collect over 100,000 Btu of useful solar energy per year, too much window area may cause overheating. Sizing and placement of windows are the most important energy-related tasks during this preliminary design phase. Here are some important guidelines:

Total Window Area Should Not Exceed 20 Percent of the Exterior Wall Area The average conventional house has 15 to 25 percent of its exterior walls taken up by windows. Figure 6.9 shows the calculated HLC for walls plus windows versus window area for two types of

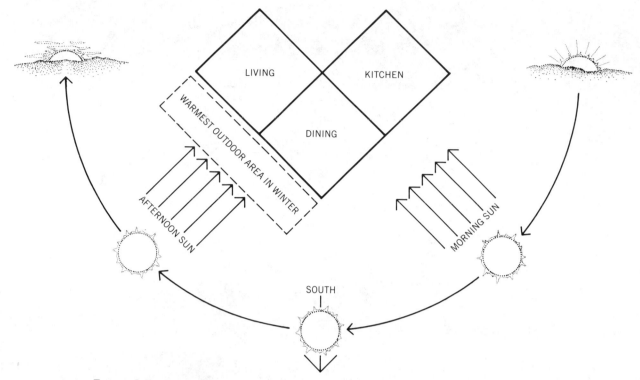

Figure 6.8 Example of room placement to take advantage of sun movement. Morning sun provides quick "solar pickup" into morning activity areas.

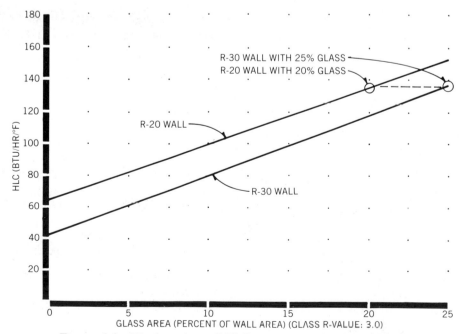

Figure 6.9 Window plus wall HLC vs. percent of wall area glass.

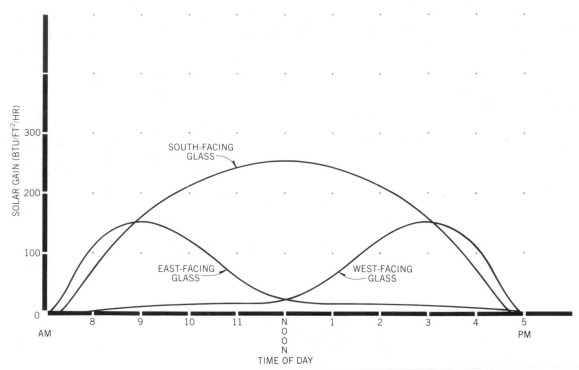

Figure 6.10 Clear-day solar gain during one day through 1 square foot of glass facing east, south, and west. Data is for January, 40° north latitude.

walls (R-20 and R-30). Notice that the HLC for the R-20 wall with 20 percent glass (256 square feet) is equal to that for the R-30 wall with 30 percent glass (320 square feet). In other words, increasing the glass area from 256 square feet to 320 square feet, an increase of 25 percent, could be balanced by increasing the wall R-value from R-20 to R-30, a 50 percent increase!

Concentrate Windows on South- and East-Facing Walls East-facing glass is naturally best for morning solar gain, which is the most valuable because outdoor temperatures are then lowest and the house is cool from the night. South-facing glass receives the most solar energy, distributed evenly around solar noon.

West-facing glass, receiving afternoon sun, is less valuable from a heating standpoint because outdoor temperatures are higher at this time of day; therefore the house needs the least heat during afternoon hours. West-facing glass can also contribute to overheating problems. North-facing glass is always a net energy loser. This is not to say that north walls must be windowless, but rather that their windows should be limited to the minimal area necessary for lighting, aesthetics, and other practical considerations.

Figure 6.10 shows the solar heat gain distribution throughout a cloudless January day for east-, south-, and west-facing glass at 40° north latitude.

Recommended Glass Distribution Although south-facing glass provides the greatest total solar heat over the

winter, it is not necessary or even best to put all the glass on the south side of a superinsulated house. Because of the low house heating load, much of the midday solar energy coming through south-facing glass will be wasted, particularly on sunny days. It is better to distribute the glass area between east and south, providing a good balance between even distribution over the day and total solar gain. The recommended distribution is as follows:

Compass Direction of Windows	Percent of Total Window Area
South	35 to 45 percent
East	25 to 35 percent
West	15 to 25 percent
North	5 to 15 percent

Figure 6.11 shows the total solar heat gain through 200 square feet of glass distributed 40 percent south, 30 percent east, 20 percent west, and 10 percent north during a clear sunny January day at 40° north latitude. Notice that the morning peak is from 9 A.M. until noon, a leveling off takes place from noon until 2 P.M., and a rapid decline occurs after 2 P.M.; this means good morning pickup, even distribution during midday; and decreased gain during the afternoon hours of potential overheating.

Other Passive Solar Strategies In discussing solar gain so far, we have been referring to "direct gain" pas-

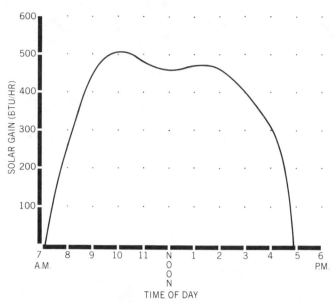

Figure 6.11 Total clear-day solar gain during one day through 200 square feet of glass distributed 40 percent south, 30 percent east, 20 percent west, and 10 percent north. Data is for January, 40° north latitude.

sive solar heating, i.e. sun shining through windows. What about other types of passive solar design? In general, most special types of passive solar design are not necessary if a house is superinsulated. But "necessary" is a relative term. If, for example, you are building a very large house with generous window area on all sides, some sort of expanded passive solar heating may be useful and cost effective. Mass walls (Trombe walls and water walls), sunspaces, and wall collectors *can* all be integrated into a superinsulated house design, using traditional passive solar design techniques. Thus superinsulation need not be an alternative to conventional passive solar design—you can have your cake and eat it too!

STEP 2: PRELIMINARY ENERGY SPECIFICATIONS

With the preliminary house design set, the next step is to specify the three most important energy-related characteristics of the thermal envelope—*R-values, window type, and airtightness.* Other energy components such as heating, cooling, hot water, and appliances, although of significant importance to an integrated design, can be left for later attention.

Selecting R-Values

If you ask ten energy experts to prescribe optimum R-value for the walls, roof, and foundation of a house, you will most likely get ten different answers. Why so much uncertainty? Because the costs and benefits of each incremental addition of R-value are very difficult to as-

sess. How much more does an R-30 wall cost than an R-13 wall? First of all, it depends on how you are going to achieve that R-30. As shown in Chapter 7, several different types of R-30 wall design are possible. For some, such as exterior foam sheathing, the extra expense is mostly for materials; for others, such as double-framed construction, labor costs may be more important. Different builders will give different estimates. Tract developers, for example, with many framing crews, may add considerable extra cost for any deviation from conventional framing techniques. Custom builders, on the other hand, may be able to accommodate unconventional designs with minimum extra cost (see Chapter 1 for a discussion of extra costs for superinsulation).

Insulation Guidelines for Walls When planning insulation, try to achieve the following R-values for areas with the following heating degree days.

Heating Degree Days (base 65°F)	R-Value
Below 5000	25 to 30
5000 to 7500	30 to 35
7500 to 10,000	35 to 40

As can be seen from the above guidelines, recommended R-values for most U.S. climates are between R-25 and R-35. The decision may be partly determined by construction preference and availability of materials. In the final analysis, a variation of R-3 or R-5 has a relatively minor effect on total energy consumption compared to other factors such as window size and placement (see Figure 6.9) or airtightness. If a particular wall construction is preferable because of cost or ease of construction, then sacrificing some R-value will be acceptable.

Insulation Guidelines for Roofs and Ceilings The R-value of the top of the house should be at least as high as that of the walls, but not necessarily higher. In houses with unheated attics, adding extra insulation is usually very inexpensive, so that attics usually have higher R-values. Cathedral ceilings and flat roofs, on the other hand, are more expensive to insulate, making the recommended R-values somewhat lower. Recommended R-values are as follows:

Type of Roof/Ceiling	R-Value
Unheated attics	2 × walls
Cathedral ceilings or flat roofs	1.0 to 1.5 × walls, depending on cost of installation

Insulation Guidelines for Foundations Because of the variability of foundation design and the complexity of below-grade heat loss, foundation R-value selection is not as straightforward as that for walls and roofs. Costs for foundation wall insulation can vary considerably, depending on materials used and whether the insulation is inside or outside the wall. Chapter 8 includes a complete discussion of the complexities of below-grade heat loss and foundation insulation. Guidelines for foundation R-values are as follows:

Component	R-value
Above grade walls	0.8 to 1.0 times main house walls
Below grade walls	
0 to 2 feet depth	0.8 to 1.0 times main house walls
2 feet to footings	0.5 to 1.0 times main house walls
floors	R-0 to R-10
	(see Chapter 8)

Window Guidelines Window-type selection boils down to R-values ranging from R-2 to about R-4, where R-2 roughly represents double glazing, R-3 is roughly triple glazing, and R-4 represents one of the new special glazing systems (see Chapter 10). Guidelines for window R-value selection are as follows:

Heating Degree Days (base 65°F)	Window R-Value
Below 5000	R-2 or R-3
Above 5000	R-3 or R-4

If the total window area is *less* than 15 percent of the floor area, then use the *lower* R-value in the above guidelines; if total window area is *greater* than 15 percent, then use the *higher* R-value.

Sometimes, a mixture of window types is best. Very small windows, for example, should usually be only double glazed because the extra cost of high R-value glazing is greater per square foot with small units. Large windows in the living room, near seating areas, are the most important candidates for high R-value glass because the inside surface temperature affects thermal comfort of people sitting nearby. In moderate climates, south-facing glass should be double rather than triple glazed because the extra heat loss through double glass is more than offset by increased solar gain. On the windward side of the house, high R-value is important for reducing the impact of wind on heat loss. Chapter 10 presents a few other factors for consideration when selecting window R-value.

Airtightness

Designing for airtightness is crucial in a superinsulated house. However, it is not possible to specify an exact level of airtightness or air leakage. One cannot confidently say, "Let's design this house with an average natural air infiltration rate of 0.2 air changes per hour." During Step 2 of the design process, one merely recognizes that the house will be reasonably airtight. For energy calculations, a safe assumption is that the average natural infiltration rate of a well-built superinsulated house will be between 0.05 and 0.15 air changes per hour.

The important aspects of designing for airtightness come in Step 4, when the air/vapor barrier is designed. Those design details are presented in Part II of this book.

STEP 3: PRELIMINARY ENERGY ANALYSIS

Annual Auxiliary Heat Requirements

The objectives of this step are to estimate the annual auxiliary heat requirements of the house as designed and to see if it meets the energy efficiency goals established during the predesign phase. Can this house be heated for $.05, $.10, or $.20 per square foot per year? If the analysis shows that energy goals are not being met, the designer returns to Step 1 to try some modifications. Only after the basic design meets the specified goals does the designer proceed to the detailed energy systems design of Step 4.

In Chapter 5, we presented a step-by-step outline of the degree-day method for calculating annual auxiliary heat requirements. Although not particularly accurate, because of uncertainty over what base degree days to use, the degree-day method is quick and easy. Unless the designer has access to computer facilities, the manual degree-day method is the best tool for preliminary energy analysis.

Microcomputer Programs With the advent of low-cost microcomputers came a wide assortment of building energy analysis programs, ranging in price from twenty-five to several thousand dollars. Some merely perform standard degree-day calculations, while others calculate hour-by-hour heat losses and gains for an entire year. Some are very simple to use, requiring no technical or computer background; others assume a solid engineering background and possibly a good working knowledge of computers as well. Some are field validated; others are not. When considering energy analysis software, the inexperienced designer should seek competent advice and references.

The HOTCAN Program Amid the jungle of available software, one program—HOTCAN—developed by the Canadian National Research Council, stands out as a very practical choice for almost any designer with access to a microcomputer. Available in several versions for the most popular personal computers, HOTCAN is very easy to learn and use. Field validation tests in Canada have shown it to be remarkably accurate.

Using monthly average data for the air temperature and solar radiation on each of eight compass directions, the program calculates the total heat loss, solar fraction, and auxiliary heat required for each month of the year. Given fuel prices, it also calculates total annual space heating and water heating costs for five different fuel types.

Figure 6.12 is a sample HOTCAN printout. The first page lists area, R-value, HLC, and percent of total heat

```
**********************************************
*                  HOTCAN!                   *
*        HEAT LOSS ANALYSIS PROGRAM          *
*           OTTAWA, CANADA - 1984            *
*          (HOTCAN RELEASE 4.02)             *
**********************************************
```

CLIENT NAME: DEMONSTRATION HOUSE
ADDRESS   : TORONTO

HOUSE DATA FILE NAME:

WEATHER DATA IS FOR TORONTO

*** BUILDING PARAMETERS ***

ELEMENTS	HOUSE VOLUME	AIR CHANGE	HT LOSS W/DEGC	% SEASONAL HT LOSS
VENTILATION	12000 FT3	.12/HR	12.58	10.15

ELEMENTS	AREA FT2	R VALUE FT2-DEGC/W	HT LOSS W/DEGC	% SEASONAL HT LOSS
CEILING	1500.00	60.00		
TOTAL	1500.00	60.00	13.18	10.64
MAIN WALLS	1088.00	30.00		
TOTAL	1088.00	30.00	19.14	15.44
DOORS	42.00	10.00		
TOTAL	42.00	10.00	2.22	1.79
BASEMENT AB.GD	320.00	20.00		
TOTAL	320.00	20.00	8.44	6.81
BASEMENT 2FT	320.00	20.00		
TOTAL	320.00	20.00	6.67	3.00
BASE. TO FLOOR	640.00	20.00		
TOTAL	640.00	20.00	24.66	11.09
FLOOR PERIMETER	444.00	5.00		
TOTAL	444.00	5.00	16.43	7.38
FLOOR CENTRE	1056.00	5.00		
TOTAL	1056.00	5.00	17.85	8.02
SOUTH WINDOWS	80.00	3.18		
TOTAL	80.00	3.18	13.26	10.70
NORTH WINDOWS	22.00	3.18		
TOTAL	22.00	3.18	3.65	2.94
EAST WINDOWS	55.00	3.18		
TOTAL	55.00	3.18	9.12	7.35
WEST WINDOWS	35.00	3.18		
TOTAL	35.00	3.18	5.80	4.68
S-EAST WINDOWS	.00	.00		
TOTAL	.00	.00	.00	.00
S-WEST WINDOWS	.00	.00		
TOTAL	.00	.00	.00	.00

Figure 6.12 Sample HOTCAN printout.

HOTCAN   PAGE 2

ADDRESS   : TORONTO

DESIGN HEAT LOSS AT -17.2C = 4.01 KW
DEGREE DAYS FOR TORONTO IS 4082
TEMPERATURES (DEG C) MAIN FLOOR = 20   BASEMENT = 18
ALLOWABLE DAILY TEMPERATURE SWING = 2.75
SENSIBLE HEAT GAIN FROM PEOPLE (KWH/D) = 0
DAILY BASE ELECTRIC CONSUMPTION (KWH/D) = 14
DAILY HOT WATER ENERGY CONSUMPTION (KWH/D) = 14
MASS LEVEL CHOSEN IS <A>
BASEMENT INSULATED PRIMARILY FROM THE OUTSIDE
WINDOW SHADING COEFFICIENTS: SOUTH = .72   NORTH = .72
                            EAST = .72   WEST   = .72
                            S-EAST = 0   S-WEST = 0
SOUTH OVERHANG GEOMETRY: AVERAGE WINDOW HEIGHT = 5 FT
                         AVERAGE OVERHANG WIDTH = 2 FT
                         AVERAGE HEIGHT ABOVE WINDOW = .67 FT
NATURAL INFILTRATION RATE (AC/HR) = .05
  FORCED VENTILATION RATE (AC/HR) = .35
HEAT RECOVERY EFFECTIVENESS ON VENTILATION AIR = 80 %

*** MONTHLY SUMMARY OF ENERGY CONSUMPTION ***

MONTH	THERMAL LOAD KWH/D	MONTHLY SOLAR FRAC	AUX HEAT REQ KWH/D	TOT CONS KWH/D
JAN	53.66	.31	37.27	65.27
FEB	53.63	.38	33.50	61.50
MAR	42.73	.46	22.96	50.96
APR	25.30	.65	8.78	36.78
MAY	10.10	.92	.78	28.78
JUN	.00	1.00	.00	28.00
JUL	.00	1.00	.00	28.00
AUG	.00	1.00	.00	28.00
SEP	.00	1.00	.00	28.00
OCT	11.31	.83	1.89	29.89
NOV	24.62	.42	14.24	42.24
DEC	45.38	.27	32.98	60.98

*** YEARLY ENERGY CONSUMPTION COMPARISONS ***

HEATING SEASON STARTS IN OCT AND ENDS IN APR.
ESTIMATED ANNUAL SPACE HEATING 16 GJ, OR   4,600 KWHRS
SEEH PROGRAM ENERGY BUDGET FOR SPACE HEATING =   4,841 KWHRS

PREDICTED ANNUAL AUXILIARY ENERGY CONSUMPTION =   10,220 KWHRS
SEEH PROGRAM AUXILIARY ENERGY CONSUMPTION =   10,600 KWHRS

TOTAL ANNUAL ENERGY CONSUMPTION =   **14,820 KWHRS**
TOTAL ANNUAL SEEH PROGRAM ENERGY BUDGET =   **15,441 KWHRS**

*** ANNUAL PREDICTED FUEL COSTS ***

FUEL COSTS ARE FOR ONTARIO   AS OF 84/10/23

ENERGY SOURCE	COST PER UNIT	SPACE HEATING	HOT WATER	LIGHTS AND APPLIANCES
NATURAL GAS	21.3C/M3	$ 99.67/YR EFF.= 94%	$ 191.2/YR EFF.= 55%	--

****

loss for each building component. The second page lists building data, monthly summaries of energy consumption, and predicted annual energy costs.

If, after running an analysis, the predicted fuel costs seem too high, the designer can look back to the first page to find which building components account for the greatest percentage of heat loss. For example, if windows account for 50 percent of the total, you can go back to design Step 1 and reduce the number or size of some windows; or go to Step 2 and increase window R-value. The new design changes are then easily entered into the computer and the program is rerun. The process can be repeated until the design is satisfactory.

The beauty of any computer application is speed. To enter complete data into HOTCAN for an average house takes about 20 minutes. To run the program takes less than 1 minute. To alter the input data and rerun again takes only 2 or 3 minutes. The designer is free to test any number of variations of R-value, window size, etc., with a relatively small investment in time.

HOTCAN can be purchased on computer disk (see Appendix E for addresses) and comes with weather data for several Canadian cities. Appendix C includes all the weather data necessary for 85 U.S. and Canadian cities. A new version that includes U.S. weather data on disk will soon be available (see Appendix E).

The Design Load

The **design load** is the heat loss under the coldest temperature experienced during the winter. Used mainly for sizing and selecting the heating system, the design load is calculated simply by multiplying the house HLC by the design indoor-outdoor temperature differential.

$$\text{Design load} = \text{HCL} \times \text{design temp. diff.} \quad [6.1]$$

The design temperature differential is calculated by subtracting the *winter design temperature* from desired interior temperature. The American Society of Heating, Refrigerating, and Air Conditioning Engineers (ASHRAE) defines two winter design temperatures, a 99 percent and a 97.5 percent value. During an average winter, the outside temperature falls below the 99 percent design value only 1 percent of the time, and falls below the 97.5 percent value only 2.5 percent of the time. The 99 percent winter design temperature is generally a few degrees lower than the 97.5 percent value. Pairs of winter design temperatures are listed in Appendix C.

Example. What is the design load of a house with an HLC of 300 Btu/hr-F located in a climate with a winter design temperature of 10°F? Assume an indoor temperature of 70°F.

$$\text{Design Load} = 300 \times (70 - 10)$$
$$= 18{,}000 \text{ Btu per hour}$$

Typical of superinsulated houses, this example shows a very small winter design heating load. The value of 18,000 Btu/hr is less than 6 kilowatts. Even on the coldest night, this house could easily be heated by a few feet of electric baseboard heaters, eliminating much of the cost of a central heating system. The situation is actually even better because some of the design heat load will be supplied by intrinsic heat and solar energy input, so that the full 18,000 Btu/hr will rarely be needed.

Rating the Thermal Envelope

In evaluating a design, one might want to look at the overall performance of the thermal envelope, perhaps for comparison with other designs in other areas, or with general standards of energy efficiency. To evaluate the thermal envelope, calculate the ratio of HLC to floor area and compare that value with those on the following chart:

HLC/Floor area (Btu/hr-F-ft²)	Rating
0.10 or less	extremely good
0.10 to 0.25	typical superinsulation
0.25 to 0.50	moderately energy efficient
0.50 or greater	back to the drawing board

STEP 4: ENERGY SYSTEMS COMPONENT DESIGN

This is the most important step in the design process. Six components constitute the household energy system:

1. Thermal envelope—insulation, windows, and airtightness
2. Air management system
3. Heating system
4. Cooling system
5. Water heating
6. Appliances and lighting

Component design and selection are often left to subcontractors and draftsmen—a mistake for a well-designed superinsulated house. Although each is designed separately, all the energy systems interact with each other. We have already seen how a passive solar system might necessitate the need for special air management to distribute excess solar heat input. Similarly, the heating and cooling systems must be designed to provide the right temperature control for each space. Water heating and appliances are also important, since they can add heat to the house and certainly affect the overall energy dynamics. To make sure that everything works together and that money isn't wasted, all the components should be carefully designed into one integrated system.

Part II of this book deals specifically with each of the six components of the overall house energy system.

STEP 5: CONSTRUCTION DOCUMENTS

No matter how well understood and designed a superinsulated house is, it will not be correctly built unless the information is effectively transferred from designer to builder. Especially for the builder who is unfamiliar with energy-efficient construction, the importance of clear, detailed drawings and specifications cannot be overestimated.

Construction sequence, for example, is not traditionally indicated on working drawings. But superinsulated construction often requires a certain sequence for the installation of the air/vapor barrier and insulation, particularly with double-wall construction. A good example of this is the construction sequence shown in Chapter 7 for the "Roki" double wall. These detailed instructions are an excellent illustration of the kind of information that can and should be transmitted through the construction documents to save time and money on the site.

PART II PRACTICE

Seven

Walls

THE WALL IS THE MOST VISIBLY DISTINCTIVE FEATURE OF A SUPERINSULATED HOUSE

Superinsulated houses typically have walls that are thicker and that have higher R-values than the walls of conventional houses. Most people describe a superinsulated house by the type and R-value of the exterior walls; for instance, "6-inch walls with R-19 fiberglass batts plus 2 inches of exterior insulative sheathing," or "double stud walls with 12 inches of cellulose insulation."

Superinsulated walls differ from conventional walls in several ways. Thick insulation alone does not make a superinsulated wall (see Chapter 2). Compared to conventional walls, superinsulated walls are much more airtight, have less thermal bridging, have a higher R-value, and are built more carefully, avoiding insulation voids and other defects.

During the evolution of superinsulated housing, designers and builders in Scandinavia, Canada, and the United States developed several basic wall designs. *No one design has yet been proven superior to all the others;* each has its own advantages and disadvantages. In selecting a wall design, one should "shop around" and evaluate each alternative according to one's own selection criteria.

In this chapter, we present four superinsulated wall designs.

1. Strapped wall.
2. Double wall.
3. Single wall with insulative sheathing.
4. Truss wall.

All four are satisfactory for a superinsulated house. Within each design type, many variations are possible and with proper understanding of how and why a wall works, the reader should be able to modify any of the basic designs to enhance ease of construction and to accommodate his or her own special needs.

Several new wall designs are being tested at the time of this writing. Although some of them might hold promise for the future, discussion in this chapter is limited to those designs and techniques that have been field tested and proven to be energy-efficient and cost-effective.

Selecting a Wall Design

As mentioned above, there is no one best wall design for superinsulated houses. What is right for one builder or homeowner may be wrong for another. Materials and labor costs vary; so do regional styles. This section presents some important evaluation factors which should be considered in selecting a wall design.

R-Value Obviously, the selected wall design must have enough thermal resistance to satisfy the requirements of a superinsulated house, usually between R-25 and R-40.

High R-value is attained in three ways: (1) through framing techniques that allow for thicker insulation inside the wall; (2) by using high R-value insulation materials such as urethane or polystyrene in the wall cavities; or (3) by using exterior or interior insulative sheathing.

In most cases, there will be more than one way to achieve a desired R-value. For example, an R-30+ wall can be built by using 2 × 6 studs with R-19 fiberglass plus 2 inches of polystyrene sheathing, or by using a double-stud wall with three R-11 fiberglass batts (Figure 7.1).

Thermal Bridging The ideal insulation system would be a continuous blanket of insulation surrounding the thermal envelope of the house (excluding windows and other penetrations) with no framing extending through the wall from inside to outside. In selecting or designing a framing system for a superinsulated house, the less framing in the exterior walls the better (from a thermal standpoint). In Figure 7.1, the wall with exterior insulative sheathing (Figure 7.1a) has less thermal bridging than the 8-inch stud wall (Figure 7.1b). The double-stud wall (Figure 7.1c) has the least thermal bridging of all the designs.

Airtightness Unless the walls of a superinsulated house are airtight, the house will not perform properly. All the wall designs presented in this chapter are capable of being very tight if properly built. They rely on some type of plastic sheeting to serve as an air/vapor barrier. To guard against air leakage through penetrations by electrical and plumbing fixtures, some of the designs locate the air/vapor barrier out of the way of those elements; other designs use special installation techniques to seal the air/vapor barrier at all penetrations.

Cost To attain superinsulation performance levels, some wall designs simply require more materials, such as thicker insulation and wider studs; other designs, such as the strapped wall, call for proportionately greater labor time. Costs for materials and labor are difficult to assess. While materials costs are relatively straightforward and easy to compute, labor costs are much more variable, ranging from 10 percent (for some manufactured housing operations) to 50 percent of the total construction cost.

Ease of Construction Construction ease or difficulty will directly affect the cost of labor. Your analysis should include not only construction of the wall itself, but also the impact on the work performed by sub-trades. When considering ease of construction, look at the entire construction sequence from framing to finish trim. With some wall designs, such as the "Saskatchewan" double wall, part of the insulation is installed before the framing is finished. Who will do it? Will they have to come back a second time? How about the air/vapor barrier? As mentioned above, some designs locate the air/vapor barrier away from plumbing and electrical components. Others do not. If you choose one that does not, which sub-trade will do the sealing and patching, and how much will it cost? The answers to these questions must be considered when evaluating ease of construction.

Building Codes Where wall design departs from conventional practice, it may be necessary to justify the design to obtain approval from the local building inspector. This has sometimes been the case with double-wall construction where one wall is load-bearing and the other isn't. Another example is the placement of the air/vapor barrier deep in the wall (as with the "Saskatchewan" double wall). In extreme cases involving very conservative building inspectors, an engineering report might be required for code approval.

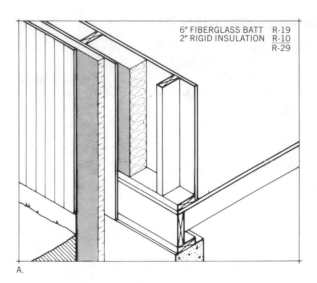

A.

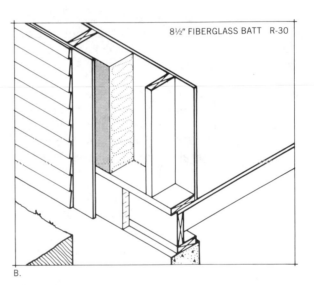

B.

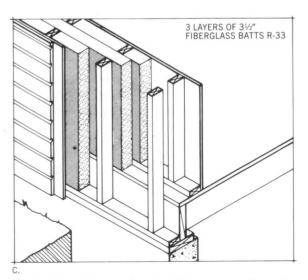

C.

Figure 7.1 Three types of R-30 (approximately) walls. A. 2 × 6 wall with insulating sheathing. B. 2 × 8 stud wall. C. Double wall.

Selecting Insulation Materials

Appendix A lists common thermal insulation materials along with technical specifications and general advantages and disadvantages. The following sections discuss the specific advantages and disadvantages of those materials for wall applications. When selecting the insulation materials for a superinsulated wall, the following criteria are important:

R-Value per Inch   The highest R-value per inch is obviously the most desirable, but this is more important in some situations than others. If, for example, wall thickness must be absolutely limited to 4 to 6 inches, then one of the rigid foams with R-6 to R-7 per inch might be best, despite the high cost. On the other hand, if wall thickness doesn't matter, then cellulose or fiberglass, with lower R per inch, might be preferable due to lower cost.

Cost per R-Value   The proper way to evaluate the cost of an insulation material is cost per R-value, not cost per inch thickness. See Appendix A for a comparison of cost per R value of different insulating materials.

Durability of Installation   As discussed in Chapter 2, the thermal performance of insulation materials can be affected by a variety of factors, such as moisture and settling. Settling is particularly important in walls because the insulation is installed as a vertical column, and any settling creates an insulation void at the top of the wall.

Health and Safety Considerations   Health and safety implications of wall insulation are important but unfortunately difficult to assess. For example, when urea formaldehyde foam was first introduced as sidewall insulation in the United States, it was heralded as "the answer" for residential energy conservation. It was later banned by the Consumer Product Safety Commission as a health hazard. In 1983, the ban was lifted. Some concern has been expressed about the hazard of breathing particles from fiberglass or dust from cellulose. At this time, there is no evidence indicating that either is a problem. One consideration which does warrant serious attention is flammability. Some of the plastic foams may support combustion, and even those that do not support combustion may give off toxic fumes when ignited.

Fiberglass Batts   Glass fiber batts are among the best materials for superinsulated walls. Their main advantages are availability at low cost, ease of installation, and good fire resistance. The R-value ranges from about R-3.1 per inch to R-3.5 per inch.

Always use unfaced batts. The kraft or foil facings on many commercially available batts are not necessary; they are intended to serve as vapor barriers and are commonly used for attachment to the framing. They are not, however, good air/vapor barriers because of the great length of their seams, which are difficult and expensive to

seal. Such facing is not necessary for attachment. Batts should fit snugly and be held in place by friction, not staples. Unfaced, friction-fit batts are easy to install.

Blown-in Fiberglass   This material has been largely overlooked as a good wall-cavity insulation, partly because the R-value is often listed as R-2.2 per inch. But the "in-place" R-value depends on *installed density*. In attic installation, where the material settles to its natural settled density of about 0.7 lb/cu.ft., the R-value is about R-2.2 per inch. However, when installed in a wall at a density of 2.0 lb/cu.ft., the R-value is R-4.0 per inch. Thus, a 5.5-inch wall cavity filled with blown-in fiberglass can have a total R-22 in the cavity, while one insulated with fiberglass batts could have only R-19.

The other advantage of this material, like any blown-in insulation, is that it can be installed in some hard-to-reach places which might be difficult to insulate with batts or rigid board.

The performance of loose fiberglass depends on quality of installation. The material must be installed at the proper density and must completely fill the wall space, leaving no voids. Care must be taken to see that the material doesn't "hang up" on nails and wiring in the wall. Since the wall is already sheathed inside and out before the insulation is installed, voids will not be visibly detectable. Skill and conscientiousness on the part of the installing contractor will ensure proper installation.

Settling is another potential problem. In a wall with 5.5 inches of loose fiberglass, if the insulation in every stud bay settles 2 inches, the overall R-value of the wall will be decreased by nearly 28 percent! However, field testing has not shown settling to be a significant problem. Again, conscientious installation should prevent problems.

Blown-in Cellulose   Cellulose shares most of the advantages and disadvantages of blown-in fiberglass. It is more impervious to air infiltration than is fiberglass, but this should not be an issue in walls with proper air/vapor barriers. As with any blown-in insulation, settling is possibly a serious problem. The R-value ranges from R-2.8 to R-3.7 per inch, depending on density.

Blown-in Rockwool   This material has basically the same advantages and disadvantages as blown-in fiberglass with one exception: rockwool's higher melting temperature. Under the intense heat of a house fire, fiberglass can melt, allowing the fire to spread through hollow wall cavities; rockwool, on the other hand, will never melt during fires, thus providing greater resistance to flame spread. A disadvantage of rockwool compared to fiberglass is that it tends to "hang up" on protrusions and nails in the wall cavity. Its R-value ranges from 2.8 to 3.7 per inch.

Extruded Polystyrene   This is an excellent material for exterior insulative sheathing: It is not affected by moisture or air intrusion; it is readily available and easy to install; and its R-value is about R-5.0 per inch. Currently, only two brands of extruded polystyrene are widely available—Styrofoam™ and Foamular™; manufactured by Dow Chemical and UC Industries, respectively.

We do not recommend using extruded polystyrene to insulate inside stud cavities. Cutting the boards for a good fit between the studs and sealing them in place is very difficult. Furthermore, since the material is rigid, any deformation of the framing members (frequently caused by drying) could cause spaces to open up around the insulation, allowing convective heat transfer within the stud cavity. Polystyrene is flammable and gives off noxious fumes upon burning. Most building codes require that it be covered with fire-rated sheathing.

Expanded Polystyrene The main advantage of this material over extruded polystyrene is in cost. It typically costs about 40 percent less than extruded polystyrene.

The disadvantages are lower R-value (R-3.6 to R-4.4 per inch, depending on density) and a tendency to break more easily. Like extruded polystyrene, it is flammable and must be covered with fire-rated sheathing.

Polyurethane and Polyisocyanurate These two materials have basically the same advantages and disadvantages as extruded polystyrene. The R-value is somewhat higher (R-6.0 to R-8.0 per inch), but so is the cost per R-value. Like polystyrene, urethane can burn and give off noxious fumes.

Spray Urethane When used in wall cavities, this material has two advantages: It has a very high R-value (R-6 to R-7 per inch); and it forms a continuous, airtight seal between joints and around penetrations. Spray urethane is its own air/vapor barrier.

There are several potential problems, however, with using foamed-in-place urethane in wall cavities. First is cost: its price is about four times that of fiberglass batts (per sq. ft. per R-value). Second is quality of installation: proper spray application requires a good deal of skill to avoid gaps and to ensure even coverage. Finally, there is the question of durability. Since the cured foam is very rigid, any deformation of the framing (as with drying and warping of studs, joints, etc.) could cause spaces to develop, which would degrade the overall performance of the insulation system.

Reflective Foil Recent research has shown that reflective foils (also called radiation barriers) are of limited value in cold climates for reducing the heat loss of a house. Published R-values for air spaces bound by very shiny foils are as high as R-11. According to the most recent findings, however, that level of thermal resistance is rarely attainable due to defects or the dulling of the foil surface. On the other hand, in warm climates, research shows that reflective foil may be very valuable for reducing heat gain through walls and thus reducing the house cooling load.

Reflective foil may therefore be acceptable in warm climates, but should not be relied on in cold areas.

Materials Not Recommended for Superinsulated Walls Except in unusual circumstances or for special applications, vermiculite, perlite, and urea formaldehyde foam are not recommended for use in superinsulated walls. Vermiculite and perlite are much lower in R-value per inch than the other insulating materials. To get a certain total R-value using these materials will require a significantly thicker and more expensive wall. They are also more porous to air flow. Urea formaldehyde insulation has generated considerable controversy because of the possibility of formaldehyde emission (see Chapter 4). Also, unless installed carefully at the right temperature, the material shrinks, thus seriously degrading the wall's thermal integrity.

DESIGN AND CONSTRUCTION DETAILS

Platform Framing and Balloon Framing Techniques

The major difference between platform framing (Figure 7.2) and balloon framing (Figure 7.3) is that with platform framing, exterior wall studs do not extend as one piece from the foundation to the roof. With balloon framing, they do.

Platform framing is far more popular than balloon framing in current United States housing. It is easier to construct and less expensive; common framing lumber comes precut for 8-foot platform-framed walls.

But platform framing, from a *thermal* standpoint, is inherently problematical. The areas around floor joists and band joists, which compose over 10 percent of the total wall area, act as significant thermal bridges (Figure 7.4). Some builders insulate the header joists on the inside, between the floor joists (Figure 7.5). But this invites moisture condensation on the cold band joist unless a vapor seal is installed on the inside of the insulation, between the floor joists—a difficult and time-consuming job.

Another significant problem with platform framing is air leakage through and around wall top plates and bottom plates. This tends to worsen over time as the horizontal plates shrink across the grain. Platform framing includes considerable cross-grain wood along the lines of vertical support, which exacerbates the problem.

From a thermal standpoint, balloon framing is better than platform framing. Look at the balloon wall section in Figure 7.6. In this two-story house, both the first-story and second-story joist headers are completely insulated on the outside, so that there is almost no thermal bridging. This standard balloon design still has one flaw: the

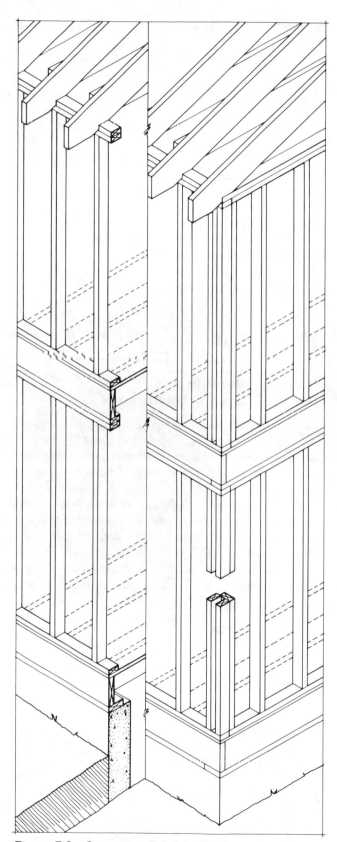

Figure 7.2 Conventional platform framing.

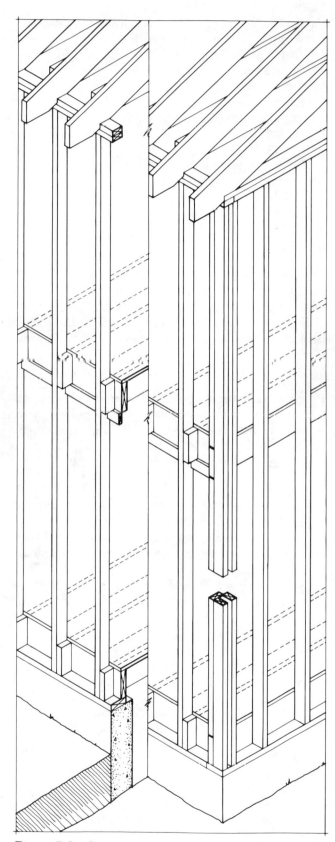

Figure 7.3 Conventional balloon framing.

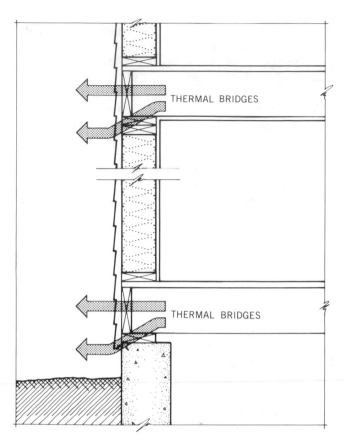

Figure 7.4 Joist detail with conventional platform framing. This area is difficult to insulate effectively.

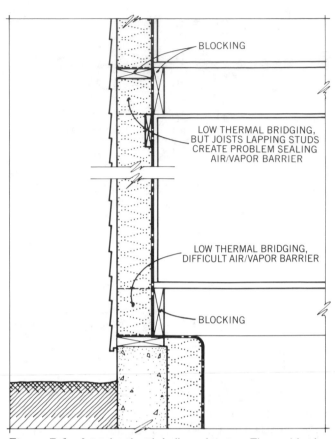

Figure 7.6 Joist detail with balloon framing. Thermal bridging is reduced.

air/vapor barrier is broken between first and second floors. Later in this chapter, we will look at how to overcome this problem.

Because balloon framing shrinks less, it is traditionally used in two-story houses with brick or stone veneer or exterior plaster; the chance of the masonry veneer crack-

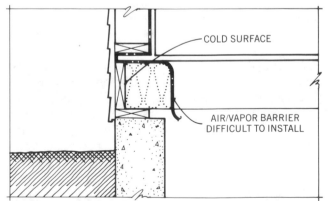

Figure 7.5 Insulated header joist. If no vapor barrier is installed, the header joist will get cold and be subject to moisture condensation. Installing a vapor barrier on the inside of the insulation is difficult.

ing due to differential movement of the veneer and the wooden frame is diminished.

But despite these advantages, balloon framing is relatively uncommon, except in the special applications mentioned above, because of certain drawbacks. It is generally more difficult and expensive than platform framing, requiring longer studs which must be precision-cut on site. (It's hard to find 20-foot long 2 × 4's that are straight and true.) Walls cannot be prefabricated on the deck as with platform framing, and with two-story construction, scaffolding is sometimes necessary. In houses with basements, the crew works over an open basement while the walls are being erected.

Hybrid Balloon Framing for Superinsulated Walls By combining balloon-type framing with platform-type framing, it is possible to enjoy the advantages of both systems. The following section will illustrate the use of balloon-type framing at the first-floor joists, the second-floor joists, and the second-floor rafters of a single-stud-wall house. Later, we will look at combining balloon and platform framing in a double-stud-wall house.

Balloon Framing at First-Floor Joists Figure 7.7 shows balloon-type framing installed at the first floor level. This design is identical to conventional balloon

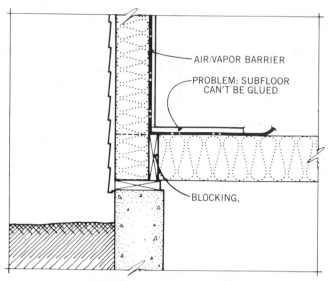

Figure 7.7 Balloon framing at first floor with insulation between the joists. Air/vapor barrier is installed under subfloor. This can be a problem if subfloor is to be glued to joists.

framing. Notice how the insulation is continuous, with very little thermal bridging.

If the floor joists are to be insulated, as in Figure 7.7, then the air/vapor barrier should be above the insulation, on top of the joists. This presents a problem, however. At first glance, it would seem easy to run the air/vapor barrier down the wall and over the floor joists. The problem is that many builders nail and glue the subfloor to the floor joists. In that case, you cannot have polyethylene between the joists and the subfloor. This is a problem to which there's no easy solution, although it's possible to install the air/vapor barrier between the subfloor and fin-

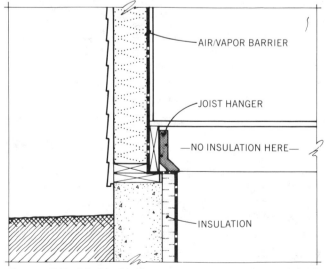

Figure 7.8 Modified balloon framing at first floor with air/vapor barrier installed around joists.

ish floor, being very careful to prevent tears during installation of the finish floor.

The preferred design is shown in Figure 7.8. Here the basement wall is insulated and the floor joists are not. The air/vapor barrier is run around the header joists and down the inside of the basement (or crawl space) wall, requiring a slight departure from conventional balloon framing. With conventional balloon framing, the floor joists are nailed to the sides of the wall studs (Figure 7.2), making it impossible to run the vapor barrier by. The modification for superinsulated design is simply to hang the floor joists from a ledger board using joist hangers (Figure 7.8) or to rest the joists on a widened sill plate. The air/vapor barrier is easily run down the wall, past the ledger, and down the inside of the basement wall.

A sequence for installing this system is as follows (Figure 7.9):

1. A 2 × 8 sill plate is installed.
2. The air/vapor barrier is draped over the sill plate with about 2 feet of plastic overhanging on each side.
3. The air/vapor barrier is covered with roofing paper, plywood, or some other suitable material to protect it during joist installation.
4. The joist system is then installed as in conventional platform construction except that the platform is brought back 5.5 inches from the edges to allow room for the exterior wall.
5. The subfloor is installed.
6. The air/vapor barrier is wrapped around the joist system and brought up onto the subfloor.
7. The wall is prefabricated on the deck with a single bottom plate, tipped up into position on the sill plate, and nailed into the sill plate.
8. Blocking is installed between wall studs for attaching gypsum board and the air/vapor barrier.
9. The vapor barrier is stapled to the blocking.

An advantage of this system over conventional balloon framing is that the deck can go on before the wall is built, making wall fabrication much easier.

Note: In every instance, be absolutely certain that the air/vapor barrier is never run on the cold side of the insulation. This is a very common and serious mistake, most typically found at the joist header region. You must not install insulation between the joists, inside the air/vapor barrier, unless there is at least twice as much insulation on the outside of the barrier as on the inside. Too much insulation on the inside will make the barrier cold and cause moisture condensation.

Balloon Framing at Second-Floor Joists Figure 7.11 shows balloon framing for second-floor joists. The joist system is completely insulated by the exterior wall, creating minimal thermal bridging. The air/vapor barrier is continuous from the first floor to the second floor.

STEPS 1, 2, 3

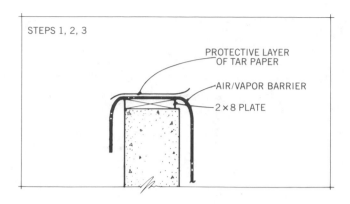

PROTECTIVE LAYER
OF TAR PAPER

AIR/VAPOR BARRIER

2 × 8 PLATE

4, 5

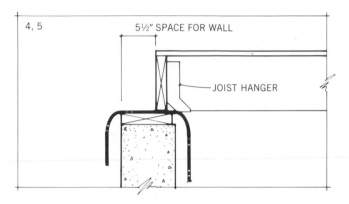

5½" SPACE FOR WALL

JOIST HANGER

6, 7

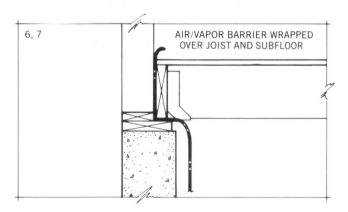

AIR/VAPOR BARRIER WRAPPED
OVER JOIST AND SUBFLOOR

8, 9

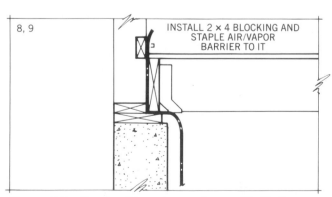

INSTALL 2 × 4 BLOCKING AND
STAPLE AIR/VAPOR
BARRIER TO IT

Figure 7.9 Construction sequence for modified balloon framing at first floor. Notice installation of tar paper to protect air/vapor barrier during joist installation.

Figure 7.10 Balloon framing at first floor. Air/vapor barrier is installed around rim joist; outer wall is assembled on deck, ready for installation. (Photo by Harold Orr.)

As with the first-floor detail, the attachment of the joists in this design differs from normal balloon construction. With conventional balloon framing, the joists are supported by a continuous 1 × 4 ribbon strip which is "let-in" to the inside edges of the studs (Figure 7.3). This wouldn't work here because there would be no easy way to run the air/vapor barrier uninterruptedly past the joists. Instead, the air/vapor barrier is first installed over the studs (Figure 7.11). A 2 × 8 ledger is then nailed to the studs over the air/vapor barrier. The floor joists are then attached to the ledger with joist hangers.

Note: The supportive strength of this type of ledger plate is derived from both the shear strength of the attachment nails and the friction strength of the ledger against the studs. The polyethylene air/vapor barrier is slippery and

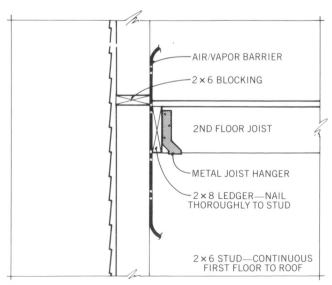

AIR/VAPOR BARRIER

2 × 6 BLOCKING

2ND FLOOR JOIST

METAL JOIST HANGER

2 × 8 LEDGER—NAIL
THOROUGHLY TO STUD

2 × 6 STUD—CONTINUOUS
FIRST FLOOR TO ROOF

Figure 7.11 Modified balloon framing at second floor joists.

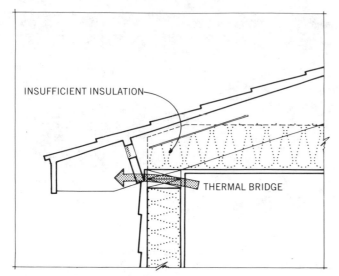

Figure 7.12 Wall-rafter juncture with conventional construction.

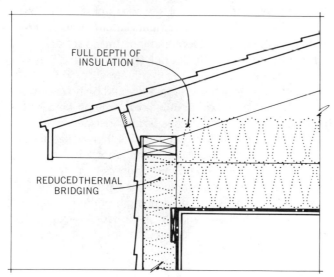

Figure 7.13 Modified balloon framing at wall-rafter juncture. This design greatly reduces thermal bridging and provides more room for insulation over wall plates.

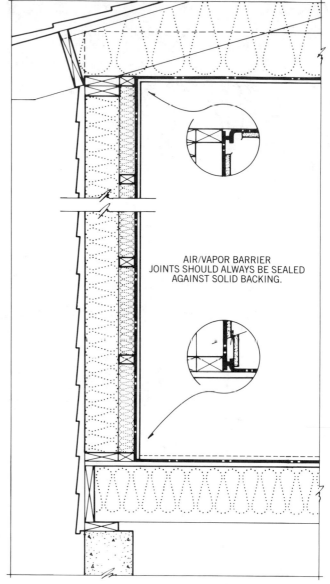

Figure 7.14 Section of strapped wall showing air/vapor barrier installed on the inner surface of the strapping, behind the gypsum board.

reduces the friction strength. This must be compensated for with extra nailing; use four 4-inch nails at each stud.

Balloon Framing at Attic Joists In conventional construction with site-built rafters, the rafters sit on the wall cap plate, fitted with a "birdsmouth" cut (Figure 7.12). This is a thermal weak spot for two reasons: first, the solid wood at the joint is a thermal bridge; second, the slope of the roof doesn't allow the placement of full thickness insulation in the ceiling.

Figure 7.13 shows the use of balloon framing to improve the thermal efficiency of the wall-rafter joint. With this design, there is almost no thermal bridging at the wall/ceiling joint; the entire joint is surrounded with insulation. In this case, unlike the design in Figure 7.11, the air/vapor barrier is not run behind the ledger plate. Instead, it is run up the wall and underneath the ceiling. Chapter 9 discusses other techniques for installing adequate insulation at this area.

The Strapped Wall

The strapped wall is a framing method for increasing the thickness and insulating value of single-stud walls. To build a strapped wall, horizontal members are nailed onto the inside of a conventionally framed stud wall (Figure 7.14). The space created by the strapping is then insu-

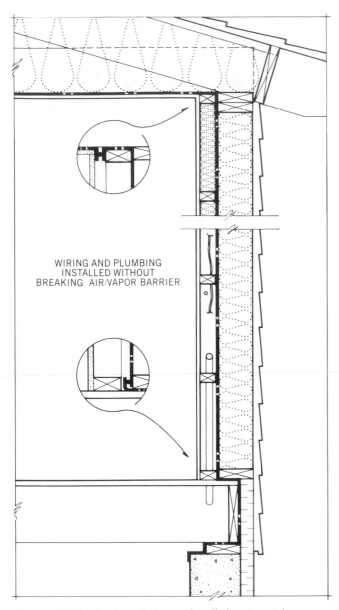

WIRING AND PLUMBING
INSTALLED WITHOUT
BREAKING AIR/VAPOR BARRIER

Figure 7.15 Section of strapped wall showing air/vapor barrier installed between the strapping and studs.

Figure 7.16 Strapped wall with air/vapor barrier between strapping and studs. Notice the quality of the insulation installation. (Photo by Harold Orr.)

lated with fiberglass batts or other suitable insulation material.

Advantages of Strapping   Strapping allows one to increase the insulation depth of a single stud wall by 1.5 inches, 2.5 inches, 3.0 inches, or 3.5 inches. The stud wall is framed using conventional techniques; very little special skill or training is required.

Compared to a wide single-stud wall—for example, a 2 × 8 or 2 × 10 wall—the strapped wall has considerably less thermal bridging. However, it is not as good in this respect as a wall with exterior insulative sheathing or a double wall (see below). The strapped wall still has thermal bridging at the top and bottom plates and at the intersection of the strapping and the wall studs.

The air/vapor barrier can be installed between the strapping and the studs, out of the way, and protected from damage caused by subcontractors and occupants.

Disadvantages of Strapping   Although not difficult, building a strapped wall can be time-consuming. Vertical blocking must be installed for attachment of electrical boxes, separate framing must be built around window and door rough openings, and vertical nailers must be installed for gypsum board joints. The most problematic drawback is that it is difficult to get batt insulation of the appropriate thickness to fill the strapping cavities.

Air/Vapor Barrier Installation in Strapped Walls
The air/vapor barrier in a strapped wall can be installed either on the inner surface of the wall directly under the gypsum board (Figure 7.14), or between the framing members and the strapping (Figures 7.15 and 7.16). The advantage of the latter design is that all the wiring can go in the strapping cavity without penetrating the air/vapor barrier. Also, the barrier is out of the way and less subject to damage by the gypsum board crew or other sub-contractors.

Keep in mind that the air/vapor barrier seams should always be over a solid member and not suspended in air. At the top of the wall, the wall air/vapor barrier should be sealed to the ceiling barrier against the wall top plate (see insets in Figure 7.15). At the bottom, it should be sealed to the floor air/vapor barrier (or the barrier from the wall below) against the bottom plate. The air/vapor barrier should, whenever possible, be sandwiched between two solid surfaces at the seams. When the air/vapor barrier is installed between the strapping and the studs (Figure 7.15), the top and bottom straps serve this purpose; when the air/vapor barrier is installed on the inner surface of the strapping (Figure 7.14), the gypsum board and the strapping do so.

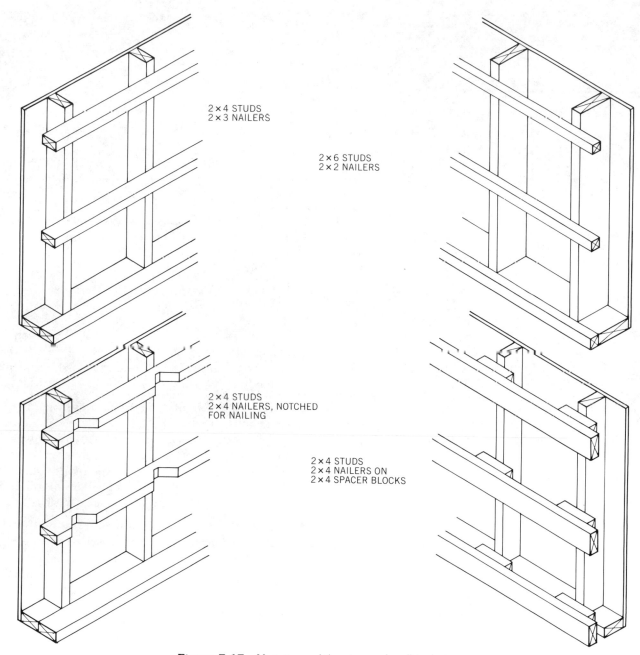

2 × 4 STUDS
2 × 3 NAILERS

2 × 6 STUDS
2 × 2 NAILERS

2 × 4 STUDS
2 × 4 NAILERS, NOTCHED
FOR NAILING

2 × 4 STUDS
2 × 4 NAILERS ON
2 × 4 SPACER BLOCKS

Figure 7.17 Variations of the strapped wall technique.

To reduce thermal bridging, some builders nail the bottom strap to the studs above the bottom plate and also nail the top strap to the studs below the top plates. This is not recommended if the air/vapor barrier is installed between the strapping and the studs because the barrier seam is not sandwiched between two solid members, thus making a good seal difficult.

Details and Variations   Strapped walls can be built with 2 × 2's, 2 × 3's, 2 × 4's on end, or even with two flat 2 × 4's (Figure 7.17). Be careful, however, when using batt insulation, to select members that create cavities that can be completely filled with insulation. If the insulation does not completely fill the cavity, convection currents may degrade the performance. On the other hand, if you compress batts into a very undersized cavity, it will be difficult to install the gypsum board.

Figure 7.18 shows design details for corners, interior partitions, and windows. Note that there are no vertical nailers at the corner. This floating corner is an approved and recommended method for installing gypsum board.

Also note the absence of a backer at the attachment

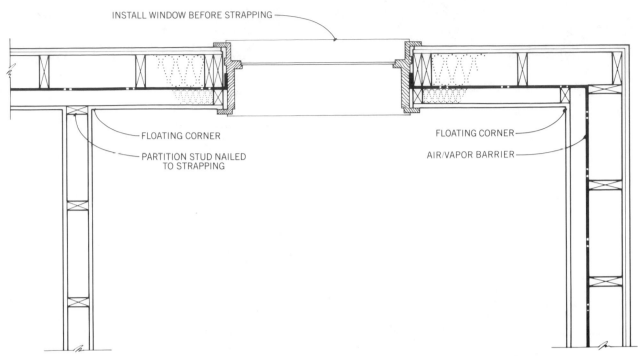

INSTALL WINDOW BEFORE STRAPPING

FLOATING CORNER

PARTITION STUD NAILED
TO STRAPPING

FLOATING CORNER

AIR/VAPOR BARRIER

Figure 7.18 Plan view of strapped wall, showing partition and corner details.

point of the interior partition. The end stud of the partition is braced by being nailed into the strapping.

Double-Wall Construction

With double-wall construction, two separate stud walls are built with a central space between. Only one wall needs be structural; the other may serve only as a "curtain wall" to create a central space for insulation and to support the wall sheathing.

Advantages of the Double Wall   The double wall can incorporate the best features of both platform framing and balloon framing. The inner wall can be built according to conventional platform techniques, and the outer wall can resemble balloon construction, reducing thermal bridging at the floor and ceiling joists as described above. Also, installing a continuous air/vapor barrier from foundation to roof is relatively easy; this barrier can be placed deep into the wall to protect it during construction and to minimize penetration by electrical wires and plumbing.

The most obvious advantage of the double wall is that it allows insulation of almost any thickness to be installed with very little increased cost. If more insulation is desired, the two walls are simply spaced farther apart; no added support structure is required. The only added cost is the insulation material.

Disadvantages of the Double Wall   Even though the materials and basic technique are not radically differ-

ent from conventional framing, the double-stud wall does require some "retooling". The cost will, of course, be greater than a conventional single-stud wall, although the cost of structural materials is only slightly more than a 2×6 single-wall with studs 16 inches on center. Building a double-stud wall may or may not be more expensive than other types of superinsulated walls. The amount of extra labor required can vary greatly and depends largely on crew training and supervision.

Double-Wall Design and Construction   Several varieties of double walls have been successfully built in Canada and the United States, with many minor variations created to increase construction efficiency, reduce cost, and conform to specific design requirements.

Much of the pioneering work with double-wall construction was done as part of the Energy Showcase project in Saskatchewan, Canada. Figure 7.19 shows a cross section of one wall design used in that project.

The inner 2×4 wall is structural and is placed at the edge of the platform. The outer 2×4 wall is non-structural and is cantilevered out from the platform. The two walls are spaced 5.5 inches apart and are connected by $\frac{3}{8}$-inch plywood top and bottom plates. The outer wall is supported from underneath by a 2×4 substructure which also contains foundation insulation.

Inner and outer wall cavities are filled with 3.5-inch (R-11) fiberglass batts, and the space between the walls is filled with 6-inch (R-19) batts installed horizontally. The total R-value of the wall is R-41+. The air/vapor barrier is

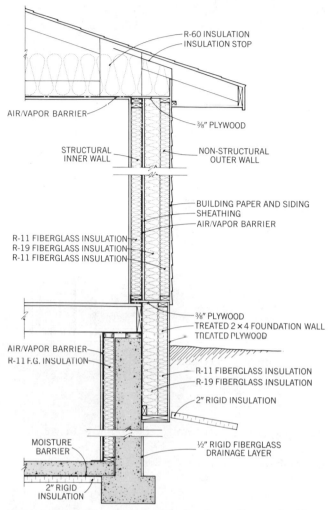

Figure 7.19 Section of the "Saskatchewan"-type double wall.

a 6-mil polyethylene sheet installed on the outer surface of the inside wall.

One of the most noticeable, and sometimes objectionable, features of this wall design is the cantilevered outer wall. An alternative is to set the outer wall back so that it is either flush with the platform (Figure 7.20a) or cantilevered only a few inches to accept exterior rigid foam foundation insulation (Figure 7.20b). Another alternative is to use balloon-type framing for the outer wall, resting the studs on the foundation, outside the platform (Figure 7.20c).

The Embedded Air/Vapor Barrier The primary rule for air/vapor barriers is that they must be installed on the *warm* side of the insulation.

However, the Saskatchewan double-stud wall appears to violate this rule: *the air/vapor barrier is near the middle of the insulation (Figure 7.19)*. Despite this apparent departure from recommended practice, the Canadians have not reported any problems. Why? According to Canadian researchers, the embedded air/vapor barrier will cause *no moisture problems as long as the insulation on the cold side of the barrier has twice the R-value of the insulation on the warm side*. In other words, the air/vapor barrier may be safely placed one-third of the way into the insulation from the warm (heated) side.

Does this technique—called the $\frac{1}{3}$-$\frac{2}{3}$ rule—actually work? It would seem to in theory. Consider the following interesting parallel between a Saskatchewan-type double wall with embedded air/vapor barrier and a double-glazed window (Figure 7.21).

The wall has three layers of 3.5-inch (R-11) fiberglass batts with the vapor barrier installed between the middle and inner batts. 66 percent of the R-value is outside the vapor barrier.

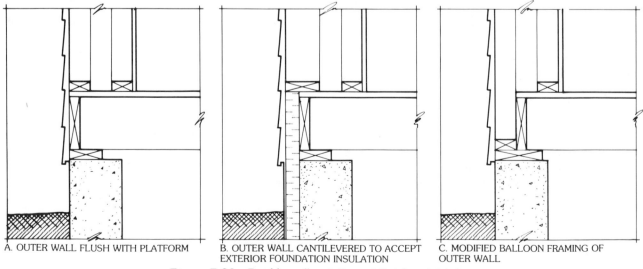

A. OUTER WALL FLUSH WITH PLATFORM   B. OUTER WALL CANTILEVERED TO ACCEPT EXTERIOR FOUNDATION INSULATION   C. MODIFIED BALLOON FRAMING OF OUTER WALL

Figure 7.20 Double-wall variations at first floor joist area.

The double-glazed window has a total R-value of 1.84, composed of the inner and outer air films, the air space between the panes, and the glass itself. The inner surface of the window is a vapor barrier. The inner air film (R-.68) is inside the vapor barrier, while the rest of the window (R-1.16) is outside the vapor barrier. As with the double wall, about two-thirds of the R-value is outside the vapor barrier.

Theoretically, the temperature of the inner glass window surface should be almost exactly the same as the temperature of the air/vapor barrier in the wall. Moreover, moisture condensation on the window should be just about identical to moisture condensation on the air/vapor barrier in the wall. Therefore, by observing moisture condensation on the window, we can deduce the amount of condensation in the wall.

Common experience has shown that double-glazed windows do not exhibit severe moisture condensation problems unless the indoor humidity is excessively high. The $\frac{1}{3}$-$\frac{2}{3}$ rule would, by extension, work for double-stud walls as well.

One of the reasons the $\frac{1}{3}$-$\frac{2}{3}$ embedded air/vapor barrier rule can be relied on is that moisture problems do not happen overnight; they take a while to develop. Consider a climate in which the 99 percent winter design temperature is say, −10°F. In an average winter, the temperature falls below −10°F. for only 22 to 54 hours, occurring as 2- or 3-hour periods on 10 or 20 days during the winter. This isn't enough time for moisture condensation to cause a real problem.

There is one important exception to the $\frac{1}{3}$-$\frac{2}{3}$ rule. In hot tub or pool enclosures, greenhouses, or any space where the relative humidity is constantly 70 or 80 percent, the air/vapor barrier *should* be installed on the winter-warm, inner surface of the insulation.

Double-Wall Assembly Sequence   The double wall is prefabricated into a single unit on the platform, then tilted into place and fastened as with conventional single-stud wall construction.

The sequence is as follows (Figure 7.22):
1. The inner wall is framed on the platform.
2. The air/vapor barrier is stapled to the outer surface of the inner wall.
3. Structural sheathing is applied over the air/vapor barrier.
4. The outer wall is framed on top of the inner wall.
5. Temporary spacers (either 3.5- or 5.5-inch) are placed between the walls.
6. $\frac{3}{8}$-inch plywood top and bottom plates are installed.
7. The insulation can now be installed in the central cavity and the outer stud cavities. Or it can be installed from the outside, later, after the wall is erected.
8. The wall is tipped up into place.

Note: The assembled wall is heavy, so it should be fabricated in position for tilting into place. Once up, it is very stable and strong.

For two-story construction, the sequence continues as follows (Figure 7.23):
9. A 3-foot wide strip of 6-mil polyethylene air/vapor barrier is attached and sealed to the top of the first floor wall air/vapor barrier. This strip is then placed over the top of the wall. The air/vapor barrier must be protected here with roofing paper or other suitable material to prevent damage when the second-floor joists are slid up for installation.
10. The second floor joists and floor are then installed over the inner wall.
11. The air/vapor barrier is then brought up around the joist header and onto the floor.

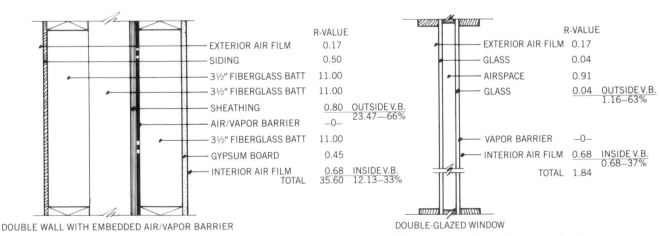

	R-VALUE	
EXTERIOR AIR FILM	0.17	
SIDING	0.50	
3½″ FIBERGLASS BATT	11.00	
3½″ FIBERGLASS BATT	11.00	
SHEATHING	0.80	OUTSIDE V.B. 23.47—66%
AIR/VAPOR BARRIER	—0—	
3½″ FIBERGLASS BATT	11.00	
GYPSUM BOARD	0.45	
INTERIOR AIR FILM	0.68	INSIDE V.B.
TOTAL	35.60	12.13—33%

DOUBLE WALL WITH EMBEDDED AIR/VAPOR BARRIER

	R-VALUE	
EXTERIOR AIR FILM	0.17	
GLASS	0.04	
AIRSPACE	0.91	
GLASS	0.04	OUTSIDE V.B. 1.16—63%
VAPOR BARRIER	—0—	
INTERIOR AIR FILM	0.68	INSIDE V.B. 0.68—37%
TOTAL	1.84	

DOUBLE-GLAZED WINDOW

Figure 7.21   Comparison of air/vapor barrier location in "Saskatchewan" double wall and double-glazed window.

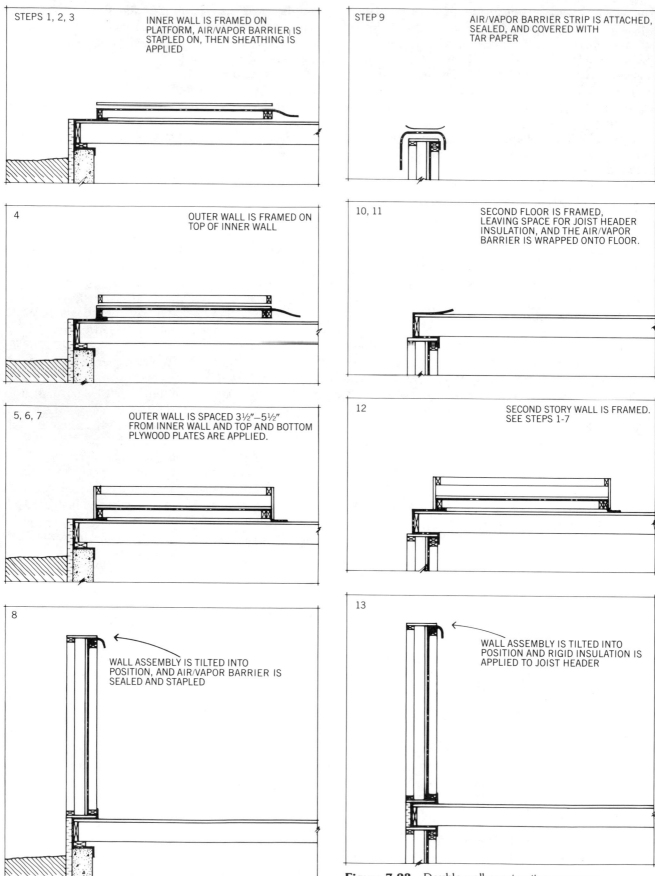

STEPS 1, 2, 3   INNER WALL IS FRAMED ON PLATFORM, AIR/VAPOR BARRIER IS STAPLED ON, THEN SHEATHING IS APPLIED

STEP 9   AIR/VAPOR BARRIER STRIP IS ATTACHED, SEALED, AND COVERED WITH TAR PAPER

4   OUTER WALL IS FRAMED ON TOP OF INNER WALL

10, 11   SECOND FLOOR IS FRAMED, LEAVING SPACE FOR JOIST HEADER INSULATION, AND THE AIR/VAPOR BARRIER IS WRAPPED ONTO FLOOR.

5, 6, 7   OUTER WALL IS SPACED 3½″–5½″ FROM INNER WALL AND TOP AND BOTTOM PLYWOOD PLATES ARE APPLIED.

12   SECOND STORY WALL IS FRAMED. SEE STEPS 1-7

8   WALL ASSEMBLY IS TILTED INTO POSITION, AND AIR/VAPOR BARRIER IS SEALED AND STAPLED

13   WALL ASSEMBLY IS TILTED INTO POSITION AND RIGID INSULATION IS APPLIED TO JOIST HEADER

Figure 7.22 Double-wall construction sequence—first story.

Figure 7.23 Double-wall construction sequence—second story.

12. The second-story wall is fabricated on the deck.

13. The wall is tilted into position and insulation is applied to the joist header.

Figure 7.24 shows a double-wall fabrication sequence for a house in Saskatchewan.

Corners   Details of corner framing in a double-stud wall are shown in Figure 7.26. Notice that the interior corners are built with only two studs. Instead of a third stud post, horizontal blocking, 24 inches on center, is put in between the last two studs. The gypsum board is nailed to the blocking 12 inches from the corner. The gypsum board of the adjacent wall is nailed vertically to the end stud as with conventional framing. This "floating" corner eliminates some of the thermal bridging at the corner, allows more insulation to be installed, and uses less lumber.

The corners are not tied together by cap plates (as they are with conventional framing) or by overlapping the plywood top plates. Some builders use metal straps over the top plywood plates. Another technique, used in Saskatchewan, is to use a 2 × 6 nailer, placed over the gable wall and tied into the eave walls (Figure 7.27). This nailer is necessary with truss roofs where the gable end truss is over the wall and does not offer a nailing surface for the ceiling gypsum board. It also helps to tie the walls together. Of course, the walls are also held together by the exterior sheathing.

Internal Angles   In Figure 7.26, wall B meets wall C to form an internal angle. Notice that the inner wall of wall B does not extend all the way to the exterior surface of the total wall assembly. There is good reason for this. If the wall did extend all the way out, its cold outer surface would come in contact with the air/vapor barrier, inviting moisture condensation. By stopping the inner wall where shown, that problem is avoided. Of course, if the air/vapor barrier is installed on the inner surface of the wall, rather than deep in the wall as shown in the illustration, then this detail is not necessary.

External Angles   In Figure 7.26, wall B meets wall A to form an external angle. This creates a situation different from that described above for internal angles. The air/vapor barrier is kept warm at all points. In this case, the

A

B

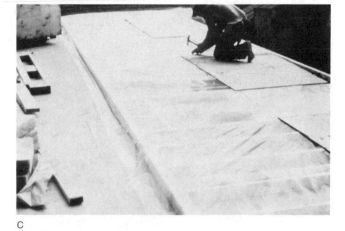

C

D

Figure 7.24   Double-wall construction sequence. A. Inner wall is assembled on the deck. (Photo by Gordon Howell.) B. Air/vapor barrier is installed over completed inner wall. (Photo by Harold Orr.) C. Sheating is installed over air/vapor barrier. (Photo by Harold Orr.) D. Outer wall is built over inner wall using inner wall as template. (Photo by Gordon Howell.)

Figure 7.24 (*continued*) E. Plywood top and bottom plates are installed, separating the two walls. (Photo by Gordon Howell.) F. Fiberglass batts are installed horizontally between the two walls. (Photo by Harold Orr.) G. Fiberglass batts are installed in outer wall stud cavities. (Photo by Gordon Howell.) H. Exterior sheathing is installed on outer wall. (Photo by Gordon Howell.) I. Completed wall is tipped up into place. (Photo by Harold Orr.)

Figure 7.25 An alternative double-wall framing technique. Insulation is installed after framing is completed. (Photo by Howard Faulkner.)

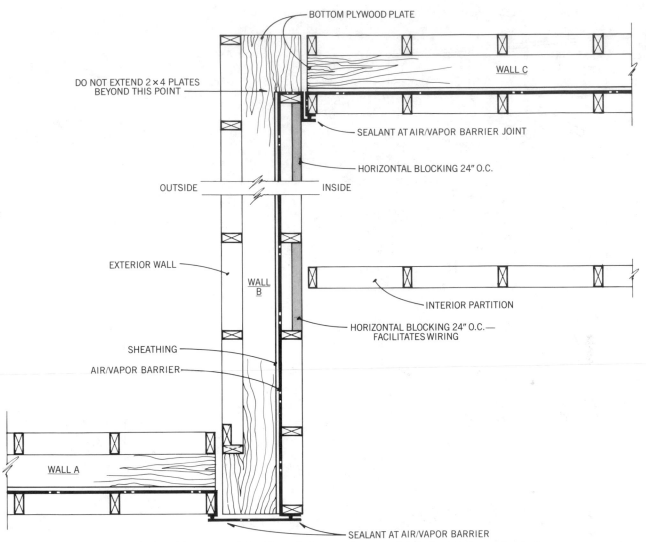

Figure 7.26 Plan view of double wall showing framing details for interior and exterior corners.

outer wall of wall B is stopped short, not to protect the air/vapor barrier, but to provide a nail base for the interior sheathing. Extending the outer wall all the way to the outside of the wall assembly would be acceptable, although this adds slightly to the thermal bridging of the wall assembly.

Rough Openings for Windows and Doors Rough openings for windows and doors are sheathed with ½-inch plywood (Figure 7.29) before the window and door units are installed. When framing the wall, the rough openings must therefore be 1 inch larger vertically and horizontally to leave room for the plywood. If the windows are to be sealed with foam caulk, it is preferable to make the rough openings even larger. Why? Even if the installed window fits tightly into the rough opening, the joint must still be caulked. Caulking a tight seam is difficult; it's hard to get any caulk, particularly the popular foam caulks, into the

joint. By intentionally creating a wide (½-inch) crack, it is easy to make a tight seal.

Outer Wall Framing If the outer wall is not structural, some of the framing can be eliminated. It need not have double headers over windows and doors or trimmer studs supporting the headers. There is also no need for double top plates on the outer walls. However, unless the outer wall studs are custom cut 1.5 inches long, the double top plate will be necessary to match the height of the two walls. Since there is insulation between them, the double top plates do not form a bad thermal bridge.

Double-Wall Variations *Staggered Studs* Theoretically, by staggering the studs of the two walls (Figure 7.30), thermal bridging is reduced to the practical minimum. But staggering the studs adds complexity, making

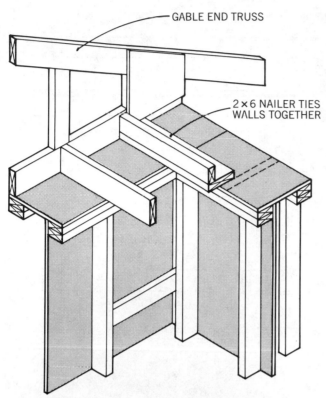

Figure 7.27 Double-wall detail showing ceiling nailer used to tie double walls together at corner.

Figure 7.28 Double-wall framing, corner detail, showing air barrier on outer surface of exterior wall. With this wall design, developed by Gene Leger, a Tyvek™ air barrier is applied over horizontal strapping on the outer wall. Diagonal siding is applied to the outside of the wall for structural strength.

it difficult to match rough openings for windows and doors in the two walls. The actual difference in heat conduction between staggered and nonstaggered studs is quite small. Therefore, we recommend matching the stud pattern in the two walls.

One or Two Batts vs Three The example of the Saskatchewan wall above showed the installation of three

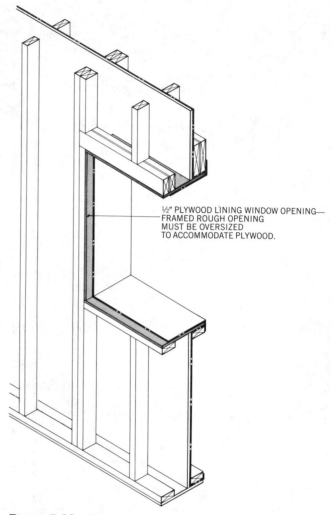

Figure 7.29 Plywood casing at double-wall rough openings.

separate fiberglass batts: two installed vertically in the stud bays of the inner and outer walls, and a third installed horizontally between the walls. If the wall studs are not staggered, it is possible to install one 3.5-inch batt in the inner stud wall and only one 6-inch batt to fill the cavity between the walls as well as the stud bays (Figure 7.31). The problem with this technique is that it leaves voids around the studs and possible gaps between the batts. It is recommended, therefore, that three separate batts be used.

Balloon-Type Framing at Floor Figures 7.32 and 7.33 show how double-wall construction can take advantage of the best features of both balloon-type and platform-type framing. The outer wall bears directly on the foundation, providing good insulation and an airtight seal at the joists. The air/vapor barrier can be run around the header joists with no problem.

Balloon-Type Framing at Ceiling Figure 7.34 shows the outer wall framing extended up beyond the second-

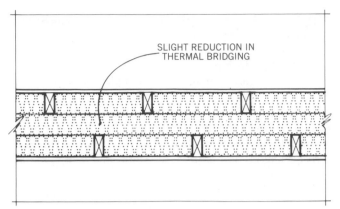

Figure 7.30 Staggered-stud double wall.

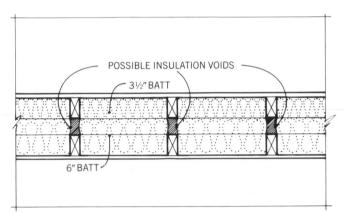

Figure 7.31 Double wall insulated with two rather than three fiberglass batts, showing possible voids created between opposing studs.

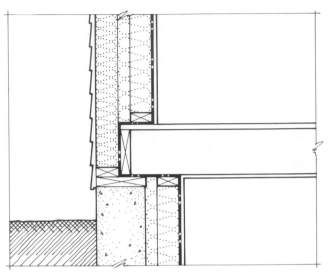

Figure 7.32 Double-wall framing showing modified balloon framing at first-floor level.

Figure 7.33 Double-wall framing with balloon framing of outer wall. Notice careful sealing of air/vapor barrier at rim joist corner. (Photo by Harold Orr.)

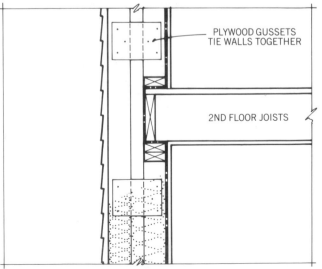

Figure 7.34 Double-wall balloon framing at second-floor joists.

floor joists. The studs could either end at the second-floor level or extend clear up to the roof. Since there are no top or bottom plates connecting the two walls, an alternative method must be used to tie them together. One good method is to use 8- × 12-inch plywood gussetts at every third stud (Figure 7.34); another method is to use a small piece of galvanized sheet metal cut exactly to the size of the wall separation distance.

Single Plate Wall With Staggered Studs The type of wall shown in Figure 7.35, often used as a common wall between units in multifamily buildings, is referred to as a "party wall"—an apt description. No framing passes through the wall, except the top and bottom plates. Sound doesn't readily pass through. There is no acoustical bridging, and no thermal bridging for the same reason. The wall is not only conducive to quiet, but also thermally efficient.

This wall design uses just as much wood as a double-stud wall. In fact, if you rip the 2 × 8 plates down the middle, you essentially have a double-stud wall.

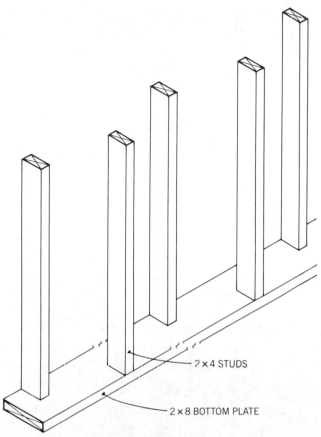

Figure 7.35 Staggered-stud double wall with single top and bottom plates.

— 2 × 4 STUDS

— 2 × 8 BOTTOM PLATE

vapor barrier is easier and also less likely to upset the construction schedule.

Insulative Sheathing As discussed later in this chapter, interior or exterior insulative sheathing is a good way to increase the thermal resistance of any type of wall. One exception is the double wall. The reason is economics. To increase the R-value of a double wall, it is cheaper and easier simply to space the two walls farther apart and add more insulation. The added insulation is the only extra cost. Some builders still justify the foam sheathing, arguing that the floor area under a double wall is worth $50 per square foot and that it is less expensive to buy and install foam sheathing than to take up valuable floor space. The validity of this argument depends on the method of economic analysis.

Construction of Interior Partitions The Canadian double wall assembly is $\frac{3}{4}$ inch taller than a normal stud wall because of the two $\frac{3}{8}$-inch plywood top and bottom plates. Interior partitions, built with standard-length studs, will all be $\frac{3}{4}$ inch too short. Provision must be made to fill that gap. One obvious solution is to attach plywood plates to the tops of the partitions. Another solution is to cut the exterior wall studs $\frac{3}{4}$ inch short. Still another approach is to install the interior partitions *after* the ceiling gypsum board is in. The $\frac{1}{2}$-inch ceiling gypsum board leaves just enough extra space to allow the partitions to be tipped up. The partitions are then shimmed and nailed into place.

Air/Vapor Barrier on the Inner Surface of Studs Although the inner surface of the studs has been the typical location for an air/vapor barrier, there are disadvantages. The barrier is relatively unprotected, both during construction and during occupancy, and it is more difficult to make it tight and continuous around electrical wiring and boxes. All holes or damages have to be sealed later.

On the other hand, the initial installation of the air/

Air/Vapor Barrier Around Interior Partitions If the air/vapor barrier is embedded deep into the exterior walls on the outside of the inner studs, interior partitions are installed the same as in standard construction. If, on the other hand, the air/vapor barrier is installed on the inner surface, behind the gypsum board, it is important to provide some means for spanning the exterior wall air/vapor barrier across the partition. There are two ways to do this.

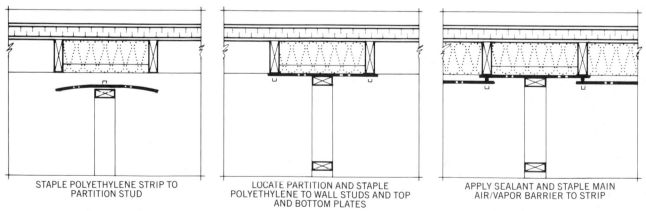

STAPLE POLYETHYLENE STRIP TO PARTITION STUD

LOCATE PARTITION AND STAPLE POLYETHYLENE TO WALL STUDS AND TOP AND BOTTOM PLATES

APPLY SEALANT AND STAPLE MAIN AIR/VAPOR BARRIER TO STRIP

Figure 7.36 One method of spanning air/vapor barrier across interior partitions when partitions are installed *before* exterior wall air/vapor barrier.

One is to attach a strip of 6-mil polyethylene to the partition before it is installed (Figure 7.36). The strip should be wide enough to span the exterior wall studs on either side of the partition. When the main air/vapor barrier is installed, it is sealed to the strip at the studs.

The second approach is to install the interior partitions *after* the walls (and ceiling) have been finished, that is, after the insulation, air/vapor barrier and gypsum board have been installed. This will cause an interruption in the framing and electrical installation schedules, but there are advantages which may more than offset that problem. First, the wall and ceiling air/vapor barrier go up very quickly since there will be few seams and very little cutting and sealing. Second, the wall (and ceiling) gypsum board can also go up quickly since long sheets can be put up in one very efficient operation. Third, there is no need to fuss with polyethylene on the interior partitions. This is discussed further in Chapter 9.

One question that always arises in reference to this technique is whether to install the gypsum board—or just the insulation and air/vapor barrier—before the interior partitions. There is a slight advantage in installing the partition walls before the gypsum board: it makes it easier to see where nails should be driven to hit the framing. But at the same time, it leaves the air/vapor barrier exposed to wind effects over a longer period.

Attachment to Outer Wall Figure 7.38 shows the best way to attach interior partitions to exterior walls. With this framing pattern, the usual three backer studs in the exterior wall are eliminated. Three horizontal 2 × 4 nailing blocks are installed between the exterior wall studs. The end stud of the interior partition is then nailed to the blocks.

The advantage of this system is that it allows more insulation to be installed in the exterior wall. It also uses

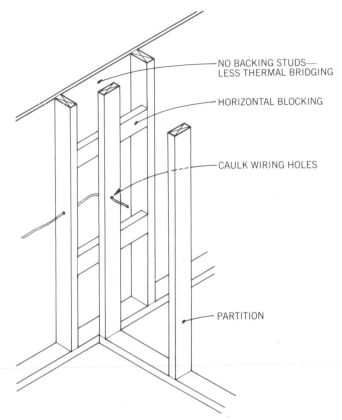

Figure 7.38 Attachment of interior partitions at exterior wall.

less wood and takes less time. Running wires between the two walls is also easier since there are fewer holes to drill.

The Roki Double Wall Design and Construction Sequence The Roki double wall is not a revolutionary wall design, but rather an innovative double wall design

Figure 7.37 Exterior double wall in place with interior partitions installed. Notice air/vapor barrier attached to top plate of all interior partitions, to be later sealed to ceiling air/vapor barrier. (Photo by Harold Orr.)

Figure 7.39 Double-wall framing; interior view. The air/vapor barrier and sheathing are installed on the outer surface of the inner wall studs. Notice horizontal nailers at left for attachment of interior partitions. (Photo by Harold Orr.)

CONSTRUCTION SEQUENCE

1. SILL SEAL APPLIED AND 2 × 8 SILL PLATE BOLTED DOWN.

2. LAY A '-6" STRIP OF POLYETHYLENE AIR/VAPOR BARRIER ON TOP OF PLATE. SEAL AND STAPLE TO BASEMENT WALL AIR/VAPOR BARRIER.

3. SET JOISTS AND USE ½" CDX PLYWOOD AS RIM JOIST. (CHECK CODE FOR FIRESTOP REQMTS.). ALLOW 3" BEARING FOR RIM AND JOISTS ON SILL PLATE.

4. APPLY PLYWOOD FLOOR DECK.

5. BRING AIR/VAPOR BARRIER UP ONTO FLOOR DECK AND STAPLE.

6. FRAME EXTERIOR WALL AND SET ON SILL PLATE LEAVING A 1" GAP BETWEEN WALL AND RIM JOIST.

7. SLIDE 1" RIGID INSULATION BETWEEN WALL AND RIM JOIST.

8. SET INTERIOR WALL IN PLACE, WITH AIR/VAPOR BARRIER APPLIED TO EXTERIOR FACE, WRAPPING BOTTOM PLATE. SEAL AND STAPLE AIR/VAPOR BARRIERS.

9. SEAL AND STAPLE A 2'-6" STRIP OF AIR/VAPOR BARRIER TO INT. WALL AIR/VAPOR BARRIER ON INSIDE OF TOP PLATE. FRAME SECOND FLOOR ON AIR/VAPOR BARRIER STRIP, AND BRING IT ONTO DECK. SECOND FLOOR DECKING SHOULD BE LEVEL WITH EXTERIOR WALL TOP PLATE.

10. ADD 16 GAUGE METAL SPACERS 4'-0" O.C.

11. FRAME AND PLACE SECOND FLOOR WALLS, WRAPPING AIR/VAPOR BARRIER OVER INNER WALL TOP PLATE BEFORE PLACING ROOF FRAMING. SEAL AND STAPLE CEILING AIR/VAPOR BARRIER TO WALL AIR/VAPOR BARRIER.

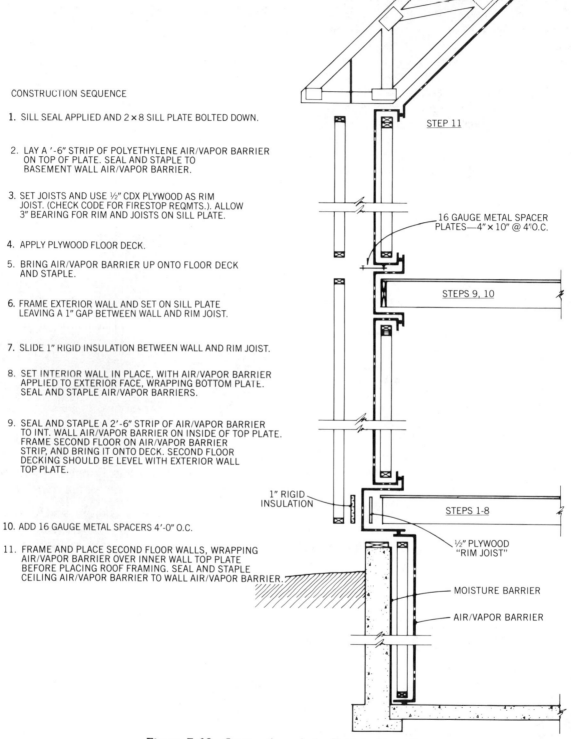

STEP 11

16 GAUGE METAL SPACER PLATES—4" × 10" @ 4' O.C.

STEPS 9, 10

1" RIGID INSULATION

STEPS 1-8

½" PLYWOOD "RIM JOIST"

MOISTURE BARRIER

AIR/VAPOR BARRIER

Figure 7.40 Section through the Roki double wall.

variation and construction sequence developed jointly by Roger Beaulieu, President of Roki Associates in Gorham, Maine, and Professor Howard Faulkner of the University of Southern Maine, the same team responsible for development of the Supertruss™ system (see Chapter 9).

A hybrid balloon/platform framing system, the Roki wall has *no top plates or bottom plates between the inner and outer walls*. The two walls are tied together with 16-gauge metal spacer plates. One advantage of this system is efficiency of the construction sequence. Another advantage

A

B

Figure 7.41 The Roki double wall construction sequence. A. Joists in place with air/vapor barrier draped over foundation. Note plywood joist header. B. Air/vapor barrier wrapped around joists and sealed at corners. (Photos by Howard Faulkner.)

is that the walls can be easily insulated with blown-in insulation from the top of the upper wall; there is a clear space (except for the metal plates) from attic to foundation. The attic insulation is blown in on top of the wall insulation, leaving almost no thermal bridging and almost no danger of voids resulting from insulation settling in the walls, particularly when using the Supertruss™ system, as pictured in the illustration.

Figures 7.40 and 7.41 show the sequence for constructing the Roki wall.

Exterior Rigid Insulative Sheathing

Exterior rigid insulative sheathing can be used instead of or in conjunction with any type of wall insulation to increase the overall thermal resistance of the wall assembly. The most common wall assembly of this type is 2×6 single stud walls with 2 inches of rigid foam installed over the studs on the outside (Figure 7.42).

Advantages of Insulative Sheathing There are two main advantages of insulative sheathing. First, it provides complete insulation coverage; there is *no thermal bridging through the insulation*. If you add 2 inches of extruded polystyrene (R-10), then the overall R-value of the entire wall is increased by R-10. Second, the insulation and framing within the stud cavity are kept warm. There is less likelihood of convection within the insulation. Also, since the wall structure is not subjected to diurnal and seasonal temperature cycling, it bears less thermal stress.

Disadvantages of External Insulative Sheathing When installed in thicknesses greater than 2 inches, insulative sheathing is sometimes difficult to install. First of all, it usually requires very long nails which can be cumbersome to handle. Corner nailing is particularly difficult since there may not be a good nail-base at the extreme corner (Figure 7.43). With compressible materials, such as expanded polystyrene, it is sometimes difficult to avoid waviness from compression when the siding is installed. Quality of workmanship becomes crucial.

Foam sheathing is not structural. Furthermore, even if a structural type of sheathing, such as plywood, is in-

C

D

E

Figure 7.41 (*continued*) C. 2 × 4's indicate where the two installed walls will go. D. Outer wall in place with rigid foam installed around joist headers. Inner wall is assembled on deck, ready to be installed. E. Inner wall installed in place. Notice how the air/vapor barrier is wrapped around corner of inner wall and sealed.

stalled over the foam, it won't provide structural racking resistance. Stud-framed walls with external insulative sheathing must therefore have some other type of racking resistance—either plywood nailed right to the studs, under the foam, or "let-in" corner bracing.

Finally, and perhaps most important, the *exterior insulation may form a vapor barrier on the outside (wrong side) of the wall.* This point warrants further discussion.

The potential danger of moisture condensation on the inner surface of exterior insulative sheathing has been the topic of considerable debate in the energy-efficient-design community. One manufacturer of rigid isocyanurate sheathing used to sell and recommend the installation of "vent strips" between the insulation and the framing to allow outside air to circulate inside the insulation and to vent moisture; some recent books on energy-efficient construction still carry that advice. The reality is that ventilation reduces the effectiveness of the insulation. Recent research at the U.S. Forest Products Laboratory has shown that venting the foam insulation can actually increase air leakage into walls and aggravate moisture problems.

So what about the moisture condensation problem? Unfortunately, our understanding of the moisture dynamics in an insulated wall is still somewhat incomplete. Theoretically, exterior insulative sheathing should cause moisture condensation problems because it places a va-

F

Figure 7.41 (*continued*) F. Interior view of completely assembled double wall. Notice diagonal bracing for racking strength. Unlike the "Saskatchewan" double wall, the Roki wall does not have sheathing on the outside of the inner wall, thus the need for diagonal bracing. However, it is not necessary to "let in" the bracing because of the hollow cavity between the two walls.

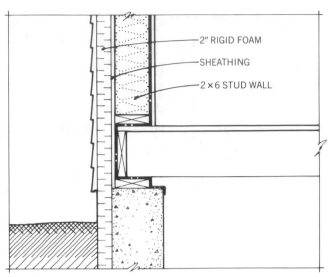

Figure 7.42 2 × 6 single wall with exterior rigid foam insulation.

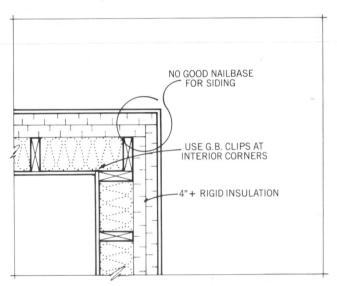

Figure 7.43 Thick exterior rigid foam insulation, showing problem of lack of nail-base at corners.

por-retarding membrane near the cold surface of an insulated wall. In practice, however, it does not seem to actually cause any serious problems. Tens of thousands of houses have been built this way with virtually no documented cases of damage where the insulation was properly installed.

To avoid any possible problems, however, certain safety precautions should be carefully adhered to when using exterior insulative sheathing:

1. Make sure the interior air/vapor barrier is continuous and carefully installed. If no moisture can get into the wall, there should be no problem.
2. Use thick insulative sheathing—at least 1.5 inches thick. The purpose of this is to keep the inner surface of the rigid insulation as warm as possible.
3. Seal the seams of the foam with tape to prevent any

cold air from getting behind the insulation. If cold air is allowed to penetrate, it will lower the temperature inside the wall and increase the likelihood of moisture condensation.

4. Install an air barrier over the rigid insulation. This will further decrease the possibility of cold air intrusion into the wall.
5. Never ventilate from inside the insulative sheathing to the outdoor air.

Exterior Insulative Sheathing as the Prime Insulation Material   Some builders allow exterior insulation to serve as the primary rather than supplemental insulation material. Figure 7.44 shows a wall with 5.25 inches

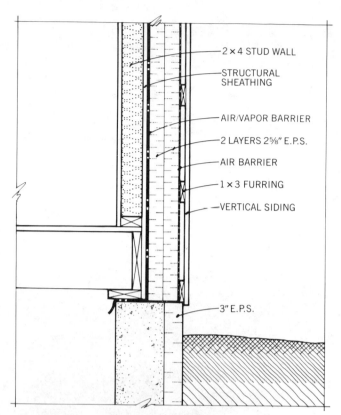

- 2 × 4 STUD WALL
- STRUCTURAL SHEATHING
- AIR/VAPOR BARRIER
- 2 LAYERS 2⅝″ E.P.S.
- AIR BARRIER
- 1 × 3 FURRING
- VERTICAL SIDING
- 3″ E.P.S.

Figure 7.44 Standard stud wall with extra thick exterior rigid foam insulation. (The "Styro House.")

of expanded polystyrene on the outside of a standard 2 × 4 single-stud wall. This wall construction was used in the "Styro House" shown in Chapter 1.

The beauty of this system is that the initial framing is absolutely conventional. The only special feature is that the exterior walls are pulled back 2.25 inches to allow part of the foam sheathing to sit on the foundation.

The "super" insulation is then installed as follows:

1. The entire house is wrapped with a polyethylene air/vapor barrier from the outside. There is very little cutting and sealing, even on a two-story house.
2. Two layers of 2⅝-inch expanded polystyrene (EPS) board are tacked onto the walls with the seams overlapping.
3. 2 × 10 window and door jambs are installed.
4. The insulation is then wrapped with a spun-bonded polyethylene air-barrier (such as Tyvek™).
5. 1 × 3 horizontal furring is attached to the outside of the walls using 8-inch spikes.
6. Vertical siding is installed, nailed into the 1 × 3 furring.
7. The foundation is insulated with 3 inches of insulation which fits neatly under the 3 inches of wall insulation extending out from the sill plate.

8. 3.5-inch (R-11) fiberglass insulation is then installed in the stud cavities.

There are several advantages to this design. The R-value of the wall is about R-32 with no thermal bridging all the way through the wall. There should be no moisture problems since two-thirds of the insulation R-value is outside the air/vapor barrier. Wiring and plumbing can be installed within the stud cavity with no worry about damage to the air/vapor barrier. The initial framing is totally conventional, so that no special skills or materials are required except around windows and doors. If the windows and doors are properly sealed, the walls should be extremely airtight.

The main disadvantage is the unusual process of applying the foam sheathing; 8-inch nails will be foreign to most carpenters and can cause cantilevering problems. Also, the cost of this system may run higher than other superinsulated wall designs of comparable R-value.

Wall Trusses

Non-Structural Trusses Non-structural trusses can be used to increase the depth of the insulation support structure of a wall. Figure 7.45 shows an innovative site-built unit called the Larsen Truss™. The trusses are installed on the outside of a conventionally framed and sheathed wall. The truss cavities are filled with insulation, and siding is then applied onto the trusses. Figures 7.46 through 7.48 show the details of the Larsen Truss and a few installation details.

Advantages The advantages of this system are similar to those for the "super" insulative sheathing listed above. The air/vapor barrier goes up in big pieces, so that there is less cutting and pasting than there is with single-wall systems. The trusses themselves are very easy to install; they are simply nailed directly to the siding. High R-values are easily attainable. With 8-inch trusses, you can install 8-inch fiberglass batts for R-30, or 8 inches of blown-in fiberglass at 2 pounds per cubic foot for R-32. These R-values are in addition to any insulation installed in the inner stud wall. The only other way to get R-values this high is with a double wall.

Disadvantages The main disadvantage of the Larsen Truss and similar systems is that they are new and very unconventional. They are commercially available only in western Canada and will usually have to be site built. The first installation for any builder will undoubtedly be slow and probably quite expensive. Some problems might be experienced with warping of the truss members. Also, extra framing is required around windows and doors. Additionally, the spacing between the truss chords can allow convective loops that might degrade the thermal performance of fiberglass batts. Blown fiberglass would seem more appropriate.

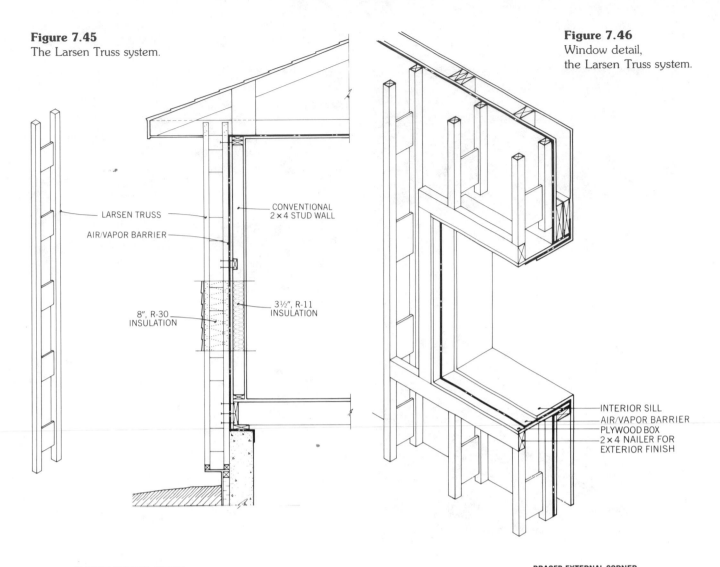

Figure 7.45
The Larsen Truss system.

Figure 7.46
Window detail,
the Larsen Truss system.

LARSEN TRUSS

AIR/VAPOR BARRIER

CONVENTIONAL
2 × 4 STUD WALL

8", R-30
INSULATION

3½", R-11
INSULATION

INTERIOR SILL
AIR/VAPOR BARRIER
PLYWOOD BOX
2 × 4 NAILER FOR
EXTERIOR FINISH

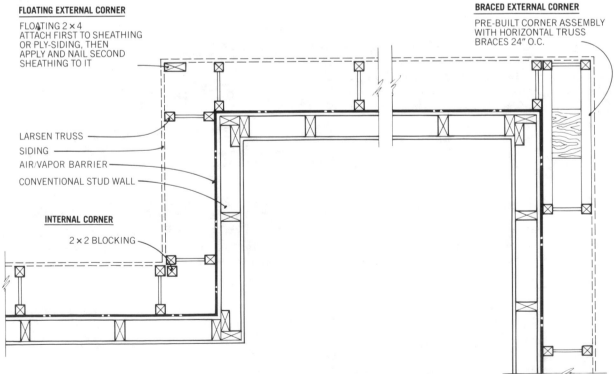

FLOATING EXTERNAL CORNER

FLOATING 2 × 4
ATTACH FIRST TO SHEATHING
OR PLY-SIDING, THEN
APPLY AND NAIL SECOND
SHEATHING TO IT

BRACED EXTERNAL CORNER

PRE-BUILT CORNER ASSEMBLY
WITH HORIZONTAL TRUSS
BRACES 24" O.C.

LARSEN TRUSS

SIDING

AIR/VAPOR BARRIER

CONVENTIONAL STUD WALL

INTERNAL CORNER

2 × 2 BLOCKING

Figure 7.47   Corner details, plan view; the Larsen Truss system.

Figure 7.48 The Larsen Truss, corner detail. (Photo by John Hughes.)

Figure 7.49 Truss frame construction. (Photo by Harold Orr.)

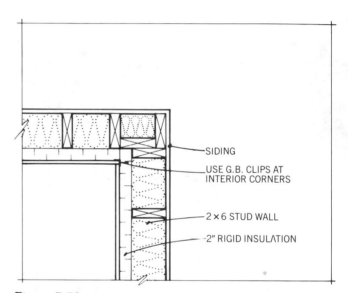

Figure 7.50 Interior rigid foam insulation; plan view.

Structural Wall Trusses Building with structural wall trusses is similar to building with very wide studs. The advantage is that there is much less wood in the truss and therefore less thermal bridging through the wall. Although popular in Scandinavia, wall trusses are still relatively rare in the United States and Canada. Truss frame systems that combine wall and roof trusses into one rigid frame (Figure 7.49) are a new variation now being tested in North America.

Interior Insulative Sheathing

Installing rigid insulation on the interior wall surface (Figure 7.50) is, from a thermal standpoint, a good technique which shares several of the advantages of exterior insulation while avoiding any possible problems with the cold-side vapor barrier.

The main disadvantage of this scheme is the difficulty of installing the gypsum board. Corners are a particular problem, since nailers must be displaced a distance equal to the thickness of the foam. The wall studs are not visible, so nailing the gypsum board is slightly harder. Plus, longer nails or screws must be used to penetrate through the rigid insulation. Electrical boxes and interior moldings are also more difficult to install. Since most rigid foams are flammable, the sheathing must be covered with a fire-rated interior finish.

Eight

Foundations

Traditionally, energy efficiency has not been an important design requirement for foundations because foundation heat loss in conventional houses is relatively small compared to the huge losses from the rest of the house. This is not the case, however, with superinsulated houses, in which an *un*insulated foundation would be a major flaw. A superinsulated foundation must be carefully designed and constructed to complement the thermal integrity of the rest of the house.

Today's houses are usually built on a slab, or over a crawl space or basement. The choice is often a matter of preference, although certain options appear to be more popular in some parts of the country (for instance, basements seem to be preferred in the northern part of the United States), and certain options may not be feasible because of conditions of a specific site (for instance, a basement is not possible at a location with a very high water table). In a superinsulated house, the choices are the same. Heat loss characteristics for these design alternatives are somewhat different, however, and so are designs for the insulation systems.

This chapter discusses how a house loses heat through its foundation to the ground, examines the basic principles for reducing that heat loss, and finally presents some specific design and construction details for superinsulated foundations.

THE GROUND IS A HEAT SINK

The thermal resistance and heat storage properties of the ground are such that the temperature remains constant year round below roughly the first 20 feet. At that depth, referred to as the "deep ground," the daily and seasonal fluctuations in air temperature are not reflected in the ground temperature. For most locations in North America, the deep ground temperature is always lower than typical house interior temperatures. Whether the house

sits on the ground, in the ground, or under the ground, heat will flow from the house into the ground (Figure 8.1). The heat sink effect of the ground creates a heat loss for the house, adding to the heating load in winter, and sometimes subtracting from the cooling load in summer.

The deep ground temperature for any area is the net effect of the ground's heat gain in summer and heat loss in winter. Therefore, the deep ground temperature is approximately equal to the average annual air temperature. Actually, in snowy regions, it is usually a few degrees above the average annual air temperature because snow cover insulates the ground against heat loss in winter. Most of the heat lost from foundations is not to the deep ground but rather to the ground at shallower depths where the temperature is affected by daily and seasonal variations in air temperature. Daily temperature fluctuations affect only the first few inches of soil, but seasonal changes affect soil temperature to depths up to 10 or 20 feet, depending on soil properties.

There are exceptions. In some warm climates, the deep ground temperature as well as shallow ground temperatures are higher than indoor air temperatures throughout the year. In Houston, for example, the ground temperature is always above indoor room temperature; the ground is a heat source, not a sink.

Heat Flows From a Foundation in Two Directions

During cold weather, heat is lost from a foundation both upward to the outdoor air and downward to the deep ground (Figure 8.2). During warm weather, heat flow is primarily downward (Figure 8.3). Foundation insulation systems can be designed to control these two flows separately and differently, according to climate and design needs.

The actual amount of heat that flows from a foundation to the ground surface or to the deep ground is very difficult to calculate. Reliable computation methods are still

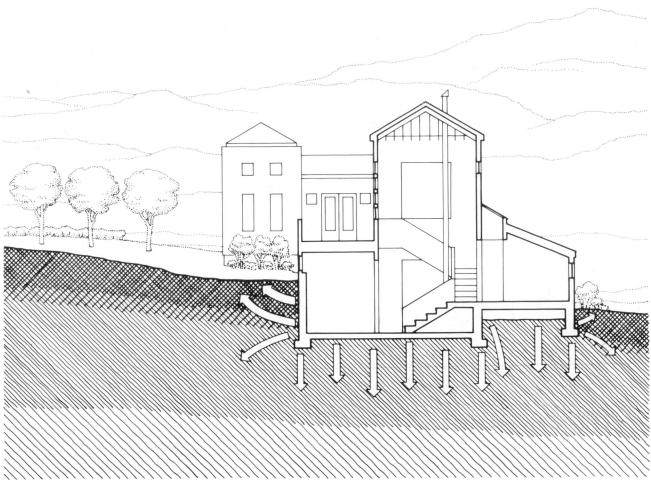

Figure 8.1 The ground is a heat sink.

being developed, but because of the relatively complex characteristics of heat transfer below grade, even the most sophisticated techniques produce uncertain results. Unlike above-grade heat loss, where the building envelope loses heat to the air, a relatively uniform medium, foundation heat loss is to the earth, a medium whose type, moisture content, ground cover, and thermal properties can vary considerably. The most significant variable is soil moisture content: wet soil has a much higher thermal conductivity than drier soil. Moisture content sometimes varies with the seasons. For example, in northern climates, ground freezing combined with heat loss from the house may dry out a soil, lowering its thermal conductivity. Another factor that is seasonally variable is snow cover. One foot of new snow adds about R-10 to R-15 to the thermal resistance between the ground and the outside air.

Upward to the Ground Surface   Heat flow through the ground upward to the ground surface is the greatest and most important heat loss from foundations. The magnitude of this heat flow depends on the distance the heat must travel to reach the surface and the temperature

and properties of the soil around the foundation (Figure 8.4). The soil actually serves as insulation between the foundation and the outdoor air. The upper sections of a foundation, near the ground surface, obviously have the shortest heat-flow path and thus the greatest heat loss; the lower foundation sections will have the longest heat-flow path and the least heat loss. There is an exception to this in the case of hollow-block foundation walls, as we shall see later in this chapter.

Downward to the Deep Earth   A secondary heat-flow path is from the foundation to the deep ground. As mentioned above, the temperature of the deep ground is constant and usually less than indoor air temperature. Foundations will lose heat by conduction to the deep earth as long as this temperature differential exists. This downward flow is typically less than the upward flow because in the former the temperature difference is smaller. Even in Fargo, North Dakota, the deep ground temperature is only about 41°F, considerably warmer than the average winter air temperature. The actual amount of heat lost to the deep ground is particularly difficult to quantify because downward flow is further

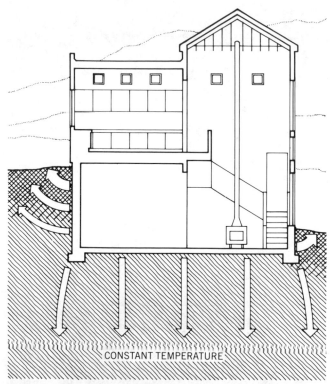

Figure 8.2 Winter foundation heat loss. The greatest heat loss is to the upper soil levels and ground surface.

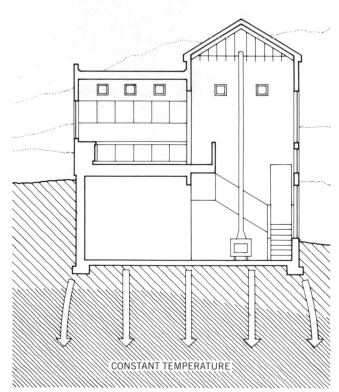

Figure 8.3 Summer foundation heat loss. Heat loss is to the deep ground only.

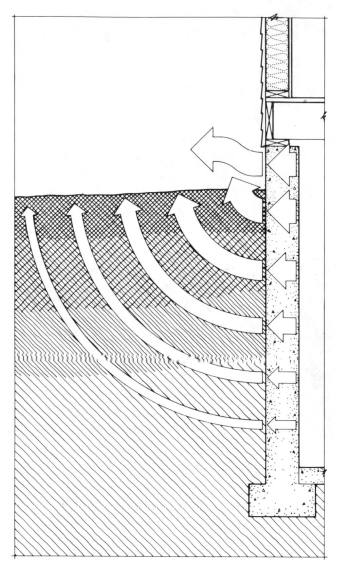

Figure 8.4 Upward heat flow to the ground surface.

complicated by the fact that the very placement of the house causes the ground under it to gradually warm up. Over the years, heat loss from the foundation warms the soil under a house (Figure 8.5). This phenomenon is well documented in permafrost regions but is less well understood for moderate climates. It is not known exactly how long it takes the subsoil temperature regime to stabilize or how much influence the effect has on foundation heat loss. Computer simulations performed at the University of Minnesota show that the stabilization period could range from a few months to three years. Soil properties, particularly groundwater, will have a significant effect. Studies in Sweden have shown that the presence of a house disturbs the temperature of the ground as far as one house width away in a horizontal direction, and more than 30 feet in depth.

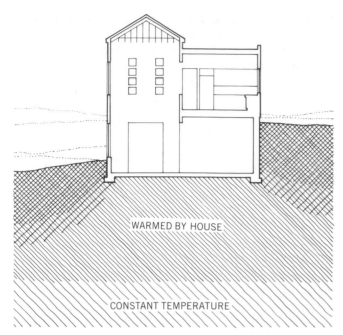

Figure 8.5 *The effect of a house on underground temperature. Over time, the house tends to warm the earth beneath.*

DESIGNING THE SUPERINSULATED FOUNDATION

The design of a superinsulated foundation is a relatively straightforward process. But it involves making several important decisions differently than one does when designing a conventional foundation. For conventional houses, the foundation provides anchor and support for the structure; then an insulation system is added. For superinsulated houses, the design process begins with defining the boundaries of the thermal envelope. The next step is to schematically design the insulation system

by deciding which surfaces are to be insulated and with how much insulation. Finally, the insulation system is designed.

A properly designed superinsulated foundation must minimize heat loss to the outdoor air and to the ground; make an airtight seal to the house superstructure; provide warm floors in the winter for thermal comfort; and take advantage of the potential cooling capacity of ground coupling. It must accomplish all of the above without leading to any moisture problems, fire hazards, or air-quality problems in the living space. Naturally, it must also provide adequate anchor and support for the house structure.

Defining the Boundary of the Thermal Envelope

The first step in designing the foundation insulation system is to define the lower boundary of the thermal envelope. This is an important process even though it may seem a bit academic. The conventional way to locate the boundary of the thermal envelope is simply to draw a line around the heated living space. With superinsulated house design, the boundary of the thermal envelope is designed a little differently: *The idea is to locate the boundary where it can be insulated and sealed most effectively and economically.* As discussed in Chapter 1, the best thermal envelope may enclose spaces that don't necessarily need to be heated. This is often the case for the lower boundary of the thermal envelope, which may include the basement.

Basements Typically, basements are not planned to be used as part of the primary living space, so the thermal envelope is planned as shown in Figure 8.6a, with the insulation system installed in the basement ceiling. A secondary insulation system might also be placed on the

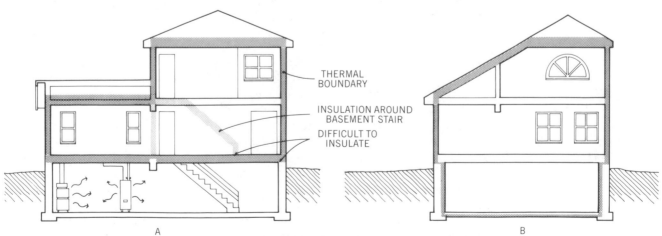

A

B

Figure 8.6 Two possibilities for defining the boundary of the thermal envelope in houses with basements. A. Basement outside the thermal envelope—unheated. B. Basement within the thermal envelope—heated.

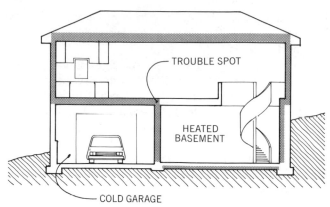

Figure 8.7 Defining the boundary of the thermal envelope in a house with a "tuck-under" garage.

basement walls to keep the basement from getting too cold. (We don't recommend this design for superinsulated houses.)

For superinsulated houses, the basement should be included in the thermal envelope, as shown in Figure 8.6b. The insulation system should be installed on the basement walls and possibly under the floor. There are several good reasons for this.

First of all, basements often contain unintentional heat sources—furnaces, water heaters, pipes, ducts, chimneys, washing machines, dryers, etc. All of these supply heat which should be captured within the thermal envelope rather than allowed to escape through an uninsulated basement.

But there is another, more important reason to place the thermal boundary at the walls and floor rather than at the ceiling of the basement: it is difficult to create an effective superinsulation system in the ceiling. Basement ceilings usually contain plumbing, wiring, ducts, and cross braces—all of which make it difficult to attain perfect insulation coverage. The joists themselves are thermal bridges which degrade the effectiveness of the insulation system. All household utilities penetrate the basement ceiling by means of wiring, plumbing, heating ducts, and flues. If that ceiling is the boundary of the thermal envelope, then it must include a continuous air/vapor barrier, which must be sealed at every penetration. This could be a monumental task. Furthermore, if the basement is to be considered outside the thermal envelope, then the boundary includes not only the basement ceiling but also the doorway, walls, and ceiling of any stairway leading to the basement—a complex geometry which is difficult to superinsulate and to make airtight. This usually becomes obvious when you sit down and plan where the air/vapor barrier will go and how it will be sealed. All these factors, when combined, virtually preclude the possibility of creating an effective superinsulation system over an unheated basement. Finally, if you install an effective insula-

tion system in the basement ceiling, the basement might become quite cold (depending on how many unintentional heat sources are located there). Not only would this make the basement uncomfortable for incidental activities but it would also risk freezing pipes as well.

Some designers decide to insulate the basement ceiling to some degree and then also insulate the exterior foundation walls above grade. This helps to reduce heat losses, but two imperfect boundaries on either side of a semi-exterior space are generally less effective than a single effective boundary on one side.

Of course, life is not always simple and neither are basements. Figure 8.7 shows a popular house design with a "tuck-under" garage. The garage should never be inside the thermal envelope, not only because of noxious fumes, but also because there is no such thing as a truly airtight garage door. So the garage ceiling must be part of the boundary of the thermal envelope. But what about the basement? In Figure 8.7, the basement is shown included inside the envelope. This is a difficult and complex construction. One troublesome spot is where the partition between the basement and garage meets the basement ceiling. The air/vapor barrier has to somehow cross through the ceiling. Although there are ways to do this (see Chapter 11), it typically requires a lot of cutting and pasting and will usually result in a less-than-perfect air/vapor barrier seal. If, on the other hand, you choose not to include the basement within the thermal envelope, you will be faced with the difficulties described above. The reality is simply that tuck-under garages are difficult to superinsulate. Similar problems sometimes arise with split-level and other complex designs.

None of these problems is insurmountable as long as properly anticipated. That is why defining the boundary of the thermal envelope is more than just academic. *When you sit down and plan where the insulation will go, where the air/vapor barrier will go, and how the insulation will be installed, the best envelope design will usually become obvious.*

Crawl Spaces As with basements, there are two approaches to crawl-space insulation design (Figure 8.8). Either the walls and floor of the crawl space are insulated, which places the crawl space within the thermal envelope (Figure 8.8a), or the overlying floor is insulated, which places the crawl space outside the thermal envelope (Figure 8.8b). Some of the arguments for enclosing a basement within the thermal envelope are equally applicable to crawl spaces. The exterior wall of the crawl space is easier to superinsulate than the overlying floor. If the overlying floor is insulated, thermal bridging through the floor joists not only increases heat loss, but also causes a cold floor above. Pipes in an unheated crawl space are subject to freezing. Also, to prevent unwanted heat loss, any ducts located there would have to be carefully sealed and insulated.

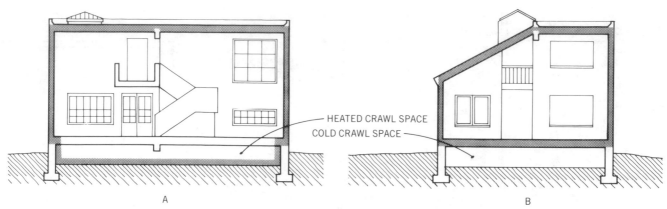

Figure 8.8 Two possibilities for defining the boundary of the thermal envelope in a house with a crawl space. A. Crawl space inside the thermal envelope—heated. B. Crawl space outside the thermal envelope—unheated.

Crawl spaces are usually ventilated to eliminate excess moisture from the ground and from the house above. When the crawl space is included inside the thermal envelope, it is essentially a heated crawl space and will require different treatment with respect to ventilation. Obviously, you can't ventilate a heated crawl space since you would be just dumping heat outdoors. Alternative methods of moisture control are discussed later in the chapter.

Slab-on-Grade Traditional slab-on-grade house design usually includes the floor within the thermal envelope (except when left uninsulated altogether). Actually, it is possible to *exclude* the slab from the envelope by installing an insulated floor over it. This, in fact, can be quite energy-efficient, but is usually impractical due to excessive cost and other problems that will be discussed later.

Selectively Placed Foundation Insulation Reduces Heat Loss

Once the thermal envelope has been defined, the next step is planning how to reduce the heat loss through it. Heat loss can be broken down into components: above-grade loss, below-grade loss to the air, and below-grade loss to the deep ground. A well thought out insulation system addresses each component individually with appropriate design strategies. The methods do not differ in principle for basements, crawl spaces, or slabs.

Reducing Above-Grade Heat Loss Since the above-grade section of a foundation is exposed to the outdoor air, it not only has the greatest conductive heat loss, but is also subject to considerable air leakage at the sill plate and band joist areas. The insulation system at this section therefore must have high R-value and must also include an integrated air/vapor barrier to stop air leakage.

The R-value of the above-grade section of foundation walls should be comparable to the R-value of the main house walls (see Chapter 6). Insulation is placed either on the outside, on the inside, or, in the case of wood foundations, within the foundation wall.

The band joist area is a particularly troublesome spot. Since the band joist normally sits on the outside edge of the foundation, the usual tendency is to stuff insulation between the floor joists (Figure 8.9a). But where does the air/vapor barrier go? To seal an air/vapor barrier between each joist is a very tedious job (see Chapter 11). But if it's left out, water vapor will be able to pass freely through the insulation. Since the insulation should keep the band joists cold, condensation is sure to occur. But the story gets worse. As mentioned above, the band joist area is also the site of considerable air leakage over and under the joists. One seemingly attractive way to seal this area is to install an air/vapor barrier around and over the band joists (Figure 8.9b). *Now we have an air/vapor barrier in the wrong place. This is a common and serious mistake and can easily result in moisture damage.* Yet the band joist area must be insulated and sealed against air leakage. What to do? Several designs that accomplish this will be presented later in the chapter.

Reducing Below-Grade Losses to the Air The section of foundation from grade level to about 3 feet below grade loses heat mainly by conduction upward through the soil to the air above. A much smaller amount of heat is also lost to the deep ground. The soil temperature at shallow depths varies with the season but is often cold enough to cause considerable heat loss. Since typical foundation materials are airtight and the foundations are covered with soil, heat loss is by conduction only. One exception is with masonry block foundations, in which convection and radiation within the block cavities account for part of the heat loss, as discussed below.

Upward heat-flow from the foundation to the air can be reduced by placing insulation vertically on the inside

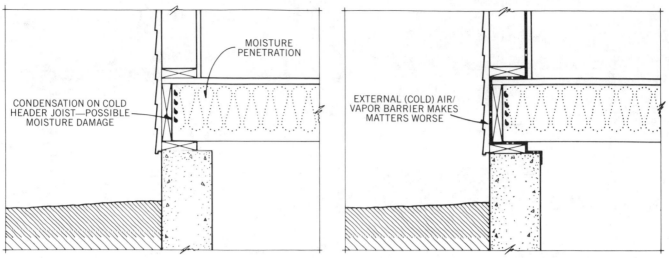

MOISTURE PENETRATION

CONDENSATION ON COLD HEADER JOIST—POSSIBLE MOISTURE DAMAGE

EXTERNAL (COLD) AIR/VAPOR BARRIER MAKES MATTERS WORSE

A. INSULATION BETWEEN THE JOISTS WITH NO AIR/VAPOR BARRIER

B. EXTERNAL AIR/VAPOR BARRIER

Figure 8.9 Unacceptable methods for insulating header joists. In both cases, the header joists will be cold and subject to moisture condensation.

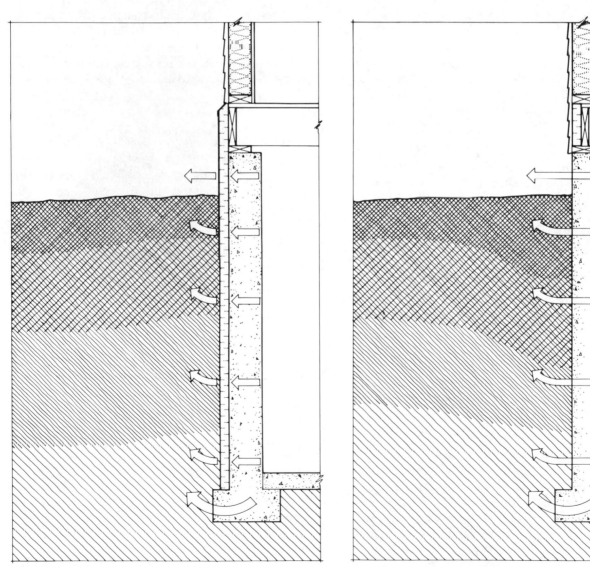

Figure 8.10 Exterior foam foundation insulation. The foundation is inside the thermal envelope.

Figure 8.11 Interior foundation insulation. The foundation will be at or near the temperature of surrounding soil.

and/or outside of the foundation wall (Figures 8.10 and 8.11). In order to reach the surface, heat must flow either through or around the insulation. Conduction through the insulation is impeded by the thermal resistance of the material; conduction around the insulation is impeded by the distance and thermal resistance through the soil. Since the insulation should effectively cut off most of the heat flow from the foundation, soil around the foundation will be almost as cold as if the house were not there.

An alternative foundation insulation scheme is shown in Figure 8.12. In this case, an almost horizontal layer of insulation extends outward from the foundation. Again, insulation has increased the thermal resistance along the shortest path from the foundation to the outside air, and the alternative heat flow path—around the insulation—is a much longer distance, thereby naturally providing addi-

tional thermal resistance. This is a "selective" insulation system: it reduces heat loss through the ground to the air but does not affect the loss to the deep ground. It is recommended for moderate climates where winter heat loss should be reduced but summer heat loss should be maintained for its cooling effect. This design scheme is also effective for keeping frost away from a foundation: the soil around the foundation will be warmed by it and will never freeze.

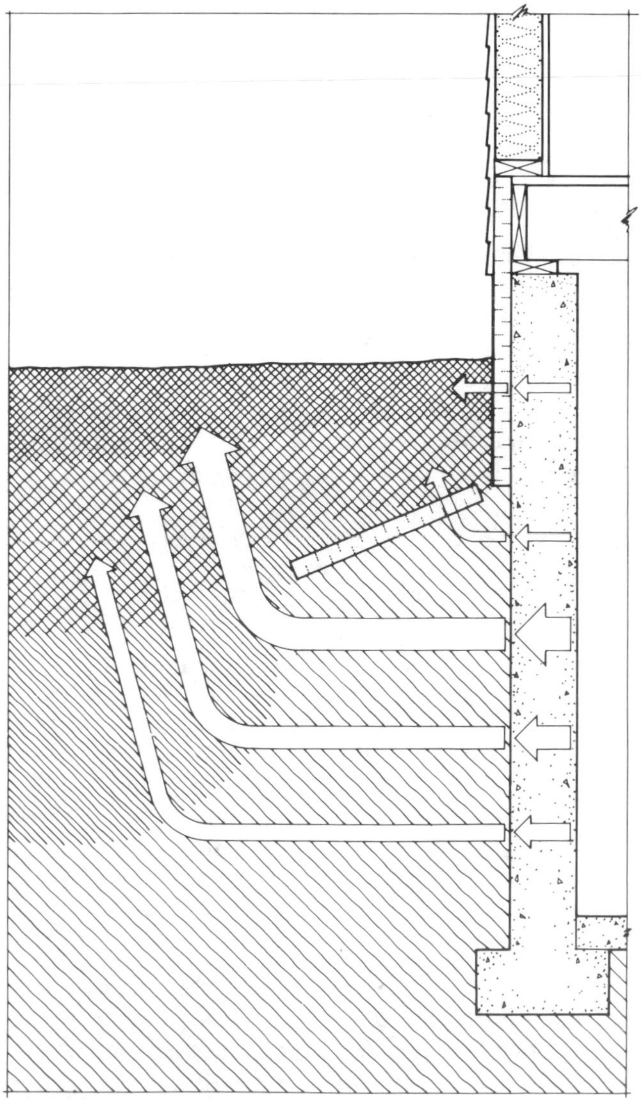

Reducing Losses to the Deep Ground   The floors of basements, crawl spaces, and slabs, as well as the deepest sections of foundation walls, all lose heat primarily to the deep ground. This heat loss is most commonly controlled with rigid foam insulation placed under the floor and/or on the walls. Optimizing the thickness of insulation for this application is not easy, since heat-load calculations to the deep earth are so uncertain. As a guideline, R-5 to R-10 should be sufficient for all but the most extreme climates.

In warm or moderate climates, where the cooling load is equal to or greater than the heating load, the bottom of the foundation may be left uninsulated to take advantage of the cooling effect of the earth. *It is too simplistic, however, to assume that the ground will always supply useful cooling in warm climates.* First of all, foundations typically only extend down 5 or 6 feet into the earth. In very warm climates, the temperature of the ground at that depth may be *warmer* than room temperature, even in the summer. Also, even in cold climates, the ground around a foundation is warmed all year by heat from the foundation and may get too warm to provide cooling. Another consideration is possible moisture condensation problems. In very humid climates with cool ground temperatures, the temperature of the inside surface of an uninsulated foundation may get below the dew point, resulting in condensation.

Figure 8.12   Horizontal insulation, installed below grade.

Figure 8.13   Exterior rigid foam foundation insulation with horizontal insulation installed below grade. (Photo by Harold Orr.)

THE INSULATION SYSTEM

Foundation Materials: The Support Structure

From a thermal standpoint, the three common foundation materials—poured concrete, masonry blocks, and wood—perform differently, not only in thermal transmission characteristics, but also in the types of insulation system they should receive. The following sections describe the characteristics of these materials that are relevant to the design of a superinsulated foundation system.

Poured Concrete The single most important characteristic of poured concrete is its R-value. An 8-inch thick concrete wall has an R-value of R-0.7; an uninsulated concrete foundation would be a thermal disaster! When designing an insulation system, careful effort should be made to avoid any concrete thermal bridges passing through or around the insulation. Even if the heat has to travel 3 feet through the concrete (R-3.1), a significant thermal bridge still exists and should be eliminated.

Concrete foundations are insulated on either the inside or outside surface, as shown in the first parts of this chapter. A few new systems actually include foam insulation in the center of a poured concrete foundation wall. These innovations, though not yet widely accepted, may hold promise for the future.

Hollow Masonry Blocks Masonry blocks are manufactured from a variety of materials with varying thermal conductivities. The R-value of hollow 8-inch blocks varies between R-1.0 and R-3.0. Although slightly higher in R-value than poured concrete, hollow blocks have a major thermal shortcoming. The hollow cores, usually connected vertically, can greatly increase heat loss through the formation of convective loops (Figure 8.14). Along its entire height, the wall collects heat from the house interior and dumps it through the top of the foundation into the cold outdoor air. Thus the entire foundation wall in Figure 8.14 is losing heat to the outdoors.

Therefore, hollow block foundations should be filled, as they are built, with an appropriate insulating material. The best material for this application is either perlite or vermiculite. Neither has very high R-value (R-2.7 per inch for perlite and R-2.3 per inch for vermiculite), but both stop the convective loop. They are both waterproof—that is, they will not damage if wetted—making them ideal for foundation application.

Filling the hollow cores with insulation will not provide enough thermal resistance to make a masonry block foundation energy-efficient. Additional insulation, either on the inside or the outside of the wall, is also necessary.

Wood Wood foundations are quickly gaining popularity for all types of house construction. From a thermal standpoint, they have two advantages over concrete. First, wood has a considerably higher R-value than concrete (R-1.25 per inch). Thermal bridging is therefore less of a problem. Second, wood foundations are basically 6- or 8-inch stud walls (Figure 8.15), which can be insulated easily with fiberglass batts for much less than it costs to insulate concrete or block foundations with rigid foam.

Wood foundations are pressure-treated with special preservatives for protection against decay and insect attack. The only preservatives accepted for use in residential wood foundations are chromated copper arsenate (CCA) and ammoniacal copper arsenate (ACA). These preservatives are often referred to as "waterborne preservative treatments" because the wood is treated with a solution of chemicals dissolved in water. As the wood dries, these chemicals become permanently fixed within the wood. Once the wood is dry, these treatments leave a dry, paintable surface.

There has been some concern about the potential for indoor air contamination from pressure-treated wood in airtight houses. The contaminant in question is arsenic, one component of both CCA and ACA. A study done by the National Bureau of Standards showed no elevated levels of arsenic in the air in basements built with pressure-treated wood. They did find traces of arsenic in dust samples in the basement, but this was not considered to be a health hazard.

Insulation Materials

In evaluating insulation materials for underground application, the following criteria are important:

1. R-value
2. resistance to water absorption
3. compressive strength
4. resistance to soil chemicals
5. cost
6. availability
7. resistance to insect and rodent attack

Appendix A includes a summary of properties of the common insulation materials. The following sections discuss specific attributes of the common insulation materials as they relate to use in foundations.

Extruded Polystyrene This is the best material for below-grade use, particularly if there is any exposure to ground water. It comes in 2×4-foot and 2×8-foot sheets and in thicknesses up to 3.5 inches.

The main advantages of this material are high R-value (R-5.0 per inch at 75°F, R-5.4 per inch at 40°F), low water absorption, and high compressive strength (5760 pounds per square foot).

Expanded Polystyrene This material is chemically the same as extruded polystyrene, but is manufactured by a different process. Often referred to as "beadboard," it is actually composed of tiny beads, fused together.

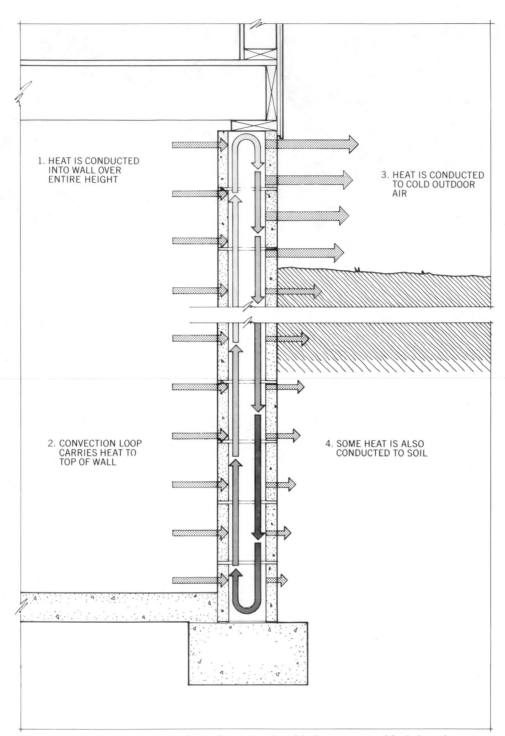

1. HEAT IS CONDUCTED INTO WALL OVER ENTIRE HEIGHT

3. HEAT IS CONDUCTED TO COLD OUTDOOR AIR

2. CONVECTION LOOP CARRIES HEAT TO TOP OF WALL

4. SOME HEAT IS ALSO CONDUCTED TO SOIL

Figure 8.14 Convective loop formed in uninsulated hollow masonry-block foundation wall.

There are over one hundred manufacturers of beadboard in the United States and Canada. It can be purchased in almost any thickness and size.

Expanded polystyrene should not be used underground unless it is completely protected from water penetration. It can absorb up to 6 percent of its weight in water, which not only degrades its R-value, but also creates a strong potential for physical damage if the water freezes into ice. For certain applications, such as interior foundation insulation, where the insulation will not be exposed to ground water, expanded polystyrene is acceptable. You must be certain, however, that the insula-

Figure 8.15 All Weather Wood Foundation insulated with 6-inch (R-19) fiberglass batts. (Photo by Howard Faulkner.)

Figure 8.17 Medium-density fiberglass in place over concrete foundation. (Photo by Harold Orr.)

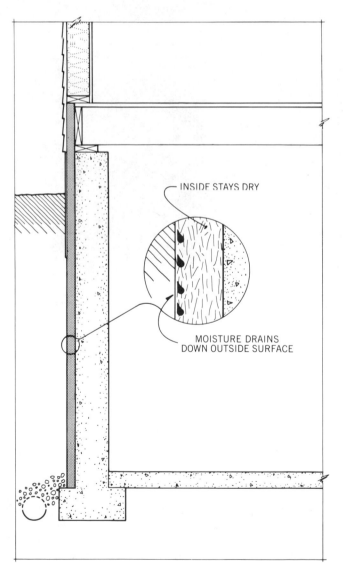

INSIDE STAYS DRY

MOISTURE DRAINS DOWN OUTSIDE SURFACE

Figure 8.16 Medium-density rigid fiberglass installed on the outside of a foundation as insulation and drainage layer.

tion will remain dry. Another problem with this material is quality consistency. Unlike extruded polystyrene, which is manufactured in the United States by only two major companies, expanded polystyrene is produced by hundreds of smaller companies. The same consistency of quality cannot be assured.

Polyurethane and Polyisocyanurate These two materials are chemically very similar. They have higher R-values than any other rigid foam insulation material, but like expanded polystyrene, they also may absorb water and are therefore not recommended for below-grade application unless completely protected from water.

Low-Density Fiberglass Fiberglass batt insulation can be used on the inside of masonry basement or crawl space walls, and is also good for wood foundations. Its low cost makes it probably the best material for those applications. When used for foundations, as for any installation, it must be protected from moisture.

Medium-Density Fiberglass This material is similar to low-density fiberglass batts except that it is manufactured at a higher density (5 to 7 pounds per cubic foot), and treated with a different binding material. It is a semi-rigid board.

Although medium-density fiberglass is a fairly good insulating material (R-4.5 per inch), its best application is as a drainage layer on the outside of foundations. When installed vertically, water will not penetrate into the board, but will simply run down the outer skin (Figure 8.16). This makes it an excellent material for keeping foundations dry.

The only commercially available medium-density fiberglass for foundation use is BaseClad, by Fiberglas Canada. Unfortunately, it is available only in Canada at the time of this writing. Some Canadian builders have used fiberglass roofing insulation as a substitute for BaseClad and report that it works just as well.

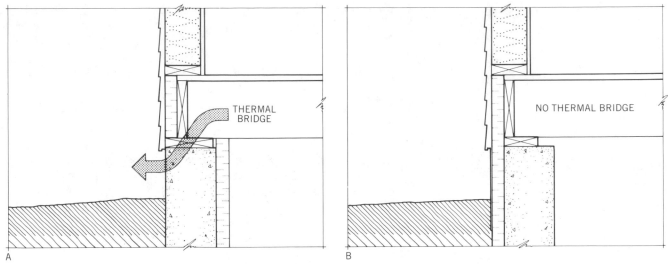

Figure 8.18 The advantage of exterior foundation insulation over interior foundation insulation for reducing thermal bridging. A. Interior insulation. Thermal bridging exists through wall's bottom plate into foundation. B. Exterior insulation. Thermal bridging is eliminated.

Note: In late 1984, Owens Corning Fiberglas was doing final market tests on a product very similar to BaseClad. If approved, the product is to be marketed in the United States under the name Warm-N-Dri.

DESIGN SPECIFICS: BASEMENTS

Basement Wall Insulation

With poured concrete or masonry block foundations, insulation is placed on the inside and/or outside of the wall. With wood foundations, the insulation is placed inside the wall, but it may be supplemented with additional exterior or interior insulation. The following sections discuss the attributes and details of several foundation wall superinsulation systems.

Insulation on the Outside *Advantages and Disadvantages* From a thermal standpoint, exterior insulation works better than interior insulation. With insulation on the outside of the foundation wall, the wall itself is kept warm and is protected somewhat from damage caused by annual freeze-thaw cycles. The inside surface of the foundation wall will also be warm and therefore less prone to condensation than with interior insulation (see the next section). Also, since the wall is inside the thermal envelope, it may serve beneficially as thermal mass, particularly if there is passive solar energy input to the basement space.

With interior insulation, the concrete acts as a thermal bridge between the sill plate and the outdoor air (Figure 8.18a). This is avoided with exterior insulation (Figure 8.18b).

Any foundation insulation will make the surrounding

soil cold because it cuts off heat from the house. This has raised some concern about frost heave (see the end of this chapter). Exterior insulation is preferable for reducing the likelihood of ground frost damage. In Figure 8.19a, the concrete wall with interior insulation acts as a thermal bridge between the outdoor air and the deep ground. Since concrete has a higher conductivity than soil, the foundation accelerates the heat loss from (or cold penetration into) the ground, thus increasing the likelihood of ground frost. With exterior insulation (Figure 8.19b), this phenomenon is eliminated.

Exterior foundation insulation is often run up past the header joist (Figure 8.20a), keeping it warm and helping to prevent condensation (Figure 8.20b), as well as helping to make an airtight seal between the sill plate and the foundation.

Exterior insulation of foundation walls has some disadvantages too, the main one being the difficulty in installing sufficient thickness. Figure 8.21 shows an example of this. The 4-inch thick foam sticks out beyond the house siding, creating an unusual and sometimes objectionable appearance. Some sort of flashing must be installed to protect the top of the foam from the weather. The installation is not impossible, just difficult.

Another disadvantage is that exterior insulation is exposed to the environment and therefore more prone to damage and degradation. Above grade, it must be covered with some type of material to protect it from sunlight (ultraviolet degradation) and mechanical damage (Figure 8.21). Below grade, there is possible damage from moisture, frost heave, insects, and animals. We've heard reports of insects burrowing into various types of foams. Although this has not been well documented, it is a po-

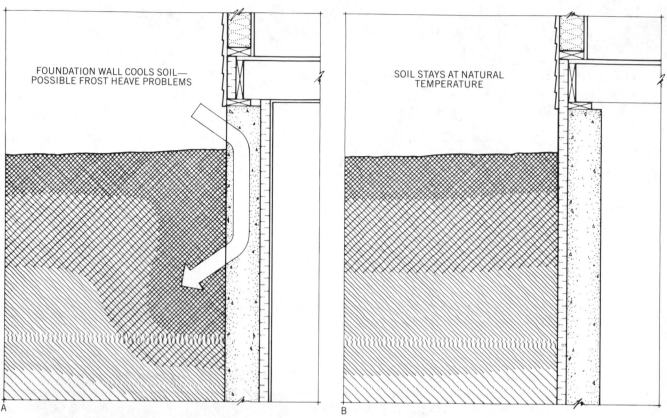

FOUNDATION WALL COOLS SOIL—
POSSIBLE FROST HEAVE PROBLEMS

SOIL STAYS AT NATURAL
TEMPERATURE

A

B

Figure 8.19 The advantage of exterior foundation insulation over interior foundation insulation for reducing the possibility of frost heave. A. Interior insulation. Concrete wall increases "cold penetration" into the soil. B. Exterior insulation. Soil remains at or near natural temperature.

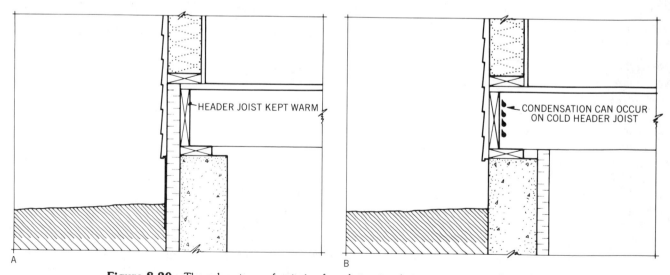

HEADER JOIST KEPT WARM

CONDENSATION CAN OCCUR
ON COLD HEADER JOIST

A

B

Figure 8.20 The advantage of exterior foundation insulation over interior foundation insulation for avoiding condensation problems on joist headers. A. Exterior insulation. Header joist is kept warm; little likelihood of moisture condensation. B. Interior insulation. Header joist is uninsulated and cold.

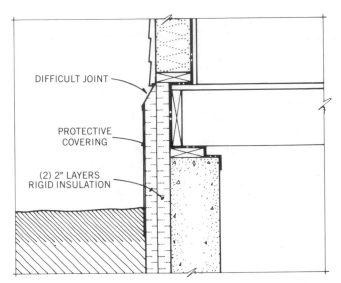

Figure 8.21 Installation of thick exterior foam insulation. One problem is the difficulty in fitting the insulation to the siding.

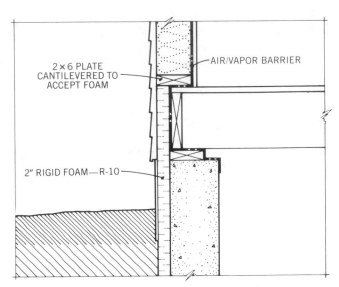

Figure 8.22 2 × 6 bottom plate cantilevered to accept foam foundation insulation.

tentially serious problem, not only because the insulation will be damaged, but because insects may build concealed pathways for travel to other parts of the house.

Design and Installation The best material for exterior foundation insulation is extruded polystyrene. It is possible to use expanded polystyrene, urethane or isocyanurate, but these materials must be absolutely protected from moisture. Another good material is medium-density semi-rigid fiberglass.

The above-grade sections of foundation wall should be insulated as close as possible to the same R-value as the exterior walls of the house. With extruded polystyrene, that means at least 4 inches of insulation, usually installed in two 2-inch thick layers. This thickness should be extended down to 2 feet below grade. In extremely cold climates, where the average annual temperature is less than 45°F, that thickness should be extended all the way down to the footing. In more moderate climates, the deeper portions of the foundation need only 2 inches. Differential thickness is sometimes a problem during backfilling, when the upper layer may get pulled down by the backfill soil.

In Figure 8.22, the 6-inch wall is cantilevered out 2 inches to allow the foam to tuck under the bottom plate. Obviously, this design can only be used with a 6-inch or wider wall. The header joist is insulated and the joint between the sill plate and foundation is sealed against air leakage. The main disadvantage of this scheme is that the R-value is only R-10. Also, it does not provide a good air seal at the wall bottom plate. An air/vapor barrier must be installed.

If the upper house wall is insulated with exterior foam sheathing, the insulation can be brought down past the joists and over the foundation wall, as seen in Figure

8.23. This is an improvement over the design in Figure 8.22 in that the joists and foundation are insulated to R-20. Also, the foam sheathing creates an airtight seal at the wall bottom plate as well as the foundation sill plate. (An air/vapor barrier is still recommended, but less crucial.)

Figure 8.24 shows another variation in which an extra thickness of foam is inserted at the joist area. Notice the plywood nailer between the two layers of foam—a simple tip that precludes the need for 5-inch nails to attach the siding at the joist area.

When installing the rigid foam sheets, place them vertically rather than horizontally. This will help to avoid possible damage from tangential frost heave grabbing the

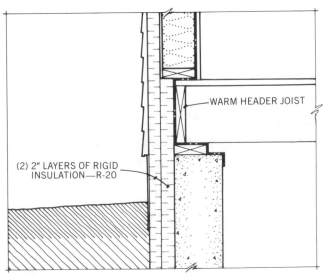

Figure 8.23 4-inch-thick foam foundation insulation with 2-inch-thick foam wall insulation.

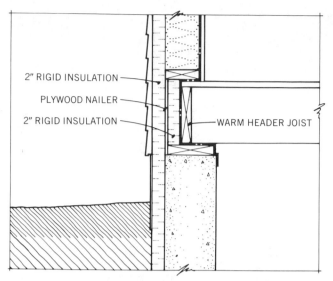

Figure 8.24 2 inches of continuous foam insulation over foundation and upper wall, with extra 2 inches inset at header joint.

upper horizontal layer and pulling it up (see the section on frost heave below). Also, it reduces the risk of damage during backfilling. The foam can be attached with either adhesive or mechanical fasteners. When using adhesive, make sure it is compatible with the type of plastic foam you are using (see the next section).

Protecting Insulation Above Grade Exterior foundation insulation must never be left exposed above grade, not only for aesthetic reasons, but also because most plastic foams will be quickly degraded by sunlight and other weathering influences.

There are several types of material suitable for covering above-grade foundation insulation, including fiberglass-

Figure 8.25 Foam foundation insulation with extra foam inset at header joint. Notice plywood nailer for attachment of siding. (Photo by Harold Orr.)

reinforced plastic, preservative-treated plywood, cement asbestos board, rigid vinyl sheets, latex-modified cement mortar, and latex-modified stucco.

Rigid Coverings Fiberglass reinforced plastic, cement asbestos board, pressure-treated wood, and similar rigid materials can be attached by nailing through the foam into the sill plate. Concrete nails and other masonry fasteners can be used if attachment to masonry is more convenient. Adhesives can also be used either as the primary means of attachment or as a supplement to mechanical fastening.

Cementitious Coatings Some cementitious coatings are applied directly to the foam insulation; others require some type of wire mesh as an attachment base. Some manufacturers of coatings recommended roughening the foam with a wire brush before the coating is applied. Contact the coating manufacturer for specific instructions. (See Appendix D for a list of manufacturers.)

A note of caution: There have been scattered reports of surface coatings failing and falling off, especially at joints and exterior corners. This shouldn't happen if the right material is selected and properly applied. One possible cause of the problem is differential thermal expansion. If, when the foundation heats up in the sun, the coating expands at a different rate than the foam underneath, something has to give. Some coating products contain a special acrylic polymer which helps prevent this problem. Check with the manufacturer.

Protecting Insulation Below Grade—Water Any foundation should be well drained, not only to protect the insulation, but also to protect the foundation itself. Aside from avoiding the deleterious effects of water, proper drainage is the best way to prevent frost heave damage. If the existing soil is clay, it should be replaced by gravel around the foundation. Footing drains embedded in crushed stone should always be installed (Figure 8.26).

Extruded polystyrene requires no protection from water below grade. It absorbs very little water and is hardly degraded. Any other rigid foam—expanded polystyrene, urethane, polyisocyanurate—must be protected with a durable waterproof covering.

Medium-density fiberglass is a special case. This material is itself a drainage layer and needs no protection. It should not, therefore, be protected against water below grade. If, for some reason, you do cover it with a waterproof membrane, such as polyethylene, the membrane must not be wrapped underneath the insulation. To do so would create a trap for water, preventing it from draining out of the insulation.

Frost Heave Frost heave can exert tremendous force, capable of damaging the foundation as well as the insulation system. With the advent of heavily insulated foundations, which prevent heat from escaping into and thawing the ground, concern has arisen that frost heave problems may increase; however, the phenomenon has

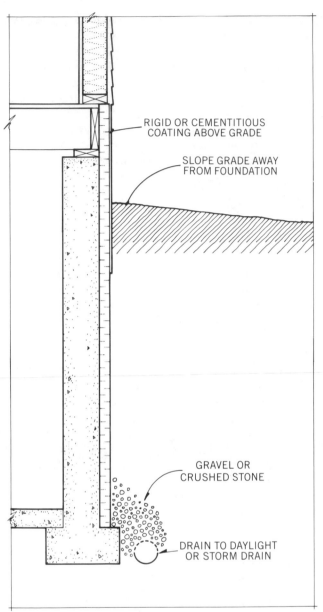

RIGID OR CEMENTITIOUS
COATING ABOVE GRADE

SLOPE GRADE AWAY
FROM FOUNDATION

GRAVEL OR
CRUSHED STONE

DRAIN TO DAYLIGHT
OR STORM DRAIN

Figure 8.26 Protection of exterior foundation insulation.

12-16"

20-24"

1" CLEARANCE

FROST-FREE
AREA

OPTIONAL INSULATION
FOR COLD CLIMATES

HEAT FLOW DOWN STILL OCCURS
(WITHOUT OPTIONAL LOWER
INSULATION)

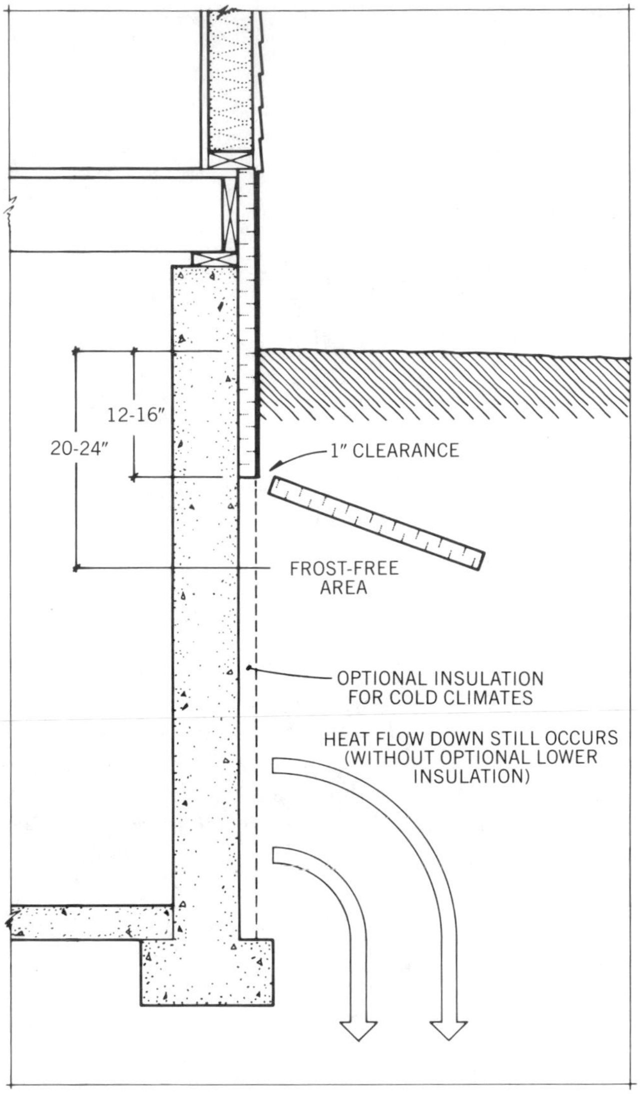

Figure 8.27 Shallow horizontal foam insulation. This is a "selective" insulation system, allowing heat to escape from lower part of foundation (without optional lower exterior foam insulation).

not occurred so long as proper precautions have been taken. Preventing frost heave is much easier than designing a foundation to withstand it. Frost heave prevention is discussed later in the chapter.

Insects There is no easy solution to the problem of insects penetrating into and behind foundation insulation. The United States Department of Agriculture publishes several pamphlets on insect control around foundations. Most methods entail soil poisons.

Construction Damage As with many aspects of building a superinsulated house, quality of workmanship can make or break the job. A rough backhoe operator could easily tear a foundation insulation system to shreds. With careful backfilling, on the other hand, it should be easy to avoid damage.

Shallow Horizontal Insulation Combined With Vertical Exterior Insulation The foundation insulation system in Figure 8.27 has some unique features and properties. A horizontal fin of rigid foam insulation is installed just below the ground surface, sloping away from the foundation; the top section of foundation is insulated with exterior foam in the conventional manner. The horizontal fin retards upward heat loss from the foundation to the air just as effectively as if it were installed on the outside of the foundation wall; the length of the heat-flow path from foundation to surface is about the same with either configuration.

The horizontal fin does not, however, affect downward heat flow from the foundation to the deep earth; the foundation is still "coupled" to the deep earth. In moder-

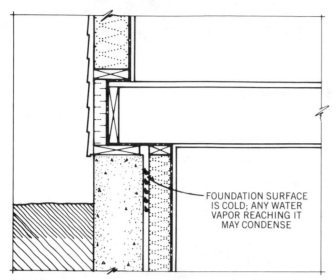

FOUNDATION SURFACE IS COLD; ANY WATER VAPOR REACHING IT MAY CONDENSE

Figure 8.28 Possible condensation problems with interior foundation insulation.

ate climates, this allows you to "have your cake and eat it too," for the horizontal insulation effectively reduces the greatest component of winter foundation heat loss (upward to the air), but still may allow summer cooling through heat loss to the deep earth.

Another advantage of this system is that the soil under the horizontal insulation will never freeze; it is therefore an effective way to prevent frost heave damage.

The only suitable material for horizontal underground insulation is extruded polystyrene. Use a 2-inch thickness and extend the insulation 4 feet out from the foundation on all sides. From a thermal standpoint, the insulation should be placed as close to the surface as possible. However, since most foundation plantings will require at least 12 inches of soil for root penetration, the insulation should be 12 to 16 inches deep next to the house and slope down away from the foundation to a depth of about 2 feet.

In moderate climates (5000 base-65 degree days or less), this installation will preclude the necessity for vertical insulation on the lower part of the foundation wall. But in colder climates, the lower half of the wall should also be insulated to reduce losses to the deep earth. In the latter case, ground-coupled summer cooling through basement walls will be somewhat lost, but it may still occur through the basement floor if it is left uninsulated.

Be careful not to damage the insulation during backfilling. Sometimes the horizontal insulation catches on the foundation and breaks at the edge. An easy way to prevent this is to place the insulation 1 inch away from the foundation (Figure 8.27).

Insulation on the Inside *Advantages and Disadvantages* Interior foundation insulation has several practical and financial advantages. First, it is relatively easy to apply almost any thickness of insulation since

there is a large amount of space inside the foundation and no siding to match up to (as with exterior insulation). Second, the insulation doesn't need to be protected above grade since it is protected from the elements by the house. Also, since interior insulation is not subjected to as many environmental hazards as exterior insulation is, less expensive materials, such as expanded polystyrene, may be used as long as there is no severe water problem.

Despite its attractive practical advantages, interior foundation insulation has several thermal drawbacks, a few of which have already been mentioned in the section on exterior insulation.

With the insulation on the inside, the foundation wall is always cold, which can cause several types of problems. When using fiberglass insulation, if any room air gets behind the insulation, water vapor condensation could occur on the cold wall surface (Figure 8.28). Here is a problem for which there is no good answer; interior foundation insulation systems are subject to moisture penetration from both sides—water vapor from the living space and ground water from the foundation wall. Another problem is thermal bridging through the top of the foundation into the sill plate (Figure 8.18a)—a minor heat loss, but one that in cold climates could cause problems with moisture condensation at the floor/wall joint.

With insulation on the inside, the unprotected foundation is subject to severe thermal and physical stresses. The temperature of the foundation walls will closely track the freeze-thaw cycles of the surrounding soil. Over time, if the wall develops any cracks, water may penetrate and freeze within the cracks and eventually cause structural damage. This is likely to occur only over the long term. The extent of the problem is not fully known since superinsulated houses haven't been around that long. Proper drainage around the foundation will probably prevent most problems.

Fiberglass Insulation Fiberglass batts are installed in a frame wall that is built adjacent to the foundation wall (Fig. 8.29). One problem is potential moisture penetration from *both* sides of the insulation—ground water from the foundation wall and water vapor from the air in the basement. If you install waterproof barriers on both sides of the insulation, you create a double vapor barrier, which is no good. If you leave out one of the barriers, you leave the insulation open to water penetration. This dilemma has no complete solution, only partial remedies. One or more of the following suggestions should help:

1. Make sure the soil around the foundation is well drained. In addition to protecting the insulation, good drainage also prevents wet basements and helps avoid potential frost heave problems.
2. Apply a good waterproofing or drainage layer to the outside of the foundation. There are a variety of good waterproofing compounds on the market; the best drainage layer is medium-density semi-rigid fiberglass boards.

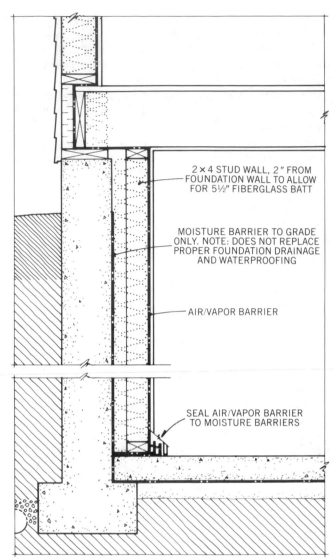

2 × 4 STUD WALL, 2″ FROM FOUNDATION WALL TO ALLOW FOR 5½″ FIBERGLASS BATT

MOISTURE BARRIER TO GRADE ONLY. NOTE: DOES NOT REPLACE PROPER FOUNDATION DRAINAGE AND WATERPROOFING

AIR/VAPOR BARRIER

SEAL AIR/VAPOR BARRIER TO MOISTURE BARRIERS

Figure 8.29 Interior foundation insulation showing concrete basement wall with 2 × 4 stud wall set off from foundation and insulated with fiberglass insulation. Notice the installation of air/vapor barrier and moisture barrier.

3. Allow the foundation concrete to cure for a couple of months before installing the interior insulation system. Concrete gives off an enormous quantity of water during curing. If a newly poured foundation is waterproofed on the outside and insulated on the inside, where will all that water go? If the foundation walls can be left exposed for a few months after construction, the water will dry out before the insulation is installed.

4. Figure 8.29 shows the best way to protect interior insulation.

Notice that there is an air/vapor barrier on the inside of the stud wall and a separate polyethylene moisture barrier between the frame wall and the concrete foundation wall. The *moisture barrier* prevents *liquid* water from penetrating the frame wall. The air/vapor barrier runs all the way up the wall, past the joist header, and is sealed to the first floor air/vapor barrier above. The moisture barrier extends only up to grade level. The idea is to seal the below-grade portion against ground-water penetration but to allow the upper exterior foundation wall to breathe in case any moisture does penetrate the insulation system.

Rigid Foam Interior rigid foam insulation on basement walls is relatively straightforward. Building codes usually require the foam to be covered with a fire-rated sheathing. A vapor barrier is not necessary.

The rigid foam can be applied either with adhesive or furring strips. When using adhesive, make sure it is compatible with the type of insulation being used. The thinners in some adhesives will attack foam plastic insulation. The adhesive should not be applied in daubs (Figure 8.30a), which may create an air space between the foundation surface and the insulation. If any warm air leaks into this space, it could condense on the inner surface of the foundation wall. It is better to apply a full bed of

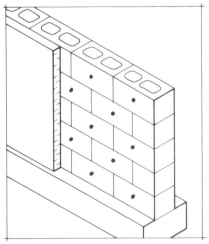

A. ADHESIVE DAUBS—NOT RECOMMENDED

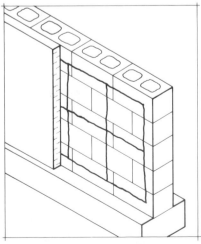

B. ADHESIVE GRID—BETTER METHOD

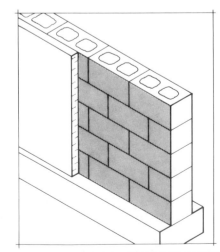

C. FULL ADHESIVE BED—RECOMMENDED METHOD

Figure 8.30 Application of interior rigid foam foundation insulation with adhesives.

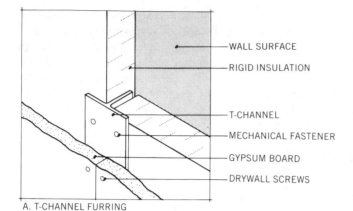

A. T-CHANNEL FURRING

— WALL SURFACE
— RIGID INSULATION
— T-CHANNEL
— MECHANICAL FASTENER
— GYPSUM BOARD
— DRYWALL SCREWS

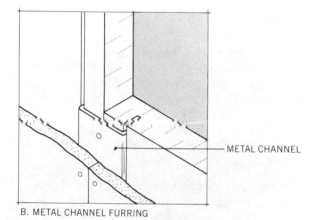

B. METAL CHANNEL FURRING

— METAL CHANNEL

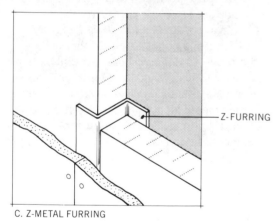

C. Z-METAL FURRING

— Z-FURRING

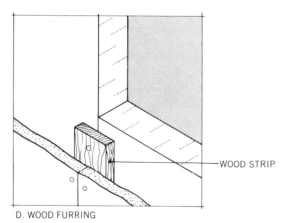

D. WOOD FURRING

— WOOD STRIP

Figure 8.31 Application of interior rigid foam foundation insulation with furring.

adhesive or a grid of beads of adhesive (Figures 8.30b and 8.30c).

A number of types of wood or metal furring can be used to attach rigid foam and sheathing to masonry walls (Figure 8.31).

Prior to application of the furring, insulation may be held in place temporarily by light daubs of adhesive. These daubs should be very light, to avoid holding the insulation away from the surface (for the reasons mentioned above). Gypsum board, like any other interior finish, is installed by being screwed or nailed into the furring.

Insulation Over the Top of the Foundation In certain design situations, an attractive option is to insulate over the top of the foundation, underneath the sill plate (Figure 8.32a). With interior foundation insulation, this application will help prevent short circuiting through the foundation into the wall. Another place where it would be useful is under brick walls (Figure 8.32b).

With a compressive strength of 5760 pounds per square foot, extruded polystyrene would *seem* to be a good material for this application. However, according to one manufacturer of that product, it should not be subjected to the kind of loading that would occur under the sill plate. The foam will evidently "creep" over long periods of time and change shape. This applies even to the special high-density foam with a rated compressive strength of over 14,000 pounds per square foot.

Insulation on Both Sides of the Foundation Wall Here's one area of a house where it is acceptable to split the insulation system. In fact, it allows the best of both worlds. The only drawback is cost. However, if costs allow, a very effective insulation system can consist of 1 or 2 inches of rigid foam sheathing on the outside of the foundation wall plus some additional insulation on the inside.

Basement Floor Insulation

The amount of heat loss through a basement floor is relatively small and may even decrease over the years as the house heats the underlying soil. In most cases, subfloor insulation is probably not cost effective. This is uncertain, however, because even the best methods for calculating seasonal heat loss through the floor are still imprecise.

The main reason for subfloor insulation in cold climates is to create a warm floor for thermal comfort. Even if the basement is not initially intended to be a living space, future use might change, and retrofit insulation is prohibitively expensive. Without insulation, the floor will be cold. Cold floors are uncomfortable and cause many finished basements to go unused. Often people raise the thermostat setting to compensate for the effect of cold floors, which causes increased energy use. Another undesirable effect of a cold basement floor is that the basement ceiling loses radiant heat to it. In the basement in Figure 8.33,

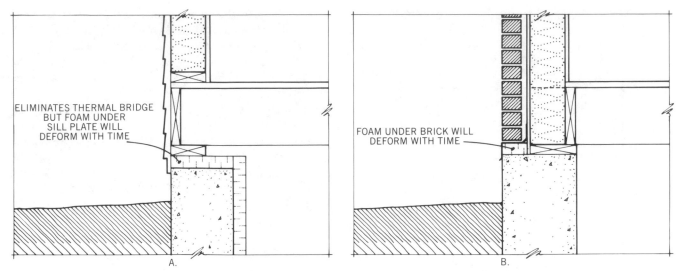

Figure 8.32 Unacceptable uses of rigid foam insulation on top of foundation wall. A. Foam under sill plate. B. Foam under brick.

which is not intentionally heated, the space temperature may range from 70°F at the ceiling to 60 at the floor surface. The warm ceiling will lose heat by radiation to the cool basement floor, possibly making the floor above feel cool and uncomfortable.

In warm climates with fewer than about 4000 base-65 degree days, the basement floor should be left uninsulated. There is probably not enough winter heat loss to justify the insulation, and the uninsulated floor may provide some beneficial ground-coupled cooling. However, in humid climates, if the basement floor cools below the dew point, condensation will occur on the floor—a most annoying situation. In those cases, the basement floor should probably be insulated to prevent condensation, despite the sacrifice of ground-coupled cooling.

The best insulation material for basement floors is extruded polystyrene. If the floor is more than 4 feet below grade, a 1-inch thickness is enough; if the floor is less than 4 feet below grade, use a 2-inch thickness. A 2- to 3-inch layer of sand should be placed underneath the foam (Figure 8.34) and spread out into a smooth, flat surface. A 6-mil polyethylene moisture barrier should be placed beneath the foam, either under or over the sand layer.

Be sure to notify your concrete contractor in advance that the basement floor is underlain by a waterproof layer of insulation and polyethylene which will prevent drainage from the fresh concrete. Set-up time will be longer, so the contractor may want to use a special mix to shorten the curing period.

There's an alternative insulation system for basement floors. Construct a wooden floor with stringers, and insulate between the stringers with fiberglass batts. This is thermally acceptable, but care must be taken to ensure that no water will penetrate the insulation from the concrete floor. Lay a polyethylene moisture barrier under the floor before the concrete is poured. A vapor barrier is also

necessary over the insulation. The situation here is similar to that of interior fiberglass insulation on walls—moisture can penetrate from either side of the insulation. Proper protection means vapor barriers on both sides; furthermore, these barriers *must* be carefully sealed at all seams and penetrations because if any moisture does get into the insulation, there's no way to ventilate it.

Under the Footings Some builders have put extruded polystyrene and even urethane insulation under-

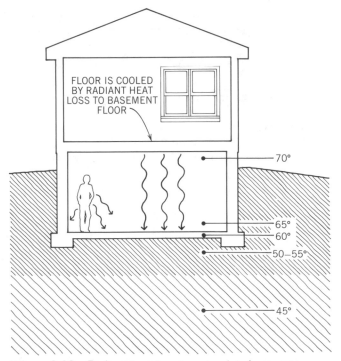

Figure 8.33 Radiant heat loss to uninsulated concrete floor.

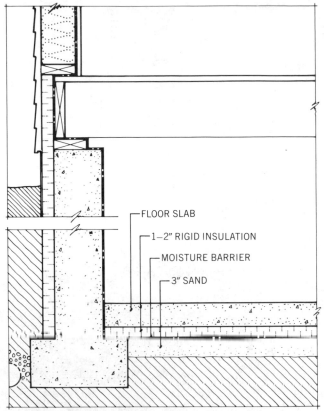

FLOOR SLAB

1–2″ RIGID INSULATION

MOISTURE BARRIER

3″ SAND

Figure 8.34 Rigid foam insulation installed under basement floor.

neath the foundation footings to avoid condensation in corners.

Unfortunately, the situation here is similar to that of insulation under the foundation sill plates. Even though extruded polystyrene should be able to take the load, we don't recommend using it because deformation of the material might occur over long periods of time.

DESIGN SPECIFICS: CRAWL SPACES

As discussed earlier in the chapter, crawl spaces of superinsulated houses should be included *inside* the thermal envelope—making them heated crawl spaces. Most of the above discussion about basements applies also to crawl spaces. Exterior foundation wall insulation is identical. Interior wall and floor insulation, however, require some special discussion.

One significant difference between basements and crawl spaces is that crawl spaces generally have exposed dirt floors, which can be a significant source of moisture. Traditionally, crawl spaces are ventilated to remove water vapor that evaporates from the earth or diffuses or leaks down from the house above. In a warm crawl space enclosed within the thermal envelope, such ventilation would degrade thermal performance. But if you can't ventilate, how do you control moisture? Recent research

at Princeton University has shown that crawl space moisture buildup can be effectively avoided by placing a polyethylene moisture barrier over the exposed soil, eliminating the need for ventilation. These studies show that if the ground under a crawl space is covered with polyethylene sheets overlapped at the seams and run up the crawl space walls (and any interior support pillars), then closing the crawl space vents has no effect on the moisture content of the wood. In fact, in houses with ground cover, opening the vents in summer appeared to *increase* the wood moisture content compared to that of other houses where the vents remain closed. A good moisture barrier over the ground is therefore a necessary component of a superinsulated crawl space.

Crawl Space Walls

Crawl space walls can be insulated with rigid foam either on the inside or the outside. Use the same methods you would for basements. One difference is that it isn't necessary to cover interior foam insulation with a fire-rated sheathing since the crawl space is not a living space.

The inside of the walls can also be insulated with fiberglass batts. It makes little sense, however, to build a frame wall as in basements. The best alternative is to attach the batts to the foundation at the sill and drape them down the inside of the foundation wall (Figure 8.35). Be careful to butt the batts closely together, leaving no space between them. A moisture barrier should be applied to the inside of the foundation wall before insulating. Attach it to the wall at grade level and run it across the entire crawl space floor.

Crawl Space Floors

Should crawl space floors be insulated? Consider the same factors you would with basement floors. Even though crawl space floors will not be as deep in the ground as basement floors, the temperature underneath will be about the same provided the foundation walls are insulated all the way down to the footings.

Crawl space floors can be insulated either with fiberglass batts or rigid foam. When using fiberglass, run the batts up the crawl space walls and attach them to the sill plate with a furring strip.

The air/vapor barrier presents somewhat of a problem. It must be sealed to the foundation sill plate, run over the inside of the insulation, and continued over the floor insulation (Figure 8.35). The problem? How to make a tight seal at the seams over the floor. The solution is to use the largest sheets of polyethylene possible to minimize seams; then seal them with a good polyethylene tape.

Whether or not it is insulated, the crawl space floor must have a continuous moisture barrier. The moisture barrier should also be sealed with tape.

If the house is in an area with high water table, install a central drain in the floor of the crawl space, with either a

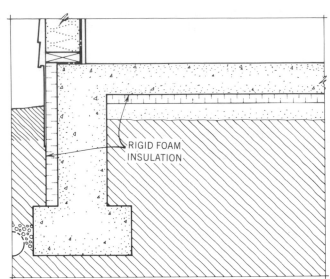

Figure 8.36 Insulated slab-on-grade, showing rigid foam beneath the slab and on the outside of foundation wall.

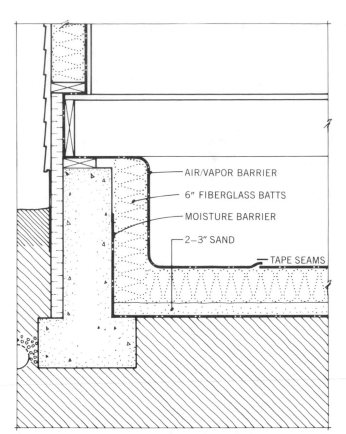

AIR/VAPOR BARRIER

6″ FIBERGLASS BATTS

MOISTURE BARRIER

2–3″ SAND

TAPE SEAMS

Figure 8.35 Interior fiberglass insulation and exterior foam insulation installed in a crawl space.

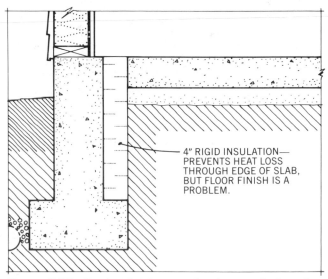

RIGID FOAM INSULATION

4″ RIGID INSULATION— PREVENTS HEAT LOSS THROUGH EDGE OF SLAB, BUT FLOOR FINISH IS A PROBLEM.

Figure 8.37 Insulated slab-on-grade, showing thick rigid foam installed on the inside of foundation wall. This technique could present a problem with interior floor finish.

sump pump or drainage to daylight. Before the drain is installed, however, consider possible problems with radon (see Chapter 4).

Another recommendation for crawl space floors is to pour a "rat slab"—a very rough concrete floor that is not smoothed or finished. It helps keep ground moisture and radon out of the crawl space and makes it easier to install insulation. The rat slab can be poured over foam insulation.

DESIGN SPECIFICS: SLAB-ON-GRADE

The insulation system for a slab-on-grade floor is also quite straightforward. The most important place to insulate is the area of greatest heat loss—the slab edge. The best system is exterior foundation wall insulation, installed as it is in basements or crawl spaces (Figure 8.36). Interior wall insulation alone is not recommended because getting enough insulation between the slab and the foundation wall is difficult. The design shown in Figure 8.37 is commonly pictured in standard construction guides. Usually, only 1 inch of foam is pictured, but in a superinsulated house, 2 to 4 inches is necessary. A problem sometimes arises with the interior wall/floor finish. What do you do with the 2 to 4 inches of exposed foam around the perimeter of the floor? If that detail can be

worked out, then the interior insulation system is perfectly acceptable.

One difference between a house with a slab-on-grade and one with a basement is that the slab is almost always the floor of the living space. This makes subfloor insulation more important; a cool slab could create considerable thermal discomfort for building occupants. In cold climates, the slab should always be insulated. The technique is the same as that used for basement floors (Figure 8.34).

One final note about slab insulation. Some designers choose to insulate above slab floors rather than under-

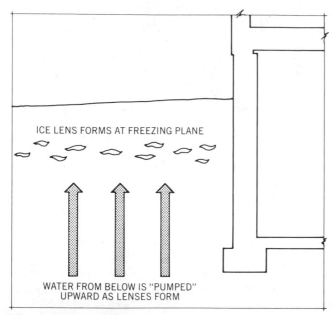

ICE LENS FORMS AT FREEZING PLANE

WATER FROM BELOW IS "PUMPED" UPWARD AS LENSES FORM

Figure 8.38 Mechanism of frost heave showing ice-lens formation at the freezing plane

neath. This was mentioned above as an acceptable method for insulating basement floors, using either wood or rigid foam. The same applies to slabs but with one minor difference. An uninsulated slab-on-grade is closer to the ground than an uninsulated basement and will, therefore, get colder. If rigid foam is used, the cold concrete slab and the warm plastic foam will expand and contract differently. When using this type of design, a "slip plane" should therefore be included between these two components.

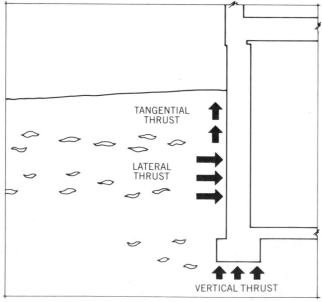

TANGENTIAL THRUST

LATERAL THRUST

VERTICAL THRUST

Figure 8.39 Frost heave thrust forces.

FROST HEAVE

Theoretically, by insulating a foundation, and cutting off the flow of house heat into the surrounding soil, you increase the chance of frost around the foundation. But in researching this book, we found no documented cases of frost damage induced by insulating house foundations.

According to some experts, *what is often believed to be frost damage is actually caused by clay expansion.* Clay expands when wetted and shrinks upon drying. Partially saturated clay soils that undergo a change in moisture content undergo a corresponding change in volume. This phenomenon causes buildings to heave up and down, rock back and forth, and even move sideways. Clay soils, however, are also very susceptible to frost.

Given the unknowns involved and the potential for problems, it would behoove the builder of low-energy homes to take extra precautions to guard against frost damage.

What Is Frost Heave?

As the mean air temperature drops in winter, the surface of the ground freezes. As winter progresses, the freezing plane slowly penetrates down into the soil.

In a fine-grained moist soil, a peculiar phenomenon occurs (Figure 8.38). At the freezing plane, the water in the soil turns to ice. This has, in effect, a drying effect, so that water in the unfrozen soil beneath moves upward toward the freezing plane in the same way that water moves from moist soil to dry soil. This water, on reaching the freezing plane, adds to the growth of an "ice lens" or layer of pure ice. The ice is thus formed not only from the freezing of the water in place but also from a type of pumping effect, bringing water up through the soil into the zone of ice-lens formation. As the freezing plane moves deeper, another lens is formed. Pressure develops, causing the ice and soil above to be lifted.

Frost heave can cause damage to foundations in three ways (Figure 8.39): vertical thrust, lateral thrust, and ad-freeze tangential thrust.

Vertical Thrust If the freezing plane penetrates beneath the foundation footings, frost heave can push the foundation up out of the ground. In the spring, when the ground thaws, the foundation will settle again, but not necessarily uniformly. This is the force that breaks sidewalks and garage floors and pushes the endless supply of boulders to the surface of farmers' fields.

Lateral Thrust Frost can push horizontally as well as vertically. Horizontal thrust increases with decreasing temperature, reaching a maximum at about 14°F. Field tests and lab experiments have shown the force of lateral thrust to range between 2000 and 6000 pounds per square foot.

Evidently, foundation damage from lateral thrust is relatively rare, even with heavily insulated foundations, unless the foundation has been very poorly drained.

Adfreeze and Tangential Thrust As soil freezes, it can form a strong bond with vertical foundation surfaces. This is called "adfreezing." As ice-lens growth forces the soil mass upward, it can drag the foundation up with it. This is known as "tangential thrust."

Adfreeze force can be considerable. One study in Canada showed a force of 6000 pounds on a 3.5-inch diameter steel post placed in clay where the frost penetration was 3.5 feet. Adfreeze heaving has also been shown to separate the upper blocks of block-wall foundations. It is probably a greater threat to insulated foundations than lateral thrust.

How To Protect Insulated Foundations

The three basic requirements for frost heave are: (1) a freezing plane in the soil; (2) a frost-susceptible soil through which moisture can move; and (3) a supply of water. Only when all three factors are present will heaving occur. Eliminate any one of these elements and you eliminate the problem.

Eliminating the Freezing Plane The traditional technique to eliminate the freezing plane is merely to bury the foundation footings below frost.

Most building codes include the basic requirement that footings be placed "below the depth of maximum frost penetration." Some local codes specify a certain depth, others don't. The intent is obviously to keep the footings out of freezing soil.

This approach to protecting against frost by simply embedding footings to an assumed maximum frost depth may not be appropriate for superinsulated foundations.

First of all, the frost depth can vary widely in any one geographic region. It is affected by many factors in addition to air temperature: soil type, soil moisture content, snow cover, vegetation, solar radiation, and wind velocity all affect the rate of heat loss from the ground. With uninsulated foundations, there is always the safeguard of heat from the foundation keeping frost away; but not with superinsulated foundations.

Also, merely embedding the footings deep in the ground does nothing to protect against adfreezing and tangential thrust. Again, this becomes more of an issue with superinsulated foundations.

An effective technique used in Scandinavia and Canada is to raise the level of the freezing plane by insulating the ground from the outdoor air. The shallow horizontal insulation shown in Figure 8.27 effectively raises the frost line to the level of the insulation (or just below it). The freezing plane will almost never penetrate below the insulation.

With horizontal insulation protecting the subsoil, there is no need to place the foundation footings 4 or 5 feet deep. The frost will only penetrate a few inches below the insulation. In Canada, foundation footings that are protected by horizontal insulation are commonly placed only 24 inches below the surface. There have been no problems with this system, even in climates with over 12,000 base-65 degree days. Shallow foundations can probably be successfully used almost anywhere in North America. The main obstacles to their use are institutional strictures, such as building codes, rather than technical problems.

Eliminating the Frost-Susceptible Soil In general, fine sand and silts are susceptible to frost heaving; they show a high rate of heave but at relatively low pressures. Clays also are susceptible; they normally heave slowly but often with tremendous pressures. Coarse sands and clean gravels do not heave.

If you have any doubts about the soil at your site, replace it with clean gravel when you backfill. This measure, combined with adequate drainage, should eliminate the danger of adfreeze and tangential thrust heave.

Eliminating the Supply of Water *Proper drainage is the surest way to avoid frost heave problems.* Every foundation should have good footing drains embedded in crushed stone.

Be careful not to damage the drains during installation. For example, flexible perforated ABS pipe often fails, not because the holes get clogged, but because the pipe gets crushed during backfilling. The pipe should first be carefully embedded in gravel before backfilling with heavy machinery. Clay or PVC pipe is acceptable as long as it is carefully installed.

In summary, insulating foundations may increase the risk of frost damage, but the protective measures described above, if properly performed, will virtually eliminate the risk of foundation damage, whether or not the foundation is insulated.

Nine

Roofs and ceilings

CAPPING THE THERMAL ENVELOPE

Where Is the Cap?

The first step in designing a superinsulated roof/ceiling system is to define the upper boundary of the thermal envelope. As we saw with foundation insulation systems (Chapter 8), the boundary of the thermal envelope need not be the same as the boundary of the living space.

With simple house designs such as ranches, the location of the thermal envelope will usually be obvious (Figure 9.1). With more complex designs such as Cape Cod houses or saltboxes, more thought is necessary to find the optimum design.

There are three general types of configuration: (1) flat ceilings below unheated attics; (2) kneewalls and half walls in Cape Cod and split-level houses; and (3) insulated roofs. Some houses will combine elements from these configurations.

We will briefly look at the advantages and special problems of each configuration.

Flat Ceilings Below Unheated Attics The unheated attic, common in the United States, is the most convenient configuration for superinsulation (Figure 9.1). The attic space is outside the thermal envelope; the entire insulation system is on the attic floor. (Except for what we call the *weather barrier,* that is, the roof, which protects the house from rain, snow, etc.) When properly insulated, the attic will be nearly as cold as the outdoors.

In superinsulated houses, the unheated attic is typically not designed as usable space; there is too much insulation in the floor to allow easy placement of floorboards. The attic floor can be the most energy-efficient component of a superinsulated house. Because of all the available space, it is easy to install large amounts of insulation.

In fact, in some ways, attic insulation is almost too easy. After piling on huge thicknesses of insulation, you might feel it unnecessary to address the seemingly minor flaws that degrade an insulation system. If a ceiling has R-50 insulation, it must be superinsulated—right? Wrong! Superinsulated ceilings, like superinsulated walls and foundations, must be designed and built correctly—airtight and vapor-tight, with minimal thermal bridging, no convective loops, and full coverage of insulation. Fortunately, flat ceilings lend themselves well to all of these requirements.

Kneewalls and Half Walls Adjacent to Unheated Attics Kneewalls and half walls may be the boundary of the thermal envelope between the living space and an unheated attic. These types of walls are found in Cape Cod and split-level houses. Superinsulating these walls is basically like superinsulating any other type of walls. An air/vapor barrier must be carefully installed on the warm side of the insulation and the thermal bridging through any framing members should be taken care of by one of the techniques used in superinsulated wall construction (see Chapter 7).

However, the complexity of kneewalls and half walls makes them harder to insulate and seal effectively than regular superinsulated walls. Consider the house shown in Figure 9.2a. Placing the boundary of the thermal envelope at the boundary of the living space, as shown, requires various joints to be airtight and free of thermal bridges.

The most troublesome spot is where a kneewall meets the floor; how does the vapor barrier cross the floor? There are solutions, but most are quite time-consuming, and more often than not, the joint ends up being leaky. Figure 9.2b shows a better alternative in which the boundaries of the thermal envelope and the living space

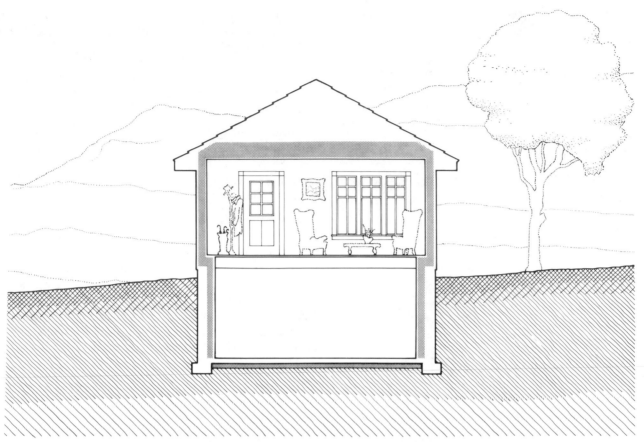

Figure 9.1 Thermal envelope of house with an unheated attic.

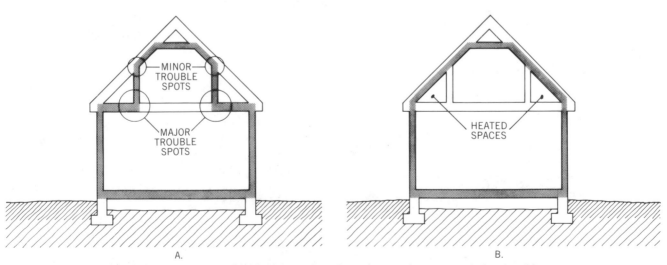

Figure 9.2 Two possible thermal envelope boundary configurations. A. Insulated knee-walls. This configuration is difficult to insulate and seal at the "trouble spots." B. Insulated roof. This is the preferred configuration, even though it encloses more heated space, because the insulation system is less likely to have defects.

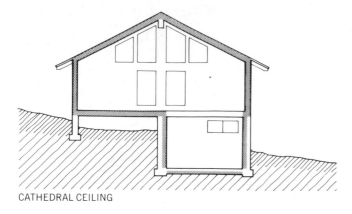

CATHEDRAL CEILING

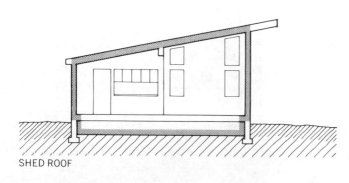

SHED ROOF

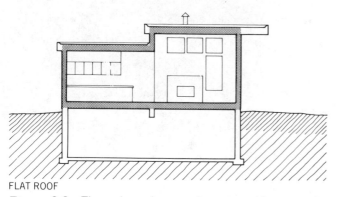

FLAT ROOF

Figure 9.3 Thermal envelope configuration of houses with insulated roofs.

are not the same. The insulation is run inside the roof as if the whole top-floor space were to be heated. In fact, the whole space *will* be heated, but since the insulation system is likely to be more effective, total energy use over the long run should be less.

For half walls between heated living spaces and attics in, for instance, split-level houses, alternative definitions of the thermal envelope may not exist, so the half wall should be superinsulated as best as possible.

Insulated Roofs: Difficult Candidates for Superinsulation Cathedral ceilings, flat roofs, and shed roofs (Figure 9.3) are all insulated roofs in which the upper-

most boundary of the thermal envelope is also the uppermost boundary of the house; there is no unheated space at the top of the house.

We saw in the example above how insulating the sloping roof offered some advantages over insulating the ceiling and kneewall. However, superinsulating the roof also has certain distinct drawbacks.

Minimal Space for Insulation Roofs are typically built with either 6- or 8-inch rafters. A special construction technique such as trusses or foam sheathing is necessary in order to attain the R-25 or higher value typical of superinsulation.

Exterior Vapor Barrier Roofing shingles and/or other roof surfaces form a vapor barrier on the wrong side of the insulation. To safeguard against moisture problems, the space between the roof and insulation must be ventilated. Some Canadian building codes require a 6-inch air space, although common practice in the United States usually calls for only 1 inch. Regardless of its thickness, the ventilation air space reduces the already limited space available for insulation.

Thermal Bridging Rafters and roof joists form thermal bridges through an insulated roof. Although bridging can be reduced by using roof trusses and/or exterior foam sheathing, both add to cost.

Difficult to Seal Penetrations Chimneys, plumbing stacks, and wiring penetrations are especially difficult to seal when the roof is the boundary of the thermal envelope.

Exposure of Roof Skin to High Temperatures When the insulation is right under the roof skin, there is some concern about overheating induced by solar radiation and leading to degradation of the roof shingles over time. If the space between the roof and the insulation is ventilated, overheating should not be a problem.

Why Do Ceilings Have More Insulation Than Walls Do?

Virtually all guidelines or specifications for house insulation recommend more insulation in the ceiling than in the walls. Why? Probably because of the common misconception that heat rises. But heat doesn't rise; only warm air rises. If you were to apply heat to the center of a solid block of stone, the heat would conduct equally to all sides, including top and bottom.

Even though warm air rises, there is typically very little temperature differential between ceiling and floor in a superinsulated house. As warm air rises to the ceiling, the ceiling gets heated slightly (Figure 9.4) and begins to radiate energy to the other room surfaces. Since the conductive heat loss from those other surfaces is low, they quickly warm up to nearly the same temperature as the ceiling. Thus the ceiling rarely gets more than a few de-

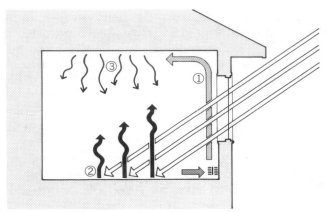

Figure 9.4 Ceiling thermal dynamics: 1) air warmed by baseboard heater rises to ceiling; 2) sunlight warms floor, which radiates heat to ceiling; 3) ceiling radiates heat back down to other room surfaces.

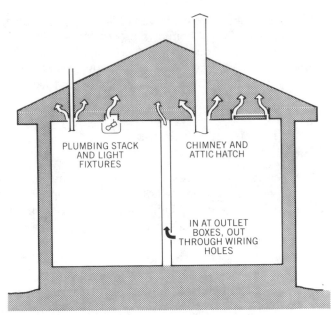

Figure 9.5 Common air leakage paths through ceilings.

grees warmer than the floor or walls, and the air temperature throughout the room stays fairly uniform. Except in spaces where there is a large amount of solar heat, the ceiling/floor temperature differential is not likely to be more than 3° to 4°F.

Nevertheless, putting more insulation into ceilings than walls generally makes sense, since ceiling insulation is easy and inexpensive to install. In an attic, the difference in cost between installing 6 inches of insulation versus 12 inches is usually no more than the cost of the extra insulation—no modified support structure, no special materials, and very little added labor is required.

In superinsulated houses, however, roofs/ceilings *need* not be more insulated than walls. Cathedral ceilings, for example, can be insulated to R-25 or R-30 without too much trouble, but to increase the insulation level to R-50 or R-60 is difficult and expensive. It is no longer simply a matter of blowing in a few more inches of insulation or adding another batt, as with attic floors. You need added support structure, insulative sheathing, or other special components. Since there are usually no windows or doors, insulating a cathedral ceiling is usually still less expensive than insulating a wall, but not by much. *If the cost per R-value for a roof insulation system is the same as the cost per R-value for a wall insulation system, then the roof should be insulated only to the same level as the walls.*

Superinsulated Ceilings Must Be Airtight

Warm air tends to rise. Heated air in a house exerts a continuous force against the top ceiling as long as the air in the house is warmer than the air outside. If there are any leakage paths at the top of the house, air will pass through, carrying moisture with it. The loss of heated air constitutes an energy loss; the loss of moisture can cause

serious condensation problems in the attic. Since ceilings don't have obvious large penetrations like windows and doors, air leakage is often overlooked. However, seemingly minor penetrations, such as light fixtures, plumbing stacks, attic hatches, and chimneys can cause significant air leakage (Figures 9.5 and 3.1). Installing very thick insulation won't stop air leakage through these areas. A superinsulated ceiling must include a properly installed air/vapor barrier, tightly sealed at all joints and penetrations.

Avoid Any Convective-Loop Heat Losses Conventional houses have another kind of defect that seriously undermines the effectiveness of attic floor insulation—convective loops. Convective loops are created when warm air contained below the attic floor insulation is not effectively sealed from cooler attic air. The lighter warm air below sets up a convection pattern which permits heat to flow past the insulation. We have seen examples of convective loops in Chapters 2 and 8. A soffited ceiling, often found above kitchen cabinets, bathtubs, stairwells, and closets, is shown in Figure 2.13. Since the ceiling is not continuous above the soffit, the pocket of warm air trapped between the insulation and the lowered ceiling can leak out into the attic through gaps in the insulation.

In superinsulated houses, this convective loop is avoided by having a well-sealed, continuous air/vapor barrier directly below the insulation.

Another type of convective loop in ordinary houses occurs where wiring holes in partition top plates permit warm interior wall air to mix with cooler attic air. Again, the problem can be avoided by a properly sealed air/vapor barrier below the attic floor insulation.

Convective loops, as we have just illustrated, are often (although not always) connected to air leaks. Eliminate the air leak *at the boundary of the thermal envelope* to eliminate the convective loop. A properly designed and built superinsulated house will have minimal air leaks and little convective loop heat loss.

Superinsulated Ceilings Must Be Vapor-Tight

There has been a great deal of controversy in the building community over whether or not to install air/vapor barriers in ceilings. Some contemporary designers insist that continuous air/vapor barriers in ceilings cause moisture problems and should be intentionally eliminated to allow excess water vapor to escape from the house by diffusion through the ceiling. This approach is *not* recommended for superinsulated houses because:

1. *Most of the water vapor flow to an attic is by air flow and not by diffusion.* If you eliminate the air/vapor barrier, both flows increase, so that while the vapor can escape, *so can heat.* Thus, eliminating the ceiling air/vapor barrier carries a high price tag in heat loss.
2. *Attic ventilation is not controllable.* Unless a powered fan is used, attic ventilation depends upon outdoor wind and temperature conditions, which cannot be counted on to be uniform or continuous. Superinsulated attics are much colder than conventional attics due to higher levels of ceiling insulation. If water vapor is allowed to diffuse up into the attic space, it may condense and, in very cold climates, even freeze before it can be ventilated out. By controlling the flow of water vapor with an air/vapor barrier, that situation is avoided.
3. *Added humidity in the attic could cause truss uplift.* Elevated humidity in attic spaces can aggravate the problem of truss uplift (discussed below) caused by the differential in temperature and moisture between top and bottom truss chords.
4. *Ceilings may not allow sufficient diffusion of water vapor to control humidity.* As an illustration, let's look at a 1500-square-foot ceiling with no air/vapor barrier, built with ½-inch gypsum board painted with two coats of latex paint. Let's assume that the indoor air is at 70°F with 40 percent relative humidity, and that the attic air is at 25°F with 70 percent relative humidity. Under these conditions, the ceiling will allow between 5 and 10 pounds of water vapor to diffuse per day. The average family of four produces about 25 pounds of water vapor per day. Under our assumed temperature and humidity conditions, this ceiling will allow less than half that amount to diffuse out. If the ceiling were painted with an oil-based paint, which has a much lower permeability than latex paint, the total vapor diffusion rate would be

even less—about 2 to 3 pounds per day. These rough calculations indicate that water vapor diffusion could be inadequate to relieve excessive interior humidity. In conventional houses, air leakage through walls, flues, etc., would probably diffuse the rest. But in an airtight superinsulated house, a mechanical ventilation system is the *only* way to control humidity, whether or not there is an air/vapor barrier in the ceiling.

5. *Mechanical ventilation is a better alternative for removing excess humidity.* Superinsulated houses *must* have mechanical ventilation systems to remove air contaminants and bring in fresh air. That same system also removes excess indoor moisture by simply dumping humid air from the house.
6. *Lost water vapor is lost energy.* Comparative laboratory tests have shown that eliminating the ceiling air/vapor barrier from a room can cause the heating requirements of that room to increase as much as 10 percent. Water vapor contains latent heat—about 8300 Btu per gallon. If allowed to diffuse or leak out of the house through the ceiling, that energy is lost and wasted. Alternatively, if exhaust air is removed through certain mechanical ventilation systems, some latent heat *can* be captured.

Thermal Bridges Must Be Reduced As Much As Possible

In houses with attics, thermal bridging through the ceiling joists is not a serious problem because sufficient insulation placed over the joists insulates them from cold attic air.

With cathedral ceilings and flat roofs, or where the sloping roof is the boundary of the thermal envelope, however, the joists normally extend through the insulation and can cause significant thermal bridging. With these roof types, special features are incorporated to reduce thermal bridging.

Full-Thickness Insulation Must Be Installed Over the Entire Area

Recent British experiments with attic insulation showed that a 5 percent uninsulated area in a test attic resulted in a 57.5 percent "worsening" of the thermal performance. Even leaving out a small area such as the attic hatch (see below) can seriously degrade the performance of the attic insulation system. As with walls, there must be absolutely no voids in the attic insulation system.

With conventional construction, you can't place full-thickness insulation over or near the wall top plates since the roof rafters, sitting on the wall plates, do not leave sufficient clearance. In superinsulated houses, however, the roof rafters or trusses are raised up to allow full-thickness insulation to be placed right over the walls.

DESIGN AND CONSTRUCTION OF SUPERINSULATED ROOFS/CEILINGS

In this section, we will look at support structure design, choice of insulating materials, air/vapor barrier installation, and ventilation for unheated attics, cathedral ceilings, and flat or shed roofs. Since unheated attics and cathedral ceilings are the most common, they are discussed in greatest detail.

Unheated Attics

Insulation System Support Structures   The support structure must provide support for the insulation and an attachment base for the air/vapor barrier and weather barrier. For houses with attics, the support structure can be composed of roof trusses or site-built rafters; ceiling strapping can be added to either of these types.

Roof Trusses   Truss design and manufacture has evolved in recent years to the point where almost any type of roof configuration can be accommodated. Aside from energy efficiency, trusses provide a very rapid and cost-effective method of roof construction.

From an energy standpoint, trusses have two advantages: (1) they can provide adequate clearance over wall plates for full-thickness insulation, and (2) they generally allow greater clear span than site-built rafters—an advantage for making the ceiling airtight.

Figure 9.6 shows a "raised heel" truss, sometimes referred to as an "Arkansas" truss. The top chord of the truss is cantilevered out over the exterior wall, leaving enough vertical clearance to install full-thickness insulation over the wall top plates. Notice how the wall sheathing is extended up to form an insulation dam at the outside edge of the wall. Other types of trusses are available that also provide this feature.

The long span of trusses allows the ceiling to be installed complete with air/vapor barrier and interior finish *before* the interior partitions are installed. The advantages are that the air/vapor barrier is put up all at once, doesn't have to be sealed and patched at each interior partition, and is more likely to be flaw-free; and that the ceiling gypsum board is put up very quickly, using 12-foot sheets with no interruptions at interior partitions. The disadvantage is that the framing crew must come back a second time to install the interior partitions.

Site-Built Rafters   When using site-built rafters, some way must be found to install full-thickness insulation over the walls at the ceiling/wall joint. One way to accomplish this is shown in Figure 9.7. Ceiling joists are installed over the wall plates as usual. But instead of resting the rafters on the wall plates, they are attached to a second plate installed on *top* of the ceiling joists. With this system, the ceiling joists can be filled with full-thickness insulation all the way over the walls. Thermal bridging is minimized.

Another design possibility is shown in Figure 9.8. The wall is built extra-tall using long studs. A ledger plate is attached to the wall framing 12 inches below the top plates, and the ceiling joists are attached to the ledger plate with joist hangers. This scheme is costly and requires extra-long wall studs. However, it is quite energy-efficient since it allows the ceiling/wall corner to be insulated with almost no thermal bridging.

When using this system, pay careful attention to the roof structure. Normally, ceiling joists help resist lateral roof forces, which tend to push the walls outward. The dropped joists, hung with joist hangers, do not provide that strength. Collar ties or other suitable reinforcements are necessary to ensure structural strength. If there are any doubts, a structural engineer should be consulted.

Strapped Ceilings   Strapped ceilings have the same general characteristics and advantages as strapped walls (Chapter 7). Horizontal strapping—1 × 2's, 2 × 3's, or 2 × 4's—are nailed, 16 inches on center, to the ceiling joists or truss bottom chords (Figure 9.9), and the cavity space is filled with insulation. This is an easy technique, involving no special tools or materials. It doesn't affect the

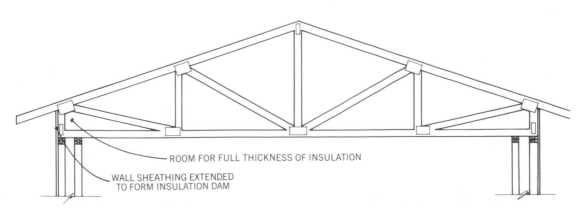

ROOM FOR FULL THICKNESS OF INSULATION

WALL SHEATHING EXTENDED
TO FORM INSULATION DAM

Figure 9.6   Raised heel ("Arkansas") truss. Extra height over wall plates allows full thickness insulation over walls.

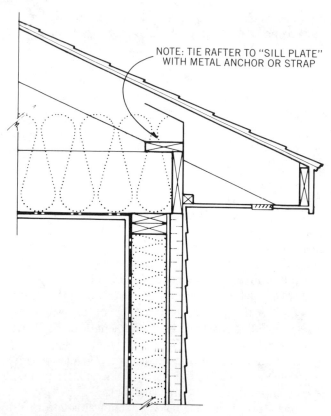

Figure 9.7 "Platform" framing rafters to increase insulation depth and reduce thermal bridging.

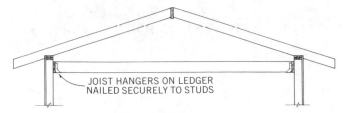

Figure 9.8 Site-built rafters with dropped ceiling joists.

appearance of the roof from the outside, though it will lower the inside ceiling height unless extra-long partitions and walls are used.

Strapping has another advantage: If the ceiling joists or trusses are installed 24 inches on center, then the 16-inch on-center strapping will provide better attachment for ceiling gypsum board and better support for the insulation above.

The air/vapor barrier in a strapped ceiling is best installed between the strapping and the ceiling framing members (Figure 9.9), allowing electrical wiring to be installed in the strapping cavity without damage to the barrier. If heavy insulation is to be installed in the ceiling, make sure the air/vapor barrier is well stapled to the ceiling joists or truss chords. Otherwise, the weight of the insulation may cause the air/vapor barrier to sag into the strapping cavity and possibly even pull the staples.

Some builders install two layers of ceiling gypsum board, one above and the other below the strapping (Fig-

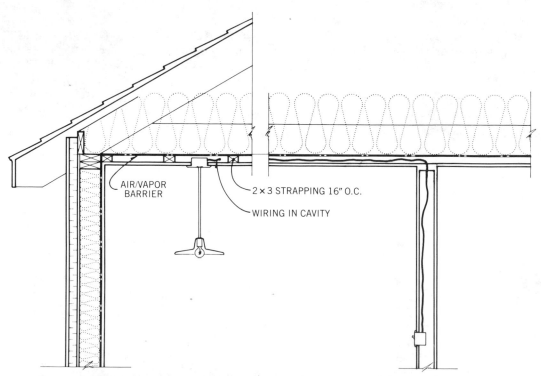

Figure 9.9 Strappped ceiling with electrical installation in strapping cavity. Air/vapor barrier is protected.

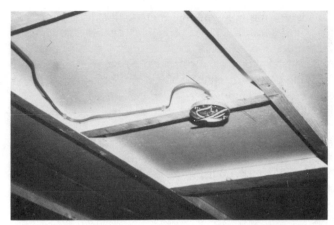

Figure 9.10 "Flush-fitting" electrical box installed in strapped ceiling. In this installation, two layers of gypsum-board are used. The air/vapor barrier has already been installed above the upper layer of gypsum board. (Photo by Harold Orr.)

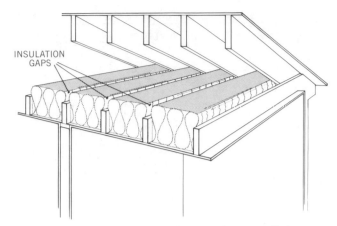

Figure 9.11 Single layer of fiberglass batts installed in attic between ceiling joists. Notice the gaps between batts.

ure 9.10). This is in effect a hung ceiling. The space between the ceilings is available for any utility runs or recessed fluorescent lighting. The air/vapor barrier is absolutely protected. This system is costly, however, and other than allowing the protection of the air/vapor barrier, it has no thermal advantage.

Insulation Materials *Batts* Fiberglass batts are commonly used in superinsulated attics. They are an acceptable choice as long as they are properly installed. Sometimes it is difficult to cut and fit batts around framing and other protrusions in the attic. Also, when only one layer of batts is installed, the joists or truss bottom chords create spaces between the batts, and since the batts are typically thicker than the framing, there may be an uninsulated gap left above the framing members (Figure 9.11). This can be somewhat overcome by installing two layers with the lower layer completely filling the joist cavities and the upper layer running perpendicular to it (Figure 9.12). The finished installation must appear as a solid unbroken blanket of insulation.

Loose Fill Blown-in fiberglass, rockwool, and cellulose are all satisfactory materials for insulating attics. When using any of the loose-fill insulations, consideration should be given to possible settling and the resultant loss in R-value. This is evidently less important with fiberglass or rockwool than with cellulose. Because of many variables in cellulose insulation manufacture and installation, the density varies, ranging typically from 2.5 to 3.5 pounds per cubic foot. If installed at a low density, cellulose is prone to settling, resulting in decreased thickness and R-value. Field measurements done at Oak Ridge National Laboratory have shown a 20 percent increase in density of cellulose within the first few years after installation.

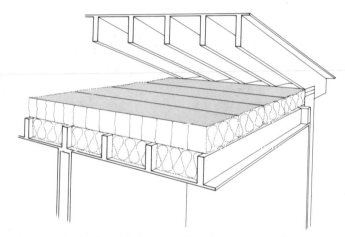

Figure 9.12 Double layer of fiberglass batts installed in attic. The two layers are installed at right angles to avoid any gaps.

Figure 9.13 illustrates the effect on R-value of increased density due to settling. In this example, cellulose is installed 15 inches thick in an attic at a density of 2.5 pounds per cubic foot (Figure 9.13a). The total installed R-value is R-55.5 (3.7 per inch × 15 inches); the installed weight per area is 3.125 pounds per square foot. If the settled density increases 20 percent to 3.0 pounds per cubic foot (a "worst case" situation), the thickness will decrease to 12.5 inches (Figure 9.13b). The R-value per inch will be somewhat less (about R-3.5 per inch) and the total R-value will be reduced to R-43.8. Thus, there is a total potential loss of 21 percent in R-value if the insulation density increases 20 percent.

Settling is not a problem as long as you know about it and compensate by installing extra thicknesses of insulation. For cellulose, it is recommended that the insulation be installed by weight rather than by thickness. Assume

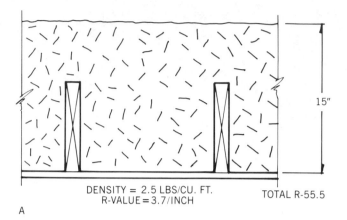

DENSITY = 2.5 LBS/CU. FT.
R-VALUE = 3.7/INCH   TOTAL R-55.5

A

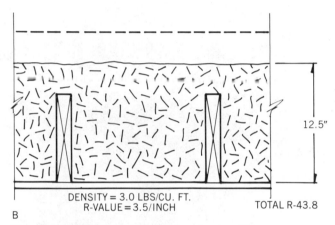

DENSITY = 3.0 LBS/CU. FT.
R-VALUE = 3.5/INCH   TOTAL R-43.8

B

Figure 9.13 Potential effect of settling on R-value using blown-in cellulose insulation. In this extreme example, a 20 percent increase in density results in a 21 percent decrease in total R-value. A. As installed. B. After settling, with 20 percent increase in density.

that the final settled density will be about 3.0 pounds per cubic foot and that the final R-value will be about 3.5 per inch. If you apply some simple arithmetic, you will see that the total settled R-value will be about R-14 per pound of insulation per square foot.

To figure out how much cellulose insulation to install, follow these steps:

1. Choose the desired R-value.
2. Divide the total R value by 14 to get the number of pounds per square foot.
3. Multiply the pounds per square foot by the area of the attic to get the total number of pounds to install.

For example, suppose we wanted to insulate a 1000-square-foot attic with blown cellulose to R-60.

1. Total R = 60
2. R-60 divided by 14 = 4.3 pounds per square foot.
3. 4.3 times 1000 = 4300 pounds of cellulose.

This is not the conventional method for installing cellulose, and your design will probably not coincide with the recommended coverage printed on the packaging. The initial installation will most likely be greater than R-60 until the cellulose settles. The cellulose may not actually settle to 3.0 pounds per cubic foot, in which case the R-value will remain greater than planned.

There has been some evidence and concern that the added weight of the cellulose insulation in superinsulated houses can lead to sagging of gypsum board ceilings. Current thinking suggests that the problem is caused principally by dampening of the gypsum board due to some combination of the following conditions:

1. Application of thick, water-based, textured finishes.
2. High humidity during winter construction due to rapid drying of building materials in tightly closed houses.
3. The use of "salamander"-type propane space heaters, which give off water vapor in the exhaust.
4. Water vapor diffusing through the gypsum board and condensing on the cold air/vapor barrier prior to installation of the insulation.

The following measures are recommended to avoid this problem:

1. Use ⅝-inch gypsum board rather than ½-inch. Never use ⅜-inch board on ceilings.
2. Install the board parallel to the ceiling framing rather than perpendicular.
3. If the roof trusses or ceiling joists are installed 24-inch on center, install strapping 16-inch on center to provide better attachment for the gypsum board.
4. Install the ceiling insulation *before* undertaking moisture-producing operations such as applying water-based finishes. This will keep the air/vapor barrier warm and prevent condensation.
5. Provide good ventilation during construction. One method used by Canadian builders is to temporarily install a "barn-type" air-to-air heat exchanger (see Appendix D) in one of the window openings during construction. This will provide good ventilation without sacrificing heat. The exchanger can be easily moved from site to site.

Rigid Foams Rigid foams such as urethane or polystyrene are not recommended for attics because of their high cost and installation difficulty. Also, since space is not a concern, the high R-value per inch of these materials is not an advantage.

Radiation Barriers Radiation barriers are reflective materials that reduce heat loss by reflecting long wave infrared radiation. They are not useful as attic insulation in cold climates but may be very effective in reducing cooling loads in hot southern climates.

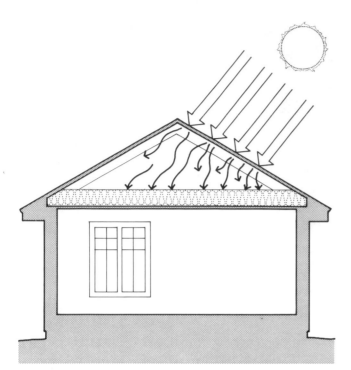

Figure 9.14 Attic overheating due to radiant energy from underside of roof. During a sunny day, the temperature of the insulation in the attic floor may be *higher* than the temperature of the air in the attic.

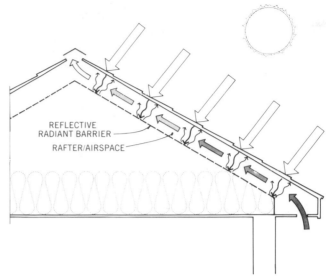

Figure 9.15 Radiation barrier, installed under roof rafters, reflects infrared radiation from underside of roof, reducing heat gain into attic.

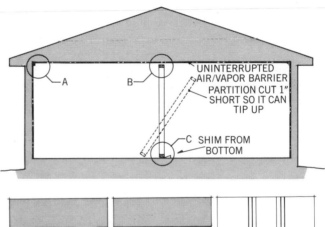

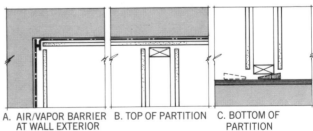

A. AIR/VAPOR BARRIER AT WALL EXTERIOR B. TOP OF PARTITION C. BOTTOM OF PARTITION

Figure 9.16 Interior partitions installed after ceiling completion. By installing the ceiling air/vapor barrier *first*, no special treatment of interior partitions is necessary.

Some interesting experiments at the Florida Solar Energy Center have shown that the main mechanism of overheating in attics is thermal radiation from the underside of the hot roof "shining" down onto the surface of the attic insulation (Figure 9.14). In the daytime, the surface of the insulation is often hotter than the air in the attic. The purpose of the radiation barrier is to intercept that radiant energy and reflect it back up to the roof.

Several available products serve well to block this downward flow of radiant energy (see Appendix D). Most are aluminum foil or aluminized Mylar. The material is stapled to the edges of the roof rafters, creating a continuous shiny surface on the underside of the roof (Figure 9.15).

Putting a radiation barrier underneath the rafters will cause the air space between the barrier and the roof to become much hotter than before. To avoid overheating, combination ridge and soffit vents must be provided as shown in Figure 9.15. The hot air will be drawn out through the ridge vents and be replaced by cooler outside air entering through the soffit vents.

The Ceiling Air/Vapor Barrier   The integrity of the ceiling air/vapor barrier is particularly important since buoyant warm air is constantly trying to force its way up through the ceiling into the attic. The barrier should be a continuous sheet of 6-mil polyethylene or other suitable material, stapled to the joists or trusses, carefully sealed at the seams and to all penetrations through the ceiling, and joined to the wall air/vapor barriers at the wall top plates.

If possible, the air/vapor barrier (and ceiling gypsum board) should be installed *before* the interior partitions (Figure 9.16), making it easier to provide a continuous barrier and alleviating the need for sealing the plastic at each interior partition. Also, this allows the gypsum board to be installed very quickly, in long sheets.

Before the gypsum board goes up, be sure to install blocking between the joists or trusses for nailing the partitions. The interior partitions should be built 1 inch shorter than normal to accommodate the $\frac{5}{8}$-inch gypsum board

Figure 9.17 Ceiling air/vapor barrier being installed before interior partitions. (Photo by Harold Orr.)

Figure 9.18 Gypsum board being installed over continuous ceiling air/vapor barrier prior to installation of interior partitions. Ceiling goes up fast using 12-foot pieces of gypsum board. (Photo by Harold Orr.)

plus about $\frac{3}{8}$-inch extra space to tip up the partition into place. Once in place, the partitions are shimmed under the bottom plate.

Interior partitions installed *before* the ceiling air/vapor barrier is installed must be prepared by placing a short strip of polyethylene between the two top plates (Figure 9.19). This strip is joined later to the ceiling air/vapor barrier. Why install the air/vapor barrier between the two top plates? To protect it against damage when installing the ceiling joists or roof trusses. To make life easier and neater, the polyethylene strip should be stapled up to the sides of the cap plate (Figure 9.19) to facilitate caulking and stapling to the ceiling air/vapor barrier later.

If the ceiling gypsum board is not going to be put up immediately after the ceiling air/vapor barrier is installed, it is wise to temporarily leave out a 10-foot by 10-foot section of air/vapor barrier to protect the plastic against wind damage. Wind blowing over the partially completed house creates a pressure differential between the inside space and the attic that can tear the air/vapor barrier. Leaving out one panel will relieve the pressure and prevent damage. The missing panel can be installed by the gypsum-board crew just prior to the installation of the ceiling gypsum board.

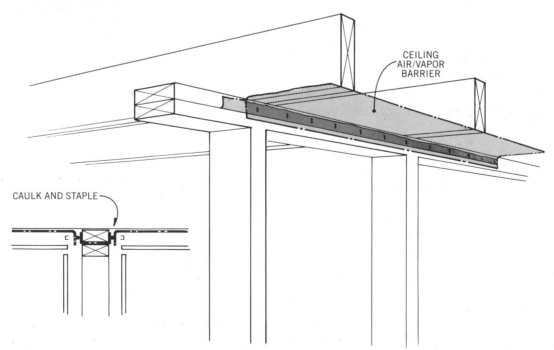

Figure 9.19 Interior partitions installed *before* ceiling air/vapor barrier. Partition is prepared with air/vapor barrier between top plates.

Sealing Penetrations Through the Air/Vapor Barrier We have already discussed how the ceiling air/vapor barrier must be sealed at all interior partitions and at the exterior walls. The next important step is to deal with penetrations up through the top of the house. Every penetration through the insulated roof/ceiling must be sealed at the air/vapor barrier.

The best way to deal with ceiling penetrations is to minimize or eliminate them altogether. Light fixtures can be mounted on interior walls, attic hatches can be installed over unheated spaces, and vent fans can be ducted down and out through the basement. Of course, some penetrations are unavoidable. The following section presents some tips for properly sealing various penetrations through the air/vapor barrier.

Electrical Wiring and Ceiling Light Fixtures All wiring penetrations through the air/vapor barrier must be sealed against a solid backing. Figures 9.20 through 9.22 show two ways to install ceiling electrical boxes. Figures 9.20 and 9.21 show installation of a standard depth box. First, three pieces of blocking are installed between the ceiling joists: one piece is recessed for attaching the electrical box; the other two side blocks, installed flush with the joists, provide backing for sealing the air/vapor barrier. The three pieces form a recessed "box" between the joists. A patch of polyethylene is stapled into the box. The wiring is brought down through a hole drilled in the recessed blocking and is sealed with caulk at the air/vapor barrier. The electrical box is then installed. When the ceiling air/vapor barrier is installed, it is sealed to the polyethylene patch at the joists and side blocks.

Figure 9.22 shows a simpler type of installation using a flush-fitting box. A single piece of blocking is installed flush with the ceiling joists. When the wiring hole is drilled

in the blocking, it is widened to accept the cable clamp. Before the box is installed, a patch of polyethylene is sealed to the blocking. The ceiling air/vapor barrier is sealed to the patch later. One drawback to flush-fitting boxes is that only one wire can be run into them. They can't be used as "spaghetti junctions," as is often done with ceiling boxes.

All of the wiring and air/vapor barrier preparation should be done prior to installation of the ceiling air/vapor barrier.

If the air/vapor barrier in a strapped ceiling is installed between the strapping and the roof joists, the electrical wiring and boxes can be installed in the strapping cavity using conventional techniques without damaging the air/vapor barrier (Figure 9.9). The type of electrical boxes used will depend on the dimensions of the strapping.

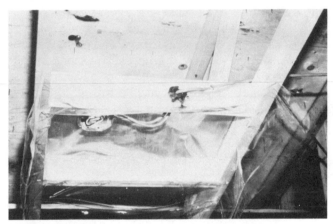

Figure 9.21 Recessed blocking installed with electrical wiring in place. The blocking is lined with polyethylene which will later be sealed to ceiling air/vapor barrier. (Photo by Harold Orr.)

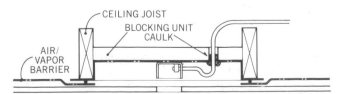

Figure 9.20 Recessed blocking for installing electrical boxes in ceiling. All wiring penetrations are caulked after electrical installation.

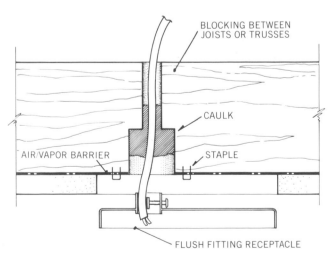

Figure 9.22 Installation of flush-fitting electrical box in ceiling. Note that blocking must be routed to receive wiring clamp.

Ceiling Light Fixtures and Overheating

Ceiling light fixtures generate considerable heat. With conventional construction and low levels of insulation, some of that heat is dissipated through the roof. With higher levels of insulation, the ceiling receptable will be hotter and may cause some deterioration or embrittlement of the air/vapor barrier and sealant over time. Since superinsulated houses are still relatively new, we can only guess how severe this problem may be. To be safe, we recommend that only suspended lighting systems or low-wattage fixtures be installed on ceilings. Recessed lighting fixtures should not be used in superinsulated houses. The best solution, of course, is to put the light fixtures elsewhere.

Plumbing Stacks   Plumbing vent stacks, typically installed in pipe chases leading from basement to attic, are notorious sources of air leakage. If a vent stack is not well sealed, the pipe chase becomes an air chimney.

Since plumbing vent stacks expand and contract as hot water is intermittently used in a house, an expansion joint should be installed under the attic floor and kept inside the heated space where it won't be subject to freezing temperatures. Don't try to clamp the stack against expansion; that could cause further problems. Even with an expansion joint, the air-seal between the stack and the house should be somewhat flexible. Use a nonhardening

caulk, oakum, and/or plastic films to seal the stack. Where the stack penetrates the top plate, the hole should be round and no more than 0.5-inch greater in diameter than the plumbing stack. Figure 9.23 shows how to seal the plumbing stack to the air/vapor barrier.

Note: Attics in superinsulated houses are almost as cold as the outdoors. If there is a long run of plumbing stack through the attic, water vapor in the stack can condense and freeze into ice. In cold climates, enough ice can build up to clog the stack, causing annoying problems in the bathrooms below. In extremely cold climates, the section of plumbing stack in the attic should therefore be wrapped with insulation to prevent ice formation. Ordinary fiberglass pipe wrap will do the trick.

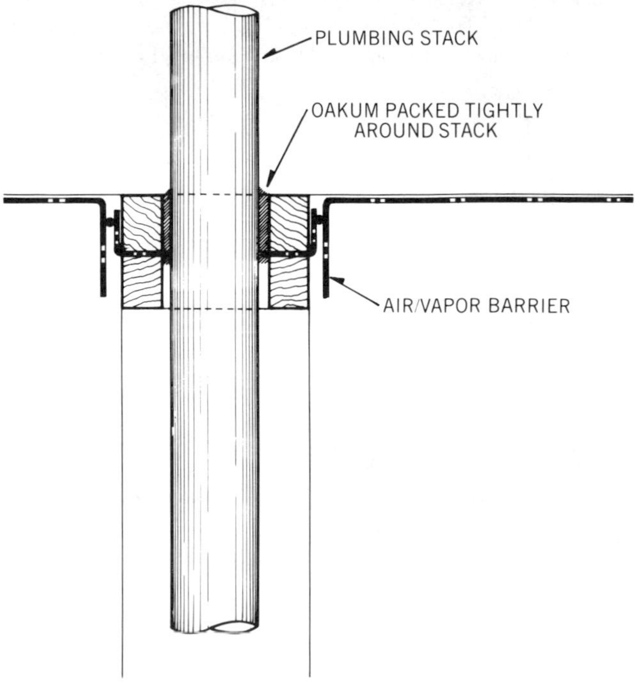

Metal Chimneys and Flues   Figure 9.24 shows the recommended way to seal around metal chimneys at the upper-ceiling level. A metal cylinder is installed around the chimney to provide clearance between the chimney and the insulation. A firestop plate, installed at the bottom of the metal cylinder, is sealed to the chimney with heat-resistant caulk. Notice how the firestop plate is extended horizontally beyond the partition wall, making it much easier to attach the ceiling air/vapor barrier than if the plate were inside the chimney enclosure.

Never use polyethylene or spray foam to seal around a chimney, even if the chimney is rated for zero clearance.

Attic Hatches   In a superinsulated house, the high level of insulation in the attic renders the floor space unusable; therefore the attic hatch is normally used only for emergency access (fire codes usually require access to the attic). Since hatches are a relatively small part of the overall ceiling area, they are often left uninsulated. A simple heat-loss analysis will show why this is a mistake. Consider a 600-square-foot ceiling insulated to R-60 with a 3-foot by 2-foot uninsulated attic hatch (R-2). Even though the attic hatch is only 1 percent of the total ceiling area, it reduces the overall R-value of the ceiling from R-60 to R-47—a loss of almost 22 percent. This calculation takes only conductive heat loss into consideration. If

PLUMBING STACK

OAKUM PACKED TIGHTLY AROUND STACK

AIR/VAPOR BARRIER

Figure 9.23   One method of sealing plumbing stack through ceiling.

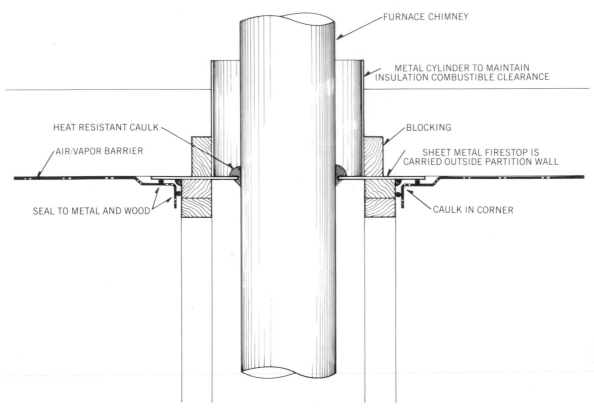

Figure 9.24 Method for sealing metal chimney.

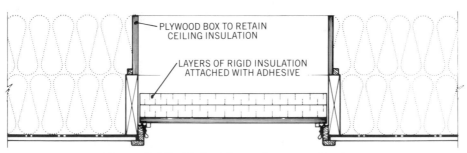

Figure 9.25 Method for insulating attic hatch.

poorly sealed, the attic hatch will also be a significant source of infiltration heat loss.

The best way to deal with hatches is to move them elsewhere, either over an unheated space or in an attic gable wall. If a ceiling installation cannot be avoided, the hatch must be both well insulated and well sealed. Figure 9.25 shows one recommended design. The plywood box should be tall enough to prevent any insulation from spilling over through the hatch. The rigid insulation is attached directly to the hatch with adhesive.

Figure 9.26 shows a detail for terminating the ceiling air/vapor barrier at the hatch. Window sash clamps provide an effective means of securing the hatch. If used only for emergency access, the hatch should be caulked around the edges with latex caulk, providing a temporary airtight seal which can be easily broken in the case of

emergencies (check with local code officials before doing this).

Vent Fans Bathroom and kitchen vent fan ducts should not be run up through the ceiling. In the first place, they

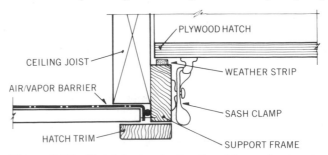

Figure 9.26 Detail for terminating the air/vapor barrier at attic hatch.

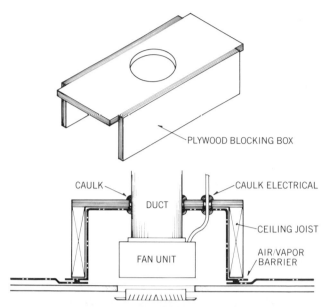

Figure 9.27 Installation of bathroom exhaust fan and duct through ceiling.

present yet another air/vapor barrier penetration that must be sealed. In the second place, these ducts are vertical air shafts connecting the living space with the outdoors. Even with good dampers, there will always be some air leakage as the buoyant warm air tries to rise up out of the house. Also, bathroom and kitchen exhaust air should, ideally, be fed into an air-to-air heat exchanger or other heat recovery device (see Chapter 12 for details).

If the fan or duct must go in the ceiling, it should be installed in a "box" similar to the type illustrated for installing ceiling electrical boxes. The installation shown in Figure 9.27 uses plywood over the joists as a backing for the air/vapor barrier. The exhaust should be vented out through the roof and never into the attic space.

The Ceiling Air Barrier   Should attic insulation have a separate air barrier installed on top? The answer is a qualified no. Theoretically it is a good idea; an exterior air barrier will not only protect the insulation from the degrading effects of air intrusion, but will also prevent loose-fill insulation from blowing around during high winds. A vapor-permeable membrane such as Dupont Tyvek should be acceptable. But researchers at the Canadian National Research Council warn that the exterior barrier could cause problems; if any water vapor leaks up through the ceiling air/vapor barrier, it may condense and collect on the air barrier before it has a chance to diffuse through. This may only be a problem in very cold climates, but should be taken into account when considering the air barrier installation. A cautious compromise is to put in a partial air barrier around the perimeter of the attic to protect against wind near eave or soffit vents.

Installing Attic Ventilation   The basic purpose of attic ventilation is to remove moisture that enters the attic from the living space. Even though a perfect air/vapor barrier eliminates the need for attic ventilation, the wise designer should assume that construction crews are less than perfect and that attic ventilation will be necessary. ASHRAE guidelines recommend installing 1 square foot of "free ventilation area" for each 300 square feet of attic. These guidelines are probably excessive for superinsulated houses but until more definitive results are available, we recommend that the 1 : 300 rule be followed. To meet these guidelines, be sure to size your vents according to their "free area," not total opening area; screens, grilles, and louvers decrease the free area between 10 and 50 percent. Vent manufacturers' data sheets will usually list the net free area for their products.

The ideal attic ventilation system has the following features: (1) it provides sufficient air exchange to remove excess humidity in winter and overheated air in summer; (2) it works independently of windspeed or direction; (3) it creates air movement along the underside of the roof; (4) it won't blow loose-fill insulation around in the attic; (5) it keeps out rain and snow; and (6) it is relatively easy and inexpensive to install.

Ridge and Soffit Vents Are the Most Effective Attic Ventilation System   Continuous ridge and soffit vents provide air circulation under the roof skin where it is most needed (Figure 9.28). They work even when there is no wind; the high/low placement of the vents allows the stack effect to draw cool air in through the soffit vents and out through the ridge vent.

Other types of ventilators are less efficient. Air flow through gable end vents depends on wind; the vents must be arranged to provide a path for cross ventilation. Even then, they work only when the wind is perpendicular to the gables; they are much less effective if the wind is blowing against the eave-side of the house (Figure 9.29). Roof louvers also depend on wind and don't ventilate the entire underside of the roof. Powered exhaust fans should be avoided; they may actually make matters worse since they induce a negative pressure in the attic, which may cause air from the house to be drawn up into the attic through imperfections in the air/vapor barrier (Figure 9.30).

Cathedral Ceilings

As mentioned at the beginning of this chapter, cathedral ceilings are relatively difficult candidates for superinsulation. They can be just as energy-efficient as attics, but at somewhat greater expense. Much of the information presented for unheated attics is also applicable to cathedral ceilings. There are, of course, some differences, mostly dealing with support structures. As with walls, the principal design requirements here are adequate space for insulation and minimal thermal bridging.

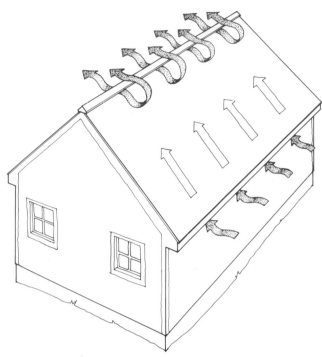

Figure 9.28 Air flow in attic with continuous ridge and soffit vents. This is the most effective type of attic ventilation because it keeps underside of roof cool, avoids air intrusion into attic floor insulation, and doesn't depend on wind.

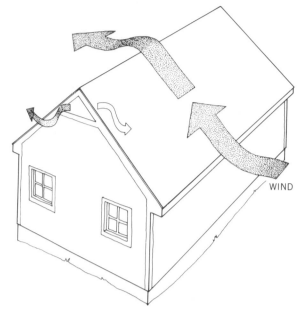

Figure 9.29 Air flow in attic with gable vents. Effectiveness of this type of ventilation varies with intensity and direction of wind.

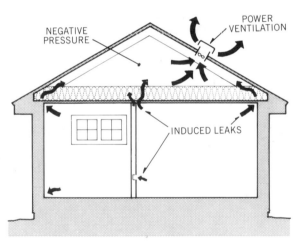

Figure 9.30 Attic with power ventilation. The negative pressure created in the attic by the fan could induce air leakage from house into attic through defects in the air/vapor barrier.

Site-Built Rafters Site-built rafters present three shortcomings for creating a superinsulated cathedral ceiling: (1) limited space for insulation, (2) extensive thermal bridging, and (3) inadequate clearance over exterior wall plates for full-thickness insulation.

If the rafters make up the entire insulation support structure, that is, there is no foam sheathing or strapping, then the minimum rafter size for adequate insulation is 10 inches. Figure 9.31 shows an R-33 ceiling using 10-inch rafters. The nominal size of this lumber is 9.5 inches; the venting baffles take up about 1.5 inches, leaving 8.0 inches for insulation. In this case, loose-fill fiberglass is blown in at a high density, giving an R-value of about R-3.5 to R-4.0 per inch, or R-28 to R-32 for the 8 inches. The gypsum board and the interior air film add another R-1.3 or so.

Despite the apparent high R-value, this roof design fails to overcome other shortcomings of site-built rafters. Thermal bridging reduces the overall R-value. Also, notice that in Figure 9.31 there is insufficient insulation over the wall top plates.

Scissors Trusses Scissors trusses (Figure 9.32) overcome the problems associated with site-built rafters. With scissors trusses, the top and bottom chords are not paral-

lel, but the sloping bottom chords still allow a vaulted ceiling effect.

The advantages of this roofing system, in addition to high R-value, are limited thermal bridging and ease of erection. The open nature of trusses allows cross-ventilation between truss spaces, providing a wider area for dissipation of moisture which might leak through an imperfect air/vapor barrier. The open webs also eliminate the need for drilling through rafters for wiring installation.

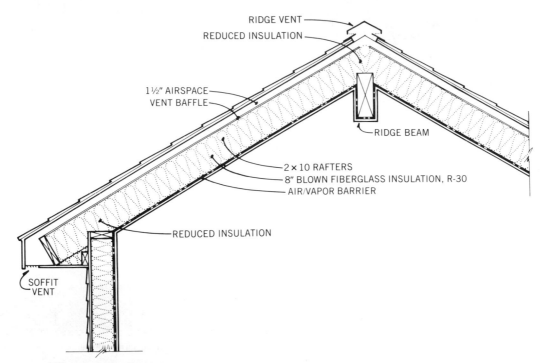

Figure 9.31 Conventional cathedral ceiling with site-built rafters.

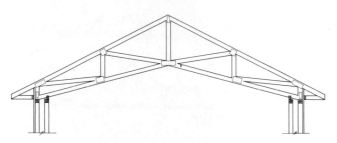

Figure 9.32 Scissors truss.

Parallel Chord Trusses Parallel chord trusses (Figure 9.33) are an improvement over scissors trusses, allowing the interior ceiling shape to follow the roof slope and avoiding excessive insulation near the peak. Installation is somewhat more difficult because they are put up in two sections rather than one, and some sort of ridge beam is usually required. The special SuperTrusses™, illustrated in Figure 9.34, provide the best of both worlds, allowing up to 24 inches of vertical space for insulation and ventilation. The only drawback is the short, flattened section at the peak.

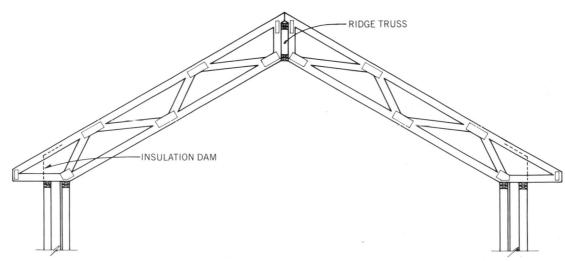

Figure 9.33 Parallel chord truss.

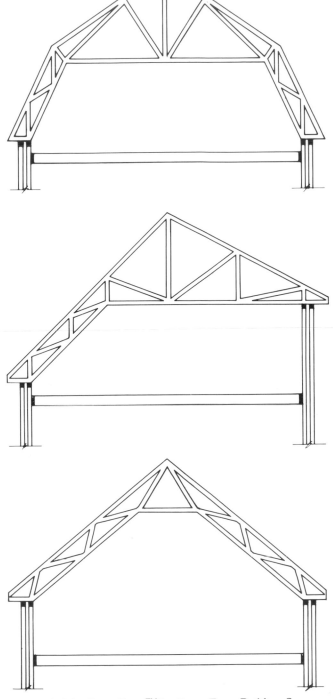

Figure 9.35 SuperTruss™ being installed. (Photo by Howard Faulkner.)

Figure 9.36 SuperTruss™ system being filled with blown fiberglass insulation. Insulation will be 22 inches thick. Notice Propervent™ ventilation baffle installed on underside of roof. (Photo by Howard Faulkner.)

Figure 9.34 SuperTruss™ by SuperTruss Building Systems, Inc.

Strapped Ceiling   Strapping can be added to any type of cathedral ceiling to increase the cavity depth for insulation and to allow the air/vapor barrier to be recessed. Techniques and features are the same as for flat ceilings under unheated attics.

Insulative Sheathing   Rigid foam insulative sheathing can be used in conjunction with trusses, rafters, or strapping and can be installed on either the outside or the inside of the roof. The most important advantage of this technique, in addition to extra R-value, is that it significantly reduces thermal bridging through the roof.

Exterior Rigid Insulation   There are two types of rigid insulation products suitable for sheathing the outside of roofs: (1) plain rigid boards, with or without facings, and (2) rigid boards bonded to nailable sheathing, made especially for roofing. Most of the available bonded prod-

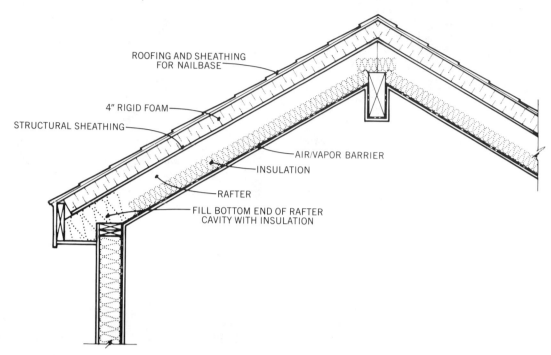

ROOFING AND SHEATHING
FOR NAILBASE

4″ RIGID FOAM

STRUCTURAL SHEATHING

AIR/VAPOR BARRIER

INSULATION

RAFTER

FILL BOTTOM END OF RAFTER
CAVITY WITH INSULATION

Figure 9.37 Cathedral ceiling with rigid foam insulation (bonded panel).

ucts use either urethane or polyisocyanurate insulation and come in thicknesses ranging from 1.5 to 4 inches. Plain rigid boards can be bought in almost any thickness up to 6 inches or more.

The main advantage of the board-bonded-to-sheathing method is that it does away with one installation step—nailing the sheathing over the insulation. Also, some of the products are applied to the roof deck with adhesive, eliminating the problem of using extra-long nails.

The separate board and sheathing route has its advantages too. The system can be made more airtight by staggering the seams of the foam and the sheathing board so that no seams run through the whole system from top to bottom. This may also produce less waste. You can use leftover pieces of insulation to fit odd roof spaces and then cover the seams with a single piece of sheathing.

Figure 9.37 shows a roof insulated with an R-29 bonded insulation panel plus 3.5 inch (R-11) fiberglass batts in the rafter space. The total R-value is about R-40. When using this type of over-the-roof system, give careful thought to potential moisture problems. *Under no circumstances should the roof be ventilated between the fiberglass and the foam sheathing,* since that would defeat the effectiveness of the foam insulation. Instead, two important precautions must be taken: (1) install a proper air/vapor barrier, and (2) install at least twice as much R-value over the rafters (foam sheathing) as between the rafters (fiberglass or other). This will keep the interior (warm) surface of the foam above the dew point and

prevent condensation. The air/vapor barrier can actually be installed between the fiberglass and the exterior foam as long as two thirds of the R-value is outside the barrier. (See Chapter 7 for a similar design using embedded air/vapor barriers in double walls.)

Interior Rigid Insulation This system is very similar to, and has the same relative advantages and disadvantages as interior foam insulation for walls (see Chapter 7). The main problems concern attachment of the interior finish at wall/ceiling joints. The placement of nailers and backers should be well thought out in advance.

Flat Roofs

Figures 9.38 and 9.39 show two types of superinsulated flat roofs. That in Figure 9.38 is simply conventional built-up roofing with rigid insulation adhered to the roof sheathing and covered by a weatherproof membrane. The most common problem with this type of flat roof insulation system is membrane damage and/or deterioration. A damaged membrane will lead to wet insulation, which is very difficult to detect and almost impossible to dry out. Commercial building owners spend millions of dollars every year for reroofing flat roofs to correct leakage. Notice how the roof is installed over the double wall—a clever design with almost no thermal bridging.

An alternative system is shown in Figure 9.39. Called a "protected roof membrane" system, this is essentially an upside-down roof. The roof membrane is applied directly to the sheathing. Rigid foam insulation is then laid over the membrane and weighted down with some type of

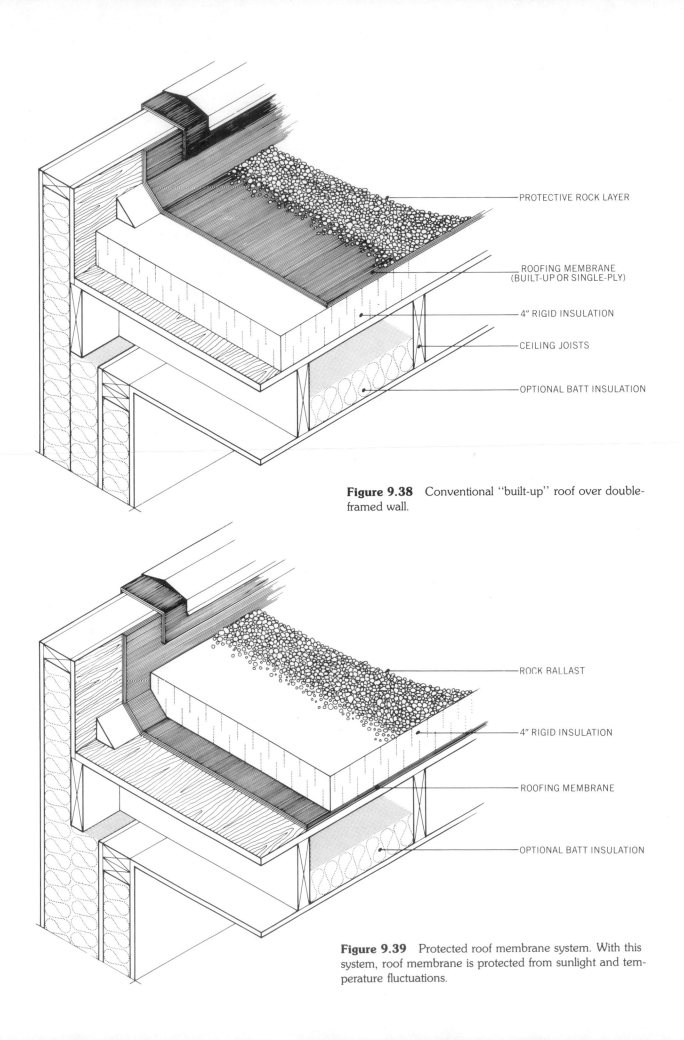

PROTECTIVE ROCK LAYER

ROOFING MEMBRANE
(BUILT-UP OR SINGLE-PLY)

4″ RIGID INSULATION

CEILING JOISTS

OPTIONAL BATT INSULATION

Figure 9.38   Conventional "built-up" roof over double-framed wall.

ROCK BALLAST

4″ RIGID INSULATION

ROOFING MEMBRANE

OPTIONAL BATT INSULATION

Figure 9.39   Protected roof membrane system. With this system, roof membrane is protected from sunlight and temperature fluctuations.

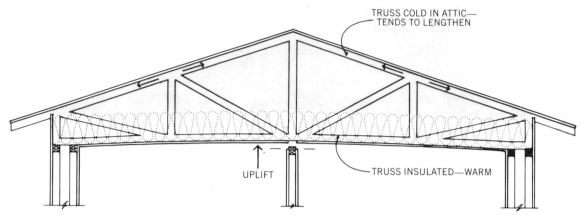

Figure 9.40 Truss uplift. Because of temperature and humidity differentials, the top chord tends to lengthen relative to the bottom chord, causing lifting at the truss center.

ballast. The advantage of this system is that the roof membrane is protected from ultraviolet radiation and large temperature variations: it is always warm. The insulation gets wet, but since it is uncovered, it easily dries again. Naturally, the insulation materials must be able to withstand continual wetting and drying cycles; the only suitable material is extruded polystyrene. The stone ballast protects the foam insulation from ultraviolet degradation. Good drainage is essential to avoid floating the insulation. The weight of the added ballast must be taken into account in the structural design of the roof.

Truss Uplift: Another Ceiling/Roof Consideration

In recent years, there have been increasingly frequent reports of cracking of gypsum board joints at the tops of interior partitions during winter. Although the condition is commonly mistaken for settling of the house, it is most often caused by an upward bowing of the bottom chord of the roof trusses. It usually occurs during the first winter after construction and corrects itself again in summer. It occurs most frequently in houses with high levels of insulation in the attic.

Truss uplift, or ceiling/floor partition separation, is an aesthetic problem, not a structural one; most truss uplift only causes a small ⅛-inch to ¼-inch crack at the ceiling partition joint. There is generally no structural threat to the building. It is, however, most disconcerting to the new homebuyer to see cracks in his/her wall during the first year, and builders often find themselves in court to explain the cause.

What Causes Truss Uplift?   Let's look at an attic space during winter. There are two environmental zones (Figure 9.40)—a cold upper zone above the insulation, and a warmer lower zone beneath the insulation. The amount of moisture in the air will be approximately the same in both zones, but the relative humidity will be

higher in the cold upper zone. The truss top chord is thus surrounded by cold air with high relative humidity; the bottom chord is surrounded by warmer air with lower relative humidity. The top chord absorbs moisture and tends to lengthen, while the bottom chord tends to remain the same length or even shrink slightly. In order for the top chord to lengthen while the bottom chord remains the same length, the truss as a whole must arch upward.

How to Prevent Truss Uplift   Unfortunately, there is no sure-fire way yet known to prevent truss uplift. However, careful consideration of the following factors should reduce its likelihood.

Lumber Quality   Trusses built with good-quality, kiln-dried lumber will be less likely to lift. Certain types of wood, including "compression wood," "juvenile wood," and wood with high slope of grain, tend to shrink and swell much more along the grain.

Moisture Content   The moisture content of the trusses should be as low as possible when installed, otherwise there could be permanent uplift due to shrinkage of the bottom chord upon drying. Trusses should be covered when stored on site, and roofing should be completed shortly after the trusses are erected. Also, the house should be ventilated during construction to keep the humidity down.

Camber   Trusses should not be ordered with positive (upward) camber because the carpenters will often force the bottom chord down to nail it to the partitions, thus building in an upward stress that adds to the uplift stress. If some trusses are delivered with unintentional camber, they should be shimmed rather than be forced down onto the partitions.

Air/Vapor Barrier   Leakage of warm moist air from the house into the attic will increase the humidity there and

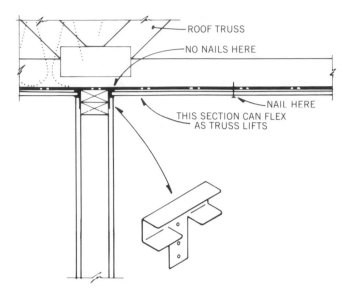

ROOF TRUSS
NO NAILS HERE
NAIL HERE
THIS SECTION CAN FLEX AS TRUSS LIFTS

ROOF TRUSS
AIR/VAPOR BARRIER
MOLDING NAILED TO TRUSS, NOT PARTITION

Figure 9.41   "Floating" joint at interior partition using drywall clips to prevent ceiling-partition separation from truss uplift.

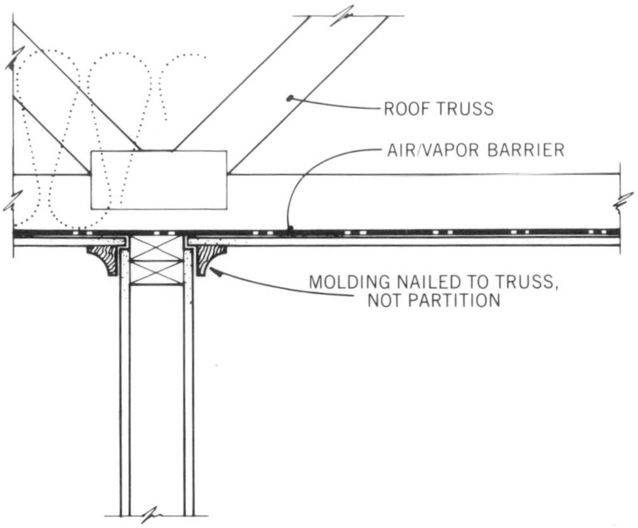

Figure 9.42   "Slip-joint" at interior partition—an alternative method for preventing ceiling-partition separation from truss uplift.

tends to increase the amount of uplift. This is yet another reason to install a complete and effective air/vapor barrier in the ceiling.

How to Decrease Potential Damage if Uplift Should Occur   Until we develop reliable methods to prevent truss uplift, we will probably have to learn to live with it by using construction techniques that allow the trusses to move up and down without damaging the interior finish. Two possible techniques are "floating interior angles" of the gypsum board and "slip joints."

The **floating angle** method for installing gypsum board is a common technique recommended by the Gypsum Association. The ceiling gypsum board is not fastened to the roof truss near the partitions. Instead, it is held in place either by the partition gypsum board or by special clips (Figure 9.41). The nearest attachment point of the gypsum board is 12 inches from the partition. If the truss does lift, the gypsum board can flex slightly over the 12 inches, preventing the ceiling and partition from separating.

Slip joints are a method for allowing the ceiling to move without cracks appearing at the wall/ceiling joint. Corner molding is nailed only to the trusses, not to the partition (Figure 9.42). If the ceiling lifts, the molding slips along the wall without showing cracks. This simple method changes the appearance of the interior considerably; its selection involves considerations of aesthetics and marketing. When this method is used, the air/vapor barrier must be applied across the top plates rather than between them (Figure 9.42).

Ten

Windows and doors

A dominant design element constituting 15 to 40 percent of the total wall area in typical houses, windows serve several important functions:

1. They allow visual communication with the outdoors, giving occupants of a room first-hand information about weather and events occurring outside. Outdoor views also provide relief from monotony and claustrophobia.
2. They admit sunshine for light and heat.
3. They allow natural ventilation.
4. They provide emergency egress in case of fire.
5. They enhance the appearance of the building exterior.

Because they are so transparent to energy flow into and out of a house, windows have always been a prime focus for energy-conserving building design and modification, sometimes resulting in houses with almost no windows and other times resulting in houses with no windows on one side but giant glass walls on the other. To increase thermal performance, windows have been covered with polyethylene, fiberglass, quilts, shutters, and shades. During the past few years, new energy-efficient glazing systems with double and triple the energy efficiency of older "insulating" windows have come onto the market.

Windows are "holes" in the insulation system (Figure 10.1). Glass, with an R-value of R-0.014 per inch, conducts heat about 90 times faster than wood and about 500 times faster than urethane insulation of the same thickness. Even double-pane insulating glass conducts heat 10 to 20 times faster than typical insulated walls. Windows are also "patches" in the air/vapor barrier. A difficult patching job, the wooden window frame must be carefully sealed to the polyethylene air/vapor barrier; movable sashes must make a tight seal against the wooden frame; and glass lites must be well sealed against the wooden sashes. Although high-quality windows usually have good seals around lites and sashes, the most important air-leakage path—between window frame and rough opening—must be carefully sealed during construction.

SELECTING WINDOWS

There are two things to consider when selecting windows—the type of glazing system, and the window style. The type of glazing system—double-glazed, triple-glazed, etc.—determines the R-value and light transmission properties. Window style—double hung, casement, slider, etc.—is important with respect to airtightness. The following sections discuss important energy-related selection criteria with recommended options for superinsulated houses.

R-Value

Determined by the type of glazing system and frame construction, window R-values range from about R-1.0 to R-4.3. When selecting R-value for windows, the most obvious consideration is relative heat loss and its effect on overall house energy consumption. Guidelines for window R-values are presented in Chapter 6. Another consideration, discussed later in this chapter, is the effect of R-value on glass interior surface temperature.

The thermal resistance of a single glazed window, about R-1, is almost entirely due to the air films that naturally hug the glass surfaces (Figure 10.2). The following sections describe various glazing systems with higher R-values, including multiple glazings, selective "low-E" coatings, interpane baffles, gas-filled airspaces, and ventilated glazing systems.

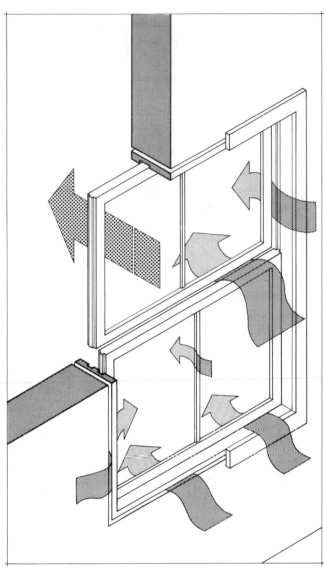

Figure 10.1 Windows are the weak spot in the house thermal envelope.

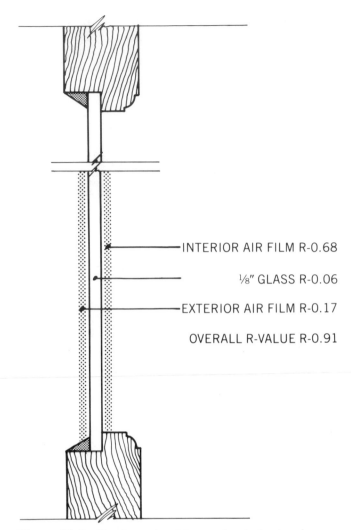

INTERIOR AIR FILM R-0.68

⅛" GLASS R-0.06

EXTERIOR AIR FILM R-0.17

OVERALL R-VALUE R-0.91

Figure 10.2 The thermal resistance of a single-glazed window is due mostly to the resistance of the air films on the glass.

Multiple Glazings The first multiple-pane window unit was patented by Thomas Stetson in 1865. Sealed double-pane insulating glass units became commercially popular during the 1950s. With the advent of the "energy crisis" during the 1970s, triple-pane windows began to appear and, more recently, quadruple-pane.

Multiple glazing increases thermal resistance by entrapping air spaces, each with an *effective R-value* ranging from R-0.7 to R-1.0, between the glass panes. Heat is transferred across the air space by infrared radiation and conduction (Figure 10.3). Infrared radiation from the warm interior glass pane is transmitted successively across each air space, absorbed by each pane of glass, and reradiated outward and inward, with the largest loss toward the cold outer glazings. Heat is also conducted across the air space by the entrapped air, which acts as insulation. Each additional air space created by adding another pane of glass increases the R-value.

Since the "insulation" in multiple-glazed windows is the entrapped air, increasing the air space thickness increases overall R-value; multiple-glazed units with ½-inch air spaces, for example, have higher R-value than those with ¼-inch air spaces. But the effect of increasing the thickness of the air space is limited. Beyond a certain thickness—about ¾-inch—interpane convection increases, carrying heat from the inner to outer pane through air circulation (Figure 10.4). Further increases in air space thickness do not result in increased R-value. The exact thickness at which convection becomes a dominant heat transfer mechanism depends on the height of the glass unit and the temperature differential between indoors and outdoors.

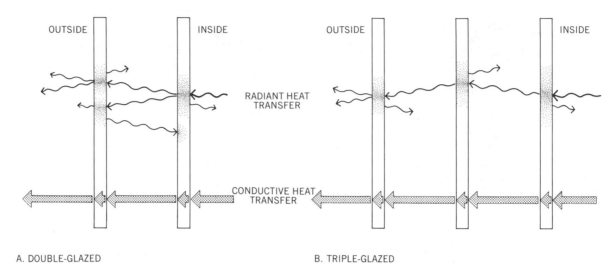

OUTSIDE   INSIDE   OUTSIDE   INSIDE

RADIANT HEAT TRANSFER

CONDUCTIVE HEAT TRANSFER

A. DOUBLE-GLAZED   B. TRIPLE-GLAZED

Figure 10.3   Heat transfer through multiple-glazed windows.

Double glazing with a $\frac{3}{16}$-inch air space has an R-value of R-1.69. With a $\frac{1}{2}$-inch air space, the R-value is about R-2.0. Triple glazing with two entrapped air spaces provides R-values ranging from R-2.5 to R-3.2, depending on the thickness of the spaces. Quadruple glazing, with three air spaces, provides R-values ranging from R-3.5 to R-4.0.

Plastic Interpanes   An all-glass triple-glazed window weighs 50 percent more than a double-glazed window; quadruple glazing is, naturally, even heavier. The heaviness of multiple glazing can be a problem.

Plastic interpanes offer a solution. Because the thermal resistance of multiple glazing is due to entrapped air rather than the glazing material itself, plastic sheeting can be just as thermally effective as glass. Several American glass and window manufacturers produce triple- and quadruple-glazed units with plastic interpanes. A quadruple-glazed window with two plastic interpanes between two outer glass panes weighs little more than conventional double-glazed windows, yet it still has the R-value of quadruple glazing.

Gas-Filled Windows   Another way to increase the thermal resistance of a multiple-glazed window is to suppress convection between the panes by substituting a heavier gas for air. Argon, sulfur hexafluoride, and carbon dioxide are three commonly used gases. The combination of gas filling and low-emissivity coatings (see below) has produced double-glazed windows with R-values as high as R-5.9. In addition to thermal efficiency, gas filling is also used for sound attenuation. Although several types of gas-filled windows are commercially available in Europe and sold in large quantities, highly energy-effi-

cient gas-filled windows are still rare in the United States and Canada.

Low-E Glass   Regular glass has an emissivity of about 0.84. Low emissivity glass or "low-E" glass has a special low-emissivity coating applied to one surface. (Emissivity, mentioned in Chapter 2, is essentially a measure of the tendency of a surface to emit and/or absorb electromagnetic radiation.) About half the heat transfer across the air space of a double-glazed unit is by radiation. When special low-emissivity coatings are applied to the glass surface, radiation is reduced and the effective R-value of the window is increased (Figure 10.6). For example, Sungate 100, a low-E double-glazed unit produced by PPG, has an R-value of R-2.86, which is equivalent to that of most triple-glazed units—but without the extra weight or bulk.

The coatings on low-E glass are "wavelength selective." That is, they reflect long-wave IR (heat radiation), but are transparent to shorter wavelength visible light. Sungate 100, for example, transmits about 90 percent as much visible light as standard clear double-glazed windows.

Low-E glass also helps reduce summer heat gain. The coated inner pane reflects long-wave infrared radiation from the warm outer pane of glass, while still allowing most visible light to pass through.

One disadvantage of low-E glass is that even though it transmits most visible light, it cuts down transmission of the near-infrared portion of the solar spectrum, resulting in lowered total solar transmission (see the next section). This is a disadvantage for passive solar heating. The total solar transmission of Sungate 100, for example, is about 55 percent, compared to 71 percent for regular double-glazed units. However, it still transmits almost as much total solar energy as triple-glazed units, which typically have a total solar transmission of about 59 percent.

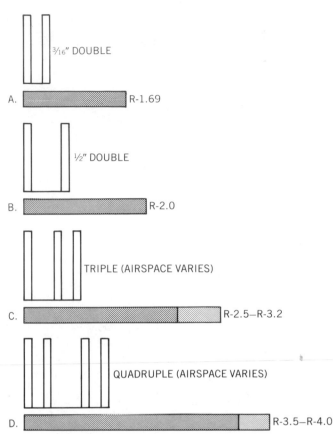

Figure 10.5 R-values for multiple-glazed windows.

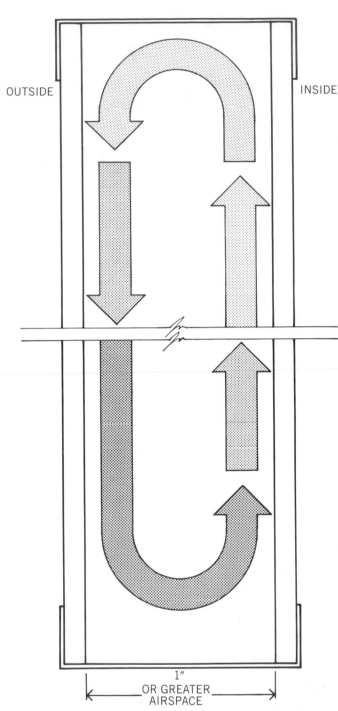

Figure 10.4 In a multiple-glazed window, convective heat transfer becomes dominant with wide interpane air spaces.

Heat Mirror Although "heat mirror" has become something of a generic term for low-emissivity coatings, it is also the trade name of a specific product consisting of a 2-mil polyester film with a low-emissivity coating, manufactured by Southwall Inc. The coating on Heat Mirror works basically like the coating on low-E glass described above, but instead of being applied directly to the glass surface, the low-emissivity film is suspended between two panes of glass. Long-wave infrared radiation from the inner pane of glass is reflected back by the Heat Mirror, reducing heat loss and increasing effective R-value (Figure 10.7). In addition to acting as a radiation barrier, the plastic film also serves as a third glazing, reducing the heat loss even further. The R-value of a glazing system with Heat Mirror suspended between two panes of glass is about R-4.3 (with 0.5-inch air spaces).

Interpane Baffles Another system that increases window thermal resistance is "interpane baffles" (Figure 10.8). But although research has shown that baffles can significantly improve window thermal efficiency, available manufactured units with baffles are actually only slightly better than regular double-glazed windows. For example, the Pella Slimshade™, with venetian blind-type baffles between the panes, has an R-value of R-2.56, compared to R-2.43 for the regular double-glazed unit. A new variation of that window is the "E Slimshade™" which has a low emissivity coating on the baffles. When the baffles are in the closed position, they act as low-emissivity thermal shutters, reflecting infrared radiation and providing an overall R-value of R-4.35.

Air-Curtain Windows An air-curtain window is actually a type of air-to-glass heat exchanger. There are several types of designs and configurations, but all work on

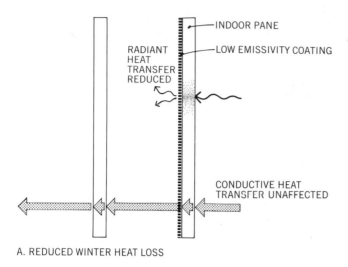

A. REDUCED WINTER HEAT LOSS

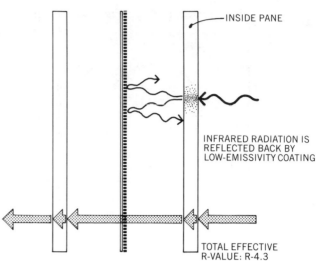

Figure 10.7 Triple-glazed window with low-emissivity plastic film as central glazing. The low-emissivity coating reflects long-wave infrared radiation from the inner pane.

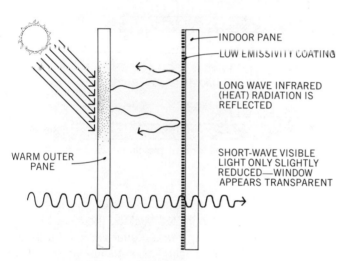

B. REDUCED SUMMER HEAT GAIN

Figure 10.6 Coated "low-E" glass increases the thermal resistance of the window by reducing radiation heat transfer.

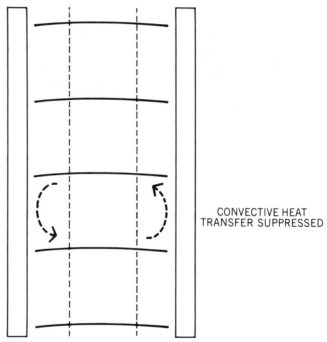

Figure 10.8 Double glazing with interpane baffles. Theoretically, the baffles increase the thermal resistance of the window by suppressing convective heat transfer.

the principle of using room exhaust air to intercept heat loss through the window. In Figure 10.9, house exhaust air is passed between the two inner panes of a triple glazed unit. Since the exhaust air is the same temperature as room air, no heat is lost across the inner pane and the inner glass is therefore kept warm. The exhaust air loses heat to the two outer panes before being vented to the outdoors. A complicated and expensive system, the air-curtain window is practical only for commercial applications at this time. One manufacturer, Ekono, has several air-curtain window installations in commercial buildings and schools in the United States.

Window Frames Window frames are typically made of wood, solid metal, or metal with thermal breaks. Wood and thermally broken metal frames have overall R-values ranging from about R-2.0 to R-4.0. Solid metal frames, particularly those made of aluminum, have extremely low

R-values and should never be used in an energy-efficient house.

Published R-values for manufactured windows are usually an average of glass and frame areas, calculated according to guidelines set forth by ASHRAE. The ASHRAE guidelines provide only a rough approximation based on a set of assumptions about frame R-value and relative areas of glass and frame. Between 1977 and 1981, ASHRAE changed those guidelines, causing some manufacturers to alter the rated R-values of their win-

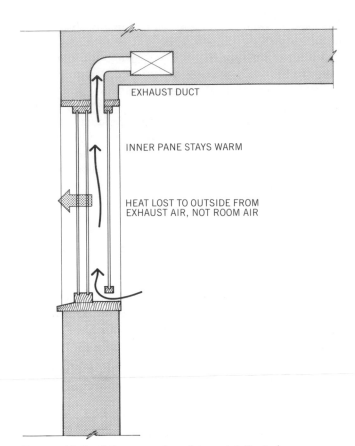

EXHAUST DUCT

INNER PANE STAYS WARM

HEAT LOST TO OUTSIDE FROM EXHAUST AIR, NOT ROOM AIR

Figure 10.9 Schematic of an "air curtain" window.

dows. The discrepancies are usually very small, usually plus or minus R-0.2. Table 10.1 lists the most recent ASHRAE guidelines for determining the R-values of window units with various frame types.

Movable Insulation Although typically not an integral part of the window proper, movable insulation is an obvious way to increase the R-value of a window system.

Window insulation can be installed on the exterior, interior, or between the panes of a window system. The most common placement is inside the window; scores of commercially produced interior thermal shutters and shades are available. A potential problem with interior window insulation is that the glass, being outside the insu-

lation, is cold and subject to condensation. Unless the insulation makes a tight seal with the window frame, interior air may leak around the insulation, and condensation may form on the glass. In extremely cold climates, another problem is thermal shock. When window shutters are opened after a very cold night, warm room air hitting the cold glass can actually cause crackage. Another problem occurs when the shutters are left shut: solar energy input can heat the air between the exterior glass and shutter to the point where the glass may crack.

Between-the-panes systems are less common. One product, the Pella Slimshade, was mentioned above. Another system called "Beadwall," manufactured by Zomeworks, Inc. uses tiny polystyrene beads that are blown between two widely spaced panes of glass. While attractive, Beadwall is costly and has practical problems which have precluded its widespread acceptance.

External shutters are an attractive option because the window glass, being on the inside of the insulation, stays warm. Another side-benefit is security. The difficulties with external shutters are making them weatherproof and providing a mechanism for operating them from the inside. One good external window insulation system was recently developed by the Syracuse Research Foundation, but it has not yet been put into commercial production.

Effect of R-Value on Interior Glass Surface Temperature Interior glass surface temperature is drastically affected by window R-value. Notice in Figure 10.10 that when the outdoor temperature is 0°F, the indoor surface of an R-1.0 window is 22°F. By comparison, an R-4.0 window under the same conditions has an indoor surface temperature of about 58°F. (The values in the figure are based on an indoor air temperature of 70°F.) Glass surface temperature is important with respect to comfort, moisture condensation, and the design of the heat distribution system.

Comfort Nobody likes to sit next to cold glass. Radiant-heat loss and drafts created by cold glass have an obvious and significant effect on thermal comfort. The extent of the chilling effect depends on window size as well as R-value.

TABLE 10.1 R-Values for Windows With Various Frame Types

Frame Type	Single Glass	Glazing System Double Glass (0.5-inch air space)	Triple Glass (0.5-inch air space)
All Glass	0.91	2.04	3.20
Wood frame	1.00–1.07	2.04–2.28	3.20–3.40
Metal frame	0.83–0.91	1.57–1.70	2.15–2.48
Thermally broken metal frame	0.91–1.01	1.77–2.15	2.58–3.20

Source: *ASHRAE Handbook of Fundamentals, 1981.*

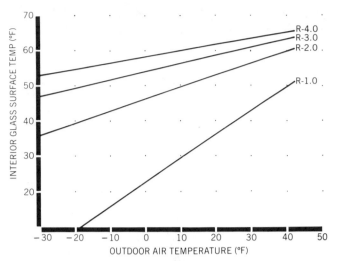

Figure 10.10 Interior glass surface temperature vs. outdoor air temperature for windows of different R-values (70°F indoor air temperature).

Moisture Condensation   The most noticeable effect of cold windows is moisture condensation on the glass. Condensation occurrence depends on the temperature of the interior surface of the glass and on the relative humidity of the room air. Figure 10.11 shows a method for determining at what indoor and outdoor temperatures, and at what indoor relative humidity, condensation will occur on windows of various R-values. It can serve as a useful design tool for selecting window R-values to avoid condensation.

Example 1.   At what indoor relative humidity will condensation occur on a window with an R-value of R-2.0 when the indoor temperature is 70°F and the outdoor temperature is 0°F.

In Figure 10.11, find 70°F on the bottom of the right-hand chart. Proceed vertically to the intersection of the sloped line marked $t_0 = 0°F$ ("t_0" is outdoor temperature). Proceed horizontally to the left-hand chart to the intersection of the sloped line marked R-2.0. Descend vertically and read 42 percent R.H. at bottom.

Under these temperature conditions, this window will have condensation whenever the indoor relative humidity is 42 percent or more.

Example 2.   Assuming that the indoor relative humidity is 40 percent, what R-value windows are necessary to prevent condensation in an area where the winter design temperature is −10°F?

Using the charts in Figure 10.11, find 70°F on the bottom of the right-hand chart, proceed vertically to the $t_0 = -10°F$ curve. Proceed horizontally to the left-hand chart to the intersection of the vertical line at 40 percent relative humidity. The necessary R-value is about R-2.25.

In airtight houses with controlled ventilation, indoor relative humidity is usually easily controllable. Most health guidelines place optimum winter humidity between 30 and 40 percent. When selecting R-values, one should assume approximately 40 percent humidity and select the appropriate R-value according to the graph in Figure 10.11.

In spaces with high indoor relative humidity, such as kitchens, bathrooms, and especially recreation areas with a hot tub or pool, higher R-values are necessary to prevent condensation. In very humid spaces, even the most efficient windows may still have condensation. In those cases, air circulation is the only way to keep windows dry. When air moves over the inner panes of glass, the R-value of the air layer on the window is reduced, so that the temperature of the glass surface becomes closer to that of the room air. Avoiding condensation by increasing air movement does not save energy; in fact, it wastes energy by decreasing window R-value. But if R-value alone cannot prevent condensation, then air circulation is recommended. Another recommendation, developed by Swedish researchers, is to avoid the recessed glass common in thick-walled superinsulated houses (Figure 10.12) because it is less exposed to natural room air currents which help keep glass defrosted.

The Effect of Window Temperature on Heat-Distribution-System Design   Windows with low heat loss can affect the design of a house's heat distribution system. In conventional houses, baseboards or heat-supply registers are often located under windows to counteract the chilling effect of drafts and radiant heat loss to window glass. But if the walls and windows are not extremely cold, perimeter heaters—or "draft heaters," as they are sometimes called—are not necessary; heat distribution can be accomplished from a central core. For example, a dropped ceiling in a central hallway can be used as a supply plenum for all the perimeter rooms of the house. Heat distribution in superinsulated houses is further discussed in Chapter 12.

Airtightness

Options   Windows are rated for air leakage in terms of cubic feet of air leakage per minute per lineal foot of crack between movable sash and window frame, under standard test pressures (equivalent to about a 25 mph wind). The industry standard is 0.50 cfm per foot, but most manufactured windows today have leakage rates well below that. Windows with compression seals, for instance, casements and awnings, typically have the lowest leakage rates. Those with sliding seals, such as double-hung windows or horizontal sliders, usually have considerably higher leakage. For example, Pella lists a leakage rate of only 0.03 cfm per foot of crack for their casement window, but 0.15 cfm per foot of crack for their double-hung window. Double-hung windows have the further disadvantage of more crack length per unit area of

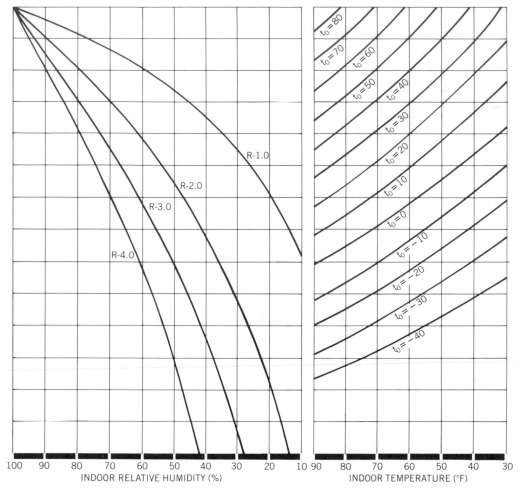

Figure 10.11 Window condensation chart (*see text for explanation*).

glass because of the central joint where the two sashes meet. Figure 10.13 shows laboratory-tested leakage rates for several common types of windows.

Selection   Obviously, from an energy standpoint, windows with the lowest air leakage rate are the most desirable. Architectural aesthetics notwithstanding, casement windows are the best choice. As for selecting between brands, manufacturers' catalogs usually list air-leakage rates for their products. In some cases, listed rates are the "best case" for the tightest unit measured; in others, an average value is used. Common judgment and reliable references are sometimes the most helpful input.

Solar Transmission Properties

Proper selection of glazing systems for solar control depends on climate and house orientation. In northern climates, west-facing windows may be candidates for sun control, but south- and east-facing glass should be clear to allow maximum solar gain. In warm southern climates, on the other hand, some type of sun control should be considered for north-, east-, and west-facing windows to

reduce the cooling load. (South-facing windows are less of a problem in southern latitudes because the summer sun is high enough to be easily shaded by moderate-sized overhangs.)

Of the total solar radiation reaching the earth's surface, approximately 3 percent is ultraviolet (UV), 44 percent is visible, and 53 percent is infrared. Different glazing types selectively transmit, absorb, and reflect each component of the solar spectrum, resulting in varying overall light and heat transmission characteristics. Manufacturers' specifications list several properties of glazing systems that are useful for characterizing their effectiveness for controlling heat gain and light transmission. The most useful specifications are *total solar transmittance, shading coefficient,* and *visible light transmittance.*

Total solar transmittance is the percent of total incident solar energy—ultraviolet, visible, and infrared—that passes through a glazing system when the incident light is perpendicular to the glass surface. Double-strength sheet glass has a total solar transmittance of 86 percent. Of the rest of the incident solar radiation, about 8 percent is reflected, and 6 percent is absorbed (Figure 10.14). The

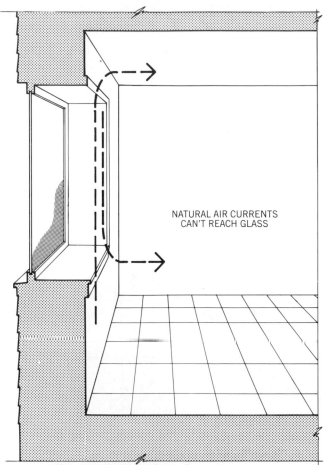

Figure 10.12 Recessed windows are more prone to condensation because indoor air currents are less able to defrost the glass.

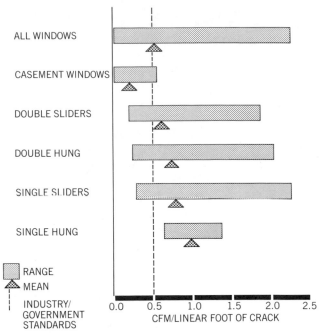

Figure 10.13 Comparative leakage rates of several common window types. Casement windows are not only the tightest, but also typically show the least variation. (Source: Lawrence Berkeley Laboratory.)

actual transmittance varies with incident angle, but the above values are used as a reference for comparative purposes. Multiple glazings, tinted glass, and reflective coatings all reduce total solar transmittance. For passive solar heating applications, the total solar transmittance is a key characteristic.

Shading coefficient is the ratio of total solar heat gain through a window to the total solar heat gain through a single sheet of double-strength glass under the same set of conditions. Shading coefficients range from 0 to 1. Clear double-strength glass has a shading coefficient of 1.00; double-glazed insulating glass has a shading coefficient of about .84; reflective and heat-absorbing glasses have shading coefficients ranging from .10 to .90.

Shading coefficient is the most useful characteristic for evaluating a window's ability to admit solar radiation. Calculation methods for estimating solar gain through windows use the shading coefficient and the Solar Heat Gain Factors (SHGF) published in the ASHRAE *Handbook of Fundamentals*. SHGF is the amount of solar energy that strikes and penetrates a single sheet of double-strength glass. SHGF varies with latitude and takes

into account both solar intensity and angle of incidence of the sunlight. To estimate the solar heat gain through any particular type of glazing, one multiplies the shading coefficient times the SHGF. The lower the shading coefficient, the less the solar heat gain. The HOTCAN computer program (see Chapter 6) uses the shading coefficient of all windows to calculate the solar contribution to the annual heating load.

Visible light transmittance is the percent of total incident visible light transmitted through a glazing system. Obviously, for providing natural lighting and views of the outdoors, light transmittance is a very important factor.

Options   Solar transmission through windows is selectively controlled through the use of reflective coatings and films, heat-absorbing glass, high-transmittance glass, and movable shading devices.

Reflective Glass and Reflective Films   The most effective glazing system for excluding sunlight is reflective glass or reflective films that are applied to the glass surface. Scores of reflective glass types and hundreds of reflective films are commercially available. Typical shading coefficients range from .10 to .90. Most commonly used on commercial buildings, reflective glazing has not been widely accepted for residential application because of its shiny exterior appearance and limited visible light transmittance. Some newer products, however, specifically targeted for the residential market, provide a reasonably low shading coefficient without high visible reflectivity.

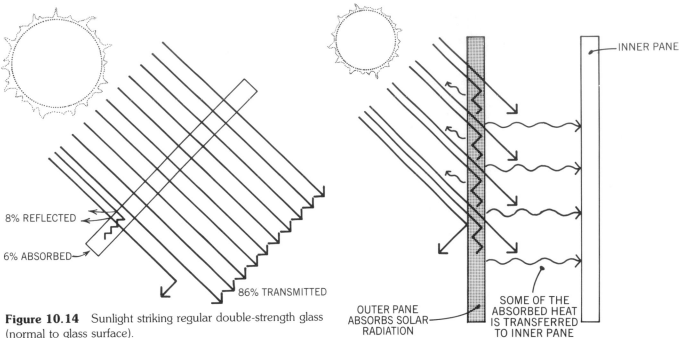

Figure 10.14 Sunlight striking regular double-strength glass (normal to glass surface).

8% REFLECTED

6% ABSORBED

86% TRANSMITTED

INNER PANE

OUTER PANE ABSORBS SOLAR RADIATION

SOME OF THE ABSORBED HEAT IS TRANSFERRED TO INNER PANE

Figure 10.15 Sunlight striking heat-absorbing (tinted) glass.

Reflective coatings reflect not only visible light but also, like the low-E coatings mentioned above, long-wave infrared radiation. Therefore, in addition to excluding solar heat, they create increased winter and summer R-values. Advertisements for reflective glass usually promote the combined merits of decreased winter heat loss as well as reduced summer solar gain; in other words, warmer in winter, cooler in summer. It should be remembered, though, that unlike low-E coatings, reflective glass is noticeable visually because of its shiny appearance.

Heat-Absorbing Glass Heat-absorbing glass is manufactured with special tints that absorb visible and near-infrared light. Available in a variety of colors and having shading coefficients ranging from 0.20 to 0.60, heat-absorbing glass is not as effective as reflective glass for reducing solar gain because the absorbed light warms the glass; absorbed heat is then transferred into the house by conduction and convection (Figure 10.15). For residential applications, however, non-reflective heat-absorbing glass is gaining popularity.

High-Transmittance Glass We have been discussing the selection of glazing to reduce unwanted solar heat gain in order to keep a house cooler. The opposite requirement, maximizing solar gain, is obviously important for south- and/or east-facing windows intended to supply useful solar heat.

Special glasses, sometimes referred to as "water white" or "low iron" (because iron impurities found in regular glass are excluded), have solar transmittance greater than 90 percent for $\frac{1}{8}$-inch thicknesses. Two commercially available products are Solarkleer by General Glass and Solarglass by AFG Industries.

Movable Shading Devices Just as the window R-value can be increased with movable insulation, the window shading coefficient can be decreased with movable interior or exterior shading devices such as blinds, curtains, screens, and awnings (Figure 10.16). Although movable shading devices are not part of the window proper, they may preclude the need for special low-shading coefficient glass to reduce solar load. However, like window insulation, their effectiveness depends on occupant action; if they are not used, they don't work.

Interior Movable Shading Devices Indoor shading devices affect not only the shading coefficient, but also many other factors that contribute to the indoor environment, such as outward vision, privacy, brightness, and sound control. Methods for selecting draperies and other indoor shading devices for sun control are described in detail in the ASHRAE *Handbook of Fundamentals*. When considering interior shading devices, keep in mind that they intercept solar heat only *after* it has penetrated through the glass. Unless the shading device has a reflective outer surface, the solar heat is absorbed and partially fed into the interior space.

Exterior Movable Shading Devices Exterior shading reduces the solar load on windows by intercepting solar radiation *before* it reaches the glass. Types of movable

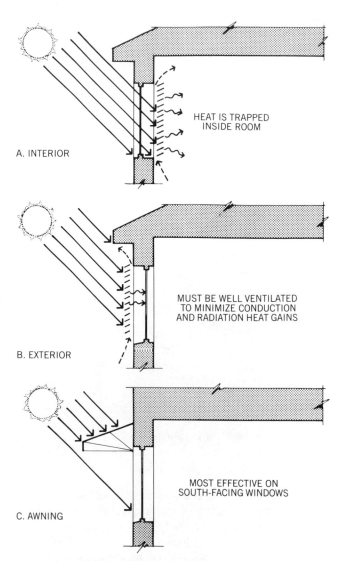

Figure 10.16 Movable shading devices for reducing solar heat gain.

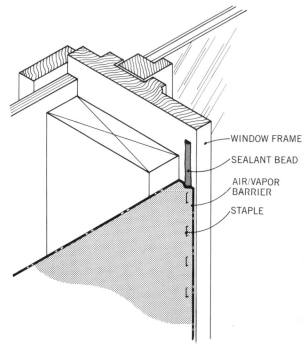

Figure 10.17 Sealing air/vapor barrier to window frame at edge.

exterior shading devices include awnings, insect screening, specially woven fiberglass screening, and sun screens made of miniaturized fixed metal louvers. Perhaps the greatest advantage of such devices is that they work with the window open, reducing solar gain while allowing outdoor air to circulate through the house.

Shade screens are particularly useful because they filter out ground-reflected sun as well as direct solar radiation. The disadvantage of screens, of course, is that they decrease visibility. One interesting product is "Shadescreen" by Kaiser Aluminum. Composed of small angled fixed metal louvers, the shading coefficient of this product changes with sun altitude angle. At 15° solar altitude, the shading coefficient is .72, but decreases to nearly 0 percent at 31° solar altitude.

INSTALLING WINDOWS

The key to proper window installation is the creation of a continuous airtight seal between the window frame and the air/vapor barrier.

Conventionally, the air/vapor barrier is terminated at the rough opening, but this leaves a major channel for air leakage between the rough opening and the window frame (see Figure 10.1). Many builders attempt to seal this area by stuffing in fiberglass insulation. While intuitively this may seem an effective sealing method, *fiberglass insulation is not an air barrier.* Under continuous pressure differential, air will leak through, no matter how tightly the fiberglass is installed.

Caulking is the most common method for sealing the joint between the window frame and rough opening. The best caulking material is expanding urethane caulk, available in small cans or bulk dispensers. The best seal is attained when the crack to be filled is at least 0.5 inch wide; narrower cracks are difficult to seal effectively. In Chapter 7, we recommended oversizing the rough opening by 1 inch to provide sufficient crack width around the window frame for good caulking.

When applied around double-hung or other types of sliding windows, the expanding caulk can actually deform the frame slightly, causing the window to bind. Care should be taken to avoid overfilling cracks.

Another approach is to extend the air/vapor barrier to the edge of the window frame and seal it to the frame as shown in Figure 10.17. If properly done this is a good

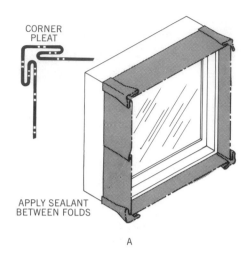

CORNER
PLEAT

APPLY SEALANT
BETWEEN FOLDS

A

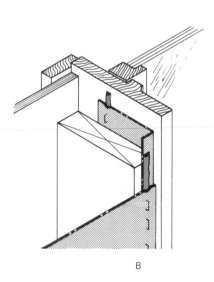

B

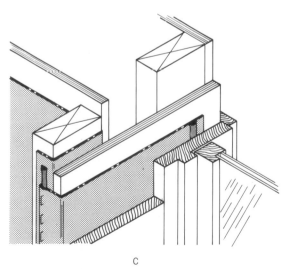

C

Figure 10.18 Installation of window air/vapor barrier. A. Attachment of air/vapor barrier to window prior to window installation. B. Installed window in a single-framed wall, with window air/vapor barrier sealed to wall air/vapor barrier. C. Installed window in a "Saskatchewan"-type double-framed wall, with air/vapor barriers sealed.

Figure 10.19 Installation of air/vapor barrier to window frame prior to window installation. Polyethylene "skirt" is sealed with acoustical caulk and stapled. Notice pleat at corner to allow the air/vapor barrier to spread out when window is installed. (Photo by Howard Faulkner.)

Figure 10.20 Window installed with air/vapor barrier sealed to wall air/vapor barrier using acoustical caulk. (Photo by Harold Orr.)

technique, but there is not much exposed frame to work on.

The best sealing technique involves attaching the air/vapor barrier to the window frame *prior* to window installation. A skirt of polyethylene is caulked and stapled to the window frame with about 6 inches of excess material extending toward the inside (Figure 10.18a). When wrapping the plastic around the frame, the corners are pleated (see inset) so that when the window is installed, the polyethylene skirt can be flared out flat against the wall without having to cut the polyethylene at the corners. After the window is installed, the polyethylene skirt is sealed to the main wall air/vapor barrier. Figures 10.18b and 10.18c show installation in a single and double wall respectively. Although time-consuming, this method—when properly done—provides the best possible seal between window and wall.

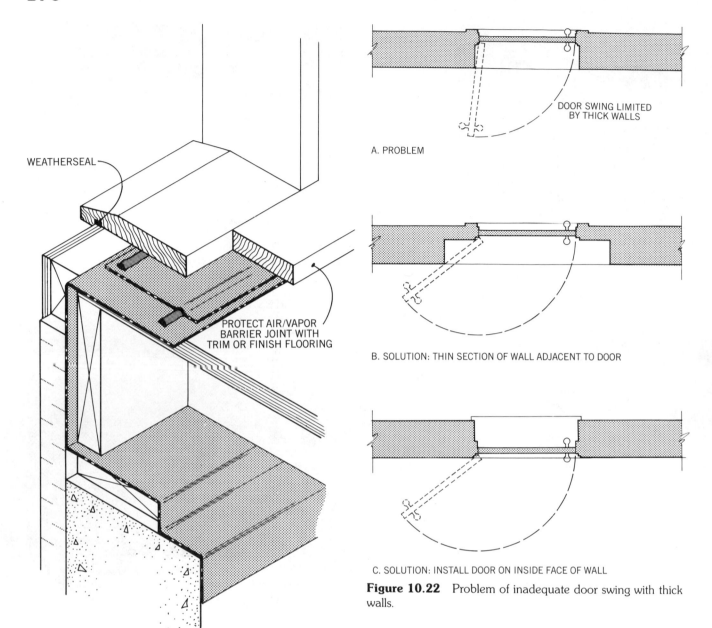

Figure 10.21 Door frame installed showing door air/vapor barrier sealed to floor air/vapor barrier. Door air/vapor barrier is installed using the same technique as for windows (Figure 10.18a).

Figure 10.22 Problem of inadequate door swing with thick walls.

DOORS

Selecting and installing exterior doors in a superinsulated house is very straightforward. The average house has two doors, constituting about 45 square feet of exterior surface and about 40 lineal feet of crack for air leakage.

R-Value

Wood has an R-value of about R-1.25 per inch. Common wooden doors have R-values ranging from about R-1.5 to R-2.5, approximately equal to double-glazed windows. The most important elements affecting the R-value of a door are glass panels, foam cores, and thermal breaks.

Glass Areas Although small decorative glass panels have only a minor impact on the overall R-value of a door they should always be double-glazed to avoid condensation problems. Sliding glass doors, composed of 60 to 80 percent glass, should be treated as windows rather than doors. Obviously, the type of glazing system is crucial with these units.

Foam Cores Several manufacturers produce steel doors with polystyrene or polyurethane foam cores. Often, the R-value is not listed in manufacturers' catalogs, but one can assume that the overall R-value of those doors is between R-5.0 and R-10.0. Because they are steel clad, it is very important that there be a thermal break between the inner and outer skins. Otherwise, interior edges will become cold and will induce moisture condensation.

Airtightness

Weatherstripping is the key to effective door airtightness. It is beyond the scope of this book to describe types of weatherstripping and their relative effectiveness. In general, common sense will be the best guide. A tight-fitting door is easy to recognize without sophisticated laboratory testing.

Installation

Door installation is similar to window installation: a good seal between the door frame and air/vapor barrier is vital. As with windows, the best method entails wrapping the air/vapor barrier around the door frame before the door is installed. Figure 10.21 shows how the plastic skirt is sealed to the air/vapor barrier at the floor.

One final consideration concerning door installation is door swing. When building a house with very thick walls, there may be a problem with opening the door all the way (Figure 10.22a). This problem can be solved either by making the wall thinner for a few feet on either side of the door (Figure 10.22b), or by installing the door flush with the inner wall (Figure 10.22c).

Eleven

The air/vapor barrier

Throughout this book, considerable emphasis has been placed on airtightness. The most important design component of an airtight house is the air/vapor barrier, about which we have already presented many facts, including its salient characteristics and installation details. This chapter discusses materials selection, installation techniques, and a few additional details.

MATERIALS

Polyethylene

Common polyethylene sheeting, the most practical material for air/vapor barriers, is available in a range of thicknesses from 2-mil to 6-mil (a mil is a thousandth of an inch). Although there is no great technical advantage in using one thickness rather than another, the 6-mil thickness is recommended in order to avoid damage during construction.

Not all polyethylene is created equal. Some is made from virgin materials, while some is made from recycled materials. Also, there are two broad chemical categories of polyethylene, low density and high density, the difference being in the molecular branching structure. Most manufacturers dope their products with special antioxidants and inhibitors to decrease sensitivity to ultraviolet radiation from the sun and to provide longer durability. Since durability of the air/vapor barrier is very important for lasting energy efficiency, one should try to use high-density polyethylene with adequate additives. Unfortunately, when buying common sheeting at a building-supply store, there is no way to know just what one is getting. Many products claim to have ultraviolet inhibitors, but without further specification, that claim has little meaning. Some specialty products, such as Monsanto 602, that are specially produced for extensive outdoor exposure, can be expected to be more durable than commonly available sheeting.

The best material for air/vapor barriers is a special type of polyethylene sheeting known as "cross-laminated" polyethylene. Although chemically the same as regular polyethylene, cross-laminated sheeting is much stronger. Cross-laminated polyethylene, 3-mil thick, is more than three times as strong as 6-mil regular polyethylene. A unique process of extrusion and lamination is used to produce the super strength of this product. Extruded polyethylene sheets are stretched, producing a molecular alignment or "grain" in the material. Two stretched sheets are then laminated together with the "grain" at right angles. This cross grain imparts strength to the laminate just as the cross grain of wood imparts strength to plywood. Although it costs slightly more than regular polyethylene, cross-laminated polyethylene is far superior: it is not only stronger, but also easier to work with. Because a 3-mil thickness is sufficiently strong, thicker material is not necessary. The most commonly available cross-laminated polyethylene is a product called Tu-Tuf™ by Sto-Cote Products (see Appendix D).

Sealants

To seal the air/vapor barrier at seams and at termination points, one should use a nonhardening sealant. Regular caulk, such as latex or oil-based products, harden over time and may lose their sealing capabilities. Canadian builders have had good success with acoustical sealant, particularly the Tremco™ brand, although any sealant made to seal polyethylene and able to retain its adhesion and flexibility should be suitable for sealing air/vapor barriers.

INSTALLATION

The following general guidelines are adapted form *Air Vapour Barriers* by Eyre and Jennings:

1. The air/vapor barrier should be installed in such a way that it provides a completely sealed envelope, except at doors, vents, and other intentional openings.

2. All joints between two sheets of polyethylene should be made against a solid wood backing. A continuous bead of caulking material should be run along the joint between the two sheets (Figure 11.1). The two sheets should then be pressed lightly together along the line of the caulk, and the joint should be strengthened with staples driven into the wood backing and along the line of the caulk (Figure 11.2). Caulk should not be treated as an adhesive; it cannot be relied upon to hold two sheets of polyethylene together without the support of staples.

3. At the joint between two large sheets of polyethylene, the two sheets should be overlapped by at least one stud space or one truss space.

4. Joints should be stapled at intervals of about 6 inches. If the polyethylene sheet is very wrinkled at the joint, an extra amount of caulking material and a closer spacing of staples will be necessary.

5. When installing a sheet of polyethylene at an inside corner, at least 2 inches of spare material should be allowed to prevent tight pulling at the corner and damage during the subsequent installation of gypsum board.

6. Generally speaking, it is better to use too much caulking material and polyethylene sheet than too little.

7. The polyethylene sheet should be protected wherever it is likely to be damaged during construction. For example, Figure 11.3 shows an air/vapor barrier protected with a strip of tar paper to prevent damage when the floor joists are slid over the walls and into place. Another example occurs when a loose strip of polyethylene is left at the foot of the walls, ready to be joined later to the wall air/vapor barrier. A temporary protective strip of material should be laid on top of this exposed barrier, particularly at exterior doors.

8. When the air/vapor barrier installation is complete, and before it is covered by other work, it should be carefully inspected for damage or poor joints. Small holes in the barrier can be repaired with polyethylene or foil tape; large holes or rips can be repaired with a generous-sized patch of polyethylene, caulked to give a thoroughly sealed joint (Figure 11.4). Wherever possible, patches should be made large enough to cover the damage and overlap any wood frame nearby so that the seal can be strengthened with staples.

Figure 11.1 Air/vapor barrier seam being sealed with continuous bead of acoustical caulk. (Photo by Harold Orr.)

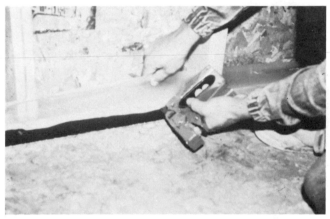

Figure 11.2 Floor air/vapor barrier being stapled in place after being sealed with acoustical caulk. (Photo by Harold Orr.)

Figure 11.3 Air/vapor barrier protected with a strip of tar paper to prevent damage during joist installation. (Photo by Harold Orr.)

Figure 11.4 Tears or holes in the air/vapor barrier are repaired with a polyethylene patch, which is sealed with acoustical caulk. (Photo by Harold Orr.)

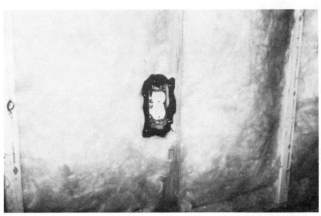

Figure 11.6 Plastic "poly-box" shown sealed to wall air/vapor barrier with acoustical caulk. (Photo by Harold Orr.)

Figure 11.5 Plastic "poly-box" installed with electrical outlet box. Wiring penetrations through the box are sealed with caulk. The air/vapor barrier will be sealed to the flange around the plastic box. (Photo by Harold Orr.)

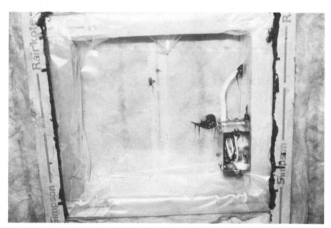

Figure 11.7 Site-built boxes lined with polyethylene for installing electrical boxes. Notice that all wiring penetrations are sealed with acoustical caulk. (Photo by Harold Faulkner.)

SPECIAL DETAILS

Electrical Receptacles in Exterior Walls

If the air/vapor-barrier is located on the inner surface of the wall directly behind the gypsum board (not embedded deep in the wall as with the Saskatchewan double wall), some method must be used to seal it to each electrical box. The recommended technique is to use one of several commercially available plastic "poly-boxes" (see Appendix D); such boxes fit around the electrical box and have a flange for sealing the air/vapor-barrier (Figures 11.5 and 11.6).

Some Canadian builders have used site-built versions of the plastic air/vapor barrier boxes. Wooden boxes are prefabricated with framing lumber and sheathed on one side with polyethylene (Figure 11.7). The boxes are installed between the studs prior to installation of the elec-

trical hardware. After wiring is installed and sealed at the holes, the cavity within the box is filled with insulation.

The "Tuck-Under" Garage

Figure 11.8 shows the problem of maintaining air/vapor barrier continuity around an attached or "tuck-under" garage. The joists create a break in the barrier. If insulation is installed in the garage ceiling, the air/vapor barrier must be placed on top of the floor. But how do you make an airtight seal across the joists? Figure 11.9 shows one recommended solution: the space between the floor joists is bridged with foil-faced rigid insulation of low permeability. The perimeter of each piece of insulation is then caulked at the joists, floor, and wall bottom plate. Although tedious and time-consuming, this technique is a

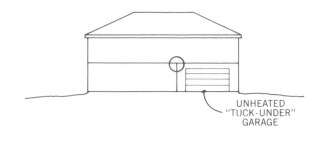

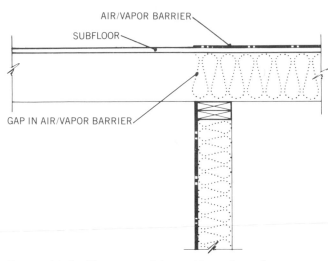

Figure 11.8 Illustration of the problem of installing a continuous air/vapor barrier with a "tuck-under" garage. The problem is how to span the air/vapor barrier across floor joists.

necessary compromise for attached garages. An alternative and slightly easier to use material is polyethylene foam. (See Appendix D for one available product.)

Overhangs

Like tuck-under garages, overhangs create a problem (Figure 11.10) in which floor joists interrupt air/vapor barrier continuity between floors. A tempting solution is to run the air/vapor barrier around and under the joist system. This is not an acceptable practice because the air/vapor barrier will be *outside* the insulation and will likely cause moisture condensation problems. The recommended practice is the same as for tuck-under garages. Each joist cavity is sealed to the floor above and to the wall below using rigid foam and caulking.

Split-Level Ceilings

The problem with split-level ceilings is to bridge the air/vapor barrier gap through the stud wall, as shown in Figure 11.11. Four strategies recommended by Eyre and Jennings are shown in Figure 11.12.

In Figure 11.12a, the gap is bridged with sealed wood blocking. Although effective, this is a tedious technique. Figure 11.12b shows a good solution with minimal extra work: the air/vapor barrier is run under and around the exterior wall. Figure 11.12c shows a solution whereby the stud wall is broken into two pony walls. Although this design provides a good air seal, it is expensive and could

Figure 11.9 Method for forming an airtight seal between floor joists using rigid foam insulation panels sealed at the edges with acoustical caulk. (Photo by Howard Faulkner.)

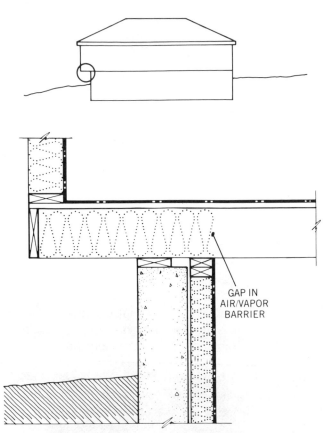

Figure 11.10 Illustration of the problem of air/vapor installation with overhangs where joists interrupt air/vapor continuity between floors.

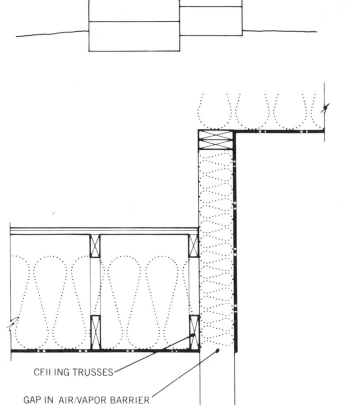

Figure 11.11 Illustration of the problem of maintaining air/vapor continuity through the stud wall in a split-level design.

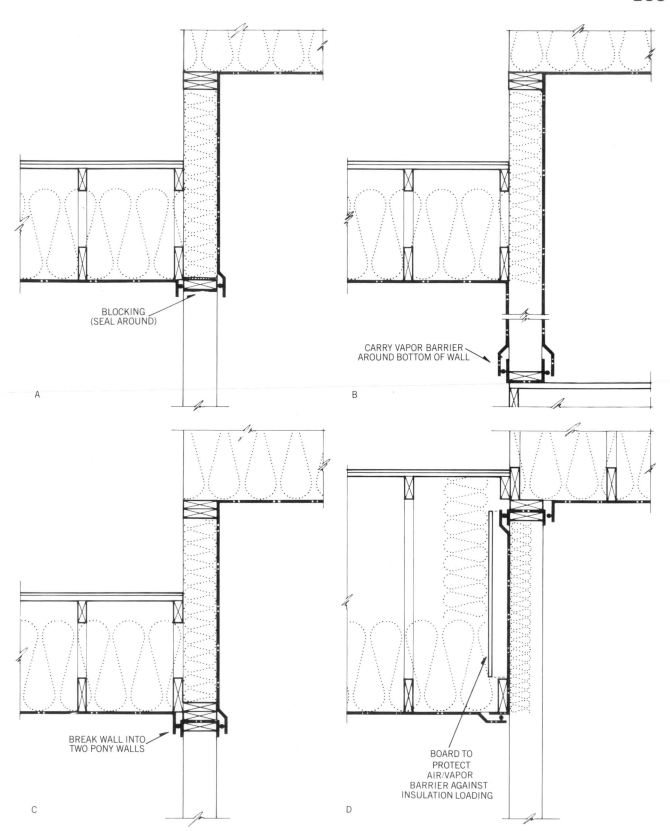

Figure 11.12 Four possible solutions to the problem of air/vapor barrier continuity through stud walls in split-level houses. A. Install and seal wood blocking in stud cavity. B. Carry air/vapor barrier around bottom of wall. C. Break wall into two pony walls. D. Install air/vapor barrier over and down the outer surface of stud wall.

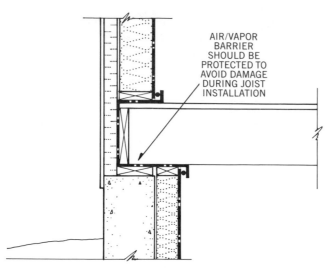

AIR/VAPOR
BARRIER
SHOULD BE
PROTECTED TO
AVOID DAMAGE
DURING JOIST
INSTALLATION

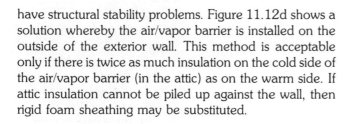

Figure 11.13 Air/vapor barrier installed on top of sill plate to prevent contact with cold foundation wall.

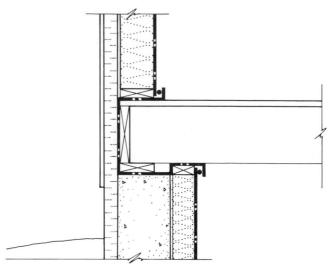

Figure 11.14 Air/vapor barrier installed under sill plate. This is an acceptable practice with exterior foundation insulation because the foundation wall will not be cold.

have structural stability problems. Figure 11.12d shows a solution whereby the air/vapor barrier is installed on the outside of the exterior wall. This method is acceptable only if there is twice as much insulation on the cold side of the air/vapor barrier (in the attic) as on the warm side. If attic insulation cannot be piled up against the wall, then rigid foam sheathing may be substituted.

The Sill Plate Problem

When installing the air/vapor barrier around joist headers, cold spots must be avoided. In Figure 11.13, the air/vapor barrier is put over the sill plate to keep it away from the cold foundation wall. When exterior foam sheathing is run over the foundation wall, the sill plate is insulated and the vapor barrier can be installed as in Figure 11.14.

Twelve

Ventilation and heating

In conventional houses, the size and performance of the heating system is important and is often carefully determined; the ventilation system however, is left to chance. In superinsulated houses, the situation is reversed in that the role of the heating system is less important, but the ventilation system must be carefully designed.

In this chapter we discuss ventilation systems first, then heating systems. The two are mutually dependent and interact in many ways.

DESIGN OF VENTILATION SYSTEMS

In a superinsulated house, the ventilation system must work independently of weather conditions. It must be intentional and controllable. It must use as little energy as possible, but provide adequate ventilation. And it must provide ventilation consistently to all parts of the house.

How much ventilation is adequate? In Chapter 4, we used the ASHRAE ventilation guideline to recommend a house ventilation rate of 0.3 to 0.4 air changes per hour. For a 2000-square-foot house with 8-foot ceilings, the ventilation requirement amounts to an air inflow rate of 4800 to 6400 cubic feet per hour, or 80 to 107 cfm. Ventilation fans should be capable of providing this rate of air flow, and may optionally have settings to provide much higher flow when needed. Significant additional amounts of air flow may be necessary if there are furnaces, woodstoves, or other combustion devices drawing air from the house interior. We discuss these air requirements later in this chapter in connection with choice of heating system.

The components of a ventilation system for a superinsulated house must be purchased and designed to provide the necessary level of air exchange.

There are two basic types of systems that best supply adequate ventilation for superinsulated houses. The first—*supply-and-exhaust system*—consists of two fans, an intake and an exhaust. The fans are connected to ducts, through which they exhaust stale air from the house and take fresh air into the house. With this type of system, the intake and exhaust air flows must be balanced. The fans are usually located in the house mechanical room with the furnace, hot water heater, and other appliances.

This system can supply adequate ventilation. But there is another consideration when ventilating superinsulated houses—heat recovery. Since the exhaust air carries heat energy to the outside, it is important to consider how this energy may be captured and returned to the house. This can be accomplished with an air-to-air heat exchanger. At the time of this writing, the easiest and most common way to install a supply-and-exhaust ventilation system is to use an air-to-air heat exchanger, which integrates many of the system's components into a single, ready-to-use package. Many air-to-air heat exchangers come equipped with an intake fan, exhaust fan, and all necessary controls. Therefore, in addition to allowing heat recovery, an air-to-air heat exchanger saves builders the unfamiliar task of putting together a supply-and-exhaust system from scratch. Note, however, that properly designed supply and return ducts are necessary to complete any ventilation system (Figure 12.1).

The second basic type of system appropriate to superinsulated houses is *exhaust-only ventilation*. To understand this system, think of a conventional bathroom or kitchen fan that exhausts stale air from the house. Air blowing out creates a negative pressure, which sucks in fresh air; if the house is conventionally built, incoming air can enter through all sorts of unintentional leakage sites. The concept of exhaust-only systems is basically the same for superinsulated houses: one fan exhausts air to the outside, creating a negative pressure. But there's one important difference. Superinsulated houses are airtight,

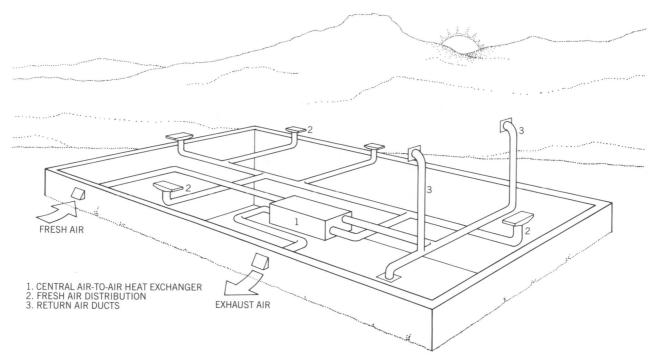

FRESH AIR

1. CENTRAL AIR-TO-AIR HEAT EXCHANGER
2. FRESH AIR DISTRIBUTION
3. RETURN AIR DUCTS

EXHAUST AIR

Figure 12.1 A fully ducted central air-to-air heat exchanger system. This is the most effective type of design for distributing air to and taking air from all parts of the house. (Source: National Center for Appropriate Technology, Butte, Montana.)

so there should be no haphazard leaks. Therefore, when designing this system for a superinsulated house, it is necessary to install special adjustable intake ports (usually above windows) through which fresh air is passively (as opposed to mechanically) drawn in by the negative pressure created by the fan. This type of system has been widely used in Sweden, but is still new in the United States. Heat recovery is possible, but depends on a device—the exhaust-air heat pump—not readily available in this country at the time of this writing.

No matter what kind of system is used, it must supply adequate ventilation to *each* room of the house. We emphasize this because it isn't enough to ventilate some rooms carefully while assuming other rooms will get fresh air indirectly; inside doors, often closed, may prevent this.

Supply-and-Exhaust Ventilation: The Air-to-Air Heat Exchanger

Air-to-air heat exchangers are devices that recover heat from the exhaust air stream and transfer it to the incoming air stream. They consist of an intake fan, exhaust fan, and central core where the heat exchange takes place, all housed in a single box. Air-to-air heat exchangers fall into two categories: wall/window-mounted or central. Central air-to-air heat exchangers (very much like central air conditioning) are usually located in the basement and connected to various rooms through ducts. Wall or window

heat exchangers, on the other hand (like wall-mounted air conditioners), are individual units directly installed in the wall or window and operating without ducts (Figure 12.2). We recommend the central heat exchanger system because it can be connected to a duct system providing fresh air directly to the rooms where it's needed and exhausting stale air from appropriate locations.

Heat Exchanger Core Types There are six types of exchanger cores available on the market: *Flat-plate*

Figure 12.2 A wall-mounted air-to-air heat exchanger. This type of installation is less effective than a fully ducted central system (Figure 12.1).

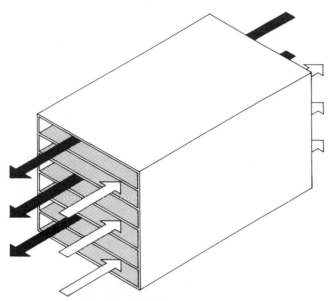

Figure 12.3 Flat plate counterflow heat-exchanger core. (Source: *Air-to-air Heat Exchangers*, National Center for Appropriate Technology.)

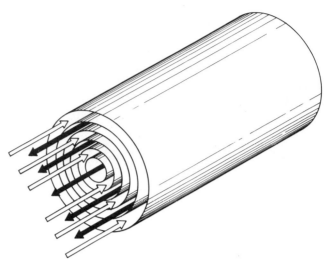

Figure 12.5 Concentric-tube counterflow heat-exchanger core. (Source: *Air-to-air Heat Exchangers*, National Center for Appropriate Technology.)

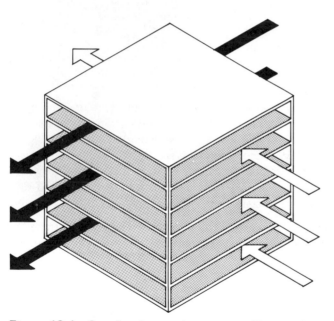

Figure 12.4 Crossflow heat-exchanger core. (Source: *Air-to-air Heat Exchangers*, National Center for Appropriate Technology.)

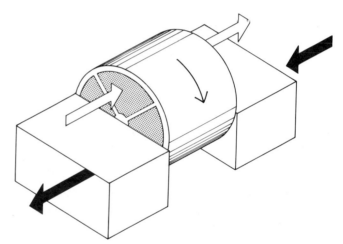

Figure 12.6 Rotary heat-exchanger core. (Source: *Air-to-air Heat Exchangers*, National Center for Appropriate Technology.)

counterflow cores are theoretically the most efficient because they allow the two air streams to run in opposite directions, a situation that makes for the best temperature profile for heat transfer between the two air streams (Figure 12.3).

In *parallel-flow* cores, where the two air streams run in the *same* direction, the maximum heat recovery efficiency is limited to 50 percent by the laws of thermodynamics.

Crossflow cores tend to be somewhat less efficient than counterflow cores because the air streams move in perpendicular directions to each other, as shown in Figure 12.4. A larger core can help improve the efficiency of this type.

Concentric-tube counterflow cores offer efficiencies similar to those of flat-plate counterflow cores, but are more difficult to manufacture and can be more expensive (Figure 12.5).

Rotary cores have been used for years in commercial or industrial applications. This type of core actually rotates between the cold and warm air streams. Rotary machines allow moisture to transfer between the two air streams (Figure 12.6).

Heat-pipe cores employ permanently sealed pipes (or

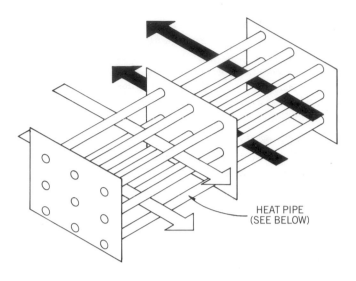

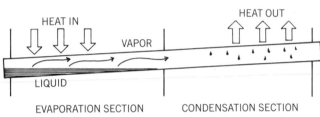

Figure 12.7 Heat-pipe heat-exchanger core. (Source: *Air-to-air Heat Exchangers,* National Center for Appropriate Technology.)

tubes) that contain a refrigerant. When one end of the tube is heated, the refrigerant vaporizes and travels to the other end of the tube, where cooling causes it to condense and flow back to the other end. The heat pipe operates through a condensation-evaporation cycle that is continuous as long as the temperature differences are sufficient to drive the process (Figure 12.7). Effectiveness depends on the number of rows of heat pipe; operation depends on installation at the proper angle. Heat-pipe heat exchangers have been suitably developed for industrial use and hold great promise for small-scale residential use. However, few manufacturers are employing this technology in the residential market.

Selecting an Air-to-Air Heat Exchanger In choosing an air-to-air heat exchanger, a prospective buyer must first determine its capacity. The capacity or the air flow rate through the unit is expressed in cubic feet per minute (cfm). The capacity depends on fan speed and the resistance to air flow in the house. Resistance can be internal, occurring in the heat exchanger core itself, or external, taking place in the ductwork that brings air to and from the heat exchanger.

Some heat exchangers have variable-speed fans that permit lower or higher capacities. At low speed, more

heat can be exchanged. At high speed, more ventilation is possible. It may, therefore, be advantageous to use an oversized multispeed heat exchanger that can recover more heat at low speeds *and* meet greater ventilation requirements at high speed. Don't choose, however, an exchanger with considerable over-capacity just to meet the occasional needs for high ventilation. For those short periods, one can always open a couple of windows.

Central air-to-air heat exchangers range in capacity from about 120 to 350 cubic feet per minute, although larger sizes are also available.

Air-to-air heat exchangers may also differ widely in *recovery efficiency* or just *efficiency*: when efficiency is higher, more heat is recovered from exhaust air and transferred to incoming air. Efficiency depends largely on the heat exchanger core. Three factors influence the efficiency of heat exchanger cores: the size of the surface area for heat transfer; the direction of air flow; and the speed at which the air moves. The greater the surface area, the greater the amount of heat that can transfer through the core to the fresh air stream. The direction in which the two air streams are moving influences temperature profiles in the various ways mentioned above in the discussion of types of exchanger cores. It should be noted that the *faster* the air is moving, however, the *lower* the efficiency. Therefore, when more ventilation is needed through a particular heat exchanger core, there is a price in lost heat recovery.

Another feature that influences efficiency is humidity-exchange capacity. Does the core allow moisture passage from the warm outgoing air to the cold incoming air? Some cores are made of specially treated paper that allows this moisture transfer to occur. Called "enthalpy" models, these heat exchangers can transfer more heat because in addition to the sensible heat transfer, they also allow latent heat transfer, that is, heat transfer through moisture transfer. Note, however, that non-enthalpy units also capture some of this latent heat during the months when water vapor in the outgoing air condenses in the core.

However, airtight houses generally retain more moisture than conventional houses do; one of the main jobs of the heat exchanger in superinsulated houses is therefore to *remove* excess moisture from the inside air. Enthalpy units may indeed be suited for warm-weather applications where high outdoor humidity is a problem. The warm, moist outdoor air passes some of its moisture, as well as part of its heat, to the outgoing, cooler exhaust air stream, thus lowering relative humidity in the house during summer. Unfortunately, you must choose between enthalpy and non-enthalpy units when selecting a machine. It is probably best to avoid the enthalpy units in cold-climate settings.

Another issue raised about heat exchangers is whether they may transfer air contaminants from the exhaust to the inlet stream. This "cross-contamination" can happen inside the heat exchanger itself (by leakage) or outside (if the inlet and exhaust streams mingle). The latter generally occurs in connection with a wall- or window-mounted unit, but it is possible even in a centralized system where intake and exhaust vents are close together outside.

One final note about efficiency: air-to-air heat exchanger fans use energy to run. One might think that this energy use significantly detracts from the gains from heat recovery. It should be noted, however, that all the power consumed by the fans is converted to heat; depending on the location of the fans relative to the exchanger core, part of this heat goes into the house, contributing to space heating. These heat gains are, however, undesirable during the summer.

Fan Characteristics Heat exchangers employ small fans to drive the two air streams. These fans are usually included with the exchanger and are an important factor in choosing one exchanger over another. When evaluating fans, note the following variables: energy use, noise, and maintenance provisions.

Choose fans that use a minimum of electricity because fans operate continuously for a large part of the year and can use a great deal of electricity. This can be expensive, especially since air-to-air heat exchangers use *two* fans. Several models of air-to-air heat exchangers employ fans that use electricity exceeding 200 watts. One popular model uses 290 watts. If the ventilation system operates for nine months a year (say 6570 hours/year), then the annual energy used by this unit would be 1905 kilowatt-hours per year. At a price of 8¢ per kWh, the annual cost of electricity for that heat exchanger would be $152.

Fortunately, much more efficient fans, which cost only slightly more than the less efficient fans commonly found in house air-moving equipment, can be purchased for air-to-air heat exchangers. Capacitive-start motors combined with certain designs can lead to much lower power consumption with the same rate of air flow. For instance, the vane-axial fans in one popular heat exchanger use only 64 watts. This heat exchanger consumes only 420 kWh and uses only $34 worth of electricity per year. However, when considering fan size, be sure to select a unit that can provide sufficient air flow through the duct system. Complex duct systems may create too much resistance to air flow for the smaller low-power fans.

Since the heat exchanger is intended to operate continuously for long periods, fan noise is an important consideration. Appropriate choice of mounting and ductwork schemes can ensure quiet operation of the machine. Generally, however, heat exchanger fans produce less noise than, say, forced-air furnace fans because the former move much less air.

Some fans are factory-sealed and require no oiling, while others require periodic lubrication. Quality machines employ fans that are expected to last from five to seven years under continuous operation. Some manufacturers sell the heat exchanger core without fans, allowing the consumer to choose the fans best suited to his or her needs. However, this cancels the advantage of buying and installing an integral unit. Another worry with do-it-yourself heat exchangers is cross-contamination from internal leakage.

Defrost Capabilities If the incoming air is cold enough, moisture in the outgoing air can freeze in the core, and ice buildup can eventually block the core. Therefore, heat exchangers should have some provision for defrosting their cores during the coldest winter days.

Note: One can preheat the incoming cold air and thus avoid freezing in the first place. In a superinsulated house, however, this preheating element may actually use more energy than the house's back-up space heating system. In addition, preheating the incoming air could reduce the overall efficiency of the heat recovery function of the heat exchanger.

An automatic defrost system requiring no attention is best. Automatic defrost mechanisms include thermostatically actuated and pressure-sensor types. Thermostatically operated defrosters sense the temperature of the incoming air stream. If the temperature is low enough, the machine will go into the defrost mode, which allows warm, stale exhaust air to run through the machine to melt the ice, while the incoming air stream is cut off temporarily.

Pressure-sensor systems monitor the pressure difference between the two air streams. When pressure increases because of ice buildup, the machine goes into the defrost mode. The incoming fan shuts down temporarily and the warm outgoing air defrosts the core.

A few brands of air-to-air heat exchangers use electric defrost rather than warm air.

Installation of Air-to-Air Heat Exchangers: Choosing a Location The basement is usually an ideal location for the heat exchanger (Figure 12.8) because of the ease of access for ductwork and the proximity to the house sewer for condensation drainage. Also, duct insulation requirements can be most easily met by locating exchangers in basements. To minimize insulation, put the heat exchanger close to the outside wall through which the exhaust duct leaves the house.

In houses without basements, a main-floor mechanical room or utility closet close to an exterior wall is a good choice. Figure 12.9 shows an air-to-air heat exchanger installed in a space behind a kneewall contained *within the thermal envelope*. A crawl space contained within the thermal envelope is also an acceptable location, although less accessible for necessary maintenance.

Although most machines feature insulated housing, it is best to avoid putting heat exchangers in cold locations, that is, outside the thermal envelope, since the condensation drain can freeze or other problems can result. For

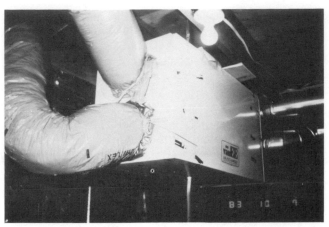

Figure 12.8 Central air-to-air heat exchanger installed in a basement ceiling. (Photo by Brian Curran.)

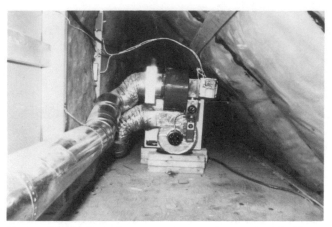

Figure 12.9 Central air-to-air heat exchanger installed in a heated attic. Note the insulation on the roof; the heat exchanger is located within the thermal envelope.

this reason, an attic location is a poor choice; attics may also present problems because ductwork must penetrate the air/vapor barrier more times from attics than from basements or other locations within the thermal envelope.

Many machines are designed to fit between or hang from the floor joists, mounted on straps or hangers. Manufacturers' instructions will indicate whether the machine should be mounted level or sloped to facilitate the drainage of condensation.

If the machine vibrates when used, it should be installed away from the floor. Rubber grommets or bushings can be used to further reduce vibration noise. Manufacturers may be able to provide other strategies for reducing fan or vibration noise.

The condensation drain should be plumbed to a drain with a trap to avoid sewer backflow. With some exchanger models, two traps are advised. Carefully note manufacturers' recommendations in this regard.

Locating Outdoor Intake and Exhaust Vents Intake vents draw in fresh air; exhaust vents expel stale air. To avoid cross-contamination, locate them at least 10 feet apart. To accomplish this, some designers run the exhaust duct out through the roof, a course we do not recommend.

If the south side of the house has an unobstructed southern exposure, air here will be several degrees warmer during the day than air on the other sides of the house. Therefore, it makes sense to locate the intake vents on the south wall whenever possible and practical.

Outside vents should not be buried under snow during winter, and should be well above soil level. *Never locate intake vents where automobile exhaust can enter.* In addition, other outside pollution sources should be considered. Avoid locating intake vents near gas exhaust vents, central vacuum cleaner exhaust ports, or where outdoor

cooking (barbecue) gases could be pulled into the port. Because this intake vent should be checked periodically for obstructions, it should never be located where one can't see it, such as under a closed deck or porch. The opening should be covered with a rain cap and insect screen, or whatever is recommended by the manufacturer.

Locating Indoor Supply and Return Vents The exhaust vents in supply-and-exhaust systems are not located in every room where there's a supply duct, but in specific locations where the most exhaust ventilation is needed: specifically, in bathrooms and the kitchen. Note the following recommendations for bathroom and kitchen exhaust vents.

The kitchen exhaust vent should never be located directly over the stove, as a traditional range hood would be. The air-to-air heat exchanger core is not meant to handle grease, which can also settle in hard-to-reach ductwork and thus create a fire hazard. Instead, the pickup point should be in a central location across the room from the range. A nonvented, filtering range hood might be installed to catch grease close to the source, to make sure that none enters the duct. Also, clothes dryers should never be vented into the duct, since this could unbalance the system, overtax the fans, and block the heat exchanger core with lint.

Sometimes building codes require additional ventilation for kitchens and baths. This task, traditionally done in kitchens with simple exhaust fans, can be taken over in a superinsulated house by the air-to-air heat exchanger which, with fans set on high speed, can provide adequate additional ventilation. Simply install timer switches to operate the heat exchanger at full speed when additional ventilation is needed. Some manufacturers also employ booster fans in the exhaust from the kitchen and bath. Although this temporarily unbalances the ventilation

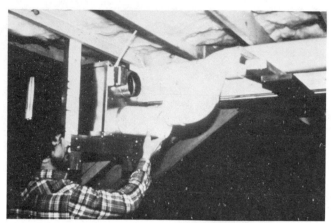

Figure 12.10 Plastic ductwork being installed on a central air-to-air heat exchanger located in a basement ceiling.

system, the short-term drop in efficiency isn't a major problem. One manufacturer uses a system that diverts air flow from little-used areas of the house to the kitchen or bathroom for a short period of time.

Fresh-air supply vents demand the most care and ingenuity in order to avoid extra costs and achieve good air mix, without creating discomforting cold-air drafts. A number of designers recommend placing supply vents high on the walls or in the ceilings to keep cooler air away from the occupants and to facilitate air movement and mixing, phenomena that are also affected by the choice of registers that cover the vents.

Ductwork in General Care should be taken to maximize air flow by choosing ductwork that has as short a run as is reasonable, is large in diameter (6 inches if possible), has few bends and elbows, and is as smooth as possible on the inside.

Many machines are designed with fittings for 6-inch ductwork. Commonly used ductwork can be made of sheet metal, PVC plastic pipe, or flexible plastic ducts (Figure 12.10). Although some local building codes mandate metal ductwork, low-cost plastic sewer pipe is probably the least expensive type of ductwork. Flexible ducts, with their ribbed surfaces, have more internal resistance to air flow, but they are easier to install and may be acceptable if ductwork resistance has been allowed for in system design.

Balancing the Air Flows Once the machine and ductwork are installed, the system's air flows must be balanced. If the incoming and outgoing air flows are not balanced, the house will be subject to positive or negative pressure when the fans are running.

Positive indoor pressure pushes air out through leakage points, which can lead to moisture condensation inside building materials. Negative indoor pressure can cause dangerous backdrafting of combustion flue gases if combustion appliances have not been isolated from the indoor air. On the other hand, negative indoor pressure causes some air to be pulled into the house at the leakage points. This reduces the risk of condensation, and if combustion appliances are absent, a slight negative pressure may be desirable.

Balancing the air flows is usually accomplished with a balancing damper in the intake air duct. Balancing is a two-person operation. It must be done on a day when the winds are calm and indoor and outdoor temperatures are similar. All windows and doors are securely closed, and one window is opened slightly. While the heat exchanger is run at high speed, one person checks air flows at the window and the other stands ready to adjust the balancing damper in the intake duct. Air flow at the window can be detected with a smoke pencil, a burning cigarette, or a length of thread held near the window opening. The balancing damper should be adjusted so that no air flow can be detected into or out of the window.

Balancing incoming and outgoing air flows can also be accomplished with an air-flow meter or hot-wire anemometer.

Summer Condensation Drainage Air-to-air heat exchangers in houses with air conditioners should run whenever the air conditioner is operating and all windows are closed. Take care, however, because some machines have been designed primarily for winter use, and if they are used in hot weather, incoming warm moist air will be cooled by the outgoing air stream and water may condense within the heat exchanger core. In such a case, the incoming air stream will require a condensation drain as well. At least one heat exchanger manufacturer offers a unit with drainage for both air streams.

Controlling the Heat Exchanger The air-to-air heat exchanger must have controls that provide the desired ventilation and also keep the heat exchanger core from freezing.

We recommend that the heat exchanger be operated continuously except when the windows and doors are left open for extended periods of time, such as in the spring and fall (and the summer in cold climates). If the house is not occupied for two or more days, the unit may be turned off. It should not be turned off, however, if the house is frequently unoccupied for shorter periods because indoor pollutant concentration can build up. After a prolonged period of being off, the unit should be run for a short time at high speed to flush out the buildup of pollutants.

If continuous operation is not desired, the exchanger can be turned on and off by timers that activate the unit for certain time periods or whenever indoor relative humidity reaches a certain point.

A certain amount of intermittent operation is necessary during the defrosting of the heat exchanger core. A well-designed heat exchanger provides this control automatically.

Exhaust-Only Ventilation

This is the alternative ventilation system for superinsulated houses. One fan—exhaust—draws stale air out of the house. Although the exhaust air leaves the house at one place, fresh air enters at many selected locations; therefore, it isn't practical to use an air-to-air heat exchanger.

Exhaust-only ventilation makes greater sense in houses located in mild climates where the cost of installing an air-to-air heat exchanger may be hard to justify in terms of potential energy savings.

Fans should be chosen for this system according to the same criteria discussed for supply-and-exhaust systems. Compared to ductwork for supply-and-exhaust, ductwork for exhaust-only is simple. Supply air ducts are unnecessary. Exhaust ducts are connected from the kitchen and bathrooms to a common duct vented through the roof or an outside wall. Instead of intake vents, passive vents are installed in the outside walls of those rooms, usually bedrooms and the living room, in which fresh air inflow is desired. Note that louvers in doors or in partitions between rooms are necessary to maintain an air flow path from the fresh air inlets to the exhaust rooms when interior doors are closed.

Since only one fan is involved, the problems arising from unbalanced flows through two fans don't exist, and the locations of the inlets and exhausts is less critical. Care should be taken, however, that ducts penetrate the thermal envelope in as few places as possible and that breaks in the air/vapor barrier are carefully sealed. Figures 12.11a and 12.11b show two types of installation: one in which exhaust is vented out through the roof; the other in which exhaust is vented out through a basement wall. In the first case, there are three breaks in the ceiling air/vapor barrier. In the second case, there's only one break. This is why we suggest locating the exhaust air vent in the basement instead of the attic. In houses that do not have a basement or crawl space within the thermal envelope, one can reduce the number of penetrations by bringing the ducts together *before* they go through the thermal envelope so that only one break is necessary (Figure 12.11c).

Exhaust-Air Heat Pumps Heat recovery with exhaust-only type ventilation is possible, though the heat is not transferred to the incoming fresh air. In one scheme, increasingly popular in Sweden, a specially designed heat pump extracts heat from the exhaust air and uses it for both domestic water and space heating. A heat pump is a mechanical device that extracts heat from one fluid and transfers it to another fluid at a higher temperature. Heat pumps are commonly used in house heating systems to extract heat from cold outdoor air and deliver it to heat the house. A major attraction of exhaust-air heat pumps is that since the heat is transferred to hot water, heat recovery is feasible even in mild weather, when one

might turn off an air-to-air heat exchanger because windows are open. The only problem is that there are, as of yet, no manufacturers of this type of heat pump in the United States, although many models are available in Sweden. Because of their considerable advantages, exhaust-air heat pumps will probably be available here soon.

HEATING SYSTEMS

Designing a heating system for superinsulated houses requires a slightly different approach than that used for designing a system for conventional houses. For conventional houses, the heating system is seen as being separate and independent from the rest of the house; except for the one basic requirement that the system supply sufficient heat, most decisions about hardware selection and distribution are made according to homebuyer preference and cost considerations. Superinsulated houses, on the other hand, have certain characteristics that must be considered during heating system design and selection; the heating system must integrate efficiently and cost-effectively with the house as a whole.

The features of a superinsulated house that must be considered when selecting a heating system are a) very low design heating load; b) reduced annual fuel consumption; c) the reduced length of the heating season; d) the presence of a controlled ventilation system; e) uniform temperature distribution (lack of cold spots) throughout the house due to the well-insulated thermal envelope; and f) the airtightness of the house.

In this section, we will look at the effect of these factors on the selection and design of the heating system of a superinsulated house. We will also present several other factors relating to energy-efficient heating that are applicable to any house, superinsulated or not. We will then take a broad look at the various types of systems and hardware available and examine their applicability for superinsulated houses.

The Design Load

The design load is the maximum *output* necessary from a heating system under the coldest conditions. Calculation of the design load was presented in Chapter 6 using the following equation:

Design load = HLC × design temperature differential
[12.1]

We use equation 12.1 to determine the design load, which in turn determines the size of the heating system. Since the furnace output must meet the design load, the required furnace input is given by:

$$\text{Heating system input} = \text{Design load}/e \qquad [12.2]$$

where e is the steady-state efficiency of the heating sys-

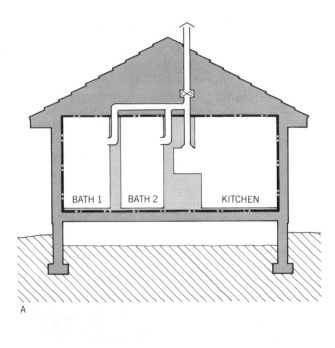

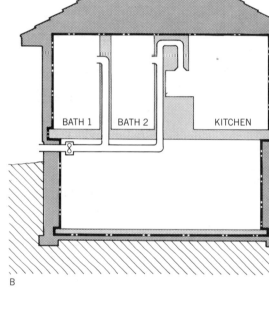

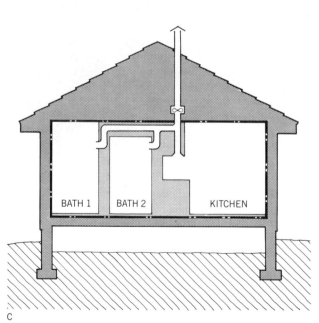

Figure 12.11 Three ducting configurations for bathroom-kitchen exhausts. A. Exhaust ducts from two bathrooms and the kitchen penetrate the thermal envelope in three places. This type of exhaust vent installation should be avoided. Not only are there three penetrations through the thermal envelope, but warm air is likely to leak up through leaky dampers. B. Exhaust from kitchen and bathrooms are ducted through interior wall cavities to the basement, where they join before being exhausted. This the best type of installation; first, be- cause there is only one duct penetration through the thermal envelope; second, because warm air will not passively leak out through the downward ducting. C. Exhaust ducts from the kitchen and bathrooms are located above a dropped ceil- ing, where they are joined and vented through the one com- mon duct. This is better than configuration ''a'' because there is only one penetration through the thermal envelope, but not as good as alternative ''b'' because warm air may still leak up through a leaky damper.

HEATING SYSTEM EFFICIENCY

There are two ways in which the efficiency of a heating unit is expressed—steady-state efficiency and annual fuel utilization efficiency (AFUE). The steady-state efficiency, measured directly while the unit is running continuously, represents the ratio of heat output to energy input. If a system has a rated input of 100,000 Btu per hour and a rated output of 80,000 Btu per hour, then it has a steady-state efficiency of 80 percent.

In actual use, the furnace does not operate continuously; its efficiency fluctuates as different parts of the heating system warm up and cool down, as pilot lights burn even when no heat is needed, as warmed air from the home escapes up the chimney, and so on. The *annual fuel utilization efficiency* (AFUE) is a more realistic measurement that tries to account for the seasonal performance of the heating system. Methods for determining the AFUE of a heating system have been developed by the U.S. Department of Energy, and every furnace or boiler sold in the U.S. has its AFUE marked on the fact sheet that accompanies the unit. When calculating energy consumption and/or cost effectiveness of a particular heating system, the AFUE should be used rather than the steady-state efficiency. However, for sizing the heating system, the steady-state efficiency is used because we are interested in the unit's performance during the coldest weather, when a properly sized heating system does operate continuously.

Electric-resistance heaters have an efficiency of 100 percent since all of the electricity is converted into heat. The performance of a heat pump is rated in the United States according to its heating season performance factor (HSPF), also determined according to U.S. Department of Energy procedures.

tem. Heating system input, like design load, is normally expressed in Btu/hr.

Traditionally, heating contractors oversize heating systems, often by as much as 50 to 100 percent, in order to be sure that the heating system will always supply adequate heat, even under extraordinarily severe weather conditions. This is a wasteful practice since the numerous on and off cycles of an oversized heating system reduce its efficiency. However, even in a superinsulated house, the heating system should be somewhat oversized above the design load. The reason for this has to do with thermal inertia and interior mass of the house. If, for example, the house is allowed to cool off during the night, the heating system, which comes on in the morning, must not only compensate for the house's heat loss, but must also supply extra heat to warm up the interior mass of the house. Calculating the exact extra capacity required is difficult and beyond the scope of this book. A safe recommendation is to oversize the system by about 25 percent.

While conventional houses often have design loads of 100,000 Btu/hr or more, superinsulated houses always have much smaller loads, typically ranging from 10,000 to 40,000 Btu/hr. Many furnace or boiler manufacturers don't even sell units that small. This may change as energy-efficient houses become more common, but for the time being, heating-plant selection will often be dictated by the availability of units small enough to match the small design load.

Annual Fuel Consumption

In selecting and designing a superinsulated house heating system, reduced annual fuel consumption is a very significant factor because it affects the cost effectiveness of the more expensive high-efficiency heating systems. If, for example, a superinsulated house has an annual heating cost of $100 or $200, it probably won't make sense to invest in a high-efficiency heating system, which may cost an extra $1000 but only save $25 or $35 per year.

Let's look at an example. In Chapter 5, we presented an equation for calculating the annual heating cost for a house, given its HLC, heating system efficiency, and cost for fuel. If a superinsulated house has an annual auxiliary energy requirement of 10 million Btu (see Chapter 5 for calculations), what will be the difference in annual fuel costs between a gas furnace with an efficiency of 78 percent and a more expensive high-efficiency unit with an efficiency of 93 percent? Assume we are burning gas at a cost of $0.60 per therm (100,000 Btu).

According to Eq. 5.13:

$$\text{Annual heating cost} = [AAH/(F \times e)] \times P$$

where AAH is annual auxiliary heat requirements in Btu, F is the energy content per purchased unit of fuel, e is the efficiency of the system, P is the unit price for purchased fuel. For the 78 percent efficient system:

$$\text{Annual heating cost} = [10,000,000/(100,000 \times 0.78)] \\ \times \$0.60 \\ = \$76.92$$

For the 93 percent efficient system:

$$\text{Annual heating cost} = [10,000,000/(100,000 \times 0.93)] \\ \times \$0.60 \\ = \$64.51$$

The savings? About $12 per year. The high-efficiency systems typically cost $800 to $1000 more than less efficient systems. Although they may be very cost effective in conventional houses with high auxiliary heating requirements, the above example shows that they may not make sense in superinsulated houses.

In a conventional house, for example, with an annual auxiliary energy requirement of say 100 million Btu, the annual costs for the 78 percent efficient and the 93 percent efficient system would be:

$$78 \text{ percent: annual cost} = \$769 \\ 93 \text{ percent: annual cost} = \$645$$

$$\text{Savings with the high-efficiency system} = \$124$$

The lower the annual auxiliary energy requirements, the less attractive are high-efficiency systems.

A similar analysis can and should be performed to compare the difference in annual energy costs between electric resistance heat, which is very expensive because of the high cost of electricity, and gas heat, which is much less expensive per Btu of purchased energy.

Let's look at two houses, both with annual auxiliary heating energy requirements of 10 million Btu, one with electric resistance heat (electricity at $.08 per kWh) and the other with gas heat (gas at $0.60 per therm). We'll assume that the gas heating system has an annual efficiency of 78 percent and that the electric resistance heat is 100 percent efficient.

For electric resistance heat:

$$\text{Annual heating cost} = [10,000,000/(3413 \times 1.00)] \\ \times \$0.08 \\ = \$234.40$$

For gas heat:

$$\text{Annual heating cost} = [10,000,000/(100,000 \times 0.78)] \\ \times \$0.60 \\ = \$76.92$$

Conclusion: In this house, gas heat costs $157 less per year. Does that mean it's the preferable system? Not necessarily. Since an electric baseboard heating system often costs several thousand dollars less (installed) than a gas-fired central heating system, many builders of superinsulated houses opt for the electric baseboard option despite the extra annual heating costs. Of course, the larger the house or the greater the auxiliary heat requirements, the bigger the difference in annual operating cost between the two systems.

The Presence of a Ventilation System

The presence of a ventilation system is another important factor in choosing and designing a superinsulated house's heating system.

One of the primary decisions when designing a heating system is the choice of type of heat distribution—individual space heaters in each room, or a central system with distribution. If a central system is used, should it be a warm air system or a hydronic system with baseboard distribution? The selection and design of the heat distribution system should take into account the presence of the ventilation system.

First of all, the ventilation system, if properly designed, creates air circulation in the house. Thus, no matter how heat is supplied to rooms, the ventilation system will tend to distribute it throughout the house. This can reduce the need for space heat distribution.

The most important implication of the presence of a ventilation system is the possibility of combining it with the heat distribution system. (This implies, of course, that the heat distribution system is the warm air type, rather than hyrdonic baseboard or others.) Combining the two, while an apparently attractive option, is not as easy as it seems at first glance. Although not impossible, there are several problems and special design considerations in attempting to combine warm air heat distribution with a ventilation duct system.

One design problem is deciding how the ventilation air will be forced through the duct distribution system. The ducts in a good warm air heating system are connected to supply and return registers in each room (except in bathrooms and kitchens, which typically have only supply registers). One option is to install an air-to-air heat exchanger with enough power to circulate air adequately through the distribution system. As discussed in the above section on ventilation, the supply and exhaust fans are balanced to provide equal intake and exhaust flows.

Let's say the heat exchanger feeds fresh air into the heating system supply ducts: what happens when the furnace fan goes on? It will tend to draw more air through the heat exchanger intake port, throwing the ventilation system out of balance. This can create two problems: first the intake air flow rate exceeds the exhaust rate, causing the house to become slightly pressurized. This is undesirable because it tends to push indoor air out through leaks in the house, and the outward leakage of warm humid air may result in condensation problems. We have heard of cases where an out-of-balance (pressurized) house has caused keyholes to freeze up; this is an annoying problem, but at least it is noticeable—it is much worse if the condensation is concealed in a wall. The second problem has to do with the air-to-air heat exchanger itself. If the intake air flow rate is greater than the exhaust rate, the humid exhaust air may get cooled too rapidly, resulting in excessive buildup of ice in the exchanger core.

Another approach might be to let the furnace fan run whenever the air-to-air heat exchanger operates and to balance the two systems against each other. In addition to the fact that this is a difficult job, there are other drawbacks. First, since the heat exchanger should run continuously, so must the furnace fan, even when no heat is needed. But furnace fans are typically more powerful than ventilation fans and will add considerably to the electricity consumption of the ventilation system. Also, furnace fans are designed to move more air than necessary for ventilation. If the system is running with the burner off, rooms will be receiving room-temperature supply air which, if directly hitting room occupants, may feel uncomfortably cool (supply air from a warm air heating system is usually at least 90° or 100°F; air at 70°F, approximately room temperature, feels uncomfortable when blowing across one's body).

Although several superinsulated houses use combined systems, some have experienced the problems described above. Most heat-exchanger manufacturers discourage combining the two systems. One heat-exchanger manufacturer recommends locating the fresh air supply duct from the air-to-air heat exchanger next to a return grille of the warm air heating system, without actually connecting the two ducts. This avoids the problem of imbalance created by the interaction of the two fans, but not the problems associated with the continuous operation of the furnace fan.

Despite the apparent problems, the integration of heating and ventilation air distribution systems is an attractive option. It eliminates system redundancy and provides fresh air to every room. This type of system, common in large commercial buildings, is an easy design job for any heating engineer. But heating engineers do not usually work on house heating systems. It is likely that we will see, in the near future, packaged combined heating and ventilation units that avoid these problems. At the time of this writing, one such system is under development by a Canadian heat-exchanger manufacturer.

The presence of a ventilation system has one other effect on heating system design. If the ventilation system is designed so that fresh outdoor air is supplied to some rooms and exhaust air is drawn from others, the rooms receiving the fresh air will need more heat because ventilation air is typically cool. The heat distribution system should take that into account, supplying proportionally more heat to the rooms receiving fresh ventilation air. The amount of extra heat needed depends on whether or not the ventilation supply air is preheated.

Uniform Temperature Distribution

A superinsulated house tends to have better temperature distribution than a conventional house does; this, too, affects the choice of heating system. House-heating experiments by the Canadian National Research Council using a space heater located at one end of a superinsulated house with no distribution system confirm the lack of an internal temperature gradient in such a house. Even with all interior doors closed, the maximum temperature difference between rooms measured in the test house was 8°F when it was about 30°F outside; with interior doors open, the gradient dropped to about 1°F.

One reason for this phenomenon is that the thermal envelope is so impervious to heat loss. Because of this, heat is much more easily transferred among rooms through interior partitions. Another important factor is that intrinsic and solar heat, important heat sources in a superinsulated house, are evenly distributed around the house. Temperatures will, of course, be more uniform in small houses than in larger ones. For example, in a large, sprawling 5000-square-foot house, the temperature in a bedroom located at one end may indeed differ substantially from the temperature in the kitchen located near the center of the house, if there is no heat distribution.

Because of the temperature uniformity, the heat distribution system may be simplified. It may not be necessary to locate heat sources along outer walls and under windows to offset the chilling effects of those cold surfaces. This has two advantages. First, ducts do not have to be placed within exterior walls, a practice that permits significant heat loss from ducts directly to the outside. Second, ducts can be located closer to the center of the house, perhaps in a central core, leading to considerable reductions in the length of supply ducts necessary for heat distribution.

In small and reasonably compact superinsulated houses, no heat distribution system may be required at all. A few space heaters may do the job. In larger houses, either space heaters or some type of distribution system—simpler and less costly, however, than those in conventional houses—will be necessary.

Airtightness

House airtightness is a crucial factor for safety reasons. Most conventional fuel-burning furnaces and boilers are atmospheric combustion types, drawing combustion air from the room in which they are located. In a superinsulated house, this can be a serious problem because the heater is competing for household air. Let's look at an example.

One cubic foot of methane, the main ingredient in natural gas, requires about 9.5 cubic feet of air for complete combustion. A natural gas furnace rated at an energy input of 30,000 Btu/hour will burn 29.1 cubic feet of natural gas in an hour, assuming a heat value of 1030 Btu per cubic foot of natural gas. This would create a combustion air requirement of 277 cubic feet per hour. However, the air actually used by the furnace would be considerably higher largely because of "secondary" air drawn up the flue. In one series of experiments on an operating furnace, researchers at Princeton University discovered that six times as much air was actually needed for operation. This implies a total air flow requirement, based on our example furnace, of 1660 cubic feet per hour. For a 2000-square-foot house with 8-foot ceilings, the air flow required would be about 0.1 air changes per hour.

While this may not be a problem for *ordinary* houses, drawing air flow at this rate from the interior of an *airtight* house would greatly unbalance the ventilation system and could create a negative pressure inside the house. A negative pressure inside could prevent combustion products from escaping up the flue and could lead to a serious indoor air pollution problem. *Because of serious potential hazards, atmospheric combustion devices should not be used in superinsulated houses.*

There are several alternative approaches. One is to locate the heater outside. Some conventional furnaces and boilers are made for outdoor installation. With that approach, no indoor air is involved in combustion.

The second approach is to use sealed-combustion, direct-venting appliances. In contrast to atmospheric combustion equipment, these units draw outside air directly into the combustion chamber through a vent pipe. The products of combustion are then vented directly to the outside through another pipe. No indoor air is involved.

A third approach is to use an "induced-draft" heater. These devices, with powered exhaust, require much less air for operation.

A fourth approach is simply to use electric heaters that don't use combustion air at all.

One final solution is to install the heater in a sealed furnace room outside the thermal envelope and isolated from the interior air. This approach has been tried for several years in Canada, but at the time of this writing, some Canadian researchers are not recommending it because of practical problems.

Now that we have examined the factors affecting heating systems in superinsulated houses, let's look at the relative advantages and disadvantages of the various types of heating systems available.

SPACE HEATERS

Electric-Resistance Space Heaters

These heaters, either baseboard or convector types, have been very popular in superinsulated houses, mostly because of their very low installation cost. Another advantage, as with any space heater, is that they provide very

good room-to-room temperature zone control. This is less important in a superinsulated house because temperatures tend to even out in the house. The main disadvantage is the cost of electricity, but as described above, this may not be an overriding drawback in superinsulated houses with extremely low annual auxiliary heat requirements.

Radiant Ceiling Heaters

Radiant ceiling heat warms room occupants by the direct transfer of long-wave infrared radiation from the ceiling (at about 100°F) to the room occupants (93 to 95°F skin temperature), making them feel comfortable even when room air temperature is cooler than normal.

Radiant electric heating is relatively inexpensive. Although it used to be installed by stringing resistance heater wires in the ceiling, there are now several systems on the market that consist of flat electric conductors sandwiched between plastic sheets. The plastic sheets are simply stapled to ceiling joists and wired before the air/vapor barrier and gypsum board go up. Another type of radiant panel, even easier-to-install, is made of ⅜ inch fire-rated gypsum board with embedded heating cables.

Gas-Fired Space Heaters

Usually mounted on an exterior wall and directly vented to the outside, gas-fired space heaters share one advantage of electric space heaters—low cost of installation. Gas space heaters suitable for use in superinsulated houses should be of the sealed combustion type which draw combustion air from the outside and vent combustion products directly outside. Unlike electric space heaters, which are inexpensive enough to install in every room, gas space heaters are likely to be limited to one or two per house. Exciting recent developments include the pulse-combustion space heater, sized just right for superinsulated houses and rated at an annual fuel utilization efficiency (AFUE) of around 95 percent. These heaters are expected to be in production soon.

Unvented space heaters, such as portable kerosene heaters, should never be used in superinsulated houses.

CENTRAL HEATING SYSTEMS

Central heating systems consist of a furnace, boiler, or heat pump located in one central location with heat distribution to individual rooms either by means of circulating warm air or hot water.

The choice between warm air distribution versus hydronic distribution with baseboards has already been discussed above in relation to the presence of a ventilation system. One additional consideration is whether or not the house will have air conditioning. Central air conditioning requires air distribution ducts. Thus, if a house is to be air conditioned, then the heating system could easily utilize the same ducts for heat distribution.

Another consideration when selecting a central heating furnace or boiler is whether or not it needs a chimney. Several units—some of which are of the sealed-combustion type—can be vented through the wall of the house. Eliminating the chimney not only saves cost, but also avoids the problems of installing the chimney through the top of the thermal envelope and of forming an airtight seal without creating a fire hazard.

Gas-Fired Systems

Gas is the most widely used fuel for space heating in the United States. Gas furnaces and boilers used in superinsulated houses, like gas space heaters, should be of the direct-vent type, in which combustion is sealed off from the house interior. Some sealed-combustion gas furnaces and boilers are of the condensing type with AFUE values exceeding 90 percent, in contrast to the 66 percent of most conventional gas furnaces and boilers. However, these high-efficiency units are much more expensive than conventional units, and as shown earlier, the extra cost would be hard to justify in a superinsulated house.

There are, however, a class of direct-venting gas boilers that are not as efficient as the super-efficient units but are well suited to superinsulated houses. These are units that provide both space heat and domestic hot water. Apart from the advantage of being one compact unit instead of two, they also require only one penetration through the thermal envelope. Consider the Heatmaker HW series of boilers manufactured by BGP Systems (see Appendix D). The smallest-capacity unit has a heat output rate of 52,000 Btu/hour, which is adequate for providing heat and hot water to the average superinsulated house. At an AFUE of 87 percent, this unit is considerably better than conventional gas boilers. Another series of direct-venting gas boilers with an optional water heater is the Netaheat units manufactured by Ener-quip (see Appendix D). These three units have heat outputs of 40,000, 53,000, and 65,000 Btu/hour, and each has an AFUE of 85 percent. The sizes of the Heatmaker and the Netaheat are appropriate to meeting the heat and hot water needs of most superinsulated houses. Since both brands are vented through a wall, installation is simple and inexpensive.

Oil-Fired Systems

The efficiency of the new oil-fired furnaces and boilers currently being developed approaches that of the most efficient gas-fired systems. As with the gas equipment, a direct-vented unit is recommended. Combination space-

and-water-heating boilers would be especially attractive, but we do not know of any commercially available at this time.

Heat Pumps

Air-to-air heat pumps extract heat from the outside air and transfer it into the house. The electricity needed by the heat pump to transfer a given amount of heat increases as the temperature outside decreases; at low enough temperatures, the system is no more efficient than an electric-resistance heater. In superinsulated houses in climates where winter temperatures often fall below 35°F, heat is called for only when it is particularly cold outside—the exact periods when the heat pump is *least* efficient. In milder climates, the performance of the heat pump may be better, but since the heat demand of a superinsulated house is so small, the added cost of the heat pump may be even harder to justify.

When operated in reverse, heat pumps can cool the house; they extract heat from inside the house and transfer it outdoors. This feature improves the economics of heat pumps in houses where air conditioners would otherwise be used. Even with this advantage, however, heat pumps remain hard to justify in houses with very small heating loads.

Ground-source heat pumps extract heat from the ground and transfer it to the air in the house. Ground temperature remains close to annual average air temperature all year round. In fact, in locations with a substantial snow cover, the ground stays considerably warmer than air temperature. Thus, when it is very cold outside, these systems are much more efficient than air-to-air heat pumps.

Superinsulated houses which only rarely require heat can be heated efficiently by ground-source heat pumps, which can also provide domestic hot water. But there is a drawback: ground-source heat pumps are even more expensive than air-to-air heat pumps and are therefore difficult to justify economically in houses with very low heating requirements. They may be economical, however, in large superinsulated houses in which heating loads are high despite efficient construction.

Electric Furnaces An electric furnace makes sense if a house is to have a warm air distribution system and if the auxiliary heat requirements of the house are extremely low. Such a device is typically less expensive than gas or oil furnaces, requires less maintenance, and, most importantly, doesn't require combustion air. Again, electricity is the most expensive type of energy, so the savings in installation cost must be balanced against increased annual energy costs.

Thirteen

Energy-efficient appliances

Throughout this book, we have concentrated on the energy required for heating and have paid little attention to the other components of house energy use. There's good reason for this focus: in ordinary U.S. houses, space heating is usually the largest component of energy use. But in superinsulated houses, the amount of energy for space heating is greatly reduced, making other uses of energy seem relatively large in comparison, comprising—if nothing is done to reduce them—about 95 percent of the total energy used in a superinsulated house.

What are these other energy uses? What are their relative magnitudes? Table 13.1 shows the amount of energy used by various electric and gas appliances in the average house in 1980. For houses with electric water heating, this was the largest energy user, consuming an average of 4000 kWh per year. (As of late 1983, the average price of residential electricity in the United States was about 8c/kWh.) Refrigerators and freezers were the next largest users of electricity, followed by clothes dryers, lights, and ranges. For houses with gas water heating, this was the largest gas user, consuming an average of 250 therms a year. (As of late 1983, the average price of natural gas in the United States was about 65c/therm.) Cooking and clothes drying were the next largest users of gas.

The relative magnitudes of energy use for purposes other than space heating are very different, however, in conventional and in superinsulated houses. First let's look at a conventional house. Figure 13.1 shows a breakdown of the different components of energy use in a typical house built in Baltimore in 1973, before the Arab Oil Embargo. With gas heat (Figure 13.1a), about 58 percent of the total energy use goes for space heating. Heating water is the second largest single component of energy use, about 17 percent, while electric appliances and cooling together make up the remaining 25 percent.

Calculating gas and electricity energy use without tak-ing into account relative costs can be misleading; on a per-unit-energy basis, electricity is much more expensive than gas because it takes gas or oil to produce electricity: about 3 units of fuel energy are needed to produce 1 unit of electricity. When we consider the origins of energy used in the home, we are discussing what is called primary energy, a way of looking at energy use that better reflects actual cost differences. To calculate the primary energy equivalent of electricity consumed in the Baltimore house, simply multiply by 3. (See Figure 13.1b.)

When working with the concept of primary energy, the relative amount of electricity use appears greatly magnified. Heating now accounts for only 38 percent of the total in the Baltimore house, while electrical appliances and cooling expand to 51 percent of the total. Thus, in terms of primary energy, electrical use was larger and probably cost more than the gas used for space heating, even in a conventional gas-heated house in 1973.

In the Baltimore all-electric house (Figure 13.1c), heated by an electric resistance furnace, space heating is slightly more than half of the total. If the house were heated using a heat pump (Figure 13.1d), the space heating energy use would be less than half of the total, but would still be the single greatest component of energy use. Thus, it can be seen that in most conventional houses, space heating uses most of the energy; the rest of the energy is consumed for hot water, appliances and lighting, and cooling loads.

Now let's look at a home designed and built to superinsulation standards, which reduce annual space heating energy requirements to 10 million Btu (10 MBTU) (Table 13.2). The other components of energy use, compared to the conventional house, remain unchanged. (The cooling energy requirement is somewhat uncertain, because several superinsulated designs reduce space heating energy use to a very small value while affecting cooling energy use in varying ways. For this reason, we show a range of numbers for cooling energy use.) Space heating has gone way down, while everything else has remained about the same, so that space heating now uses a very small part of the total energy. *Of the total energy used in the superinsulated house, about 95 percent is for water heating, lights, and appliances.* These energy uses, relatively unimportant in a conventional house, now acquire greater significance.

Is reducing them desirable? If so, how can it be done cost-effectively? In this chapter, we will try to provide answers to these questions.

ENERGY-EFFICIENT APPLIANCES FOR SUPERINSULATED HOUSES: YES OR NO?

As was pointed out in Part I of this book, superinsulated houses are super energy-sensitive: the intrinsic heat provided by appliances and people can supply a significant portion of a superinsulated house's space heating requirements. (*Note:* In this chapter, we use the word "appliances" to mean water heaters and lights as well as common household appliances.)

Energy-efficient appliances use less energy. But they also generate less heat. So is it productive or counterproductive to use them in a superinsulated house?

In our opinion, energy-efficient appliances make sense in superinsulated houses for several reasons. While intrinsic heat from appliances is important in reducing the amount of energy a superinsulated house needs for auxiliary heating and in shortening the heating season, the improved thermal envelope and larger solar heat input (compared to conventional houses) more than compensate for any heat lost by using energy-efficient appliances. In other words, with or without energy-efficient appliances, a superinsulated house will need auxiliary heat much less and be subject to a much shorter heating season than a conventional house will. Higher intrinsic heat from regular appliances is important for only a few months, while high energy consumption from regular appliances goes on all year.

Moreover, the same factors that shorten the heating season in superinsulated houses lengthen the cooling season, thus energy-efficient appliances help reduce the cooling load. Furthermore, much of the energy consumed by appliances is electrical, which is expensive. Whereas auxiliary space heating is usually provided by gas or oil, intrinsic space heating from electrical appliances is much more costly than the fuel displaced. So, while the use of energy-efficient appliances *does* increase auxiliary heating energy requirements, it ultimately decreases the *total* energy requirements of a house.

Figure 13.2 shows the results of computer simulations carried out at Lawrence Berkeley Laboratory to determine the magnitude of this effect. The heating, cooling,

TABLE 13.1   Average Annual Energy Consumption of typical Residential Appliances in the 1980 Housing Stock[a]

	Electricity—kWh/yr
Refrigerator	1700
Freezer	1300
Range	800
Water heater	4000
Clothes dryer	1000
Lighting	1000
Other	1000
Gas—therms/yr[b]	
Range	90
Clothes dryer	50
Water heater	250
Other	50
Oil—gallons/yr[c]	
Water heater	260

[a] Source: Geller, H.S., *Energy Efficient Appliances,* American Council for an Energy-Efficient Economy and the Energy Conservation Coalition, Washington, DC 1983.
[b] A therm is equal to 100,000 Btu or approximately 100 cubic feet of natural gas.
[c] A gallon of fuel oil has an energy content of approximately 139,000 Btu.

and total energy requirements of a house are shown as a function of appliance heat for a house in a hot climate (Houston) and one in a temperate climate (New York). In each case, as appliance energy drops, space heating energy use increases slightly, cooling energy use decreases somewhat, and total energy use drops significantly. The conclusions is that *reduced appliance energy use reduces overall energy consumption.* For houses using both fuel *and* electricity, the effect of energy-efficient appliances can be calculated in terms of primary energy, which will account for the energy lost in the generation of electricity. Now the savings appear even more spectacular (Figure 13.3). Although similar computer calculations have not been carried out for superinsulated houses, the results are likely to be similar, with the one difference that the space

TABLE 13.2   Components of Primary Energy Use in a Typical 1973 House and a Superinsulated House Located in Baltimore, MD[a] (in Million Btu)

	Typical 1973	Superinsulated
Space heating	100	10
Water heating	30	30
Appliances and lighting	100	100
Cooling	35	25–50

[a] Typical 1973 house data from Fig. 7b (p. 32), *Residential Energy Conservation,* Office of Technology Assessment, U.S. Congress, 1979.
The superinsulated house is assumed to have the same water heating, appliances, and lighting energy use as the 1973 house; space heating energy use is an estimate of what might be expected through superinsulation.

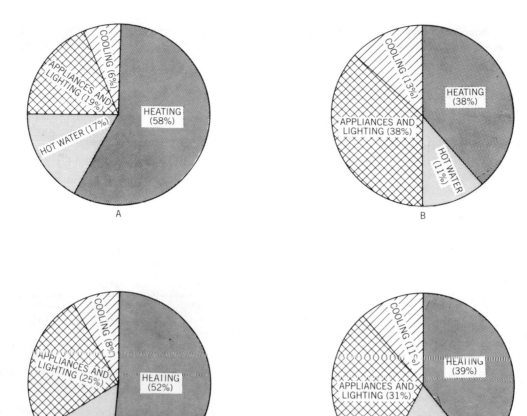

Figure 13.1 Breakdown of energy use in a typical house built in 1973 in the Baltimore climate for three different heating and hot water systems. A. Gas heat and hot water. B. Gas heat and hot water (primary energy use). C. Electric furnace and hot water. D. Heat pump and electric hot water. (Source: *Residential Energy Conservation*, Office of Technology Assessment, U.S. Congress, 1979.)

heating energy use and the total energy use will both be much smaller in a superinsulated house.

It can be seen that intrinsic heat from appliances is an expensive way to heat a house.

Moreover, much appliance energy use does not contribute to intrinsic heat at all. Very little of the heat contained in the hot water going down the drain, for instance, contributes to intrinsic heat. Neither does an outside light or, for that matter, the portion of the light energy that leaves the house through windows. In these cases, whatever energy is saved by the appliance is net savings in a house's total energy use.

REDUCING APPLIANCE ENERGY USE

Conservation measures for appliances may be grouped into three categories: management, sacrifice, and investment. Management involves better utilization of the appliance in question, for instance, turning off lights when

not in use and turning off water heaters when people are away on vacation. Sacrifice involves giving up something, for instance, unplugging a second, rarely used refrigerator. Energy conservation by management and sacrifice, extensively promoted since the Arab Oil Embargo, will not be pursued here.

In this chapter, we focus instead on those opportunities that involve more efficient utilization of appliances. Rather than involving any behavioral adaptations, these options require an additional investment for energy efficiency, and so are chosen on the basis of cost effectiveness.

For comparable operating conditions and energy prices, energy-efficient appliances are roughly equally cost-effective for all households. In many appliance categories, such as refrigerators, the energy use is essentially independent of appliance usage pattern. In these categories, we find that the most energy-efficient model available today is invariably the most cost-effective for energy

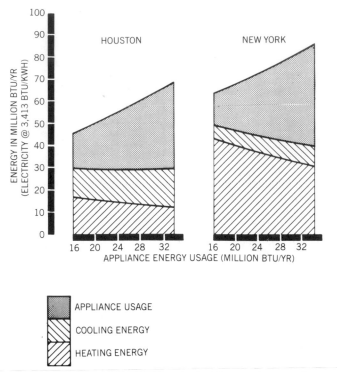

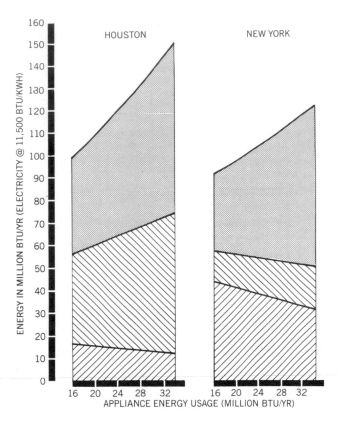

Figure 13.2 Total energy use (at building site) vs. appliance energy use. (Source: Lawrence Berkeley Laboratory.)

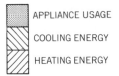

Figure 13.3 Total primary energy use vs. appliance energy use. (Source: Lawrence Berkeley Laboratory.)

prices anywhere in the country. Where the consumption depends on other factors—for example, water heater energy use depends on the quantity of hot water used—the most energy-efficient unit may be the most cost-effective, but a calculation of economics needs to be made.

Water Heating Is Generally the Largest Energy User in a Superinsulated House

Water heating is likely to be the single largest energy use in a superinsulated house and thus deserves special attention. The energy needed to heat water can be reduced in a number of ways: (1) Reduce hot water consumption; (2) reduce distribution losses; (3) recover heat from the gray water going down the drain; (4) use more efficient water heater; and (5) use a solar water heater.

Reducing hot water consumption need not involve sacrifice. Among the effective options are energy-efficient shower heads and water conserving dishwashers and clothes washers.

Water-Conserving Showers Unknown to most people, a quiet change has been going on in the nation's bathrooms over the last ten or fifteen years: shower flow rates have been dropping. This change has been motivated by a desire not only for energy conservation but also for water-conservation; the newer, better showers use less water. When water-efficient (and therefore energy-efficient) showers are turned on at full force, they use about 2 gallons a minute, compared to about 5 gal-

lons for the average shower and between 3 and 4 gallons for typical showers now being installed in new houses. Even pulsating showers can be frugal with water; some use only a little more than 2 gallons a minute. The following example illustrates the energy savings potential of low-flow shower heads.

Example. Consider a family of four, each taking an average of 5 showers a week. They have a conventional shower head using a maximum of 5 gallons per minute, but they turn it on only enough to get a 4.2 gallons per minute flow while showering. The parents take six-minute showers and the children 12-minute showers. All of them prefer a shower water temperature of 105°F. The house is supplied with well water that comes into the house at an average temperature of 55°F. They use an electric resistance water heater that is 80 percent efficient (including standby and distribution losses). How much electricity do they use annually for heating shower water? How much would they save if they switched to a shower head that used a maximum of 2 gallons per minute, and

ENERGY LABELS

The U.S. Federal Government requires manufacturers of major residential appliances to attach a label on each appliance sold showing information about the cost of its energy use. Appliances covered by the requirement, set forth by the Federal Trade Commission, are refrigerators, freezers, room air conditioners, water heaters, dishwashers, and clothes washers. The yellow-and-white label, marked "energyguide," indicates the relative energy consumption of the model compared to other models in its category, as well as the typical annual cost for operating the particular model at various energy prices.

Some appliances, principally dishwashers and clothes washers, use hot water, so that their energy use depends not only on the electricity they directly consume but also on the hot water they use. For these appliances, the energy cost depends not only on the electricity cost but also on the cost of the energy source used to heat the water and on the efficiency of the water heater. In fact, most of the energy they use is in the form of hot water. For clothes washers and dishwashers, the "energyguide" gives sets of values corresponding to water heated by gas or electricity. Figure 13.4 illustrates the "energyguide" label for a clothes washer.

The "energyguide" presents information in a convenient format. This type of information was extremely difficult for appliance purchasers to obtain before the labeling requirement was instituted in 1980. It has some drawbacks, however. The "energyguide" informs the reader about the performance of the most efficient unit, but does not mention its make or model number. To partially overcome this problem, we have provided a list of the most efficient appliances in each category in Appendix D.

A smaller problem is that the cost figure shown most prominently on the label has been calculated for national average energy prices and not those specific to a given area.

---

they opened it fully during showers? Assume that they take showers for the same duration and at the same water temperature as before.

Answer. The family runs the shower for a total of (6 + 12) × 2 × 5 or 180 minutes each week. The total hot water use is 180 × 4.2 or 756 gallons per week. With the present shower head, the energy required to heat this water is:

756 gal/wk × 8.34 lb/gal × (105 − 55)°F × 1 Btu/1b-°F
= 315,000 Btu/wk

The electricity requirements are:

315,000/(3413 × 0.8), or 115 kWh/wk or 6004 kWh/yr

With the low-flow showers, the weekly consumption of shower water would drop to 360 gallons and the electricity requirements would be (360/756) × 6004, or 2859 kWh/yr.

Thus electricity savings would be 3145 (6004 − 2859) kWh/yr. At an electricity price of 8¢ per kWh, *the savings would amount to $250 per year.*

With a gas water heater, savings would be less, but still likely to greatly exceed the few dollars that a low-flow shower head would cost. These water-efficient shower heads are probably the most cost-effective energy conservation investments around.

Because of the large potential for energy savings, some people have developed exotic showers that use even less water. Notable among these is the MINUSE shower, which uses compressed air to push the water and to maintain both the illusion of greater water flow as well as its cleaning potential. The MINUSE system includes a specially designed shower head as well as the associated hardware for generating the compressed air. The water flow rate is regulated to $\frac{1}{2}$ or $\frac{3}{4}$ gallons per minute and thus saves more than half of the energy used even in other low-flow shower installations. Although shower quality has been reported as acceptable, one problem is that the shower does not significantly heat the bather. This may not be a problem in warm climates or in the summer, but if the house is cool, people apparently depend on the heat of the water to help keep warm during showering.

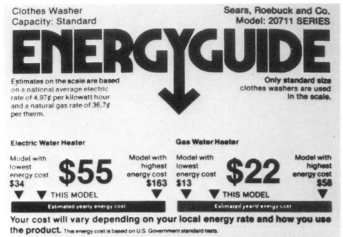

Clothes Washer
Capacity: Standard

Sears, Roebuck and Co.
Model: 20711 SERIES

ENERGYGUIDE

Estimates on the scale are based on a national average electric rate of 4.97¢ per kilowatt hour and a natural gas rate of 36.7¢ per therm.

Only standard size clothes washers are used in the scale.

Electric Water Heater

Model with lowest energy cost
$34

$55

Model with highest energy cost
$163

▼ ▼ THIS MODEL ▼

Estimated yearly energy cost

Gas Water Heater

Model with lowest energy cost
$13

$22

Model with highest energy cost
$58

▼ ▼ THIS MODEL ▼

Estimated yearly energy cost

Your cost will vary depending on your local energy rate and how you use the product. The energy cost is based on U.S. Government standard tests.

How much will this model cost you to run yearly?

with an electric water heater

Loads of clothes per week		2	4	6	8	12
Estimated yearly $ cost shown below						
Cost per kilowatt hour	2¢	$6	$11	$17	$22	$33
	4¢	$11	$22	$33	$45	$67
	6¢	$17	$33	$50	$67	$100
	8¢	$22	$45	$67	$89	$134
	10¢	$28	$56	$84	$111	$167
	12¢	$33	$67	$100	$134	$201

with a gas water heater

Loads of clothes per week		2	4	6	8	12
Estimated yearly $ cost shown below						
Cost per therm (100 cubic feet)	10¢	$2	$5	$7	$10	$15
	20¢	$4	$7	$11	$15	$22
	30¢	$5	$10	$14	$19	$29
	40¢	$6	$12	$18	$24	$35
	50¢	$7	$14	$21	$28	$42
	60¢	$8	$16	$25	$33	$49

Ask your salesperson or local utility for the energy rate (cost per kilowatt hour or therm) in your area, and for estimated costs if you have a propane or oil water heater.

Important Removal of this label before consumer purchase is a violation of federal law (42 U.S.C. 6302)

(Part No. 382165)

Figure 13.4 Example of an ENERGYGUIDE label for a clothes washer. Note that there are two sets of figures corresponding to water heated by gas and electricity.

Water-Conserving Dishwashers and Clothes Washers Together, dishwashers and clothes washers account for up to half of the hot water used in a household; their consumption of hot water represents most of their energy use. The electricity used directly by the appliances may be small, but they transfer their energy demand to the water heater. Thus an energy-efficient dishwasher or clothes washer must be a hot-water-efficient one. Dishwashers are now available with a shortened cycle option that results in a hot water savings of 16 to 33 percent.

For standard-size clothes washers, the energy use (primarily for heating water) of the least efficient is four times greater than that of the most efficient. In particular, front-loading models use about 40 percent less water than conventional top-loading designs.

Recent advances have made it possible to wash clothes without using hot water at all by laundering with specially formulated cold-water detergents. However, although these work well, most people still prefer to use warm water.

Better Plumbing Layout The energy used to heat water can also be reduced through lower distribution losses. Pipes carrying hot water from the heater tank lose heat to the surrounding air; this heat is wasted, except during a portion of the winter when it contributes to a house's intrinsic heat. Insulating the pipes may help, but not as much as one might think. Consider the following sequence. Someone uses hot water, leaving the pipes filled with it. Between uses, the water cools down in the pipes and thus heat is lost. If the pipes are insulated, the water will not cool down as fast, but it *will* still cool down. If enough time elapses before someone else needs water, he/she will still have to drain out the relatively cool water before reaching hot water. Thus, pipe insulation helps but does not completely solve the problem.

Other ways of reducing distribution losses may be more effective. House plumbing should be arranged so that hot water pipe runs are minimized. Shorter pipe runs not only reduce hot water distribution losses but also bring hot water to the faucet faster. In many conventional houses, this feature is not considered; water heaters are placed so that they are convenient to inlet gas and/or water lines or according to some other criterion.

Another contribution to increased pipe losses is thermosiphoning from the water heater storage tank. This phenomenon is shown in Figure 13.5a. As the hot water in the outlet pipe from the tank cools down, it becomes denser than the hot water in the tank. This cooled water falls back into the tank and is replaced by hot water from the tank. This cycle continues and draws heat out of the storage tank. Thermosiphoning can be avoided using a heat trap, as shown in Figure 13.5b. As the water in the pipe cools, it falls to the bottom of the trap. If the trap is installed close to the water heater tank, thermosiphoning losses can be largely eliminated. Some new water heaters have built-in devices to prevent thermosiphoning. Check manufacturer's product literature.

One case where insulation is clearly helpful is around the first few feet of pipe adjacent to the tank. Why? A certain amount of heat is *conducted* along both the hot and cold water pipes leading from the tank. You may have noticed that both pipes feel hot, especially if no hot water has been drawn from the tank for some time. Proper insulation will help reduce this conduction heat loss.

To virtually eliminate distribution heat loss, use a "point-of-use" water heater. We discuss this device later in the chapter.

Heat Lost Down the Drain Can Be Recovered, but Not Easily Much heat energy is lost when hot water runs down the drain (only a small part adds to intrinsic heat). Various schemes for recovering some of the wasted heat in "gray" water have been proposed. Recovered heat can be used either to heat the house or to preheat incoming cold water for the water heater.

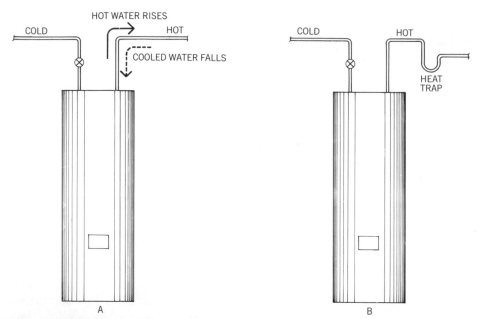

Figure 13.5 Domestic water heater installations. A. Thermosiphoning from hot water storage tank. Hot water convects up along the pipe, gets cooled, and the cooled water falls back into the tank. B. Installation of heat trap to prevent thermosiphoning. Some new water heaters come equipped with heat traps; if not, they can easily be added.

Using the waste to heat the house involves retaining the hot water within the thermal envelope longer before letting it flow down the drain. One can use a holding tank into which all the gray waste water flows. When the tank is full, excess water drains out of it. If the tank is big enough and the inlet and outlet are well located, the water will give off most of its heat before being drained from the house. There are, however, several problems with this type of approach. First, the waste water is a mixture of hot and cold water. Since the cold tap water is cooler than the house's interior temperature, some of the heat gets used up in warming this cold water. The higher the proportion of cold water in the mixture, the higher the loss. Second, the water in the holding tank is dirty and warm and can thus provide an excellent environment for biological activity, which could be a health hazard. Third, since the waste heat adds to intrinsic heat, it is useful only for a part of the year. And for a superinsulated house, this period can be short.

The second and third of these problems can be avoided by using a water-to-water heat exchanger that transfers waste heat into the new water coming into the water heater. This might be accomplished by running the waste water in a pipe through a water heater preheat tank. Cold water enters this tank and is preheated by the waste water, thereby avoiding the hazards of biological growth. Also, with this method, waste heat can be recovered all year long.

Gray-water heat recovery devices are being used effectively in some Swedish houses. However, for the American building community, their implementation and a more thorough understanding of their advantages and potential problems remain in the future. Until these devices have been thoroughly tested, we do not recommend their use in superinsulated houses.

Energy-Efficient Water Heaters   Another important way to reduce hot water energy use is an energy-efficient water heater. As was established in the previous chapter, many superinsulated houses are likely to be electrically heated. We will therefore consider electric water heaters first. Until recently, only the resistance type of electric water heater, which converts all electrical energy input to hot water, was available. Recent development of heat-pump units has made it possible to exceed even the 100 percent conversion efficiency of electric resistance water heaters.

Heat-Pump Water Heaters   For the same electricity use, heat-pump water heaters (HPWH) deliver more hot water than do electric-resistance water heaters. These devices work on the same principle as space-heating heat pumps, refrigerators, and air conditioners. Heat-pump water heaters extract heat from the surrounding air, transfer the heat to the water, and cool the space in which they are located.

The heat-pump water heaters currently available can be retrofitted onto existing electric-resistance water heaters or purchased as integral units. For new houses, the integral units are preferable, since they are less expensive overall and their installation is much simpler.

TABLE 13.3 Performance of a Typical Heat-Pump Water Heater

Ambient Temperature (°F)/ Relative Humidity (%)	Average gal/h	Average Btu/h	Average kW	Average COP	Average kW Input	Average Cooling Btu/h
90/50	26.3	15,300	4.48	3.28	1.37	10600
80/50	22.9	13,300	3.90	2.92	1.33	8750
70/80	19.3	11,200	3.28	2.56	1.28	6830
60/62	15.7	9,100	2.67	2.20	1.21	4960

Based on performance of E-Tech 100 Series heat-pump water heater; inlet water temperature is 55°F.; hot water storage temperature is 125°F.

Heat-pump water heaters can be located within the living space or in a garage or other unheated space. The performance factor or coefficient of performance (COP) of a heat-pump water heater (that is, the ratio of heat energy delivered to electricity used) depends on the temperature and humidity of the space where the unit is located. Table 13.3 shows the expected performance of an E-Tech heat-pump water heater at several ambient air temperatures and humidity values. The water is assumed to come in at 55°F and be heated to 125°F. The COP decreases from 3.28 to 2.20 as the ambient temperature drops from 90°F to 60°F at the humidity values specified in the table.

Example: Consider a household of four, equipped with water-conserving appliances and showers that use 38 gallons of 125°F hot water per day. The inlet water temperature is 55°F. If the household uses a heat-pump water heater with a performance as shown in Table 13.3, what is the daily electricity consumption rate for heating water when the space around the heater stays at a temperature of 60°F and a relative humidity of 62 percent? What is the average daily cooling delivered by the heater? How are the results different if the ambient temperature is 80°F and the relative humidity is 50 percent?

Answer: From Table 13.3, note that the electricity input rate at a hot water consumption rate of 15.7 gallons per day is 1.21 kW if ambient temperature is 60°F and relative humidity is 62°F. If the household uses 38 gallons per day, then the daily electricity consumption is:

(38/15.7) × 1.21 kWh per day = 2.93 kWh/day

the cooling delivered is:

(38/15.7) × 4960 Btu/day = 12,000 Btu/day

If the ambient temperature is 80°F and relative humidity is 50 percent, the electricity input rate would drop to 2.21 kWh/day, and the cooling would increase to 14,520 Btu/day.

First-generation heat-pump water heaters used only 50 percent of the electricity used by conventional resistance-type electric water heaters in a study carried out by the Oregon utility, Portland General Electric. In another

study carried out by Puget Sound Power and Light, a savings of 44 percent was measured. Both these studies were based on retrofit-type HPWHs. Integral, higher-performance HPWHs have now become available and should result in larger savings. For instance, an advanced HPWH manufactured by Dairy Equipment Corporation International (DEC) is significantly more efficient than other models. In field tests in a not-intentionally heated basement in Wisconsin, the DEC unit used only 35 percent as much electricity as electric-resistance water heaters. Brand names and model numbers of the most efficient HPWHs available as of mid-1984 are listed in Appendix D.

To determine the impact of HPWHs on total energy use, one must consider heating *and* cooling, since HPWHs have a cooling effect. William Levins of the Oak Ridge National Laboratory has done an analysis of the effect on total energy consumption of locating HPWHs in heated and unheated spaces. According to his calculations, for a conventional house with electric-resistance space heat and a high-performance air conditioner, an HPWH uses a certain-factor less electricity than a resistance water heater does. This factor depends on the geographic location of the house and the location of the HPWH within the house. Table 13.4 shows the value of this factor for eighteen cities and for HPWHs located within a heated space, in an "unheated" basement, and in an "unheated" garage. For a location within the thermal envelope, the factor varies between 1.25 and 1.88 depending on the city, with most values being around 1.4. *Thus the net effect of using a heat-pump water heater instead of an electric-resistance water heater is to reduce the electricity needed to heat water by a factor of 1.4, or by (1 − 1/1.4) × 100%, that is, by about 28 percent.*

The situation in a superinsulated house would be different from Levins's calculations in the following ways:

1. The heating season of a superinsulated house is considerably shorter than that of a conventional house. Thus, the cooling provided by the heat-pump water heater creates less of a penalty in the heating season and more of a savings during the cooling season.

2. Because the thermal envelope encloses it, the basement of a superinsulated house is likely to be at a

TABLE 13.4 Annual Performance of Heat-Pump Water Heater Relative to Electric Resistance Water Heater[a]

City	HPWH Location		
	Inside Thermal Envelope[b]	In Unheated Garage[c]	In Unheated Basement[d]
Albuquerque, NM	1.40	1.71	1.80
Atlanta, GA	1.49	1.82	1.82
Boston, MA	1.31	1.56	1.81
Chicago, IL	1.34	1.55	1.81
Denver, CO	1.30	1.57	1.80
Ft. Worth, TX	1.56	1.84	1.81
Knoxville, Tn	1.45	1.77	1.81
Los Angeles, CA	1.45	1.90	1.79
Minneapolis, MN	1.34	1.47	1.82
Newark, NJ	1.36	1.68	1.81
Pittsburgh, PA	1.34	1.59	1.81
Portland, OR	1.25	1.78	1.78
San Francisco, CA	1.27	1.88	1.77
Seattle, WA	1.24	1.80	1.78
Tampa, FL	1.88	1.96	1.84
Washington, DC	1.38	1.68	1.81
Wilmington, DE	1.36	1.67	1.81

[a] The numbers in the table are ratios of electricity used by an electric-resistance water heater to the electricity used by a HPWH. A hot water consumption rate of 64.3 gallons per day at 140°F is assumed.

[b] House is assumed to have electric-resistance space heat and a high performance air conditioner.

[c] Garage is assumed to be at the same temperature as the outside if outside temperature is above 65°F; 10°F above the outside temperature when it is between 30°F and 65°F, and 40°F when outside is below 30°F.

[d] Basement is assumed to remain at 70°F if outside is warmer than 70°F; to equal the outside temperature when it is between 55°F and 70°F; and to remain at 55°F when the outside temperature is lower.

Source: Levins, W. P., *The Effect of Location on the Predicted Performance of a Heat Pump Water Heater*, ASHRAE Transactions Vol. 88, Pt.1.

temperature close to that of the house interior. Thus there would be little difference between locating the HPWH in the basement or anywhere else in the house. Many HPWHs do not have any protection from freezing, and in a cold climate, there is a risk of freezing. It would not be advisable to install a unit in the garage. In warmer climates, it would be more appropriate to keep the HPWH inside the thermal envelope to benefit from the cooling.

One would therefore expect a larger electricity savings with an HPWH (relative to an electric-resistance water heater) in a superinsulated house than in a conventional house in the same climate. The savings could amount to about 35 percent or more in cooler parts of the United States. The HPWH makes more sense in warmer climates, where the savings would be larger.

Heat-Pump Water Heaters Can Operate on Waste Heat One type of heat-pump water heater is particularly promising in colder climates as well. In this device, the heat pump extracts energy from the exhaust ventilation air instead of from the surrounding air. Thus, it does not cool the interior of the house.

This kind of heat pump is an alternative to using an air-to-air heat exchanger to recover heat from ventilation air. The amount of heat available from the exhaust air stream is generally greater than the energy required for water heating. In winter, the excess hot water may be circulated through a baseboard system for space heating when necessary. Heat-pump water heaters operating off exhaust ventilation air are becoming popular in Sweden, but as of 1984 there were no U.S. manufacturers. However, in mid-1984, forty heat-pump water heater models were being made by U.S. manufacturers. Although these units extract heat from the surrounding air, a relatively minor design change would permit them to extract heat from exhaust air. We can undoubtedly look forward to the eventual U.S. manufacture of these products, if there is sufficient demand from builders of energy-efficient houses.

Gas Water Heating Most gas water heaters available today are relatively inefficient: in addition to the heat losses by conduction through the outside walls of the storage tank, these water heaters also lose heat into the inside of the tank, through the flue. When the burner is not operating, the tank remains hot, and hot air is drawn up the flue. Moreover, the pilot light, which stays on all the time, consumes a significant part of the total gas used by the water heater. If we include the conduction heat losses from the hot water distribution system, a conventional gas water heater is only about 44 percent efficient.

Many of the options for making gas water heaters more efficient are obvious. The continuous pilot can be replaced by spark ignition. A stack damper, which closes the stack when the main burner is off and opens when the burner comes on, can be installed. The jacket insulation can be upgraded. The most efficient conventional atmospheric residential water heater available at the time of this writing is the Nautilus, manufactured by Mor-Flo/American, which utilizes a better pilot, combustion chamber, and flue baffle design as well as higher insulation levels. Its estimated efficiency is 62 percent, including losses from the distribution system. While this is a significant improvement, much higher efficiencies are possible.

For superinsulated houses, certain problems are associated with the use of gas water heaters with atmospheric combustion. Two types of gas water heaters do not involve atmospheric combustion. One type is combined with or attached to a space heating furnace or boiler as described in Chapter 12. The other is a sealed-combustion, direct-vented, stand-alone unit. In the sealed combustion gas water heater, combustion air is drawn from

ATMOSPHERIC-COMBUSTION WATER HEATERS

Conventional residential gas water heaters are of the atmospheric-burner type and draw air for combustion from the space where they are located. If the water heater is located within the thermal envelope, the air is drawn from the house interior. In ordinary, leaky houses, the combustion air requirements for a water heater inside are met by air leaking in through numerous openings in the building envelope. In a house that is extremely airtight, this may cause a problem: there may not be enough air to support combustion safely. *Thus, atmospheric gas (or oil) water heaters should not be located within the thermal envelope in superinsulated houses without making special provision for combustion air.*

the outside, and exhaust gases are vented directly to the outside through an exterior wall, with minimal interruption of the thermal envelope. These characteristics are ideal for superinsulated houses. In addition, expensive chimneys are avoided. One high efficiency sealed combustion water heater is the stand-alone pulse combustion water heater, which will probably become available in the near future.

Because of the interactions between a house's space heating and water heating systems in many cases, the best water heating option must be determined by an analysis of the economics of alternative combinations of technologies for space and water heating.

Propane and Fuel-Oil Water Heaters When natural gas is unavailable, propane and fuel-oil water heaters are sometimes used instead of electric water heaters. Propane appliances are generally similar to natural gas appliances; choices, therefore, are also likely to be similar. The economics of the propane option depend on the availability as well as the relative costs of fuel.

Stand-alone oil water heaters are uncommon. Because they do not have continuous pilot, their performance is likely to be somewhat better than conventional gas water heaters. Once again, if such a heater is located within the thermal envelope, combustion air supply is a problem; options include isolating it in a room with a separate supply of outside air, or using a direct-vented unit or one that is attached to an efficient furnace or boiler. As discussed in Chapter 12, the option of a separate room with its own air supply is not recommended. We know of no direct-vented stand-alone oil-fired water heater. However, an efficient water heater attached to a Hadwick condensing oil boiler is available in Canada and is expected to be manufactured in the United States shortly.

Solar Water Heaters Solar domestic water heaters have become popular in the United States during the last decade.

Most solar water heaters for houses use flat plate solar collectors; some are thermosiphon systems, and some require pumps for moving hot water from the collector to the storage tank. A thermosiphon system works on the principle that hot water is slightly less dense than cool water. Therefore, it requires that the hot water storage tank be located above the collector. If the collector is mounted on the roof of the house, this requirement can be quite inconvenient, offsetting the advantage of saving pump energy.

In a pump-type solar water heater, the hot water is pumped from the collector into a storage tank located within the house, for example, in the basement. Appropriate temperature sensors and controls turn on the pump when necessary. Such solar systems can be divided into several types: direct or indirect systems, and those with single or double hot water storage tanks. In a direct system, water stored in the tank and used in the house also flows through the collector. Various methods of draining the collector are used to avoid freezing. In an indirect system, a mixture of antifreeze and water is circulated through the collector, and the heat collected is transferred into water in the storage tank(s) through a (double-wall) heat exchanger. Water can also be heated in a hot-air solar collector; heat is transferred from the air to the water using a heat exchanger. Some results of comparative tests conducted by the National Bureau of Standards on these types of solar water heaters are shown in Table 13.5.

Innovative solar heating systems include evacuated-tube solar collectors, which offer much higher efficiency and are potentially capable of being mass produced at low cost. One British manufacturer, Thermomax of Bangor, Wales, has recently introduced an evacuated heat pipe solar collector system with an integral tank and no moving parts; it is also relatively inexpensive. The heat pipe, like a thermosiphoning system, allows heat transfer without the need for a pump and thus increases net efficiency. The collector itself is made of evacuated tubes with a flat surface inside that is painted with a selective coating. Heat losses from the collector assembly are considerably lower.

TABLE 13.5   Comparison of Performance of Six Solar Water Heating Options[a]

System	Collector Area (ft²)	Thermal Efficiency (%)	System Efficiency (%)	Solar Fraction[b]	Net Solar Fraction[d]
Thermosiphon	54	26.4	25.7 (24.3)	0.57	0.56 (0.52)
Single, direct[c]	36	35.3	28.5 (14.9)	0.51	0.42 (0.22)
Single, indirect	54	24.7	22.3 (17.5)	0.54	0.49 (0.38)
Double, direct	54	23.3	18.1 (7.7)	0.52	0.41 (0.17)
Double, indirect	54	22.5	20.0 (15.4)	0.50	0.44 (0.33)
Air system	80	11.5	8.1 (1.3)	0.38	0.26 (0.03)

[a] Source: Farrington, R., Murphy, L. M. and Noreen, D., *An Analysis of Solar Domestic Hot Water Systems from a Systems Perspective*, Proc. of 1980 Annual Meeting of the American Solar Energy Society, Vol 3.1. (Reprinted with permission). Figures in parentheses represent values if energy used by pumps, fans, and controls were considered in terms of fuel required to generate the electricity (i.e., the primary energy).

[b] Collector areas must be considered when comparing solar fractions.

[c] Single or double refers to the number of storage tanks in the system; direct or indirect refers to the method of heat transfer—in a direct system the stored water flows through the collector.

[d] The *solar fraction* indicated here is the ratio of heat energy captured by the sun to the total heat requirement for heating water. In calculating the *net solar fraction*, the energy consumed by the pumps and other auxiliary equipment is subtracted from the heat provided by the solar system. The net solar fraction is highest for the thermosiphon and lowest for the air system: The first because there's no need to pump the fluid; the second because of the power needed to move air and also because of low efficiency of heat transfer from air to water.

Point-of-Use Water Heating   An alternative to the storage-type water heaters common today is point-of-use water heaters with very little storage. These heaters are generally located close to where the hot water is to be used. When the hot water faucet is turned on, the heater also comes on and continues to heat water to meet the demand. This type of heater has very little distribution or standby losses. Point-of-use water heaters can operate on gas or electricity. Those using gas create a host of problems: Are they getting enough air? Are the combustion products being vented outside? Only electric and sealed-combustion gas units should be considered in superinsulated airtight houses.

Despite the lower heat losses from point-of-use water heaters, there are several disadvantages. Since there may be several locations in a house where hot water is used, more than one unit may be needed. (In small one-bathroom houses with the kitchen and bathroom sharing a common wall, one unit may suffice.) This not only uses up space in the living area of the house but also increases the cost. Point-of-use electric water heaters often cost as much as storage-type electric-resistance heaters, but still considerably less than heat-pump water heaters. Point-of-use water heaters are also limited in their capacity to deliver hot water. We recommend point-of-use water heaters for households with low hot water consumption and hot water locations near each other. In such cases, the high cost of the higher performance heat-pump water heater may be hard to justify.

There is one case in which a point-of-use water heater may be particularly useful—for dishwashers. Some dishwashers require very hot water (140° or 150°F), and rather than keeping all the hot water in the house at this temperature, a point-of-use booster water heater may be used. However, this type of water heater is often an integral part of the dishwasher itself, so it may be more economical to purchase an appropriately equipped dishwasher instead of a separate point-of-use water heater.

Fuel Choice for Water Heating   We have discussed many ways of heating water, using electricity (resistance water heaters, heat-pump water heaters, solar water heaters with electric-resistance backup), gas (conventional and energy-efficient stand-alone units, attached units, and possibly solar with gas backup), as well as propane and oil heaters. When there is a choice, an important question is: which is the preferred alternative? The economics depend on a number of factors, such as fuel and water heater cost, the expected lifetime of heater, the expected hot water demand, as well as the specifics of the space heating involving not only the type of heating system but also in some cases the thermal envelope characteristics. Consider all of these factors in your fuel choice.

Refrigerators and Freezers

After space conditioning and water heating, refrigeration is usually the next biggest consumer of electricity. Over the years, combination refrigerator/freezers have gotten larger and fancier, so that by the early 1970s the typical unit was a frostfree 16-cubic-foot refrigerator with a top freezer, consuming about 1700 kWh per year. In the last couple of years, however, there have been major technological advances, allowing some new units of the same size and with the same features to use considerably less energy. For instance, the top-rated Amana frostfree

HEAT-PUMP WATER HEATERS WOULD BEAT CONVENTIONAL SOLAR WATER HEATERS (IN A FAIR WORLD)

Heat-pump water heaters offer strong competition to solar water heaters. A study carried out by the Oregon utility, Portland General Electric, showed that first generation HPWHs saved more energy than solar water heaters did (50 percent vs. 37 percent), and at less than half the installed cost. Typical installed costs for heat-pump water heaters are about $1500; for solar systems about $4000.

In a comparison of solar and heat-pump water heaters, another factor that should be considered is reliability. Solar water heater installations are fairly complex, and proper functioning depends on the construction of the components as well as on the skill and experience of the installer. Improper installation can not only reduce the savings but also increase the risk of damage from freezing. While one study, conducted by the Puget Sound Power and Light utility company, found a relatively large number of problems with heat-pump water heater installations, all were in the more complicated retrofit-type HPWH, and none in the integral-type HPWH recommended here. In fact the unit we recommend is essentially a single piece; installation is hardly more complicated than installing a conventional electric-resistance water heater.

Thus, heat-pump water heaters are cheaper to buy and likely to be more reliable than solar water heaters, and they save about as much energy. They would thus make more sense in superinsulated houses where the alternative would be an electric-resistance water heater. However, one factor considerably distorts the economics—the existence of a Federal income tax credit for solar domestic water heaters. With the 40 percent federal tax credit, a $4000 solar water heater costs only $2400. Even with that tax credit, a heat-pump water heater would still be more cost-effective. However, many states offer additional credits for solar water heaters, which can make them more cost-effective. Comparable incentives to encourage the use of HPWHs exist only in a few places, such as in the service areas of the Tennessee Valley Authority and certain west coast utilities.

refrigerator with a top freezer is an 18-cubic-foot model consuming only about 870 kWh/year. That is only about half as much energy as models sold in the early 1970s and a third less than the typical model sold in 1980. The Amana design features better insulation, a more efficient condenser fan motor, and a separation of the refrigerator and freezer compartments so that defrosting takes place much less often. An added benefit of this last feature is that food does not dry out in the refrigerator as fast as in a conventional frostfree unit.

The energy use of refrigerators is rated by using a test procedure set up by the U.S. Department of Energy. The energy consumption of each unit appears on the Energyguide label. (see sidebar on Energy Labels). Some of the most energy-efficient models of refrigerators available in mid-1984 are listed by style and capacity in Appendix D.

There have been significant improvements in the energy efficiency of freezers as well. The average model sold in 1981 consumed much less energy than the typical 1972 model, 850 kWh/yr vs. 1460 kWh/yr, although a part of this savings was because of a 10 percent reduction in average size. The most efficient models sold today use somewhat less energy. For example, several models with 15- or 16-cubic-foot capacity consume between 745 and 765 kWh annually.

Energy-Efficient Refrigerators And Freezers Are Cost-Effective   Calculating the economics of these appliances is relatively simple because the energy use does not depend greatly on such factors as use pattern and climate. The evaluation is made especially simple because several manufacturers offer pairs of models that are similar in size and features and differ only in their energy efficiency. The result of this analysis is unambiguous: *the more efficient unit is always the best buy when compared to its less efficient counterpart.* For instance, the more efficient 18-cubic-foot Amana frostfree refrigerator costs $100 more than a less efficient frostfree Amana unit of the same capacity. At an electricity price of 6.8c/kWh, the extra investment yields a rate of return of 34% (inflation-corrected), which is tax free. The energy-efficient Kenmore 16-cubic-foot upright freezer yields a real rate of return of 58 percent on an extra investment of $40. These and other energy-efficient refrigerator and freezer models are very cost-effective compared to their less efficient counterparts, even in places where electricity prices are still relatively low.

Although energy-efficient refrigerators are very cost-effective, consumers have generally preferred the less efficient models. In fact, at least one large appliance store in central New Jersey did not stock the more energy-efficient Amana refrigerator. When asked why this was so, the store manager wondered who would want to pay $100 extra for a refrigerator with no additional features except energy efficiency! Note that in New Jersey, with electricity prices around 10c/kWh, the more efficient model would be even more cost-effective than shown in the calculation above.

New Lamps of Old: Energy-Efficient Lighting

Lighting accounts for only a small part of the household energy consumption—about 10 percent.

Lights have received lots of attention as energy conservation targets because they are more visible and easily controlled—we can turn them on and off at will. The more we turn them off the more we save. This is in sharp contrast to refrigerators, which go on and off automatically. The most you can do to save refrigerator energy is to not stand in front of it with the door open while deciding upon your midnight snack.

The efficiency of light bulbs is expressed in units of lumens per watt. *Lumens* are a measure of light output, and watts are a measure of electric power input. The higher the lumens per watt, the more efficient the bulb. The following is a discussion of the features, advantages, and disadvantages of some of the new high-efficiency light bulbs.

Ordinary incandescent light bulbs are very inefficient, converting less than 20 percent of the electricity they consume into visible light. The circular screw-in fluorescents ("Circline" or "Circlite") are bulky and can only be used in a limited range of fixtures. Efficient compact fluorescent lights recently introduced by Westinghouse and Norelco, however, look like incandescent bulbs and can screw into a wide range of fixtures. The compact fluorescents have an efficacy of 40 to 61 lumens per watt, considerably higher than incandescents. The 18-watt Norelco bulb has a light output equivalent to that of an ordinary 75-watt bulb. These fluorescents have a "warm" color rendition similar to that of incandescents instead of the color quality of tube-type fluorescents that many people find objectionable. The high-frequency electronic ballast used in the Norelco bulb also eliminates the flicker that is often a problem with fluorescents.

The other new lighting technology for residential use involves a compact high-intensity discharge bulb: General Electric's Miser Maxi-light, a higher-power bulb with a light output somewhat higher than an ordinary 100-watt bulb. The bulb can only be installed with its base down (to prevent overheating) and is therefore limited to certain kinds of fixtures.

See Table 13.6 for a comparison of lighting technologies.

More Efficient Lighting Is Generally More Cost-Effective To determine if a bulb is relatively economical, we need to know its price, efficiency, how long it will last, how much it will be used, and the price of electricity. The performance characteristics and economics of alternate lighting technologies are compared in Table 13.6. The comparative economics are presented as cost per million lumen-hours, but this measure is oversimplified and may be misleading because of several factors. To date, several of the light bulbs shown in Table 13.6. have only been test-marketed; since these bulbs are not in full production, the prices shown may change. Another difficulty in making comparisons is that lighting requirements vary, and each type of bulb is not yet available in all sizes to meet these various needs. However, certain pairs may be compared: the 28W Westinghouse, 18W Norelco, and an ordinary 75W incandescent are roughly comparable in light output, although the Westinghouse and Norelco cost much more and have a considerably longer estimated lifetime. At an electricity price of 6.8c/kWh, the cost effectiveness of the three bulbs are 4.10, 4.30, and 4.70 dollars per million lumen-hours, respectively; that is, the more efficient bulbs are somewhat more cost-effective than the incandescent bulb, although the light efficacy (measured in lumens per watt) varies almost by a factor of four.

Of all the light bulbs currently available, GE's Miser Maxi-light is the most cost-effective under our assumptions of cost and electricity price, but as we have seen, it has applicability limitations.

One new technology now being developed is worthy of mention. This is an incandescent light in which the inside surface of the bulb is coated with "heat mirror" material that is infrared-reflecting but light transparent. This coating reflects near-infrared radiation back into the bulb, allowing the filament to become hotter and thus radiate more light. Since the radiant power is proportional to the fourth power of the absolute temperature, the relatively modest increase in temperature of the filament allows a doubling of the light output without increase in electric power input. These bulbs are likely to cost much less than other energy-efficient bulbs currently available and be comparably cost effective.

Ordinary light bulbs cost between $0.50 and $1.00,

TABLE 13.6 Performance and Economics of Alternative Lighting Technologies[a]

Bulb[b]	Status[c]	Efficacy (lumens/watt)	Light Output (lumens)	Lifetime (hours)	First Cost ($)	Cost Effectiveness[d] ($ per million lumen-hours)
150 W (I)	A	18	2,740	750	0.80	4.10
100 W (I)	A	17	1,700	750	0.50	4.40
100 W long-life (I)	A	15	1,500	2,500	0.80	4.70
75 W (I)	A	16	1,200	850	0.50	4.70
60 W (I)	A	15	900	1,000	0.50	5.10
40 W (I)	A	11	470	1,500	0.50	6.50
22 W G.E. circlite with ordinary ballast (F)	A	40	870	12,000	16.00	3.20
44 W G.E. circlite with ordinary ballast (F)	A	40	1,750	7,500	20.00	3.20
28 W Westinghouse compact fluorescent with ordinary ballast (F)[e]	A	42	1,170	7,500	22.00	4.10
18 W Philips/Norelco compact fluorescent with electronic ballast (F)	P/A	61	1,100	7,500	25.00	4.30
55 W General Electric Halarc (HID)	P/A	41	2,250	5,000	12.00	2.70
50 W Duro-Test heat mirror (I)	P	30	1,500	2,500	5.00 (est)	3.60 (est)
30 W Litec with electronic ballast (EF)	E	50	1,500	10,000	15.00 (est)	2.40 (est)

[a] Source: Geller, H. S., *Energy Efficient Appliances*, American Council for an Energy Efficient Economy and Energy Conservation Coalition, 1983.

[b] I—incandescent; F—fluorescent; HID—high intensity discharge; ER—electrodeless fluorescent.

[c] A—available; P—prototype; E—experimental.

[d] Cost effectiveness is based on the first cost plus operating cost assuming an electricity price of 6.8 c/kWh. No charge is included for bulb replacement. Also operating costs are not discounted in this evaluation.

[e] Westinghouse Lamp Division was acquired by Philips/Norelco in March 1983.

whereas the advanced bulbs by GE, Westinghouse, and Norelco vary between $12 and $25 each. Even though these advanced bulbs are more cost-effective and save a great deal of energy, one question remains: Are people ready to pay $25 for a light bulb?

Cooking Ranges and Ovens

The energy efficiency of different gas or electric ranges is roughly comparable, although energy use will vary depending on the cook and the type of meal prepared. In terms of the energy delivered to a house, electric ranges are somewhat more efficient than gas units. In terms of *primary* energy, however, the electric range uses more energy and costs more to operate. Nevertheless, the energy required for cooking is a small part of the total energy use, even in a superinsulated house. The main question centers around the choice of gas or electricity for cooking fuel. If gas is not used for either space or water heating, then the costs of hooking up to a natural gas pipeline just for a gas stove and possibly a clothes dryer may be unrealistically high. In such situations, natural gas may be considered unavailable for all practical purposes.

When gas is available, the principal factors in the choice between gas and electricity are convenience and indoor air quality. The relative convenience of gas and electric ranges is certainly a subjective matter, so it will not be discussed here. There has been considerable concern, however, regarding the indoor air quality implications of unvented gas appliances such as ranges. Studies have documented the health effects resulting from the presence of gas as a cooking fuel in houses. Some have even recommended that gas ranges should not be used in any house. This would be an unpopular recommendation, considering that 41 percent of U.S. households in 1980 chose to cook with natural gas or propane. The ventilation strategy recommended in Chapters 4 and 12 should be adequate to eliminate the bulk of pollutants generated by cooking with natural gas.

Clothes Dryers

In the past, most energy consumed by clothes dryers was used for the pilot light. However, pilots were eliminated in the 1970s, and all models are now electrically ignited. No further energy-efficient features are commercially available, but significant opportunities for improved efficiency exist for both gas and electric dryers. For instance, the minimum energy needed for drying appears to be the energy needed to evaporate the water in the clothes, plus a certain amount to heat the water to room temperature. In actual use, dryers use about twice this minimum amount. However, if the latent heat from the evaporated water could be recovered, then the energy requirements could be much lower.

One way to recover heat from a clothes dryer is to vent the exhaust indoors. Although this practice captures heat energy, it is not recommended in superinsulated houses. The exhaust contains a large amount of airborne fibers (lint), humidity, as well as residues from laundry chemicals. With natural gas dryers, there are combustion products as well.

The exhaust from a dryer should not be vented into the return air duct of an air-to-air heat exchanger. If done, not only would the ventilation system be unbalanced, but the lint would rapidly block up the heat exchanger core. The dryer should be separately vented outdoors or into a house's exhaust airstream just before it leaves the house. In the latter case, the dryer exhaust duct should be fitted with a backdraft damper to prevent house exhaust air from returning through the dryer when it is not in operation.

Fourteen

Testing and evaluating the superinsulated house

THE QUALITY OF CONSTRUCTION CAN BE VERIFIED

With a well thought out design and careful construction, superinsulated houses will be comfortable and use little energy. However, there may be flaws in design or construction that keep the house from performing as well as intended. Assumptions made in calculating energy flows may be incorrect. Even a properly designed house may not realize its full potential if there are defects in construction. Fortunately, defects can be found easily with appropriate diagnostic equipment. Many hard-to-calculate insulation deficiencies found in conventional houses are unlikely to be present in superinsulated houses, so calculating heat losses should be easier and more accurate.

In this chapter, we describe ways that the performance of a superinsulated house and its components can be diagnosed. Such diagnosis is done in two ways: by testing the house itself and by evaluating its performance. Methods that test the house itself include the blower-door pressurization method, the tracer-gas method, and infrared thermography. Performance evaluation methods include analyses of billing data, interpretation of heat energy use, and monitoring of ventilation and indoor air quality. In both testing and evaluation, certain techniques are more the province of the builder and others are more appropriate to the researcher. For instance, the blower-door method is useful to the builder, while the tracer-gas method is used more extensively by researchers; simple energy bill analysis can be done by builders or homeowners, but extensive monitoring using automated equipment to record interior temperatures, space and water heating usage, weather variables, and so forth is more likely to be done by researchers.

The Importance of Testing and Evaluation

Diagnosis may not be necessary for every house, because many defects can be checked visually during construction. However, some potential problems may be missed in a visual inspection. For those inexperienced in superinsulation design and construction, it would be worthwhile to have the first few complete houses tested extensively. This may help uncover generic flaws in design, for instance, thermal bridges where framing members have not been properly insulated. Although it may not be possible to correct the problem on that particular house, a slight modification in design and/or construction technique can help to avoid the problem in houses built later.

Even after the first few houses have been thoroughly diagnosed to identify design flaws, many builders continue to carry out some diagnostics on at least a sample of houses they build, as a form of construction quality control. Measuring the airtightness of each completed house may reduce the need for extensive visual inspection during construction. Testing each house permits the builder to certify the construction quality. If such testing were commonly available, it could become part of building codes. Swedish building codes, for instance, specify an airtightness standard based on house pressurization tests.

TESTING THE HOUSE ITSELF
The Blower-Door Pressurization/Depressurization Method

Superinsulated houses are designed to be airtight. The airtightness of the thermal envelope can be checked by house pressurization with a device commonly called a *blower door.* This method was briefly introduced in Chapter 3.

The blower door can either pressurize or depressurize the house, creating a pressure difference between inside and outside of up to 50 pascals (the pascal is the International System of Units measurement for pressure; 50 pascals is equivalent to 0.2 inches of water in Imperial Units). The blower door is equipped with instruments to measure the inside-outside pressure difference and to determine the flow rate through the fan.

Consider a house being pressurized to 50 Pa; this house's air flow rate is measured as being 600 cubic feet per minute through the fan, or what is referred to as a flow rate of Q(50). The air that flows into the house through the fan leaves the house through cracks and openings in the thermal envelope. Thus the flow of 600 cubic feet per minute tells us how much the house leaks at an inside-outside pressure difference of 50 Pa. Q(50) = 600 cubic feet per minute.

Air leakage under pressurization is usually expressed in terms of air changes per hour (acph). This is referred to as the q(50) rate. q(50) is calculated using the following equation:

$$q(50) = [Q(50) \times 60]/V \qquad [14.1]$$

where Q(50) is the leakage rate in cfm, and V is the house volume in cubic feet. The constant 60 represents 60 minutes per hour.

If the house in our example has a volume of 12,000 cubic feet, and the leakage rate under pressure, Q(50), is 600 cfm, then q(50) is given by:

$$q(50) = [600 \times 60]/12{,}000$$
$$= 3.0 \text{ acph}$$

The test and measurements are frequently carried out for both pressurizing and depressurizing the house, and the leakage flows are averaged. For instance, if under depressurization the same house leaked 540 cfm under 50 Pa pressure, then q(50) would be given as:

$$q(50) = [540 \times 60]/12{,}000$$
$$= 2.7 \text{ acph}$$

The average leakage rate of the house at 50 Pa would then be:

$$(3.0 + 2.7)/2$$
$$\text{or } 2.85 \text{ acph}$$

Most blower doors in use today (see Appendix D) are designed for testing conventional houses. Since conventional houses are much leakier than superinsulated houses, some of these blower doors may not work very well at the low leakage flow rates of airtight houses. These will need to be either fitted with adapters or completely redesigned in order to measure the air leakage of superinsulated houses.

The air leakage rates of superinsulated houses are likely to range from 0.5 to 3.0 acph at a pressure difference of 50 Pa. Typical houses with floor areas of 1000 to 3000 square feet and 8-foot ceilings will have volumes of 8000 to 24000 cubic feet. Thus the expected flow rates will range from 4000 to 72,000 cubic feet per hour or from about 65 to 1200 cubic feet per minute. For the measurement to be accurate, the blower door should have a valid calibration in this range of flow rates.

Measuring the leakage at several pressure differences can be used to calculate another indicator of a house's leakage, its *equivalent leakage area* (ELA). The ELA concept was developed at Lawrence Berkeley Laboratory in connection with research relating blower-door data to a house's natural air infiltration rate under the pressure differences created by wind and temperature difference.

An accurate prediction of the natural air infiltration equivalent to specific blower-door measurements is far less useful for a superinsulated house than for a conventional house, because natural air infiltration in the former case is very small—most of the air entering or leaving the envelope is accounted for in the controlled ventilating system. For this reason, even a crude formula relating pressurization leakage to natural air infiltration should suffice for a superinsulated house. Such a crude relationship is:

$$
\begin{array}{ll}
\text{Typical winter natural} \\
\text{air infiltration rate} & = \dfrac{\text{Average leakage at 50 pascals}}{20} \\
\text{(acph)}
\end{array}
$$

The natural air infiltration rate is roughly one twentieth of the leakage measured by a blower door at an inside-outside pressure difference of 50 pascals.

We call this the "divide by 20" formula.

Example: If a house has an air leakage rate of 1.5 acph at 50 Pa pressure, what would be the natural air infiltration rate of the house using the "divide by 20" formula? If the house ventilation is designed to provide an additional air flow rate of 0.5 acph, what percent of the total air leakage of the house is accounted for by natural air infiltration?

Answer: The natural air infiltration rate of the house is 1.5/20 acph, or 0.075 acph, using the "divide by 20" rule.

If the ventilation system provides an additional 0.5 acph, then the total air flowing in or out of the house is 0.575 acph. Of this, only 0.075/0.575, or 13 percent, is due to natural air infiltration.

The measured air leakage under pressurization q(50) of superinsulated houses should be below 3 air changes per hour and preferably around 1 acph. 1 to 3 acph at 50 Pa corresponds to natural air infiltration rates of about

Figure 14.1 Use of smoke gun to detect air leaks between window frame and sill. Test is performed while house is pressurized with a blower door. (Photo by Gadzco, Inc.)

0.05 to 0.15 acph. Intentional ventilation supplied by the ventilation system should supplement this to provide the total ventilation desired. If a total ventilation of 0.5 acph is desired, the ventilation system should be designed to provide 0.4 (± 0.05) acph. The uncertainty of ± 0.05 acph, corresponding to different airtightness levels, is probably as good as the accuracy with which the ventilation air flow rate can be designed in any case. Thus, ventilation design is determined by intended ventilation rate, independent of the house's airtightness, provided that the house is airtight enough.

A blower door can thus be used to *measure and verify* the airtightness of a house. It serves another purpose as well. Since the blower-door fan induces larger-than-normal pressure differences across the house's envelope, air leaks are exaggerated, making them easier to find. Those conducting the test can use smoke from a smoke gun to pinpoint small leaks (Figure 14.1). Leaks can also be detected by using infrared thermography in conjunction with the blower door, a subject covered later in this chapter.

The Tracer-Gas Decay Method

The blower door method is a useful technique: it quantifies the leakage characteristics of the building envelope and locates air leakage sites. But because the tests are done at artificially high imposed pressure differences, the leakage measurements do not directly correspond to the house's normal, natural air leakage rate, which can only be estimated. It is possible to measure the ventilation rate *directly* by using the tracer-gas method.

The technique involves mixing a very small quantity of a tracer gas into the house air and then monitoring the changes in its concentration. As air leaves the house, it carries some tracer gas with it, while air entering the house brings none in. *In a house with a high ventilation rate, the tracer gas will be quickly diluted.* If the ventilation rate is low, tracer gas concentration will decrease slowly.

A desirable tracer gas is one that is not toxic or flammable, does not occur naturally in any significance, and is easy to detect even in small concentrations.

The tracer-gas decay technique has been used extensively in research programs to measure the ventilation rate of houses. In most cases, the ventilation is provided entirely by air infiltration without any fans, so the technique provides a measurement of natural air infiltration. Natural air infiltration is, of course, dependent on weather; therefore, the results of a single tracer-gas decay measurement are only valid for those particular conditions. Since air infiltration rates vary greatly in a conventional house, many measurements are required for accurate characterization. In a superinsulated house, on the other hand, natural air infiltration is insignificant. Most of the ventilation, typically provided by fans, is fairly steady. Thus, only one or two tests are needed.

These measurements tend to be expensive. They require equipment and trained personnel for gas analyses. But the expense is much greater, and unavoidable, in conventional houses, which require many consecutive measurements. Airtight houses, which require only one or two tests, can be evaluated much less expensively. Instead of setting up the instrumentation in the house, the entire test can be done by a "mail order" bottle sampling technique.

In bottle-sample tracer-gas measurements, a plastic bottle containing a small quantity of tracer gas and several sample bottles are sent to the house with a set of detailed instructions. The resident opens the tracer bottle and releases the gas into the house air; at certain intervals, perhaps half an hour apart, the resident collects house air samples in the remaining bottles. The bottles are returned to the laboratory for analysis. Since neither the equipment nor the technician need to leave the lab, the expense is reduced considerably. The bottle sampling technique was developed at Princeton University and has been extensively used. Although it is not yet available from many commercial laboratories, we expect that it will soon be.

Infrared Thermograpy

Unlike the blower door, which is a calibrated fan that one can learn to use relatively easily, an *infrared viewer* is both technologically complex and difficult to use correctly. An infrared viewer creates an image as in a camera's viewfinder. But unlike the image in a camera, what we see in an infrared viewer corresponds not to visible light but to infrared radiation given off by surfaces. The infrared viewer electronically converts invisible infrared radiation into visible images.

The type of infrared radiation emitted by most surfaces of a house is in the so-called *far-infrared* range; this is in contrast to *near-infrared* radiation, which is close to visible light and detectable by putting infrared film in a regular camera. No kind of film in any ordinary camera will produce images of the far-infrared radiation.

Seen through an infrared viewer, shades of gray or other colors correspond to variations in temperature on the surfaces being examined. It is these temperatures that tell us what we need to know about a house's thermal envelope.

An infrared viewer is fairly expensive—the cheapest unit costs about $10,000, and units of heightened sensitivity cost much more. Features such as video compatibility, temperature calibration, and additional lenses add considerably to the cost of the equipment (Figure 14.2).

Using infrared viewers in detecting variations in surface temperature is called *infrared thermography,* or just *thermography.* A photograph of what is seen through the viewer is called a *thermogram.* And while we are defining terms, a person who carries out the thermography is called a *thermographer.*

A thermogram is merely a picture of the temperature distribution on a surface. Knowing what the picture means requires considerable training and expertise. We do not expect many of our readers to acquire thermographic equipment, and a discussion on how to interpret thermograms is beyond the scope of this book. We describe below the uses of thermography in testing superinsulated houses. We outline the procedures used only to the extent that it could be useful in specifying the kind of diagnosis one might expect from a thermographer.

Infrared thermography can be used to locate air leaks, identify thermal bridges, locate air intrusion sites, convective loops, and hidden moisture problems, all of which degrade the performance of the thermal envelope.

A complete thermographic inspection is carried out from both inside and outside the house. Thermography from inside the house is easier to do, more sensitive, and therefore more useful.

Interior thermography is best done when the house is empty, since furniture, pictures, etc., make it difficult to inspect certain parts of the thermal envelope. Interior thermography can be done in the daytime, although solar radiation makes interpretation difficult in some instances.

Certain areas, such as the perimeter of the space between the ceiling of the first floor and the second floor, cannot be viewed from inside the house, so exterior inspection is required. Exterior thermography is best done late at night to avoid interference from the effects of solar radiation and heat storage in the building materials. This makes exterior thermography inconvenient and possibly more expensive as well.

Locating Air Leaks   To locate air leaks, it's best to use thermography in conjunction with house depressurization. If a blower door is unavailable, the house can be depressurized by using an exhaust fan. Surfaces adjacent

Figure 14.2   A thermographic inspection of an attic. (Photo by Gadzco, Inc.)

to air leaks will be chilled (during winter) by cold air leaking into the house and will therefore show up as cold in an infrared viewer. A quick scan with the viewer will reveal even those leakage sites that may be inconvenient to reach and check with a smoke gun.

Locating Insulation Deficiencies   Places in the thermal envelope where the insulation is missing or thin— for example, at a thermal bridge, will appear cold when viewed inside the house through an infrared viewer. Although such locations should be clear from design drawings (if available) or from visual inspection during construction, thermography provides a quick check for any omissions. Certain thermographic equipment will also permit an approximate numerical calculation of the effect of insulation voids or thermal bridges on the overall heat loss through the thermal envelope.

Locating Other Defects in the Thermal Envelope
The detection of air intrusion sites and convective loops is very difficult, if not impossible, without thermography.

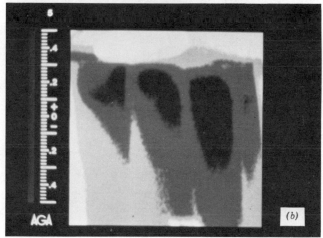

Figure 14.3 An interior wall-ceiling joint looks fine visually (a), but the thermogram (b) reveals the presence of major convective-loop heat losses through interior partition. (Photo by Gadzco, Inc.)

Recall that air intrusion refers to air entering through a break in the air barrier, penetrating the insulation, and degrading its performance. This creates a cold spot in the insulation, one that is not detectable by pressurization techniques because there's no air leakage all the way through the envelope (see Figure 14.3). Thermography, however, can detect it. Convective loops, as described in Chapter 2, can also be detected with thermography.

Both air intrusion and convective loops are detectable by thermography because they cause a slight localized cooling of the interior surface of the thermal envelope. However, even with thermography, these defects are difficult to detect; as of now, very few thermographers know how to identify them.

The best way to find air intrusion sites and convective loops with thermography is to look while the house is being depressurized with a blower door or an exhaust fan, because pressurization exaggerates an air leak that may be connected to the air intrusion or convective loop problem. Even then, though, detection is difficult. If an air intrusion site or convective loop is connected to an air leakage site, the latter may divert attention from the former.

EVALUATING PERFORMANCE
Energy-Consumption Billing Data

Defects in the thermal envelope can be discovered using the instrumentation and techniques described above. It is possible to evaluate the *effects* of defects, known or unknown, by examining a house's overall *performance*, which can be done by analyzing the house's energy consumption billing data: space heating, water heating, and air-conditioning bills. Using billing data, there are different ways to calculate energy performance, ranging from crude, easy methods to a more rigorous statistical procedure developed at Princeton University's Center for Energy and Environmental Studies.

These measures of performance take into account the effects of both design and construction quality; thus, for a group of buildings of different designs, all well built and having minimal defects, measuring performance can help determine the relationship between specific design features and energy use. Better designs can follow. If cost data are available, these relationships also help develop more cost-effective designs.

Gauging construction and design variables by performance data serves another purpose as well: it helps develop accurate energy-consumption calculation procedures, which at the time of this writing are still largely in the developmental phase. Once firm calculation procedures are proven and standardized, the science of building energy-efficient houses precisely and successfully will be even further developed.

Study of energy consumption data can apply to all kinds of houses: those heated by electricity, natural gas, or some other fuel; those that are air conditioned; those with gas or electric appliances. When examining energy bills, energy use is broken down by fuel into major components for heating, cooling, and other uses. Corresponding energy parameters are then derived.

The simplest case is an electrically heated house with no air conditioning. Here there are only two parameters: space heating electrical consumption and a "base-level" consumption for all other uses. For an electrically heated house with air conditioning, there's another parameter, the energy consumption for cooling.

For gas-heated houses with air conditioning, there are three parameters: the base-level consumptions of gas *and* electricity, and the space-heating gas consumption. For a gas-heated house with (electric) air conditioning, there's a fourth parameter, the electricity consumption for cooling.

With other fuel sources such as oil, wood, propane, and coal, the number of parameters required to characterize a house's energy consumption can become very complex.

Billing Data Analysis: The Easy Way *Base-Level Consumption* Consider the simplest case, an all-electric house with no air conditioning. Electricity provides the energy requirements for auxiliary heat, hot water, cooking, lights, and appliances. Space heating is the primary load. We assume, although this isn't strictly accurate, that the energy use for purposes other than heating or cooling, that is, for *base-level* consumption, is constant all year long.

Base-level electricity use can be estimated by looking at the electricity consumption data from June to September. Base-level consumption has very little to do with the design of the thermal envelope, since it involves non-space-conditioning energy use. However, in a well-designed superinsulated house, the base-level consumption accounts for most of the energy usage and is therefore important (see Chapter 13).

Unfortunately, there is no common yardstick against which the base-level consumption of a house can be compared, since it depends on the appliances used in the house and on the number of residents.

In an all-electric house with air conditioning, there may be no extended period during which the monthly consumption is steady. One is therefore forced to estimate base-level consumption from energy use during months such as May and September, when neither air conditioning nor heating use is expected.

Space-Heating Consumption In winter, electricity consumption increases above base level because of space-heating requirements. If the house does not have air conditioning, then the heating energy use can be calculated simply by subtracting the annual base-level energy use from the total annual energy use: Heating energy use equals total annual energy use minus annual base-level energy use. From this, we determine space-heating energy consumption for the particular year corresponding to the billing data.

Since the weather varies from year to year, a correction is used to adjust the consumption to the severity of a typical winter. The common procedure consists of dividing the actual annual heating energy use by the degree days (calculated to base 65°F) and multiplying by the average number of degree days for the location (also at 65°F). This gives us the weather-normalized space-heating consumption, WNSH:

$$WNSH = \frac{\text{heating energy use}}{\text{actual degree days}} \times \frac{\text{average degree days}}{\text{(base 65°F)}}$$
$$\text{(base 65°F)}$$

Superinsulated houses do not require heat at a rate proportional to the degree days to base 65°F, and that is not intended in the calculation. Instead, we are using the base-65°F degree-day value as a measure of the severity of winter and use this value to scale the actual consumption up or down to the consumption that might be expected in an average winter. As long as the total number of degree days for the actual year is not very far from the average, this is a reasonably accurate procedure. The actual base temperature for degree-day calculation would depend on the house design and would vary from house to house. Adjusting for these variations requires a more rigorous, statistical procedure and the use of a computer. Such a procedure has been developed and widely used at Princeton University (see below). However, base-65°F degree days are commonly compiled and are made readily available at many weather stations, rendering the procedure described above relatively easy to do using only a hand calculator.

Normalized Energy Consumption Sometimes the base-level and weather-normalized heating-energy consumption are added together to provide a single measure of a house's energy performance. This index is called *normalized energy consumption.* Here the term normalized, short for weather-normalized, refers to the adjustment of consumption in a particular year to the expected consumption in an average year.

Note: These analysis procedures are somewhat different for houses heated with natural gas, since the fuel may also be used for heating water, cooking, and other purposes. The remaining appliances and lighting are electric. Gas-heated houses use two forms of energy, so energy consumption indexes for each energy source must be calculated separately.

Common Index of Space-Heating Performance The space-heating energy performance of houses is often expressed as space-heating energy use (Btu) per square foot of living-space floor area per 65°F-base degree day. For instance, if a 2000-square-foot house used 15 million Btu during a heating season with 5600 degree days (base 65°F), the space heating performance would be:

$$\frac{15 \text{ million Btu}}{2000 \text{ ft}^2 \times 5600°\text{F-days}}$$

or, 1.34 Btu/ft^2/deg. day.

Although this index is commonly used, it has no commonly accepted name. It is frequently referred to as Btu per square foot per degree day. We refer to this index unimaginatively as BFD, the letters taken from some of the words in the units.

Conventional houses have average balance-point tem-

A SURPRISE IN MINNESOTA

Billing data analysis can yield useful information to designers, as illustrated by the following example from Minnesota.

Starting in 1980, the Minnesota Housing Finance Agency carried out an Energy-Efficient Housing Demonstration Program (EEHDP). Twenty-three builders put up 144 houses that were designed to meet a maximum heat loss coefficient (HLC) normalized by living-space floor area of 0.12 Btu/hr-°F. While builders were free to choose among a wide range of superinsulated and passive solar designs, the HLC was calculated from the plans, and only those that met or exceeded the target were built.

After the houses had been occupied for about a year, an analysis of their billing data was carried out by Gary Nelson of the Minnesota Department of Energy. The average house did perform better than the target, although there was virtually no correlation between measured HLC and the HLC calculated using the computer program. This raised questions about the usefulness of this and other computer programs for predicting energy use in low-energy houses.

The more interesting, and unexpected, result of the analysis was that houses with moderate-to-high south-glass-to-floor area ratio (that is, more passive solar heating) were more likely to have higher heat loss coefficients. Ironically, these were also more expensive to build because of their supposedly energy-efficient features. Thus, the more expensive houses were also the least efficient.

The Minnesota EEHDP experience shocked many people at first, but it helped to promote an energy-efficient housing industry that did not depend greatly on large expanses of south glazing.

---

peratures around 65°F, so that the BFD provides some sort of weather normalization. A house with a BFD of 9 Btu per square foot per degree day (base 65°F) in Minneapolis would probably have a similar BFD if located in Atlanta. But the average balance-point temperature is much lower for a superinsulated house. The heating energy use is proportional to degree days calculated to a much lower temperature. Colder climates tend to have relatively more degree-days to a lower base temperature than mild climates do. Consider Minneapolis and Atlanta, for example. Minneapolis has an average 8178 base-65°F degree days (see Appendix C) and slightly less than half as much, 3730, at base 45°F. Atlanta has 3309 base-65°F degree days, but only 639 at base 45°F, less than one-fifth as much.

The result is that a superinsulated house in a warm climate would have a lower BFD than an identical house located in a colder climate. Thus, using BFD values to compare houses in different climates can be misleading. For instance, one popular self-help housing magazine proclaimed a house in the Washington, D.C., area as the most energy-efficient house in the United States on the basis of its BFD value. But many Minnesota superinsulated houses, if placed in the Washington, D.C., climate would have lower BFD values.

Billing Data Analysis: The Princeton Scorekeeping Method The Princeton Scorekeeping Method (PRISM) is easiest to apply in electrically heated houses without air conditioning; it is also used to measure gas-consumption parameters in gas-heated houses. A regression technique calculates three parameters: a base-level consumption, a *heating slope,* and a *reference temperature.* As in the simple methods described earlier, base-level consumption is the energy used for purposes other than space heating and cooling. The *heating slope* is the extra energy input to the auxiliary heating system if the outside temperature falls by 1°F; it has units of Btu/hr-°F. Let's compare the heating slope to the house's heat loss coefficient, which is the heat loss per degree difference between inside and outside temperatures. The heat-loss coefficient and heating slope could be identical if the auxiliary heating system had an efficiency of *one:* Then energy input to the auxiliary heater would equal heat output from the auxiliary heater, which in turn would equal heat loss from the house.

The *reference temperature* calculated by the Princeton Scorekeeping Method is actually an estimate of the average balance-point temperature. Both the heating slope and reference temperature are indicators of the house's performance. Of course, the reference temperature depends on interior temperature and appliance energy use as well, so it is not related exclusively to the house's thermal performance. The heating slope depends on the efficiency of the auxiliary heating system, so it is not strictly a measure of the house's thermal envelope either. Nevertheless, the heating slope and reference temperature are useful parameters that cannot be determined by the simpler method of billing data analysis outlined earlier.

The annual space heating energy consumption can be calculated by multiplying the heating slope by the number of degree days calculated to a base temperature equal to the reference temperature:

$$\text{Annual space heating} = \text{heating slope} \times \text{HD(R)}$$

where HD(R) equals the number of heating degree days in a year calculated for the reference temperature. The heating degree days may be for a specific year or an average year. The latter number is more useful because it is weather-normalized.

The Princeton Scorekeeping Method has been extensively applied to the analysis of billing data for conventional houses heated by gas, oil, and electricity, and is currently being used for the analysis of superinsulated houses. As of this time, the computer code is not widely available, but we expect will be in the near future.

What Billing Data Does Not Tell Us Billing data, useful as it is, does not tell the whole story. One important omission is the interior temperature of the house. The interior temperature and its variations determine both comfort and energy use. Some people are skeptical of low energy consumption figures, since they suspect that the figures may appear small because the residents kept their house cold and shivered all winter long. Therefore, a record of interior temperatures throughout the winter would add considerably to the credibility of a house's low energy-consumption figure.

Such a record has traditionally involved the use of expensive data-acquisition equipment and has been carried out in connection with some research project. The alternative is for a person to measure the interior temperature several times a day from a nonrecording thermometer. This process obviously requires an inordinate amount of diligence, and few people would be inclined to carry out such measurements over any extended length of time.

Alternative and less laborious ways of recording temperature involve chart recorders that either are wound once a week or operate on a battery or house current. Although much less expensive than data-acquisition systems costing thousands of dollars, such recorders, sometimes called *thermographs,* are not cheap (they typically cost several hundred dollars). Another problem is that one has to look through yards of chart paper or tape just to get an idea of what kind of interior temperature the house averaged. One manufacturer markets a thermograph in which paper tape moves very slowly and records interior temperatures over a ninety-day period; this recorder is also one of the cheapest. The manufacturer is Ryan Instruments of Kirkland, Washington, and the unit cost about $200 in 1984.

The development of microprocessor technology permits other ways of condensing and storing useful data.

Other Measurements

Evaluating the Performance of Components of the House We have already referred to house pressurization and infrared thermography as ways of testing the thermal envelope of superinsulated houses. If more resources were available—for instance, through a superinsulated house demonstration program—some additional measurements would be warranted. Important performance characteristics that can be evaluated with a modest increase in effort are ventilation flow rate, levels of some of the more common indoor air pollutants, and moisture levels in the air and in building materials. The electricity consumed by individual appliances can be monitored using relatively inexpensive electric meters. Gas used by individual devices, such as water heaters, can be separately metered. Many of these measurements are being carried out in an in-depth evaluation of houses constructed under Minnesota's Energy-Efficient Housing Demonstration Program (EEHDP). These results will provide much more information on the performance of the EEHDP houses than was available in the first round of analysis based on billing data.

Other aspects of house performance would require much more extensive measurements and expensive equipment and are therefore likely to be limited to very few research programs. Examples of measurement programs in this category are the evaluation of the seasonal performance of natural gas-fired furnaces and the evaluation of the dynamic (that is, time-varying) thermal response of the house under the influence of variations in outside temperature and solar radiation.

Metering Individual Gas and Electric Appliances Researchers are sometimes interested in monitoring the energy performance of specific appliances. For instance, one may want to know how much energy was consumed by a gas-fired heating system or a gas water heater. One may be interested in how much electricity is used by an electric appliance, for example, a refrigerator.

The least expensive way of measuring energy consumption by individual appliances is by submetering. In the case of natural gas, this involves cutting into the gas line to the appliance and installing a gas meter similar to one used by the utility for billing purposes. The meter is normally installed by the utility or under utility supervision. The meter can then be read periodically by the resident or a researcher in order to determine the gas used by the appliance. The *rate* at which gas is used by a particular component—for example, the main burner of the furnace, or an oven—can be determined by timing the rotation of the meter dials. The smallest dials generally register half a cubic foot per revolution.

Submetering electric appliances can be much easier. A billing kWh meter, normally calibrated at 220V, can be converted to read electrical energy at 110V, and circuitry can be added to the meter so that it can be plugged into a wall outlet and have one or more appliances plugged into it. The meter, plugged in between the appliance and the wall outlet, records the energy consumed by the appliance. The *rate* at which electricity (or electrical power, measured in watts or kilowatts) is used can be measured by timing the rotation of a disk. The meter is normally calibrated to indicate the number of watt-hours corresponding to one complete revolution of the disk. The cumulative meter reading over a period of time gives the average energy consumed by the appliance.

The Performance of Heating Systems Can Be Measured by Electric Coheating

The efficiency with which a unit of energy consumed by the heating system is delivered to spaces where heat is needed is generally not easy to measure. Until recently, this quantity could be estimated only from other data. For instance, the efficiency of heat delivery from a gas furnace depends on the amount of gas energy input lost up the stack and lost to spaces other than those intended to be heated. Since the furnace operates intermittently as the thermostat calls for heat, the losses depend not only on the steady-state performance of the furnace, but also on its warm-up and cool-down characteristics as well.

One method that permits such a measurement is called *electric coheating*. In this method, the house is heated partly by the furnace and partly by electric-resistance heaters located in the rooms intended to be heated. The electric resistance heaters are 100 percent efficient in converting their electric input into useful heat. The heating system efficiency can be determined by comparing the fuel input of the gas furnace with and without the operation of the electric heaters, while maintaining the house interior temperature. The actual experiment is more complicated than the description suggests and is beyond the scope of this book.

Measuring the Dynamic Response

To understand when and why overheating occurs and to estimate cooling load in a superinsulated house, it's important to understand the house's dynamic behavior; that is, its behavior not just on one occasion but over a period of time.

During the heating season, the thermostat-controlled heating system maintains a certain minimum temperature. At other times, heat from the sun, appliances, and people—and the ability of building materials and house contents to absorb heat—keep the house warm. During such periods, the interior temperature rises *above* the thermostat setting. Superinsulated houses are likely to undergo many periods during which intrinsic heat exceeds the heat loss at a given thermostat setting. Therefore, even when it is relatively cool outside, overheating can occur.

Extensive measurements of interior temperature can help determine the circumstances under which this happens. They can also determine the house's need for cooling over a certain period of time.

A common energy-monitoring strategy involves installing a data-acquisition system and monitoring and recording various interior temperatures and other quantities. This is the basis of an extensive monitoring program of solar-heated houses that has been carried out by the Solar Energy Research Institute. Such data are frequently condensed into daily and/or weekly averages and related to energy used for space heating. Or, data collected hourly over a few days can be compared with theoretical calculations of the dynamic behavior of the house.

HISTORY

Techniques and materials for separating man from the heat and cold of his external environment are as old as civilization itself. The thatched roofs of tropical settlers and adobes developed by American Indians were early versions of insulations. They performed, to some degree, their intended functions—isolating man from the heat of the sun in summer and cold of winter winds and snow.

In the 19th century, the types of insulation used were natural materials, largely vegetable and principally wood and its derivatives. Early in the 20th century, what is today the insulation industry began with the development and manufacture of materials specifically designed to retard the movement of heat.

The first materials manufactured on a large scale were **rock wool** and **slag wool**. Natural rocks or industrial slags were melted in a furnace, fired with coke, and the molten material was spun into fibers and formed into felts or blankets. These were used in buildings of all types and also for industrial processes, but on a very limited basis, generally limited to areas where temperatures of an extreme nature existed. The use of these materials gradually increased during the first half of the 20th century, and at the end of that period they were being used in most houses as well as industrial/commercial buildings, although still limited in terms of the quantities and thicknesses used. In 1928, there were about eight plants manufacturing these products in the United States. This number increased to twenty-five by 1939 and eighty to ninety in the 1950s, but has since declined to about fifteen to twenty today.

Glass fibers were successfully developed on a commercial scale in the United States in the 1930s by Owens-Illinois, Corning Glass Company, and Owens-Corning Fiberglas Company (formed by the first two companies). **Fiberglass** insulations were developed during the 1940s and 1950s by melting inorganic materials, principally sand, and fiberizing the molten glass into a blanket-type material. Owens-Corning Fiberglas was the only producer of fiberglass insulation in the United States until 1950. An antitrust action filed in 1949 by the U.S. Department of Justice resulted in a settlement in which Owens-Corning Fiberglas agreed to license qualified companies to produce glass fibers. In addition, alternative processes have since been developed and are now being used to produce glass fibers.

In the mid-1940s, the domestic **perlite** industry began. Crude perlite was processed and expanded so that it could be used as thermal insulation. At the same time, some entrepreneurs in various parts of the United States began grinding waste paper into a fibrous state for use as an insulating material. This was the start of the **cellulose** insulation industry.

The commercial production of plastic foams began in the mid-1940s with **extruded polystyrene** developed by Dow Chemical Company. It was followed in the late 1950s by the commercial production of **urethane** foam, **expanded polystyrene,** manufactured from beads, and **urea formaldehyde**. **Phenolic** foam, which never played a significant commercial role in the United States, has been produced in Europe since the 1950s and in Canada since about 1972. During the first ten to fifteen years of production, it was primarily used in particularly severe insulating applications, such as in low-temperature space facilities, because of its moisture resistance and stable, high thermal resistance. Phenolic foam is just now gaining popularity as a building insulation in the United States; its major manufacturer is the Koppers Company.

During the last ten to fifteen years, the uses for plastic foams, particularly the polystyrenes and polyurethanes, have expanded rapidly into building insulation applications.

The 1960s saw a rapid development of fiberglass as an insulating material. As fiberglass use grew, that of rock wool (and slag wool) declined. The small rock wool factories, approximately eighty to ninety in number in the 1950s, have declined to about fifteen to twenty today, their product being replaced by fiberglass.

Although patents for cellulosic fiber insulation were issued in the 19th century, the product did not find a firm foundation in the marketplace until the late 1950s. The primary use of the material was for retrofitting attics and, to a lesser degree, for insulating existing wood-frame sidewalls.

Spurred by the economic pressures of the "energy crisis" of the 1970s, the insulation industry grew considerably, not only in quantity of materials, but also in types and brands. New insulation materials are still being introduced into the residential and commercial market, and future years are sure to see continued expansion of the industry.

TYPES OF INSULATION MATERIALS

Rock or Slag Wool

Rock wool and slag wool are terms commonly used to denote glassy fibrous substances made by melting and fiberizing the slag obtained from smelting iron and other metal ores (slag wool), or by melting and fiberizing naturally occurring rock (rock wool). Mineral wool is a generic term that refers to fiberglass as well as rock and slag wool.

In the United States, this product is almost always made from steel, copper, or lead slag, as opposed to the natural rock used extensively in Europe. The slag is melted using coke as a fuel, then spun into fibers by pouring the molten material onto rotating disks. The fibers are attenuated with steam, and then rapidly cooled to room temperature. The fibers are sprayed with a phenolic resin, which serves as a binder, then they are compressed and cured by being passed through an oven. The resulting "slabs" are cut to desired sizes to make batts. Another additive is mineral oil, which serves to seal the surface against dust production and to provide water-repellency.

Fiberglass

Fiberglass insulation is made of thin glass fibers felted in batts or nodules. It falls into two major classifications as a result of different manufacturing processes. In the first process, the fibers are produced by melting glass marbles into primary fibers, which are attenuated into relatively long fibers. The second process, known as the rotary process, produces fibers by flowing molten glass into a spinning perforated disk, thus projecting glass fibers; this process produces shorter fibers. In both processes, the fibers are sprayed with a binder and collected into wool-like mats. The process is controlled to produce mats of varying densities. The matts are formed into batts, with or without kraft paper or foil facings.

Fiberglass itself is an inorganic, noncombustible material, but flammable organic binders are used in the production of batts and blowing wool. Facings on fiberglass building insulation usually consist of an asphalt-coated kraft of foil-kraft paper laminate, which is also flammable.

Glass-fiber loose-fill insulations (for blowing and pouring) are usually produced by hammer-milling glass-fiber blanket material, thereby retaining the bonded fiber quality, which ensures good loft and R-value.

Cellulose

Cellulose insulation is made by converting used newsprint, other paper feedstock, or virgin wood to fiber form by shredding and milling it to produce a fluffy, low-density material. Chemicals are then added to provide resistance to fire, water absorption, and fungal growth. The most common chemicals used are borax, boric acid, ammonium sulfate, calcium sulfate, and aluminum sulphate at a loading of approximately 20 percent by weight.

Polystyrene Foam

Polystyrene foam insulation is manufactured in two forms, extruded and expanded.

The extruded form is manufactured by flowing a hot mixture of polystyrene, solvent, and pressurized gas (blowing agent) through a slit into the atmosphere. Due to the reduction in pressure, the gas expands, resulting in a foam with a fine, closed-cell structure. The blowing agent is usually a fluorocarbon.

The expanded (or molded) form is made by placing polystyrene beads (containing a blowing agent) into a mold and exposing them to heat. The vapor pressure of the blowing agent causes expansion of the beads, resulting in a predominantly closed-cell foam. The blowing agent is usually pentane. The R-value of molded polystyrene is lower than that of extruded polystyrene, since the former has air in the cells, while the latter has a mixture of air and fluorocarbon.

Polyurethane and Polyisocyanurate Foams

Polyurethanes are plastics that are the reaction product of isocyanates and alcohols. Polyisocyanurates are made from isocyanates in the presence of a catalyst, resulting in the formation of a more thermally stable isocyanurate ring structure.

Originally, polyurethane foams were formed during the chemical reaction by release of carbon dioxide. However, halocarbons are now used as blowing agents, resulting in an essentially 100-percent closed-cell foam. Either rigid or flexible foam can be produced, depending on the functionality of the isocyanates and alcohols and the molecular weight. For thermal insulations, the rigid foam is used.

Polyurethane and polyisocyanurate foams are produced by several different processes. Continuous slab stock is made by mixing the necessary components and continuously metering the mixture onto a moving conveyor, where it forms a continuous foam that can be cut to various lengths. Laminates can be made by a similar process, dispensing the mixture between sheets.

Foamed-in-place polyurethanes and isocyanurates are prepared by mixing or metering the components and dispensing them manually or automatically. Specially designed units are available for spray-on applications.

Perlite

Perlite is a naturally occurring, siliceous, volcanic glass containing 2 to 5 percent water by weight. Perlite ore is composed primarily of aluminum silicate. Crushed ore particles are expanded to 4 to 20 times their original volume by being rapid heated to a temperature of 1000°C, which vaporizes the occluded water and forms vapor cells in the heat-softened glass.

Perlite is used primarily in industrial/commercial buildings as a roof insulation board material. The next largest use is in lightweight insulating concrete, in which expanded perlite is mixed with Portland cement. A wide range of densities is possible. Perlite insulating concrete, both preformed and cast-in-place, is used primarily for roof decks, floor slabs, and wall systems. Low-density expanded perlite is used as loose-fill insulation.

Vermiculite

Vermiculite is a micalike hydrated laminar mineral consisting of aluminum-iron-magnesium silicates with both free and bound water. When the mineral is subjected to high temperatures, it expands due to formation of steam that is driven off, thereby causing the laminae to separate.

By controlling the degree of exfoliation, a density range of typically 4 to 10 pounds per cubic foot can be produced in the expanded material. The lower-density material is commonly used as loose-fill insulation.

Vermiculite is noncombustible and melts at 1315°C. Being an inorganic material, it is resistant to rot, vermin, and termites, and is not affected by age, temperature, or humidity.

Reflective Foils (Radiation Barriers)

Reflective materials act as insulation by reflecting infrared radiation rather than by reducing conduction as conventional bulk insulations do. The most common types of radiation barriers are aluminum foils and aluminized Mylar. They are most effectively used in applications in which radiation heat transfer is dominant, such as on the underside of roofs in hot climates.

GENERAL ADVANTAGES AND DISADVANTAGES

Table A.1 lists the common thermal insulation materials, their relative advantages and disadvantages, and appropriateness ratings for various applications.

PHYSICAL PROPERTIES AND COSTS OF INSULATION MATERIALS

Table A.2 lists important physical properties, approximate costs, and available forms of the common thermal insulation materials. Note that costs for insulation are highly variable, particularly for contractor-installed products. The most useful measure of insulation cost is cents per square foot per R-value. Figure A.1 shows graphically the approximate relative costs, in cents per square foot per R-value, of various insulation materials.

Parts of this Appendix are excerpted from *An Assessment of Thermal Materials and Systems for Building Applications*, published by the U.S. Department of Energy and prepared by Brookhaven National Laboratory with Dynatech R/D Company.

Tables A.1 and A.2 and Figure A.1 are reproduced with permission from *Rodale Product Report—Insulation Materials*, copyright 1982 by Rodale Press, Inc.

TABLE A.1 Advantages, Disadvantages, and Applications of Insulation Materials

Form	Material	Advantages	Disadvantages	Roof, Cathedral Ceiling
Rolls, Batts, and Blankets	All types	easy to install in many locations, especially standard frame construction. fairly inexpensive. good fire resistance. widely available.	hard to install properly in tight or cramped spaces. cannot be installed in already enclosed cavities. "vapor barrier" facings are hard to install effectively; additional vapor/infiltration barriers usually required. moisture and infiltration can degrade R-value of insulation. insulation "dust" during installation can irritate eyes, skin, and lungs. installer should wear eye protection, respirator, gloves, and full-coverage clothing. most facings are flammable; some "non-flammable" facings may be available. multiple "layering" of batts/blankets in horizontal spaces (attic floors) can degrade R-value of lower layer due to compression.	
	Fiberglass	good fire resistance.	see above	E
	Rock wool	excellent fire resistance.	see above	E
Loose Fill (pouring/ blowing)	All types	can be poured or blown into enclosed, inaccessible, and oddly shaped cavities. in horizontal spaces like attic floors, pour-in is faster to install than batts/blankets. blown insulation is often the only retrofit option for woodframe walls. widely available.	loose-fill has lower R-value per inch than the same material in batt/blanket form. does not provide a vapor/infiltration barrier. condensation and infiltration in cavity can degrade R-values. blow-in installation is not usually practical for homeowners; contractor or experienced help usually needed. generates more "dust" during installation than batts/blankets. installer should wear eye protection, respirator, gloves, and full-coverage clothing.	

Attic Floor, Flat Ceiling	Walls: Between Framing	Walls: Sheathing	Floors Over Unheated Spaces	Masonry Walls (Interior Surface)	Masonry Walls (Exterior Surface Above Ground)	Masonry Walls (Exterior Surface Below Ground)
			Applications Key: E = Excellent; G = Good; D = Doubtful; N = Not Recommended			
E	E	N	G	D	N	N
E	E	N	G	D	N	N

(Continued)

TABLE A.1 (*Continued*)

Form	Material	Advantages	Disadvantages	Roof, Cathedral Ceiling
	Fiberglass	good fire-resistance. does not absorb water. can be blown or poured.	blown fiberglass has lowest R-value per inch of all loose-fill materials. blown fiberglass can hang up on wires and nails. settling and voids can occur if blown at too low density.	D
	Rock wool	about 25 percent higher R-value per inch than loose-fill fiberglass. can be blown or poured. can be blown through smaller holes than fiberglass. good fire-resistance.	settling and voids can occur if blown at too low density.	D
	Cellulose	highest R-value per inch of all loose-fill materials. can be blown through smaller holes than fiberglass. more impervious to air infiltration than fiber-glass or rock wool. can be blown or poured.	potentially combustible; cannot be installed near chimneys or flues. absorbs water, dries very slowly. can deteriorate under prolonged exposure to moisture. settling and voids can occur if blown at too low density.	D
	Perlite	very good fire-resistance.	must be poured, not suitable for blow-in installation.	N
	Vermiculite	exceptionally good fire-resistance	absorbs water, dries slowly. seldom used in house insulating due to low R-value and heavy weight.	N
	Expanded Polystyrene (beads or shredded)	high R-value per inch. can be blown or poured. does not absorb moisture. settling is not a serious problem.	potentially combustible, cannot be used near chimneys or flues. not widely available. must be covered with fire-resistant sheathing.	N
Rigid Board	All Types	higher R-value per inch than batts/blankets or loose-fill materials. can be bonded to a variety of special facing materials to provide heat-reflective surface, vapor/infiltration barrier, fire resistance, finished wall surface, etc. air infiltration does not degrade R-value of board insulations as much as loose fills or batts/blankets.	hard to install in complex corners and odd-shaped spaces. plastic foams are not resistant to sunlight. some products contain fluorocarbons that can damage the environment.	

| | | | Applications | | | |
| | | Key: E = Excellent; G = Good; D = Doubtful; N = Not Recommended | | | | |

Attic Floor, Flat Ceiling	Walls: Between Framing	Walls: Sheathing	Floors Over Unheated Spaces	Masonry Walls (Interior Surface)	Masonry Walls (Exterior Surface Above Ground)	Masonry Walls (Exterior Surface Below Ground)
E	G	N	G	N	N	N
E	G	N	G	N	N	N
E	G	N	D	N	N	N
E	D	N	N	N	N	N
G	N	N	N	N	N	N
G	G	N	N	N	N	N

(Continued)

TABLE A.1 *(Continued)*

Form	Material	Advantages	Disadvantages	Roof, Cathedral Ceiling
	Expanded Polystyrene (EPS)	lowest cost per R-value of all board insulations. available in several density grades; higher density provides better thermal resistance and moisture resistance.	combustible; must be covered with fire-resistant sheathing. less mechanical strength and rigidity than extruded polystyrene.	G
	Extruded Polystyrene	good for exterior insulation of foundations and basement walls because of high moisture resistance and compresssive strength. closed-cell structure provides excellent moisture resistance.	combustible; must be covered with fire-resistant sheathing, cannot be used near chimneys or flues.	G
	Urethane	has highest R-value per inch of all insulation materials.	combustible; must be covered with fire-resistant sheathing, cannot be used near chimneys or flues.	G
	Phenolic	very good fire-resistance.	highest cost per R-value of all rigid board insulations. brittle; easily crumbles and forms "dust." may tend to warp due to moisture absorption. not readily available.	D
	High-Density Fiberglass	highest R-value per inch of all forms of fiberglass. good fire resistance. will conform to slight irregularities in the framing better than plastic foam boards, which are more rigid.		G
Aluminized Foil/Paper	Reflective Foil/Paper	lightweight.	must face a dead air space at least $\frac{3}{4}''$ thick to provide rated R-value. air infiltration can seriously degrade effective R-value. air spaces can provide pathway for rapid fire spread in house.	N

			Applications Key: E = Excellent; G = Good; D = Doubtful; N = Not Recommended			
Attic Floor, Flat Ceiling	Walls: Between Framing	Walls: Sheathing	Floors Over Unheated Spaces	Masonry Walls (Interior Surface)	Masonry Walls (Exterior Surface Above Ground)	Masonry Walls (Exterior Surface Below Ground)
D	G	E	G	E	E	D
D	D	E	G	E	E	E
D	D	E	G	E	E	D
D	D	D	D	G	G	D
D	D	E	E	E	D	N
N	D	N	G	N	N	N

(Continued)

TABLE A.1 (*Continued*)

Form	Material	Advantages	Disadvantages	Roof, Cathedral Ceiling
			difficult to install properly, tears easily, and requires careful sealing at all joints and penetrations. dust on reflective surfaces reduces R-value.	
Sprayed in Place	Cellulose	Useful as a fire-resistant covering for sprayed urethane. provides a continuous air-tight seal around penetrations, gaps in framing, etc. ideally suited for rough, irregular surfaces	must be installed by qualified contractor with special equipment. potentially combustible.	N
Foamed in Place	Urethane	high R-value per inch. provides a continuous air-tight seal around penetrations, gaps in framing, etc. ideally suited for rough, irregular surfaces. very useful in specialty designs (e.g. earth-bermed walls, underground construction, etc.).	must be installed by qualified contractor with special equipment. combustible; must be covered with fire-resistant sheathing; cannot be used near chimneys or flues.	E

| | | | | | Masonry Walls | Masonry Walls |
Attic Floor, Flat Ceiling	Walls: Between Framing	Walls: Sheathing	Floors Over Unheated Spaces	Masonry Walls (Interior Surface)	(Exterior Surface Above Ground)	(Exterior Surface Below Ground)
N	N	N	N	E	E	N
D	E	N	D	E	E	N

(Concluded)

TABLE A.2 **Physical Properties of Insulation Materials**

Form 1	Material 2	Nominal 3	Typical Range 4	Nominal R-Value N 5	Nominal Thk. 6	Likelihood of Achieving Rated R-Values 7	$ Per Sq. Ft. Per Inch Thick 8	$ Per Sq. Ft. Per R-Value 9	Density lbs. Per Cu. Ft. (PCF) 10
Rolls, Batts and Blankets	Fiberglass	3.17	3.0–3.8	R-11 R-13 R-19 R-22 R-30 R-38	3½″ 3⅝″ 6½″ 7″ 9″ 13″	F	0.04 to 0.05	0.013 to 0.016	1.5 to 2.5
	Rock wool	3.17	3.0–3.7	R-11 R-13 R-19 R-22	3½″ 3⅝″ 6½″ 7″	F	0.4 to 0.05 0.05	0.013 to 0.016 0.016	1.5 to 4.0 4.0
Loose-Fill: Poured or Blown	Fiberglass	2.2	2.2 @ 0.7 PCF 4.0 @ 2.0 PCF	depends on thickness poured or blown		F	d-i-y poured: 0.03 to 0.04 0.014–0.018 blown-in-wall: 0.20 to 0.28 0.05 to 0.07 blown-in-attic: 0.03 to 0.06 0.015–0.027		0.61 to 2.5
	Rock wool	3.1	2.8–3.7	depends on thickness poured or blown		F	d-i-y poured: 0.03 to 0.04 0.014–0.018 blown-in-wall: 0.20 to 2.28 0.05 to 0.07 blown-in-attic: 0.03 to 0.06 0.015–0.027		1.5 to 2.5
	Perlite	2.7	2.5–4.0	depends on thickness poured or blown		F	0.9 to 0.15	0.033 to 0.056	2 to 11
	Cellulose	3.2	2.8–3.7	depends on thickness poured or blown		F	blown-in-wall: 0.20 to 0.26 0.063–0.081 blown-in-attic: 0.04 to 0.06 0.013–0.019		2.2 to 3.0

Applications

Key: E = Excellent;   G = Good;   F = Fair;   P = Poor;   N.A. = Not Applicable

Permeability to Moisture Vapor Perm-Inches 11	Effect-iveness as a Vapor Barrier 12	Resistance to				Max. Service Temp (°F) 17	Fed Spec HH-I- 18	Availability	
		Water Absorption 13	Moisture Damage 14	Direct Sunlight 15	Fire 16			Packaging 19	(Trade Assns.) Manufacturers, Trade Names 20
Unfaced: more than 100 Faced: depends on facing	Unfaced: not a vapor/in-filtration barrier Faced: fair vapor barrier	G	E	E	G	180°	521 F	Batts up to 8' long Rolls up to 70' long Widths 11″ to 48″ Thicknesses 1″ to 13″ Available with Kraft paper or aluminized paper facings, or unfaced	"Fiberglas" by Owens-Corning (OC) "Microlite" by Manville Bldg. Matl. (MA) Plus products by AT, CER, and others
More Than 100	Unfaced: not a vapor/in-filtration barrier Faced: fair vapor barrier	G	E	E	E	Over 500°	521 F	Batts and rolls Widths 11″ to 14″ Thicknesses 3″ to 8″	Products by CEL, RI, USG, and others
More Than 100	Not a vapor/in-filtration barrier	G	E	E	G	180°	1030 B	Bags: 15 to 30 lbs.	"Fiberglas" by Owens-Corning (OC) "Insul-Safe II" by Certainteed (CT) "Retrofil" by Manville Bldg. Matl. (MA) plus others
More Than 100	Not a vapor/in-filtration barrier	G	E	E	E	Over 500°	1030 B	Bags: 25 to 35 lbs.	Products by CEL, RI, USG, and others
100	Not a vapor/in-filtration barrier	F	G	E	G	200°	574 B	Bags	Products by GAF, GF, RD, and others
High	Not a vapor/in-filtration barrier	P	P	G	F	180°	515 D	Bags: 15 to 30 lbs.	Manufacturers and brand names too numerous to list

(Continued)

TABLE A.2 (*Continued*)

Form 1	Material 2	R-Value/Inch Nominal 3	R-Value/Inch Typical Range 4	Products Commonly Available Nominal R-Value N 5	Products Commonly Available Nominal Thk. 6	Likelihood of Achieving Rated R-Values 7	Typical Cost $ Per Sq. Ft. Per Inch Thick 8	Typical Cost $ Per Sq. Ft. Per R-Value 9	Density lbs. Per Cu. Ft. (PCF) 10
Rigid Board	Fiberglass	4.4	3.85–4.76	4.4	1″	F	0.32	0.073	4
				8.7	2″		to	to	to
				12.0	3″		0.38	0.086	9
	Perlite	2.8	2.06–3.7	2.8	1″	F	0.20	0.071	2
				5.6	2″		to	to	to
				8.3	3″		0.25	0.089	11
	Expanded Polystyrene (EPS)	4.0	3.6 @ 0.9 PCF	4.0	1″	G	0.14 to 0.18	0.035 to 0.045	0.9
			4.0 @ 1.3 PCF	8.0	2″				1.3
			4.4 @ 1.6 PCF	12.0	3″				1.6
	Extruded Polystyrene	5.0	5.0	5.0	1″	E	0.30	0.06	1.6
				7.5	1.5″		to	to	to
				10.0	2″		0.40	0.08	2.0
	Urethane, Isocyanurate	7.2	7.1–7.7	7.2	1″	E	0.40	0.055	1.6
				14.4	2″		to	to	to
				21.6	3″		0.60	0.083	2.0

		Applications							
	Key:	E = Excellent; G = Good; F = Fair; P = Poor; N.A. = Not Applicable							

Permeability to Moisture Vapor Perm-Inches 11	Effectiveness as a Vapor Barrier 12	Resistance to				Max. Service Temp (°F) 17	Fed Spec HH-I- 18	Availability	
		Water Absorption 13	Moisture Damage 14	Direct Sunlight 15	Fire 16			Packaging 19	(Trade Assns.) Manufacturers, Trade Names 20
More Than 100	F	G	E	E	G	180°	N.A.	Panels: 4′ × 8′ Thicknesses: 1″ to 3″ Available with facings of paper, plastics, metals, and unfaced	"Insul-Quick" by Owens-Corning (OC) Plus products by AT, FE, MA, KN and others
High	N.A.	F	G	G	G	Over 500°	N.A.	Thicknesses: ¾″ to 3″	Products by CEL, GF, LU, MA, and others
5.0 @ 0.9 PCF 5.5 @ 1.3 PCF 1.5 @ 1.6 PCF	P	G	G	P	P	165°	524 C Types I, II, III	Panels: 2′ × 8′, 4′ × 8′, Many other sizes Thickness: ¾″ to 6″ T&G edges, foil facings, composite panels, and many other special treatments available	"Cellulite" by Gilman Brothers Co. (GIL) "R-Wall" by Vertex (VER) "Insulform" by Western Insulfoam (WI) "Zonolite" by W. R. Grace & Co. (GR) Plus products by AT, BE, CP, KR, PT, and others
0.6 to 0.9	G	E	E	P	P	165°	524 C Type IV	Lengths: 8′, 9′ Widths: 16″, 24″, 48″ Thicknesses: ¾″ to 2″ T&G edges, special mastics and fasteners available	"Styrofoam" by Dow Chemical (DO) "Foamular" by US Gypsum (USG)
2 to 3	G	G	E	P	P	200°	530 and 1972	Lengths: 8′, 9′, others available Widths: 4′, others available Thicknesses: ½″ to 3″	Isocyanurate: "Thermax" by Celotex (CEL) "High-R" by Owens-Corning (OC) "R-Max" by R-Max Co.

(Continued)

TABLE A.2 (*Continued*)

Form 1	Material 2	R-Value/Inch Nominal 3	R-Value/Inch Typical Range 4	Products Commonly Available Nominal R-Value N 5	Products Commonly Available Nominal Thk. 6	Likelihood of Achieving Rated R-Values 7	Typical Cost $ Per Sq. Ft. Per Inch Thick 8	Typical Cost $ Per Sq. Ft. Per R-Value 9	Density lbs. Per Cu. Ft. (PCF) 10
	Phenolic	5.0	N.A.	N.A.	N.A.	G	0.40 to 0.60	0.080 to 0.120	2.5
Aluminized Foils/Paper		**(R-Value Per Inch Not Applicable)**				P	not applicable	0.03 to 0.05	low
Sprayed in place	Cellulose	3.5	3.0–4.0	not applicable		G	0.40 to 0.80	0.11 0.23	varies
Foamed in place	Urethane	6.2	5.8–6.8	not applicable		G	0.60 to 0.90	0.10 to 0.15	approx. 2

Aluminized Foils/Paper — Direction of Heat Flow:

	Frame	Up	Horizontal
2 Reflective Layers	2 × 4	R-6.4	R-9.8
	2 × 6	R-6.6	R-9.7
3 Reflective Layers	2 × 4	R-8.8	R-11.0
	2 × 6	R-9.0	R-10.0

Applications
Key: E = Excellent; G = Good; F = Fair; P = Poor; N.A. = Not Applicable

Permeability to Moisture Vapor Perm-Inches 11	Effectiveness as a Vapor Barrier 12	Resistance to				Max. Service Temp (°F) 17	Fed Spec HH-I-18	Availability	
		Water Absorption 13	Moisture Damage 14	Direct Sunlight 15	Fire 16			Packaging 19	(Trade Assns.) Manufacturers, Trade Names 20
								T&G edges, foil facings, composite panels, & many other special treatments available	(RM) plus others *Urethane:* "Permatherm" by Evans Products Co. (EV) "R-Board" by GAF (GAF) plus others
N.A.	N.A.	N.A.	N.A.	N.A.	G	300°	N.A.	Various widths & lengths available Thicknesses: 2″, others available Foil facings, paper facings, other special treatments available	"Isophenol" by Lisi, America (LA) plus others
0.1 to 0.3	G	E	E	E	N.A.	N.A.	1252 B	Widths: 16″, 24″, others Lengths: 30′, 60′, others Available with 1, 2, 3, or 4 reflective layers Aluminum-clad sheathing board also available	"Foilpleat" by Foilpleat Co. (FO) "Roifoil" by Roy & Sons Co. (RS) plus others
N.A.	G	P	F	G	F	180°	N.A.	Many different formulations available for specific applications	Manufacturers and brand names too numerous to list
2 to 3	E	E	E	P	P	165°	N.A.	Many different formulations available for specific applications	Manufacturers and brand names too numerous to list

(Concluded)

COST PER R-VALUE COMPARISON OF INSULATION MATERIALS

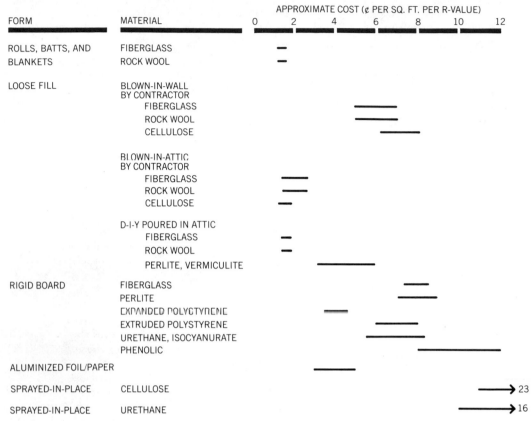

Figure A.1 Relative costs of common insulation materials.

TABLE B.1   Building Materials

Material Description	Density (lb/ft³)	R-value Per-Inch Thickness	R-value For Listed Thickness
Building Boards, Panels, Flooring			
Gypsum or plaster board, ⅜ in.	50	—	0.32
Gypsum or plaster board, ½ in.	50	—	0.45
Gypsum or plaster board, ⅝ in.	50	—	0.56
Plywood (Douglas Fir)	34	1.25	—
Plywood or wood panels, ¾ in.	34	—	0.93
Hardboard, medium density	50	1.37	—
Particle board			
Low density	37	1.85	—
Medium density	50	1.06	—
High density	62.5	0.85	—
Wood subfloor, ¾ in.		—	0.94
Finish Flooring Materials			
Carpet and rubber pad		—	1.23
Cork tile, ⅛ in.		—	0.28
Terrazzo, 1 in.		—	0.08
Tile—asphalt, linoleum, vinyl, rubber		—	0.05
Wood, hardwood finish, ¾ in.		—	0.68
Insulating Materials			
See Appendix A			
Masonry Materials—Concretes			
Cement mortar	116	0.20	—
Gypsum-fiber concrete			
87.5% gypsum, 12.5% wood chips	51	0.60	—
Lightweight aggregates including expanded shale, clay or slate; expanded slags;			
cinders; pumice; vermiculite; also cellular concretes (by density)	120	0.19	—
	100	0.28	—
	80	0.40	—
	60	0.59	—
	40	0.86	—
	20	1.43	—
Sand and gravel or stone aggregate			
oven dried	140	0.11	—
not dried	140	0.08	—
Stucco	116	0.20	—

(Continued)

TABLE B.1 *(Continued)*

| | | R-value | |
Material Description	Density (lb/ft³)	Per-Inch Thickness	For Listed Thickness
Masonry Units			
Brick, common	120	0.20	—
Brick, face	130	0.11	—
Concrete blocks, rectangular core			
Sand and gravel aggregate			
2 core, 8 in., 36 lb.		—	1.04
same with filled cores		—	1.93
Lightweight aggregate (expanded shale, slate or slag, pumice)			
3 core, 6 in., 19 lb.		—	1.65
same with filled cores		—	2.99
2 core, 8 in., 24 lb		—	2.18
same with filled cores		—	5.03
3 core, 12 in., 38 lb.		—	2.48
same with filled cores		—	5.82
Stone, lime or sand		0.08	—
Plastering Materials			
Cement plaster, sand aggregate	116	0.20	—
Sand aggregate, $\frac{3}{8}$ in.		—	0.08
Sand aggregate, $\frac{3}{4}$ in.		—	0.15
Gypsum plaster			
Lightweight aggregate, $\frac{1}{2}$ in.	45	—	0.32
Lightweight aggregate, $\frac{5}{8}$ in.	45	—	0.39
Lightweight aggregate on metal lath, $\frac{3}{4}$ in.		—	0.47
Perlite aggregate	45	0.67	—
Sand aggregate	105	0.18	—
Sand aggregate, $\frac{1}{2}$ in.	105	—	0.09
Sand aggregate, $\frac{5}{8}$ in.	105	—	0.11
Sand aggregate on metal lath, $\frac{3}{4}$ in.		—	0.13
Vermiculite aggregate	45	0.59	—
Roofing Materials			
Asbestos-cement shingles	120	—	0.21
Asphalt roll roofing	70	—	0.15
Asphalt shingles	70	—	0.44
Built-up roofing, $\frac{3}{8}$ in.	70	—	0.33
Slate, $\frac{1}{2}$		—	0.05
Wood shingles		—	0.94
Siding Materials			
Shingles			
Wood, 16 in., 7.5 exposure		—	0.87
Wood, double, 16 in., 12 in. exposure		—	1.19
Siding			
Asphalt roll siding			0.15
Hardboard siding, $\frac{7}{16}$ in.	40	—	0.67
Wood, drop, 1 × 8 in.		—	0.79
Wood, bevel, $\frac{1}{2}$ × 8 in., lapped		—	0.81
Wood, bevel, $\frac{3}{4}$ × 10 in., lapped		—	1.05
Wood, plywood, $\frac{3}{8}$ in., lapped		—	0.59
Aluminum or steel, over sheathing		—	0.61
Woods			
Maple, oak, and similar hardwoods	45	0.91	—
Fir, pine, etc.	32	1.25	—
.... $\frac{3}{4}$ in.	32	—	0.94
.... 1.5 in.	32	—	1.88
.... 5.5 in.	32	—	7.14

TABLE B.2   R-Values of Air Films

Type and Orientation of Air Film	Direction of Heat Flow	R-Value of Air Film on Surface Nonreflective in Long-Wave Infrared
Still air:		
Horizontal	up	0.61
Horizontal	down	0.92
Vertical	across	0.68
Moving air:		
15 mph wind	any	0.17
7.5 mph wind	any	0.25

The weather data presented here are from two sources—the United States weather information is from a compilation by David Jacobson of Princeton University. The Canadian weather data are from the National Research Council of Canada. The data from the two sources are somewhat different, as outlined below. However, both groupings have enough information for running HOT-CAN and other house energy analysis computer programs. The data can also be used to estimate a house's energy requirements using the simplified method shown in Chapter 5.

U.S. WEATHER DATA

The data for the United States are in Imperial units. The data base includes monthly average outside temperatures expressed in degrees Fahrenheit. These are broken down into daytime (8 A.M. to 8 P.M.) and night-time (8 P.M. to 8 A.M.) values. Annual average heating degree days are listed corresponding to degree-day bases of 40 to 70°F in 5°F increments. Average annual cooling degree days are listed only to a 65°F base temperature. The 99 and 97.5 percent values of the winter design temperatures are listed for each location where such data were available. Monthly average solar radiation flux on horizontal as well as vertical surfaces facing different directions are also presented. These are in units of 1000 Btu per square foot per month. For some of the locations, estimates of deep-

ground temperature are also listed. The data are tabulated in alphabetical order by state. Since design temperature and deep-ground temperature were not available for all locations listed, some of these entries are blank. A rough estimate of the deep-ground temperature may be obtained by averaging the twenty-four monthly-average day and night temperatures. For locations where the design temperature value is missing, data from another location with a comparable climate may be substituted.

CANADIAN WEATHER DATA

Canadian weather data are expressed in S.I. units and include monthly-average temperatures, solar radiation flux on vertical surfaces facing different directions, deep-ground temperature, and winter design temperature *difference*. Temperatures are in degrees Celsius and solar flux in MJ/ m^2.day. The data are tabulated alphabetically by province.

Sources:

1. *Monthly Average Weather Data for Selected U.S. Cities,* Princeton University Center for Energy and Environmental Studies Working Paper 62, January 1984.
2. *Weather Data for the HOTCAN Computer Program,* National Research Council, Ottawa, Canada, 1983.

TABLE C.1 Weather Data for U.S. Cities

City: Annette, Alaska **Latitude:** 55.0°
Winter Design Temp.: **Deep Ground Temp.:**

Month		JAN	FEB	MAR	APR	MAY	JUN	JUL	AUG	SEP	OCT	NOV	DEC
Average Air Temperature	(Day)	31.1	36.2	41.1	45.2	51.2	55.1	60.0	59.9	54.7	47.6	39.6	37.0
	(Night)	30.5	34.4	37.0	40.1	46.2	50.2	55.0	55.3	50.5	44.9	38.6	36.4
Solar Flux (Horiz.)		3.6	6.5	17.0	24.7	36.8	37.7	36.6	29.1	15.5	9.2	4.6	2.5
VERTICAL	SOUTH	8.2	11.2	24.1	23.7	29.8	29.5	29.6	26.0	17.9	13.6	9.4	5.1
	SW/SE	6.2	8.8	20.0	21.8	31.3	30.3	30.8	25.1	16.4	11.0	7.3	4.0
	WEST	2.7	5.0	12.8	17.2	27.6	27.5	27.8	21.1	11.9	6.8	3.5	1.9
	EAST	2.7	5.1	12.9	17.7	23.4	25.1	24.8	21.0	10.9	7.0	3.4	1.8
	NW/NE	1.5	2.9	7.0	11.6	17.9	20.1	19.9	15.1	7.1	4.2	1.9	1.2
	NORTH	1.5	2.7	5.6	8.8	15.1	17.5	17.1	11.9	5.8	3.8	1.9	1.2

Base Temperature	40	45	50	55	60	65	70	Cooling Degree Days
Heating Degree Days	753	1531	2591	3944	5576	7341	9147	(Base 65) = 27

City: Bethel, Alaska **Latitude:** 60.7°
Winter Design Temp.: **Deep Ground Temp.:**

Month		JAN	FEB	MAR	APR	MAY	JUN	JUL	AUG	SEP	OCT	NOV	DEC
Average Air Temperature	(Day)	5.7	6.0	17.8	24.5	44.7	55.7	57.6	54.0	48.9	31.1	16.7	5.1
	(Night)	5.5	3.7	13.4	18.9	35.3	46.9	50.6	48.3	42.1	27.6	15.4	4.3
Solar Flux (Horiz.)		1.8	7.0	15.5	20.5	32.2	35.4	29.1	19.6	14.0	6.5	2.7	1.1
VERTICAL	SOUTH	6.1	20.3	26.0	22.0	28.0	29.2	25.0	18.7	17.8	11.4	9.2	5.2
	SW/SE	4.3	15.0	22.0	20.8	28.4	29.8	26.2	19.2	15.6	9.2	6.8	3.8
	WEST	1.4	6.1	13.3	16.3	24.5	26.7	23.8	16.5	11.0	5.2	2.3	1.0
	EAST	1.6	6.2	11.9	15.7	22.7	24.3	19.6	13.8	11.2	5.0	2.3	1.0
	NW/NE	0.7	2.0	5.6	10.0	16.5	19.1	15.8	10.4	6.9	2.9	1.0	0.4
	NORTH	0.7	1.9	4.2	7.3	13.1	16.6	14.6	9.0	5.3	2.7	1.0	0.4

Base Temperature	40	45	50	55	60	65	70	Cooling Degree Days
Heating Degree Days	5644	6862	8252	9845	11570	13352	15162	(Base 65) = 17

(Continued)

TABLE C.1 (*Continued*)

City: Big Delta, Alaska   Latitude: 64.0°
Winter Design Temp.:   Deep Ground Temp.:

Month		JAN	FEB	MAR	APR	MAY	JUN	JUL	AUG	SEP	OCT	NOV	DEC
Average Air	(Day)	-3.9	3.8	15.1	32.0	52.9	62.6	64.8	61.2	47.9	27.7	9.6	-5.8
Temperature	(Night)	-5.5	-1.4	3.9	22.2	41.5	51.9	54.2	51.1	38.9	23.5	5.1	-6.7
Solar Flux (Horiz.)		0.9	4.3	15.9	21.8	33.5	37.0	34.0	22.9	16.0	6.2	2.0	0.3
V E R T I C A L	SOUTH	5.2	14.2	31.4	25.6	29.3	30.2	28.7	23.6	23.8	12.7	8.6	1.8
	SW/SE	3.8	10.4	24.9	23.5	28.4	29.5	28.3	22.0	20.5	9.8	6.3	1.3
	WEST	1.0	3.9	13.5	17.3	24.3	26.0	24.7	17.3	13.0	5.1	1.9	0.2
	EAST	0.8	4.1	13.7	17.2	27.2	28.2	25.1	17.5	12.2	5.2	1.8	0.2
	NW/NE	0.3	1.3	5.5	10.1	18.5	21.1	18.4	11.7	6.5	2.4	0.6	0.1
	NORTH	0.3	1.2	3.9	6.7	12.4	16.2	14.3	8.7	4.8	2.2	0.6	0.1

Base Temperature	40	45	50	55	60	65	70	Cooling Degree Days
Heating Degree Days	6811	7989	9301	10742	12301	13967	15709	(Base 65) = 125

City: Fairbanks, Alaska   Latitude: 64.8°
Winter Design Temp.: -51, -47   Deep Ground Temp.:

Month		JAN	FEB	MAR	APR	MAY	JUN	JUL	AUG	SEP	OCT	NOV	DEC
Average Air	(Day)	-13.5	-3.3	13.5	34.3	55.9	64.9	66.3	60.4	49.1	27.6	3.2	-9.6
Temperature	(Night)	-15.9	-6.8	2.6	25.2	43.9	54.8	57.1	52.9	41.3	21.5	1.3	-9.2
Solar Flux (Horiz.)		0.5	3.4	15.1	20.1	28.6	33.5	31.0	19.9	12.4	5.9	1.1	0.1
V E R T I C A L	SOUTH	2.4	11.4	30.4	23.3	25.1	27.9	26.7	20.1	18.8	14.0	4.7	0.9
	SW/SE	1.8	8.5	24.4	21.4	24.8	26.8	25.3	19.5	16.0	11.1	3.5	0.6
	WEST	0.5	3.2	13.4	15.9	21.7	24.0	21.7	16.1	10.3	5.3	1.0	0.1
	EAST	0.5	3.2	13.0	15.7	22.8	26.1	23.8	15.1	9.9	4.7	1.0	0.1
	NW/NE	0.2	1.1	5.2	9.6	16.1	19.5	17.4	10.6	5.5	2.1	0.4	0.0
	NORTH	0.2	1.1	3.7	6.8	11.7	15.5	13.4	8.5	4.4	2.0	0.4	0.0

Base Temperature	40	45	50	55	60	65	70	Cooling Degree Days
Heating Degree Days	7501	8642	9884	11253	12769	14409	16144	(Base 65) = 131

(*Continued*)

TABLE C.1 (*Continued*)

City: Gulkana, Alaska   Latitude: 62.1°
Winter Design Temp.:   Deep Ground Temp.:

Month		JAN	FEB	MAR	APR	MAY	JUN	JUL	AUG	SEP	OCT	NOV	DEC
Average Air	(Day)	-1.8	5.4	24.2	37.6	49.6	59.3	63.7	57.8	48.9	29.5	9.0	-3.6
Temperature	(Night)	-6.3	-2.2	12.0	24.8	37.6	47.9	53.4	47.4	38.7	22.9	5.1	-4.8
Solar Flux (Horiz.)		1.3	4.9	14.9	21.9	34.3	37.9	36.2	23.9	16.2	7.0	1.7	0.6
V E R T I C A L	SOUTH	6.2	13.0	26.3	24.5	30.3	30.5	30.3	24.8	23.3	15.3	5.0	2.6
	SW/SE	4.5	9.7	22.4	21.2	28.2	29.2	29.3	22.7	20.6	11.8	3.9	1.9
	WEST	1.3	4.3	13.2	15.7	23.3	25.2	25.4	17.3	13.4	5.6	1.6	0.5
	EAST	1.2	4.3	11.4	18.5	26.8	28.9	26.6	17.0	11.5	5.4	1.3	0.5
	NW/NE	0.4	1.7	5.5	11.0	18.2	21.7	19.5	10.8	6.3	2.5	0.7	0.2
	NORTH	0.4	1.5	4.3	7.3	12.7	16.3	15.3	8.2	5.0	2.3	0.7	0.2

Base Temperature	40	45	50	55	60	65	70	Cooling Degree Days
Heating Degree Days	6366	7565	8905	10400	12031	13755	15539	(Base 65) = 61

City: Homer, Alaska   Latitude: 59.6°
Winter Design Temp.:   Deep Ground Temp.:

Month		JAN	FEB	MAR	APR	MAY	JUN	JUL	AUG	SEP	OCT	NOV	DEC
Average Air	(Day)	21.2	25.8	29.7	39.9	47.2	53.5	57.6	56.6	49.7	38.3	28.6	20.9
Temperature	(Night)	19.1	22.0	23.1	32.7	39.6	47.0	50.0	49.7	44.5	34.0	27.2	19.4
Solar Flux (Horiz.)		2.6	6.2	15.2	25.9	35.2	40.6	36.9	22.8	16.5	9.4	3.3	1.7
V E R T I C A L	SOUTH	9.7	14.5	25.6	28.3	29.6	31.6	29.5	22.1	22.7	19.8	10.2	7.4
	SW/SE	7.2	11.1	20.2	25.3	29.1	32.0	29.3	21.0	18.9	15.2	7.5	5.9
	WEST	2.3	5.2	11.7	18.4	25.1	28.7	26.2	16.8	12.5	7.5	2.8	1.5
	EAST	2.2	5.1	12.6	19.3	26.3	28.7	27.7	16.8	13.4	7.7	2.8	1.5
	NW/NE	0.9	2.1	5.9	11.3	19.0	21.7	20.7	11.8	7.3	3.4	1.1	0.6
	NORTH	0.8	1.9	4.6	7.7	14.2	17.1	15.9	9.2	5.4	2.9	1.1	0.6

Base Temperature	40	45	50	55	60	65	70	Cooling Degree Days
Heating Degree Days	2839	3951	5261	6818	8552	10361	12185	(Base 65) = 1

(*Continued*)

TABLE C.1 (*Continued*)

City: Kodiak, Alaska Latitude: 57.8°
Winter Design Temp.: 10, 13° Deep Ground Temp.:

Month		JAN	FEB	MAR	APR	MAY	JUN	JUL	AUG	SEP	OCT	NOV	DEC
Average Air	(Day)	33.4	32.2	33.2	39.9	45.1	51.2	57.2	55.9	51.4	42.6	34.6	30.2
Temperature	(Night)	32.1	30.1	29.9	35.7	40.6	46.6	52.2	52.1	47.8	38.3	32.8	29.3
Solar Flux (Horiz.)		3.4	6.4	15.5	22.9	33.8	40.6	37.6	24.8	14.5	9.5	4.2	1.9
V E R T I C A L	SOUTH	11.9	14.5	23.7	23.8	28.3	31.4	30.7	23.2	18.4	19.2	12.7	6.3
	SW/SE	8.5	10.7	19.0	22.0	28.5	32.5	30.1	22.5	15.6	14.7	9.1	4.6
	WEST	2.7	5.0	11.6	16.8	24.8	29.5	26.4	18.6	10.9	7.4	3.3	1.6
	EAST	3.0	5.4	12.4	16.6	23.6	27.7	27.6	17.9	11.7	7.6	3.7	1.6
	NW/NE	1.0	2.2	5.8	10.4	17.9	21.5	21.2	12.9	7.2	3.4	1.3	0.7
–	NORTH	1.0	2.1	4.4	7.6	14.5	17.8	17.0	10.4	5.7	3.0	1.3	0.7

Base Temperature	40	45	50	55	60	65	70	Cooling Degree Days
Heating Degree Days	1458	2514	3808	5366	7103	8899	10714	(Base 65) = 13

City: Yakutat, Alaska Latitude: 59.5°
Winter Design Temp.: Deep Ground Temp.:

Month		JAN	FEB	MAR	APR	MAY	JUN	JUL	AUG	SEP	OCT	NOV	DEC
Average Air	(Day)	24.8	28.9	31.8	37.4	44.5	49.6	54.6	54.1	49.3	40.2	31.3	25.1
Temperature	(Night)	23.9	26.5	30.5	33.9	43.3	48.4	52.8	52.5	47.3	40.0	30.7	24.0
Solar Flux (Horiz.)		2.2	6.4	13.1	23.1	29.3	36.2	34.0	19.7	13.2	6.8	2.5	1.3
V E R T I C A L	SOUTH	7.3	16.6	19.7	25.2	25.9	29.5	28.4	18.8	15.8	11.4	5.9	4.7
	SW/SE	5.5	12.0	17.7	23.3	24.8	29.1	27.6	18.3	14.9	9.4	4.4	3.5
	WEST	1.9	5.1	11.4	17.6	21.1	25.6	23.9	15.5	11.1	5.5	2.0	1.1
	EAST	1.8	5.6	9.2	17.3	21.9	25.3	24.5	14.9	9.8	5.1	2.0	1.1
	NW/NE	0.8	2.1	5.5	10.5	16.8	19.7	18.9	11.3	6.6	3.1	1.1	0.5
–	NORTH	0.8	2.0	4.7	7.6	13.9	16.5	15.6	9.6	5.5	2.9	1.1	0.5

Base Temperature	40	45	50	55	60	65	70	Cooling Degree Days
Heating Degree Days	2147	3212	4512	6073	7824	9637	11457	(Base 65) = 6

(*Continued*)

TABLE C.1 (*Continued*)

City: Tucson, Arizona   Latitude: 32.1°
Winter Design Temp.: 28, 32   Deep Ground Temp.:

Month		JAN	FEB	MAR	APR	MAY	JUN	JUL	AUG	SEP	OCT	NOV	DEC
Average Air	(Day)	57.5	59.8	68.0	75.3	83.3	91.9	90.9	89.8	85.2	77.7	64.5	58.3
Temperature	(Night)	45.4	43.6	51.2	58.7	64.6	77.2	79.9	78.0	74.0	62.1	51.0	45.0
Solar Flux (Horiz.)		26.5	33.2	46.2	58.1	70.0	68.5	56.3	56.1	52.8	44.0	28.7	23.5
V E R T I C A L	SOUTH	39.3	39.2	37.6	31.1	25.3	22.4	24.9	29.6	37.2	45.2	40.2	37.2
	SW/SE	30.2	32.1	34.1	34.9	35.1	31.7	29.0	32.8	35.2	38.7	32.0	28.5
	WEST	16.8	20.7	26.9	33.2	39.2	36.9	30.7	32.0	29.1	27.0	18.8	15.3
	EAST	17.3	21.2	29.7	35.8	40.0	39.9	34.1	34.6	31.9	27.3	18.5	15.5
	NW/NE	6.9	9.3	17.0	24.2	30.7	32.7	28.1	25.8	18.5	12.7	7.4	5.9
	NORTH	5.8	6.5	10.7	13.3	17.9	20.7	19.9	16.8	10.7	8.1	5.8	5.0

Base Temperature	40	45	50	55	60	65	70		Cooling Degree Days
Heating Degree Days	69	185	416	794	1329	2025	2879		(Base 65) = 3167

City: Little Rock, Arkansas   Latitude: 34.8°
Winter Design Temp.: 15, 20   Deep Ground Temp.:

Month		JAN	FEB	MAR	APR	MAY	JUN	JUL	AUG	SEP	OCT	NOV	DEC
Average Air	(Day)	44.2	48.0	56.7	69.1	77.4	83.7	84.8	85.5	79.6	67.9	55.5	46.3
Temperature	(Night)	36.6	40.0	47.9	58.2	65.0	72.6	74.3	75.3	67.7	58.7	45.1	40.0
Solar Flux (Horiz.)		18.7	21.5	35.1	43.4	49.9	51.7	56.1	52.0	40.7	32.8	21.7	18.6
V E R T I C A L	SOUTH	28.9	25.7	32.4	29.9	27.2	23.5	26.3	30.1	32.8	36.9	31.3	30.9
	SW/SE	23.6	21.9	29.9	30.7	31.0	29.6	32.0	33.8	32.3	30.8	25.2	24.8
	WEST	13.5	14.3	23.1	27.8	31.8	32.8	34.6	33.1	27.0	20.9	14.9	13.4
	EAST	11.9	13.5	22.1	27.6	31.3	32.3	35.8	34.2	25.8	21.4	14.4	11.9
	NW/NE	5.5	7.2	14.0	20.0	25.1	26.9	29.2	25.5	16.6	10.8	6.5	5.1
	NORTH	4.9	5.9	10.9	14.8	18.7	19.8	20.6	17.0	11.8	8.0	5.3	4.5

Base Temperature	40	45	50	55	60	65	70		Cooling Degree Days
Heating Degree Days	361	683	1140	1737	2455	3315	4345		(Base 65) = 2133

(*Continued*)

TABLE C.1 (*Continued*)

City: Fresno, California
Winter Design Temp.: 28, 30

Latitude: 36.8°
Deep Ground Temp.:63

Month		JAN	FEB	MAR	APR	MAY	JUN	JUL	AUG	SEP	OCT	NOV	DEC
Average Air	(Day)	47.2	54.6	61.9	66.4	75.8	84.5	90.3	87.3	81.9	72.0	57.4	46.0
temperature	(Night)	39.5	44.4	48.9	52.2	60.4	67.7	72.9	70.3	63.9	55.4	46.2	39.2
Solar Flux (Horiz.)		13.7	21.1	38.8	47.8	65.3	73.8	72.4	66.7	55.0	42.9	21.3	13.5
V E R T I C A L	SOUTH	20.8	26.5	35.7	31.8	29.2	25.4	27.4	34.1	43.0	50.4	32.7	21.9
	SW/SE	17.1	22.0	32.5	33.3	36.2	36.1	37.7	39.7	41.0	41.9	26.1	18.1
	WEST	10.3	14.2	25.0	29.9	37.7	41.1	41.7	38.4	32.5	26.8	14.5	10.4
	EAST	9.6	14.3	25.7	30.1	38.5	41.3	40.0	38.5	33.3	26.7	13.7	9.0
	NW/NE	5.1	7.1	14.9	20.8	28.6	32.0	30.3	25.7	18.0	11.3	5.0	4.8
	NORTH	4.7	5.5	10.3	13.7	17.3	19.3	18.5	14.0	9.6	7.2	4.9	4.4

Base Temperature	40	45	50	55	60	65	70	Cooling Degree Days
Heating Degree Days	127	342	740	1356	2170	3172	4342	(Base 65) = 1698

City: Los Angeles, California
Winter Design Temp.: 39, 40

Latitude: 33.9°
Deep Ground Temp.:

Month		JAN	FEB	MAR	APR	MAY	JUN	JUL	AUG	SEP	OCT	NOV	DEC
Average Air	(Day)	57.5	60.8	58.5	62.8	64.2	69.0	70.0	70.9	69.4	67.8	61.9	60.8
Temperature	(Night)	51.0	55.3	52.9	55.7	58.2	62.0	63.4	64.8	63.2	59.7	55.3	53.6
Solar Flux (Horiz.)		21.8	22.3	39.5	47.7	52.3	49.3	55.3	53.5	37.6	28.9	27.9	22.5
V E R T I C A L	SOUTH	34.5	27.0	36.5	30.2	26.0	23.5	24.1	28.5	30.1	31.6	41.2	37.7
	SW/SE	27.0	23.5	33.4	32.4	31.4	29.1	31.5	34.5	29.6	26.8	31.0	27.2
	WEST	14.9	16.1	26.1	30.4	33.6	32.4	35.1	34.9	25.7	18.9	17.0	13.7
	EAST	14.5	14.9	26.8	31.5	35.3	33.4	35.7	33.6	27.0	19.7	18.8	16.1
	NW/NE	5.8	7.8	16.0	22.0	28.4	28.5	29.1	24.7	17.8	10.9	7.1	5.6
	NORTH	4.9	6.1	11.2	14.1	19.4	21.1	19.7	15.7	12.1	8.3	5.6	4.8

Base Temperature	40	45	50	55	60	65	70	Cooling Degree Days
Heating Degree Days	0	6	44	238	817	1850	3299	(Base 65) = 538

(*Continued*)

TABLE C.1 (*Continued*)

City: Mount Shasta, California   Latitude:41.2⁰
Winter Design Temp.:   Deep Ground Temp.:

Month		JAN	FEB	MAR	APR	MAY	JUN	JUL	AUG	SEP	OCT	NOV	DEC
Average Air	(Day)	35.0	41.2	46.6	51.4	58.3	66.8	74.7	75.8	69.2	56.1	44.8	38.8
Temperature	(Night)	30.7	35.0	41.5	42.6	52.3	59.3	67.9	61.5	57.8	44.2	39.8	33.3
Solar Flux (Horiz.)		13.3	17.4	30.5	41.8	52.2	60.8	73.0	65.4	46.8	28.7	11.7	12.3
V E R T I C A L	SOUTH	23.0	25.3	30.7	31.5	30.6	28.6	31.7	38.7	41.4	38.1	18.2	23.9
	SW/SE	18.0	20.5	27.7	34.0	33.9	34.9	40.1	42.6	38.7	31.6	14.3	17.9
	WEST	9.6	12.4	20.5	30.3	33.1	36.8	42.0	39.1	29.3	19.7	8.2	8.6
	EAST	9.4	12.1	20.4	27.0	34.2	38.4	42.6	39.3	28.8	18.6	8.5	8.9
	NW/NE	4.5	6.0	12.1	18.7	25.9	29.8	31.0	25.3	15.4	8.2	4.5	3.6
	NORTH	4.2	5.1	8.7	13.2	17.8	19.5	18.0	13.9	9.0	6.0	4.2	3.4

Base Temperature	40	45	50	55	60	65	70	Cooling Degree Days
Heating Degree Days	661	1304	2176	3222	4441	5816	7321	(Base 65) = 742

City: San Francisco, California   Latitude: 37.6⁰
Winter Design Temp.: 38,40   Deep Ground Temp.:

Month		JAN	FEB	MAR	APR	MAY	JUN	JUL	AUG	SEP	OCT	NOV	DEC
Average Air	(Day)	50.5	52.7	55.0	57.8	58.6	63.1	65.2	65.7	64.3	64.4	56.6	50.6
Temperature	(Night)	46.2	46.6	50.1	50.3	50.6	54.6	57.3	57.5	56.5	56.3	50.7	46.5
Solar Flux (Horiz.)		16.6	22.2	38.0	49.8	60.8	64.1	68.5	60.1	51.0	34.8	19.8	14.7
V E R T I C A L	SOUTH	26.7	29.1	37.0	32.7	29.3	25.7	27.5	33.1	41.0	42.0	30.8	25.3
	SW/SE	21.6	22.7	33.5	34.8	35.9	34.1	37.1	38.8	40.6	36.9	23.7	20.3
	WEST	11.7	13.6	24.6	31.4	36.9	37.5	40.5	36.9	32.1	24.2	13.0	10.6
	EAST	10.5	15.2	23.8	30.7	33.6	33.8	34.0	31.2	28.1	20.4	13.8	9.4
	NW/NE	5.0	6.8	13.3	20.6	25.0	26.4	25.4	21.3	15.7	9.5	5.8	4.5
	NORTH	4.6	5.2	9.4	13.3	17.0	18.3	17.3	13.9	9.8	7.0	4.8	4.2

Base Temperature	40	45	50	55	60	65	70	Cooling Degree Days
Heating Degree Days	10	89	330	981	2175	3703	5394	(Base 65) = 213

(*Continued*)

TABLE C.1 (*Continued*)

City: Colorado Springs, Colorado   Latitude: 38.8°
Winter Design Temp.:-3,2   Deep Ground Temp.:

Month		JAN	FEB	MAR	APR	MAY	JUN	JUL	AUG	SEP	OCT	NOV	DEC
Average Air	(Day)	36.5	38.1	42.3	52.2	62.3	72.4	76.8	75.6	70.2	58.8	42.6	39.5
Temperature	(Night)	25.3	26.0	29.6	40.3	49.5	57.9	63.9	62.5	55.1	45.9	33.1	27.7
Solar Flux (Horiz.)		17.9	22.3	34.5	43.5	50.6	57.5	54.9	53.4	41.9	33.0	20.5	15.8
V E R T I C A L	SOUTH	32.0	30.9	34.6	30.9	28.9	26.2	28.8	32.9	35.1	40.9	33.8	29.4
	SW/SE	25.4	25.0	31.0	29.5	30.5	30.8	31.2	33.1	31.4	34.3	25.7	22.1
	WEST	13.0	14.9	22.8	25.9	29.6	32.4	31.3	30.1	24.0	21.8	13.3	11.1
	EAST	11.6	14.7	22.1	31.2	32.3	35.5	37.8	35.6	26.7	20.9	13.4	11.4
	NW/NE	4.7	6.7	12.4	21.5	25.0	28.0	29.8	25.1	15.6	9.7	5.2	4.4
	NORTH	4.2	5.3	9.1	14.2	17.9	18.8	19.9	15.9	10.0	7.0	4.4	4.1

Base Temperature	40	45	50	55	60	65	70		Cooling Degree Days
Heating Degree Days	1414	2097	2931	3933	5096	6439	7935		(Base 65) = 757

City: Denver, Colorado   Latitude: 39.8°
Winter Design Temp.: -5, 1   Deep Ground Temp.:

Month		JAN	FEB	MAR	APR	MAY	JUN	JUL	AUG	SEP	OCT	NOV	DEC
Average Air	(Day)	36.1	45.7	42.5	55.0	61.9	73.7	80.7	76.1	66.5	54.7	43.6	40.1
Temperature	(Night)	26.3	33.9	32.5	42.9	49.8	59.3	67.3	63.1	55.8	41.0	32.1	29.0
Solar Flux (Horiz.)		20.3	23.8	39.6	48.5	54.8	64.1	65.2	55.9	40.2	34.7	21.3	19.5
V E R T I C A L	SOUTH	35.9	33.3	39.7	36.9	34.3	30.7	32.9	36.5	35.1	43.8	34.5	37.5
	SW/SE	26.8	26.2	34.6	34.8	36.2	34.6	35.3	36.2	32.8	36.7	26.9	29.0
	WEST	13.5	15.7	25.1	29.8	35.2	35.5	34.8	32.5	26.1	23.3	14.6	14.2
	EAST	14.7	17.0	26.8	34.5	38.5	41.2	43.7	37.7	26.7	22.3	14.6	13.2
	NW/NE	5.9	7.9	15.5	24.1	30.5	32.4	33.7	26.7	17.5	10.3	6.6	5.3
	NORTH	5.3	6.3	11.2	16.9	22.4	21.5	21.3	17.7	12.8	7.6	5.8	4.9

Base Temperature	40	45	50	55	60	65	70		Cooling Degree Days
Heating Degree Days	1240	1890	2693	3661	4804	6123	7600		(Base 65) = 814

(*Continued*)

TABLE C.1 (*Continued*)

City: Grand Junction, Colorado   Latitude: 39.1°
Winter Design Temp.: 2, 7   Deep Ground Temp.:52

Month		JAN	FEB	MAR	APR	MAY	JUN	JUL	AUG	SEP	OCT	NOV	DEC
Average Air	(Day)	27.3	36.3	44.6	56.1	69.7	79.2	87.3	83.5	73.1	57.8	45.6	32.4
Temperature	(Night)	20.6	27.8	35.2	45.0	57.0	65.4	72.2	69.8	58.9	47.2	34.1	25.9
Solar Flux (Horiz.)		16.7	19.0	35.1	42.3	54.2	61.1	61.4	54.8	44.2	29.3	20.1	15.9
V E R T I C A L	SOUTH	29.2	26.1	35.2	30.7	28.9	27.6	29.3	32.5	37.3	35.6	32.8	30.4
	SW/SE	22.5	21.7	30.6	32.5	30.9	32.7	33.7	33.4	35.1	29.4	25.0	22.1
	WEST	11.8	13.3	22.1	29.2	30.2	34.5	34.3	30.3	27.2	19.2	13.0	10.2
	EAST	11.5	12.3	23.3	26.9	36.6	38.7	37.8	34.0	27.4	19.2	13.6	11.5
	NW/NE	4.6	6.0	13.1	19.2	27.4	30.5	28.9	23.2	15.7	8.8	5.4	4.1
	NORTH	4.2	4.9	9.3	14.1	17.2	19.8	18.7	14.2	9.7	6.5	4.6	3.7

Base Temperature	40	45	50	55	60	65	70	Cooling Degree Days
Heating Degree Days	1397	2076	2890	3820	4870	6040	7347	(Base 65) = 1398

City: Pueblo, Colorado   Latitude:38.3°
Winter Design Temp.:-7, 0   Deep Ground Temp.:

Month		JAN	FEB	MAR	APR	MAY	JUN	JUL	AUG	SEP	OCT	NOV	DEC
Average Air	(Day)	33.1	42.2	45.4	57.6	69.9	79.5	83.2	82.9	73.4	65.6	49.4	42.6
Temperature	(Night)	20.8	27.4	30.9	43.3	54.2	62.9	68.1	66.6	58.1	47.7	34.8	26.6
Solar Flux (Horiz.)		20.0	22.3	36.2	46.8	56.4	57.6	58.8	52.5	45.1	32.7	19.2	19.2
V E R T I C A L	SOUTH	35.1	30.9	34.6	32.5	30.1	27.0	28.3	32.5	37.6	39.8	30.6	36.7
	SW/SE	27.2	23.7	29.6	32.2	32.9	31.2	31.3	32.7	35.7	32.4	23.4	27.7
	WEST	13.9	13.9	21.7	28.2	32.5	32.6	31.8	30.1	28.0	20.6	12.4	13.2
	EAST	13.3	15.5	24.6	31.5	37.1	38.2	39.4	36.1	27.8	21.5	13.2	13.1
	NW/NE	5.1	6.5	13.9	21.4	28.0	30.6	30.5	25.1	16.2	9.6	5.4	4.5
	NORTH	4.5	5.0	9.5	13.8	18.2	20.2	19.2	15.6	10.2	6.7	4.5	4.1

Base Temperature	40	45	50	55	60	65	70	Cooling Degree Days
Heating Degree Days	1448	2035	2755	3614	4612	5773	7106	(Base 65) = 1339

(*Continued*)

TABLE C.1 (*Continued*)

City: Washington, District of Columbia Latitude: 39.0°
Winter Design Temp.: 14, 17 Deep Ground Temp.:

Month		JAN	FEB	MAR	APR	MAY	JUN	JUL	AUG	SEP	OCT	NOV	DEC
Average Air	(Day)	33.8	37.3	47.9	60.3	68.2	76.1	81.6	80.3	74.9	61.8	51.1	39.1
Temperature	(Night)	27.6	28.6	38.8	49.7	58.8	63.9	70.2	68.3	63.7	51.8	42.2	32.5
Solar Flux (Horiz.)		17.2	18.1	31.2	42.2	48.9	49.5	51.3	49.2	37.5	24.8	17.0	14.1
V E R T I C A L	SOUTH	30.1	23.9	30.1	30.6	27.7	26.8	28.0	31.3	32.0	30.2	26.9	25.4
	SW/SE	23.4	19.0	27.4	32.3	31.2	29.9	32.7	33.2	29.1	25.1	19.9	20.0
	WEST	12.2	11.8	20.7	28.8	31.3	30.7	33.7	30.8	22.7	16.5	10.8	10.1
	EAST	11.9	12.9	20.5	27.0	31.2	32.9	33.8	31.9	24.5	16.7	12.5	9.3
	NW/NE	4.8	6.3	12.6	19.2	24.2	27.0	27.2	23.2	15.1	8.6	5.3	4.1
	NORTH	4.3	4.9	9.5	14.0	17.4	20.0	19.8	16.0	10.6	6.7	4.4	3.9

Base Temperature	40	45	50	55	60	65	70	Cooling Degree Days
Heating Degree Days	893	1429	2112	2930	3887	5004	6283	(Base 65) = 1256

City: Jacksonville, Florida Latitude: 30.5°
Winter Design Temp.: 29, 32 Deep Ground Temp.:

Month		JAN	FEB	MAR	APR	MAY	JUN	JUL	AUG	SEP	OCT	NOV	DEC
Average Air	(Day)	56.3	59.6	67.9	75.8	80.4	82.5	84.2	84.6	80.7	73.5	64.5	59.2
Temperature	(Night)	47.5	49.7	57.5	64.9	70.7	74.1	75.7	76.3	74.1	64.2	56.7	49.6
Solar Flux (Horiz.)		21.5	28.3	41.1	50.2	57.0	53.7	51.7	49.7	38.4	35.9	23.3	20.2
V E R T I C A L	SOUTH	29.4	32.1	33.7	28.6	26.1	24.2	25.7	28.4	29.6	36.6	30.2	29.1
	SW/SE	24.0	27.5	32.0	31.9	32.4	30.2	30.6	30.1	28.9	31.9	24.3	23.2
	WEST	14.4	18.7	25.8	30.5	35.1	33.9	33.1	29.5	25.1	23.0	15.0	13.3
	EAST	13.6	17.7	25.1	30.8	35.9	35.2	35.4	34.4	26.2	23.0	15.0	12.8
	NW/NE	6.6	9.2	16.3	22.0	29.4	30.8	30.6	26.8	19.1	12.7	6.8	5.9
	NORTH	5.8	7.1	12.3	14.1	20.6	23.4	23.0	18.3	14.7	9.5	5.7	5.3

Base Temperature	40	45	50	55	60	65	70	Cooling Degree Days
Heating Degree Days	84	187	353	615	1003	1560	2320	(Base 65) = 2654

(*Continued*)

TABLE C.1 (*Continued*)

City: Miami, Florida
Winter Design Temp.: 44, 47
Latitude: 25.8°
Deep Ground Temp.:

Month		JAN	FEB	MAR	APR	MAY	JUN	JUL	AUG	SEP	OCT	NOV	DEC
Average Air	(Day)	71.4	72.8	75.8	78.2	80.4	83.2	84.4	85.5	84.1	79.9	76.6	71.0
Temperature	(Night)	64.6	65.5	69.3	71.1	75.0	77.6	77.5	79.1	78.7	74.3	69.8	62.8
Solar Flux (Horiz.)		25.0	35.2	46.8	48.9	51.9	48.1	53.3	52.9	42.7	38.4	28.7	27.3
VERTICAL	SOUTH	31.2	36.1	34.9	27.0	23.5	22.8	24.9	26.9	30.0	34.7	33.9	36.5
	SW/SE	24.4	29.8	34.2	29.9	29.4	27.2	30.8	30.6	30.5	30.8	26.9	28.7
	WEST	15.5	21.3	29.4	29.5	32.5	30.5	34.7	31.7	27.4	23.9	17.5	17.3
	EAST	17.1	23.7	30.5	31.1	33.4	32.2	36.0	35.7	28.1	25.2	18.9	17.7
	NW/NE	7.7	12.0	20.1	23.9	28.9	29.5	32.3	29.0	20.6	15.4	8.7	7.5
	NORTH	6.1	8.6	13.8	16.5	21.8	24.4	25.8	20.1	15.2	11.8	6.8	6.2

Base Temperature	40	45	50	55	60	65	70	Cooling Degree Days
Heating Degree Days	0	4	20	59	133	264	506	(Base 65) = 4054

City: Atlanta, Georgia
Winter Design Temp.: 17, 22
Latitude: 33.7°
Deep Ground Temp.:

Month		JAN	FEB	MAR	APR	MAY	JUN	JUL	AUG	SEP	OCT	NOV	DEC
Average Air	(Day)	43.7	46.4	54.8	68.8	74.2	78.6	81.6	81.3	76.5	66.2	55.8	47.4
Temperature	(Night)	37.4	39.8	46.4	58.6	63.3	69.1	72.2	71.8	68.4	56.5	47.1	40.4
Solar Flux (Horiz.)		18.6	21.8	37.5	46.8	54.7	53.4	53.3	53.0	39.4	34.2	22.6	19.2
VERTICAL	SOUTH	27.2	25.5	32.2	30.0	26.7	25.2	25.1	29.7	31.4	36.9	32.6	30.8
	SW/SE	21.4	21.7	29.7	31.5	32.4	30.8	30.1	33.7	29.8	31.2	26.8	24.0
	WEST	12.5	14.6	23.5	29.3	34.4	33.8	32.0	32.9	24.9	21.4	15.7	13.1
	EAST	12.8	14.0	23.8	30.9	34.2	34.6	34.6	32.5	26.3	22.0	14.2	12.7
	NW/NE	6.1	7.6	15.1	22.2	27.4	29.5	28.6	24.4	17.6	11.0	6.1	5.4
	NORTH	5.3	6.3	11.2	14.9	19.2	21.9	19.9	16.5	12.8	7.9	5.0	4.8

Base Temperature	40	45	50	55	60	65	70	Cooling Degree Days
Heating Degree Days	331	639	1078	1656	2392	3309	4416	(Base 65) = 1609

(*Continued*)

TABLE C.1 (*Continued*)

City: Boise, Idaho   Latitude: 43.6°
Winter Design Temp.: 3, 10   Deep Ground Temp.:51

Month		JAN	FEB	MAR	APR	MAY	JUN	JUL	AUG	SEP	OCT	NOV	DEC
Average Air	(Day)	34.3	35.6	47.4	55.5	68.8	71.3	80.9	79.4	72.6	54.5	45.0	32.4
Temperature	(Night)	30.3	30.4	38.1	42.8	55.2	58.7	66.2	66.0	59.8	42.9	40.0	29.7
Solar Flux (Horiz.)		10.5	14.6	24.0	39.2	53.1	54.6	67.2	55.9	37.6	24.6	10.9	9.1
V E R T I C A L	SOUTH	19.2	22.6	26.1	30.5	32.0	28.8	32.9	36.6	34.6	33.4	17.7	17.6
	SW/SE	15.2	17.0	22.7	29.5	35.3	33.7	39.6	37.8	31.1	27.6	13.7	13.3
	WEST	7.8	9.7	16.4	25.1	33.7	34.4	40.5	33.5	23.3	16.8	7.5	6.7
	EAST	7.2	11.4	17.1	26.9	32.3	33.5	40.5	35.7	24.6	16.3	7.8	6.8
	NW/NE	3.6	5.2	10.3	18.5	23.8	26.0	29.5	23.2	13.7	7.5	4.0	3.2
	NORTH	3.5	4.3	8.1	13.1	16.9	18.5	18.5	13.7	8.9	5.6	3.7	3.1

Base Temperature	40	45	50	55	60	65	70	Cooling Degree Days
Heating Degree Days	973	1651	2493	3503	4667	5980	7429	(Base 65) = 1012

City: Chicago, Illinois   Latitude: 41.8°
Winter Design Temp.: –8, –4   Deep Ground Temp.:

Month		JAN	FEB	MAR	APR	MAY	JUN	JUL	AUG	SEP	OCT	NOV	DEC
Average Air	(Day)	27.0	29.9	40.2	55.1	59.8	71.6	80.2	76.3	66.1	57.8	42.9	33.0
Temperature	(Night)	23.7	25.2	36.6	48.1	53.7	62.6	70.9	67.4	56.7	49.5	39.0	30.4
Solar Flux (Horiz.)		14.5	18.9	29.1	44.0	50.3	58.1	63.5	49.8	40.8	26.3	15.9	11.2
V E R T I C A L	SOUTH	24.4	25.9	30.0	34.5	34.5	32.7	34.1	36.6	37.5	33.2	25.1	18.0
	SW/SE	19.4	21.5	26.5	32.9	35.8	36.5	37.8	36.6	33.8	27.0	19.1	13.9
	WEST	10.6	13.7	20.0	28.1	34.4	37.1	37.8	33.1	26.1	17.1	10.6	7.8
	EAST	10.0	13.1	20.9	30.1	37.0	37.3	40.8	35.0	27.9	17.9	11.7	8.4
	NW/NE	5.2	7.3	14.0	21.3	29.8	30.3	31.2	26.2	17.1	9.3	5.0	4.8
	NORTH	5.0	6.4	11.5	16.0	22.9	22.9	21.4	19.8	12.1	7.4	5.3	4.6

Base Temperature	40	45	50	55	60	65	70	Cooling Degree Days
Heating Degree Days	1393	2106	2943	3897	4989	6238	7656	(Base 65) = 865

(*Continued*)

TABLE C.1 (*Continued*)

City: Indianapolis, Indiana   Latitude: 39.9°
Winter Design Temp.: -2, 2   Deep Ground Temp.:

Month		JAN	FEB	MAR	APR	MAY	JUN	JUL	AUG	SEP	OCT	NOV	DEC
Average Air	(Day)	28.6	30.1	42.8	54.3	71.5	73.1	78.9	77.5	72.1	54.4	41.3	32.1
Temperature	(Night)	24.0	25.3	36.6	47.2	59.8	62.7	69.8	68.1	64.8	47.8	38.7	30.3
Solar Flux (Horiz.)		17.5	19.7	32.1	45.5	58.7	55.1	55.8	51.1	34.7	25.4	14.1	11.9
– SOUTH		29.2	26.2	32.2	34.5	34.6	33.2	33.9	35.3	31.1	29.4	19.0	17.9
V E SW/SE		23.4	21.3	29.6	33.3	37.4	36.4	36.8	35.9	29.7	24.8	15.2	13.5
R T WEST		12.9	13.4	23.1	29.0	36.8	37.4	37.0	33.1	24.6	17.3	9.6	8.0
I C EAST		11.9	13.6	22.4	31.5	39.7	39.0	38.7	34.7	23.9	18.0	10.3	9.1
A L NW/NE		5.9	7.4	15.0	22.6	30.9	32.6	31.6	25.6	17.2	10.6	6.6	5.3
– NORTH		5.5	6.5	12.4	16.8	22.0	25.5	24.3	18.7	14.2	8.6	6.2	5.1

Base Temperature	40	45	50	55	60	65	70	Cooling Degree Days
Heating Degree Days	1468	2139	2936	3836	4864	6038	7361	(Base 65) = 1096

City: Dodge City, Kansas   Latitude: 37.8°
Winter Design Temp.: 0, 5   Deep Ground Temp.:55

Month		JAN	FEB	MAR	APR	MAY	JUN	JUL	AUG	SEP	OCT	NOV	DEC
Average Air	(Day)	31.1	39.0	46.0	59.5	71.0	82.0	83.3	85.0	72.0	62.2	46.7	35.7
Temperature	(Night)	24.3	29.1	33.0	47.2	59.3	68.8	70.6	70.6	59.8	51.3	38.4	28.6
Solar Flux (Horiz.)		17.3	20.8	35.4	43.6	53.2	60.1	56.5	55.0	43.3	32.3	21.2	18.0
– SOUTH		29.4	28.0	33.9	30.4	28.8	26.7	27.3	32.0	36.0	38.9	33.1	32.6
V E SW/SE		23.0	23.4	30.0	32.2	32.5	33.2	33.2	35.6	35.3	32.5	26.1	24.4
R T WEST		12.1	14.6	22.5	29.5	32.8	35.9	35.0	33.9	28.4	21.1	14.4	11.8
I C EAST		11.7	13.6	23.6	28.2	34.5	36.1	34.0	33.0	26.2	20.6	13.9	12.2
A L NW/NE		4.9	6.6	13.7	20.0	26.8	28.9	26.9	23.2	16.1	9.3	5.7	4.7
– NORTH		4.3	5.3	9.7	14.3	18.5	19.9	18.8	15.0	11.0	6.7	4.8	4.3

Base Temperature	40	45	50	55	60	65	70	Cooling Degree Days
Heating Degree Days	1254	1860	2579	3419	4392	5505	6774	(Base 65) = 1507

(*Continued*)

TABLE C.1 (*Continued*)

City: Louisville, Kentucky   Latitude: 38.2°
Winter Design Temp.: 5, 10   Deep Ground Temp.:

Month		JAN	FEB	MAR	APR	MAY	JUN	JUL	AUG	SEP	OCT	NOV	DEC
Average Air	(Day)	35.3	36.4	48.3	59.3	71.3	77.5	81.0	80.2	74.8	61.7	50.4	40.9
Temperature	(Night)	30.3	29.9	40.6	51.9	61.8	69.1	72.8	71.5	64.2	52.6	43.9	36.9
Solar Flux (Horiz.)		15.4	17.3	30.4	42.3	51.7	53.9	53.0	53.8	40.9	27.0	15.6	12.3
V E R T I C A L	SOUTH	25.9	22.5	29.8	30.1	29.1	27.5	28.7	32.3	33.0	32.3	24.1	20.6
	SW/SE	20.2	19.1	29.3	30.6	33.3	32.8	32.8	37.5	32.3	28.2	18.7	15.9
	WEST	10.8	12.4	21.9	27.3	33.8	34.7	33.7	35.9	26.2	19.0	10.6	8.8
	EAST	10.6	11.4	19.8	27.7	33.4	33.8	34.4	30.9	25.1	17.4	10.9	8.9
	NW/NE	4.8	6.2	12.7	19.7	26.4	27.8	27.8	21.9	15.6	9.1	5.0	4.3
	NORTH	4.3	5.2	10.0	14.0	19.2	20.8	20.5	15.1	10.4	6.9	4.4	4.1

Base Temperature	40	45	50	55	60	65	70	Cooling Degree Days
Heating Degree Days	872	1397	2047	2817	3718	4758	5989	(Base 65) = 1496

City: New Orleans, Louisiana   Latitude: 30.0°
Winter Design Temp. 29,33   Deep Ground Temp.:

Month		JAN	FEB	MAR	APR	MAY	JUN	JUL	AUG	SEP	OCT	NOV	DEC
Average Air	(Day)	57.6	58.1	64.6	73.1	79.0	82.3	84.4	84.8	78.1	76.7	63.5	59.1
Temperature	(Night)	50.3	51.2	57.1	65.0	69.3	74.3	77.5	77.5	70.8	66.4	56.6	52.2
Solar Flux (Horiz.)		17.5	23.4	40.1	47.1	57.2	51.3	49.5	50.8	46.9	40.7	24.7	19.3
V E R T I C A L	SOUTH	22.7	25.0	32.8	28.8	23.9	22.0	24.2	27.8	33.5	40.3	32.4	27.6
	SW/SE	18.9	21.8	31.1	31.7	30.6	27.5	27.8	31.2	32.8	35.6	26.3	22.2
	WEST	12.0	15.3	25.3	30.6	33.5	31.0	29.8	31.2	28.2	25.4	16.3	13.2
	EAST	11.5	14.9	25.4	29.8	34.3	32.8	34.2	33.6	30.0	24.3	16.1	12.8
	NW/NE	6.5	9.2	16.3	22.3	27.7	28.5	29.3	26.2	19.6	12.8	7.3	6.1
	NORTH	5.9	7.8	11.9	15.8	18.7	21.5	21.7	17.8	12.9	9.2	5.9	5.3

Base Temperature	40	45	50	55	60	65	70	Cooling Degree Days
Heating Degree Days	44	123	280	543	940	1526	2322	(Base 65) = 2610

(*Continued*)

TABLE C.1 (*Continued*)

City: Shreveport, Louisiana Latitude:32.5°
Winter Design Temp.: 20,25 Deep Ground Temp.:67

Month	JAN	FEB	MAR	APR	MAY	JUN	JUL	AUG	SEP	OCT	NOV	DEC
Average Air (Day)	51.8	54.4	61.7	70.6	77.6	82.6	87.2	86.5	81.2	71.5	58.3	50.8
Temperature (Night)	43.6	45.5	52.3	61.8	69.0	73.1	76.9	76.0	72.4	61.0	49.7	42.6
Solar Flux (Horiz.)	20.7	24.3	41.8	43.3	54.5	56.8	59.9	52.6	44.4	34.2	22.7	19.6
SOUTH	29.2	28.3	34.8	28.0	26.6	24.9	24.9	28.6	32.3	36.3	31.3	30.1
SW/SE	24.2	24.0	34.7	30.8	31.9	32.1	33.7	32.6	32.8	32.1	25.1	23.3
WEST	14.5	16.2	28.2	29.2	33.6	36.5	38.1	32.4	28.3	22.7	15.0	13.0
EAST	12.9	15.8	25.2	27.2	33.4	34.9	34.4	34.1	27.8	21.5	15.0	13.3
NW/NE	6.4	8.5	15.8	20.6	27.0	29.6	28.2	25.9	18.1	11.6	6.7	5.9
NORTH	5.7	6.9	11.3	15.4	19.5	22.6	20.5	17.0	12.0	8.7	5.5	5.2

Base Temperature	40	45	50	55	60	65	70	Cooling Degree Days
Heating Degree Days	105	283	612	1086	1688	2443	3369	(Base 65) = 2442

City: Caribou, Maine Latitude: 46.9°
Winter Design Temp.: -18, -13 Deep Ground Temp.:37

Month	JAN	FEB	MAR	APR	MAY	JUN	JUL	AUG	SEP	OCT	NOV	DEC
Average Air (Day)	14.7	15.6	28.5	38.1	54.6	63.2	67.3	63.8	57.0	46.0	33.3	17.9
Temperature (Night)	10.1	11.2	22.3	33.4	48.1	57.5	62.0	59.2	52.6	42.1	31.5	15.7
Solar Flux (Horiz.)	8.9	13.4	22.7	35.2	45.1	46.3	45.0	37.5	27.3	15.7	9.0	8.1
SOUTH	18.7	22.1	27.3	30.3	30.7	29.8	30.5	29.4	27.9	22.0	15.6	18.4
SW/SE	15.6	19.2	25.0	31.6	33.6	33.9	33.2	31.4	27.3	18.9	13.5	15.0
WEST	8.0	11.5	17.8	26.8	31.6	33.6	32.0	28.4	20.7	12.4	7.7	6.7
EAST	6.0	8.9	15.5	22.2	28.7	29.9	30.1	24.5	16.9	11.2	5.9	4.9
NW/NE	2.9	4.3	9.0	15.4	21.8	24.4	24.1	18.4	10.4	6.1	3.5	2.5
NORTH	2.8	3.7	6.9	12.1	16.8	19.7	19.3	15.0	7.8	5.1	3.3	2.4

Base Temperature	40	45	50	55	60	65	70	Cooling Degree Days
Heating Degree Days	3292	4263	5376	6621	8018	9569	11235	(Base 65) = 283

(*Continued*)

TABLE C.1 (*Continued*)

City: Portland, Maine Latitude: 43.7°
Winter Design Temp.: -6, -1 Deep Ground Temp.: 45

Month		JAN	FEB	MAR	APR	MAY	JUN	JUL	AUG	SEP	OCT	NOV	DEC
Average Air	(Day)	22.9	25.4	37.5	47.0	60.9	70.3	73.9	71.9	63.7	52.0	40.1	30.9
Temperature	(Night)	17.5	19.9	29.7	36.3	49.4	57.3	60.3	60.5	53.4	43.3	34.0	24.9
Solar Flux (Horiz.)		13.0	15.9	27.7	36.7	47.7	50.2	51.7	44.3	33.2	22.8	13.0	11.6
V E R T I C A L — SOUTH		25.5	23.8	29.8	29.8	29.6	28.8	30.5	31.3	31.4	31.4	23.1	24.6
SW/SE		20.3	19.1	26.2	28.1	31.9	31.9	32.9	32.1	28.0	25.0	18.2	18.0
WEST		10.2	11.2	18.9	23.3	30.6	32.3	32.0	28.7	21.0	14.8	9.3	8.0
EAST		8.8	11.0	19.3	24.8	31.4	32.8	33.7	28.4	22.8	15.6	8.6	8.6
NW/NE		3.7	5.1	10.8	17.2	24.0	25.9	26.2	19.8	13.7	7.1	3.8	3.2
NORTH		3.5	4.2	7.7	12.8	17.4	19.4	18.9	14.1	9.5	5.4	3.5	3.1

Base Temperature	40	45	50	55	60	65	70	Cooling Degree Days
Heating Degree Days	1831	2627	3582	4696	5975	7420	0997	(Base 65) - 447

City: Baltimore, Maryland Latitude: 39.2°
Winter Design Temp.: 14, 17 Deep Ground Temp.:

Month		JAN	FEB	MAR	APR	MAY	JUN	JUL	AUG	SEP	OCT	NOV	DEC
Average Air	(Day)	32.8	35.3	44.5	53.0	63.9	73.8	78.0	75.8	71.0	60.0	49.0	36.2
Temperature	(Night)	29.7	32.0	41.5	48.8	59.6	70.3	74.5	73.1	67.4	53.7	44.9	34.1
Solar Flux (Horiz.)		18.1	23.0	38.4	44.2	52.6	54.9	53.6	49.6	37.3	30.2	17.8	15.3
V E R T I C A L — SOUTH		32.1	33.0	38.6	31.8	29.3	26.0	28.5	31.5	32.6	37.8	28.8	28.8
SW/SE		25.1	27.6	35.8	33.7	32.5	32.1	33.7	36.0	30.5	32.2	23.3	23.0
WEST		12.7	16.7	25.9	29.8	32.1	34.6	34.9	33.8	24.1	20.9	12.8	11.5
EAST		11.8	14.7	22.8	27.0	33.4	32.9	33.4	27.8	23.9	19.2	11.5	9.9
NW/NE		4.7	6.3	12.6	19.0	25.4	26.2	26.6	20.1	14.8	8.8	4.9	4.1
NORTH		4.1	5.0	9.0	13.9	17.6	18.9	19.6	14.8	10.6	6.5	4.2	3.8

Base Temperature	40	45	50	55	60	65	70	Cooling Degree Days
Heating Degree Days	911	1480	2194	3037	4017	5137	6418	(Base 65) = 1267

(*Continued*)

TABLE C.1 *(Continued)*

City: Boston, Massachusetts   Latitude: 42.4°
Winter Design Temp.:6,9   Deep Ground Temp.:51

Month		JAN	FEB	MAR	APR	MAY	JUN	JUL	AUG	SEP	OCT	NOV	DEC
Average Air	(Day)	30.9	30.7	37.3	53.2	60.9	72.1	73.1	77.9	66.4	57.0	46.6	34.5
Temperature	(Night)	27.7	28.3	32.9	46.8	55.0	64.7	67.9	70.1	60.4	51.3	43.6	32.1
Solar Flux (Horiz.)		16.2	17.7	32.1	48.4	56.0	57.2	52.2	56.1	37.7	27.3	14.7	13.2
– SOUTH		29.9	25.6	33.5	36.7	34.5	31.8	33.3	38.8	35.6	36.3	24.2	24.7
V E SW/SE		23.6	20.3	29.9	36.8	38.9	35.7	36.1	39.9	32.3	29.9	19.0	18.0
R T WEST		12.2	12.4	22.3	31.3	38.0	36.4	35.6	36.0	24.4	18.6	10.3	8.9
I C EAST		11.1	13.0	22.2	31.3	36.1	36.8	35.1	36.1	24.7	18.3	10.2	10.2
A L NW/NE		5.1	6.8	13.3	21.3	27.9	29.2	28.7	25.4	14.9	9.1	5.4	4.5
– NORTH		4.9	5.9	10.4	14.7	20.5	21.8	22.8	18.0	10.9	7.3	5.1	4.4

Base Temperature	40	45	50	55	60	65	70	Cooling Degree Days
Heating Degree Days	1138	1794	2574	3513	4600	5874	7332	(Base 65) = 760

City: Alpena, Michigan   Latitude:45.0°
Winter Design Temp.:-11, -6   Deep Ground Temp.:

Month		JAN	FEB	MAR	APR	MAY	JUN	JUL	AUG	SEP	OCT	NOV	DEC
Average Air	(Day)	20.5	20.9	30.8	46.2	57.0	68.7	73.9	72.6	61.7	53.0	39.7	25.3
Temperature	(Night)	16.4	15.1	25.3	37.0	44.8	58.1	61.8	63.1	52.1	45.5	35.4	22.9
Solar Flux (Horiz.)		9.0	13.8	23.8	37.4	53.2	51.8	56.2	45.1	27.8	19.7	10.3	7.2
– SOUTH		16.2	21.4	26.7	30.5	32.6	30.1	32.2	33.0	27.2	26.7	17.2	12.9
V E SW/SE		12.4	17.3	23.5	30.6	34.8	34.6	36.0	33.5	24.9	23.7	13.5	10.0
R T WEST		6.3	10.1	17.0	25.9	32.6	34.8	35.3	29.3	19.0	15.4	7.3	5.4
I C EAST		6.5	9.6	17.0	25.0	35.6	32.1	35.9	29.8	19.4	12.9	7.1	5.5
A L NW/NE		3.3	4.7	9.9	17.1	26.0	25.4	27.1	20.8	12.1	7.0	3.8	3.0
– NORTH		3.2	4.1	7.4	12.4	17.0	19.4	18.6	14.6	8.8	5.7	3.6	2.9

Base Temperature	40	45	50	55	60	65	70	Cooling Degree Days
Heating Degree Days	2457	3337	4361	5519	6801	8230	9804	(Base 65) = 490

(Continued)

TABLE C.1 *(Continued)*

City: Detroit, Michigan   Latitude: 42.2°
Winter Design Temp.: 3, 6   Deep Ground Temp.:

Month	JAN	FEB	MAR	APR	MAY	JUN	JUL	AUG	SEP	OCT	NOV	DEC
Average Air (Day)	22.9	26.4	41.1	56.1	60.1	72.9	77.3	77.4	70.5	58.2	44.2	30.4
Temperature (Night)	20.5	21.6	33.4	46.0	51.5	63.0	66.5	67.5	60.4	49.3	38.7	27.2
Solar Flux (Horiz.)	14.3	21.6	33.9	47.1	51.5	56.6	63.2	52.8	38.1	26.5	14.5	10.7
V E R T I C A L — SOUTH	24.1	31.4	35.6	36.8	34.9	33.1	36.0	37.8	35.5	33.5	21.6	16.7
SW/SE	18.5	24.9	30.7	36.4	36.2	36.6	39.6	39.3	32.3	26.9	17.7	13.1
WEST	9.8	15.1	22.6	31.0	34.5	37.0	39.5	35.8	25.1	17.4	10.6	7.4
EAST	10.2	15.8	24.5	31.7	37.1	37.8	42.4	35.7	26.4	19.2	10.3	7.8
NW/NE	5.3	7.6	14.9	22.2	29.4	30.6	33.1	26.1	17.2	9.9	6.1	4.8
— NORTH	5.0	6.2	11.4	16.0	22.4	23.4	23.5	19.1	13.0	7.8	5.7	4.7

Base Temperature	40	45	50	55	60	65	70	Cooling Degree Days
Heating Degree Days	1718	2419	3244	4202	5296	6550	7976	(Base 65) = 859

City: Grand Rapids, Michigan   Latitude: 42.9°
Winter Design Temp.: 1, 5   Deep Ground Temp.:47

Month	JAN	FEB	MAR	APR	MAY	JUN	JUL	AUG	SEP	OCT	NOV	DEC
Average Air (Day)	25.8	25.5	36.6	51.3	64.7	73.2	78.2	74.2	66.0	56.8	42.0	28.1
Temperature (Night)	22.7	21.7	31.0	42.6	53.8	62.0	65.6	62.6	55.8	49.2	37.9	24.8
Solar Flux (Horiz.)	9.1	15.1	22.4	39.6	46.2	52.6	52.0	43.4	30.4	21.4	11.1	8.4
V E R T I C A L — SOUTH	14.8	22.0	23.3	30.8	29.0	29.1	29.2	30.9	28.6	27.5	17.8	14.3
SW/SE	11.6	18.0	21.1	31.6	30.6	33.5	33.4	32.4	27.0	23.7	14.1	11.1
WEST	6.6	11.3	16.0	27.1	28.7	34.4	34.0	29.4	21.1	15.4	7.9	6.0
EAST	6.6	11.2	16.1	25.5	29.7	34.6	34.3	28.4	19.7	14.0	7.8	6.1
NW/NE	3.8	5.5	10.4	17.8	22.8	27.6	26.4	20.6	12.5	7.3	4.2	3.4
— NORTH	3.6	4.5	8.3	12.9	16.7	20.0	18.8	15.1	9.5	5.7	3.9	3.3

Base Temperature	40	45	50	55	60	65	70	Cooling Degree Days
Heating Degree Days	1792	2570	3469	4501	5654	6947	8393	(Base 65) = 791

(Continued)

TABLE C.1 (*Continued*)

City: Duluth, Minnesota   Latitude:46.8°
Winter Design Temp.:-21, -16   Deep Ground Temp.:

Month		JAN	FEB	MAR	APR	MAY	JUN	JUL	AUG	SEP	OCT	NOV	DEC
Average Air	(Day)	8.8	17.5	25.5	40.3	54.4	64.3	70.3	68.3	59.2	48.8	30.1	16.5
Temperature	(Night)	3.8	10.3	18.9	33.2	44.7	52.8	59.8	57.7	51.5	41.8	27.1	12.7
Solar Flux (Horiz.)		10.9	13.6	22.2	35.1	43.7	45.8	52.2	41.7	27.0	16.8	8.7	8.4
V E R T I C A L	SOUTH	24.1	22.2	26.2	30.2	30.6	28.6	32.1	32.0	27.5	23.9	15.0	19.4
	SW/SE	17.9	18.1	22.1	29.1	32.6	31.0	36.4	32.5	24.8	19.5	11.9	14.4
	WEST	7.9	10.4	15.1	23.7	30.7	30.5	35.7	28.2	18.5	12.3	6.5	6.2
	EAST	8.1	9.4	16.0	23.8	29.9	31.2	33.7	26.6	18.5	12.4	6.3	6.5
	NW/NE	3.1	4.5	9.2	16.2	22.6	24.5	25.9	18.8	11.0	6.2	3.4	2.6
	NORTH	2.9	3.9	7.1	11.9	17.0	18.6	19.0	14.3	8.0	5.0	3.2	2.5

Base Temperature	40	45	50	55	60	65	70	Cooling Degree Days
Heating Degree Days	3715	4704	5823	7080	8473	10012	11668	(Base 65) = 302

City: Minneapolis, Minnesota   Latitude: 44.9°
Winter Design Temp.: -16, -12   Deep Ground Temp.:

Month		JAN	FEB	MAR	APR	MAY	JUN	JUL	AUG	SEP	OCT	NOV	DEC
Average Air	(Day)	8.2	18.8	28.8	50.0	62.3	76.3	81.3	77.4	65.7	52.8	34.3	19.4
Temperature	(Night)	4.7	13.8	23.9	42.1	54.7	67.0	70.1	66.6	57.3	46.3	31.0	17.1
Solar Flux (Horiz.)		10.4	17.0	26.4	35.6	47.1	52.4	52.0	44.5	32.7	20.4	11.7	8.7
V E R T I C A L	SOUTH	20.6	27.1	30.0	29.1	30.7	28.9	30.7	31.6	31.0	28.7	20.7	17.5
	SW/SE	15.6	21.1	26.6	27.7	32.9	33.2	35.1	32.9	29.1	22.9	15.6	13.4
	WEST	8.0	11.9	18.8	23.1	31.0	33.4	34.8	29.4	21.8	14.3	8.3	6.5
	EAST	8.3	12.4	18.2	25.2	28.6	32.0	33.2	29.1	20.1	15.2	9.1	6.4
	NW/NE	3.5	5.4	10.1	17.4	21.4	24.7	25.5	20.3	11.7	7.1	4.1	3.1
	NORTH	3.3	4.5	7.3	12.5	16.7	18.0	18.6	14.3	8.1	5.4	3.7	3.0

Base Temperature	40	45	50	55	60	65	70	Cooling Degree Days
Heating Degree Days	2909	3730	4659	5705	6874	8178	9621	(Base 65) = 881

(*Continued*)

TABLE C.1 (*Continued*)

City: Jackson, Mississippi   Latitude:32.3°
Winter Design Temp.:21,25   Deep Ground Temp.:

Month		JAN	FEB	MAR	APR	MAY	JUN	JUL	AUG	SEP	OCT	NOV	DEC
Average Air	(Day)	49.2	49.0	61.6	72.6	81.3	84.8	85.2	85.3	83.1	68.8	64.9	52.6
Temperature	(Night)	42.6	40.6	50.8	62.5	67.2	73.4	75.3	75.5	70.7	55.3	53.7	45.8
Solar Flux (Horiz)		21.6	27.0	41.4	47.1	59.2	58.6	57.0	51.6	46.4	38.7	24.5	18.7
V E R T I C A L	SOUTH	29.6	31.3	35.3	30.9	29.0	26.1	27.6	31.8	34.1	40.6	32.2	26.3
	SW/SE	23.5	25.5	33.1	32.6	34.6	31.9	32.5	34.4	33.5	35.4	26.6	22.0
	WEST	14.3	17.3	26.7	30.7	36.7	35.3	35.0	33.8	28.9	24.9	16.5	13.3
	EAST	14.8	18.9	26.8	30.8	37.8	38.3	36.9	35.1	30.1	23.8	15.4	12.0
	NW/NE	7.9	10.0	17.8	23.4	30.3	32.6	30.9	27.9	20.0	12.6	7.8	7.0
	NORTH	7.1	8.0	13.8	17.5	21.7	23.8	23.0	20.7	13.8	9.5	6.7	6.4

Base Temperature	40	45	50	55	60	65	70		Cooling Degree Days
Heating Degree Days	227	446	785	1246	1047	2502	3484		(Base 65) = 2495

City: Kansas City, Missouri   Latitude: 39.1°
Winter Design Temp.: 2, 6   Deep Ground Temp.:56

Month		JAN	FEB	MAR	APR	MAY	JUN	JUL	AUG	SEP	OCT	NOV	DEC
Average Air	(Day)	30.4	34.7	50.9	61.7	67.3	81.7	83.9	81.0	74.2	63.8	45.2	32.9
Temperature	(Night)	26.3	29.6	42.5	52.2	58.2	72.8	75.3	74.1	64.1	55.0	39.9	28.7
Solar Flux (Horiz.)		16.8	21.6	40.2	49.2	56.3	61.3	60.0	51.6	44.9	30.5	17.3	15.5
V E R T I C A L	SOUTH	27.1	28.9	40.3	35.8	32.9	31.7	33.5	33.8	38.7	37.2	25.1	25.9
	SW/SE	21.9	24.1	36.7	36.7	35.7	37.1	38.6	36.8	35.9	31.2	20.7	20.1
	WEST	12.4	14.8	27.5	32.4	35.3	39.0	39.8	34.7	28.5	20.6	12.3	10.9
	EAST	11.5	14.1	26.5	32.0	38.5	38.8	38.3	33.4	29.4	20.5	11.4	11.0
	NW/NE	6.0	7.8	16.0	22.8	29.8	31.6	31.1	24.9	18.1	10.6	6.0	5.6
	NORTH	5.6	6.8	12.1	16.4	21.1	23.5	23.8	18.0	12.6	8.4	6.0	5.3

Base Temperature	40	45	50	55	60	65	70		Cooling Degree Days
Heating Degree Days	1213	1778	2444	3215	4115	5160	6361		(Base 65) =1648

(*Continued*)

TABLE C.1 (*Continued*)

City: St. Louis, Missouri   Latitude: 38.4°
Winter Design Temp.: 2, 6   Deep Ground Temp.:

Month		JAN	FEB	MAR	APR	MAY	JUN	JUL	AUG	SEP	OCT	NOV	DEC
Average Air	(Day)	32.8	36.6	50.1	59.2	73.3	79.9	82.1	81.1	75.5	58.6	42.2	32.2
Temperature	(Night)	26.6	29.4	41.0	50.7	60.9	66.8	73.0	71.0	67.7	51.5	38.3	28.7
Solar Flux (Horiz.)		19.8	21.7	37.3	46.1	58.2	59.5	54.7	52.3	37.7	26.1	14.5	13.4
V E R T I C A L	SOUTH	32.8	28.0	36.7	34.6	33.9	31.6	32.8	35.1	32.8	29.3	19.3	20.6
	SW/SE	26.2	23.1	32.9	33.4	36.8	36.5	35.6	36.3	30.3	24.5	15.8	16.4
	WEST	14.0	14.6	24.8	29.6	36.5	38.7	36.1	33.9	24.8	17.2	10.6	9.5
	EAST	13.0	14.6	25.3	33.0	39.2	40.0	39.9	35.6	25.7	18.5	10.9	9.5
	NW/NE	6.1	8.0	16.0	24.0	30.8	33.0	32.9	26.7	17.7	10.8	6.9	5.5
	NORTH	5.5	6.8	12.4	17.8	22.3	24.7	24.6	19.5	14.1	8.8	6.4	5.2

Base Temperature	40	45	50	55	60	65	70	Cooling Degree Days
Heating Degree Days	1215	1794	2495	3312	4259	5342	6558	(Base 65) = 1572

City: Billings, Montana   Latitude: 45.8°
Winter Design Temp.:-15,-10   Deep Ground Temp.:

Month		JAN	FEB	MAR	APR	MAY	JUN	JUL	AUG	SEP	OCT	NOV	DEC
Average Air	(Day)	25.7	29.5	37.5	46.9	61.9	70.1	79.9	78.7	64.8	55.9	39.1	23.7
Temperature	(Night)	21.1	24.5	28.7	37.3	51.0	57.3	65.9	65.4	53.4	46.6	34.8	20.2
Solar Flux (Horiz.)		10.3	13.1	21.7	32.2	44.9	53.2	59.4	51.2	31.0	21.1	12.5	8.5
V E R T I C A L	SOUTH	20.5	20.2	24.9	27.8	31.0	29.9	33.2	36.0	31.7	30.8	24.0	18.6
	SW/SE	16.1	16.3	21.6	25.9	31.6	32.5	37.2	36.2	29.0	24.6	18.4	14.0
	WEST	7.8	9.8	15.3	21.2	29.1	31.9	36.2	31.0	21.5	14.6	9.2	6.4
	EAST	7.1	9.5	15.5	22.8	30.6	35.0	37.5	32.6	20.6	14.8	9.2	6.4
	NW/NE	3.4	4.8	9.0	16.1	23.4	26.7	27.7	21.2	11.9	6.5	3.7	2.7
	NORTH	3.2	4.1	7.0	12.5	17.8	18.4	18.3	13.2	8.5	4.9	3.3	2.6

Base Temperature	40	45	50	55	60	65	70	Cooling Degree Days
Heating Degree Days	2078	2843	3781	4864	6095	7464	8959	(Base 65) = 817

(*Continued*)

TABLE C.1 *(Continued)*

City: Great Falls, Montana Latitude: 47.5°
Winter Design Temp.: -21, -15 Deep Ground Temp.:

Month		JAN	FEB	MAR	APR	MAY	JUN	JUL	AUG	SEP	OCT	NOV	DEC
Average Air	(Day)	22.9	25.9	37.6	46.6	58.0	70.4	75.2	71.3	64.9	52.3	40.8	31.7
Temperature	(Night)	19.5	20.8	29.5	36.8	47.7	57.8	62.7	59.5	52.5	44.7	34.7	27.9
Solar Flux (Horiz.)		12.7	15.4	26.8	43.2	49.5	61.5	65.1	50.1	35.8	22.0	14.1	9.5
V E R T I C A L	SOUTH	27.7	24.5	31.7	37.3	36.1	36.8	38.8	37.6	36.7	31.0	28.7	20.2
	SW/SE	21.5	19.1	27.5	35.1	37.5	38.7	42.7	37.7	32.9	25.3	21.6	15.3
	WEST	9.9	10.6	19.1	28.2	34.9	37.1	40.8	32.4	23.6	15.5	10.2	6.9
	EAST	9.0	11.1	18.7	28.8	34.1	40.8	40.5	33.4	23.6	15.4	10.5	7.0
	NW/NE	3.9	5.7	11.0	19.0	26.7	31.1	30.7	23.0	13.8	7.9	4.4	3.4
	NORTH	3.8	5.2	8.9	14.0	21.6	22.0	20.9	16.0	9.9	6.6	4.1	3.3

Base Temperature	40	45	50	55	60	65	70		Cooling Degree Days
Heating Degree Days	2161	2943	3880	4986	6266	7700	9253		(Base 65) = 618

City: Miles City, Montana Latitude: 46.4°
Winter Design Temp.: -20, -15 Deep Ground Temp.:

Month		JAN	FEB	MAR	APR	MAY	JUN	JUL	AUG	SEP	OCT	NOV	DEC
Average Air	(Day)	15.0	20.8	32.7	44.1	57.2	68.3	79.7	77.8	63.0	52.9	35.8	22.3
Temperature	(Night)	11.3	17.4	29.4	40.0	50.8	63.8	72.4	70.4	55.5	45.0	29.6	19.5
Solar Flux (Horiz.)		10.6	13.3	22.5	34.9	45.0	50.6	59.5	49.5	31.1	20.7	11.5	8.9
V E R T I C A L	SOUTH	23.0	21.9	26.5	29.8	31.3	29.6	33.9	35.2	32.1	30.2	23.0	20.7
	SW/SE	18.6	19.2	24.4	30.8	34.2	33.1	37.0	36.4	30.3	24.9	18.4	16.1
	WEST	9.0	11.5	17.3	26.1	32.7	33.1	35.8	31.9	22.6	15.4	9.5	7.4
	EAST	7.2	8.8	14.9	22.6	29.8	32.5	39.0	32.2	20.1	14.8	8.2	6.6
	NW/NE	3.2	4.5	8.4	15.8	23.0	25.1	28.4	21.2	11.6	6.6	3.5	2.6
	NORTH	3.0	4.0	6.3	12.1	18.2	18.6	18.5	13.4	8.2	5.0	3.2	2.5

Base Temperature	40	45	50	55	60	65	70		Cooling Degree Days
Heating Degree Days	2838	3693	4669	5755	6961	8297	9754		(Base 65) = 975

(Continued)

TABLE C.1 (*Continued*)

City: Missoula, Montana   Latitude:46.9°
Winter Design Temp.:-13, -6   Deep Ground Temp.:

Month		JAN	FEB	MAR	APR	MAY	JUN	JUL	AUG	SEP	OCT	NOV	DEC
Average Air	(Day)	25.1	33.8	38.5	48.6	57.7	66.2	76.5	74.4	60.8	47.7	36.7	27.7
Temperature	(Night)	22.6	28.6	30.9	37.7	46.4	51.9	58.9	57.3	47.3	37.8	31.7	24.5
	Solar Flux (Horiz.)	7.4	10.5	18.6	32.9	43.9	49.6	61.6	46.6	31.0	17.4	8.6	6.3
V E R T I C A L	SOUTH	12.8	15.7	21.3	28.5	30.5	30.6	34.2	34.0	31.5	24.8	14.8	11.6
	SW/SE	10.0	12.8	17.9	27.6	31.5	32.6	38.7	34.2	28.6	20.3	12.8	9.3
	WEST	5.5	7.8	12.9	22.7	29.0	32.1	37.6	29.3	20.7	12.3	7.0	4.8
	EAST	5.5	7.8	14.6	22.1	30.4	34.6	38.0	30.0	20.1	12.2	5.3	4.4
	NW/NE	3.1	4.5	8.9	15.5	23.0	27.1	27.3	20.0	11.5	6.1	3.3	2.6
	NORTH	3.0	4.1	6.9	12.1	17.0	20.0	17.4	13.3	8.1	5.0	3.2	2.5

Base Temperature	40	45	50	55	60	65	70	Cooling Degree Days
Heating Degree Days	1770	2680	3765	5011	6408	7925	9540	(Base 65) = 486

City: Omaha, Nebraska   Latitude: 41.3°
Winter Design Temp.: -8,-3   Deep Ground Temp.:

Month		JAN	FEB	MAR	APR	MAY	JUN	JUL	AUG	SEP	OCT	NOV	DEC
Average Air	(Day)	20.8	32.3	49.0	53.6	68.3	77.6	83.7	77.0	68.7	60.0	43.4	31.6
Temperature	(Night)	15.8	24.2	39.0	43.9	55.5	67.7	74.7	65.3	57.8	46.9	35.4	24.2
	Solar Flux (Horiz.)	17.2	22.8	35.4	42.9	61.3	59.0	64.3	55.1	39.6	32.3	19.2	14.8
V E R T I C A L	SOUTH	30.2	32.2	35.9	33.5	35.6	33.6	34.0	36.9	35.5	41.1	31.1	27.3
	SW/SE	22.8	26.4	31.3	32.8	40.2	38.8	40.3	39.1	34.3	33.8	23.6	20.6
	WEST	11.9	16.1	23.2	28.8	39.6	40.2	41.4	36.0	27.5	21.6	12.6	10.1
	EAST	12.7	15.6	24.6	30.2	38.2	38.5	39.2	35.9	25.7	21.9	13.6	10.7
	NW/NE	5.8	7.8	14.9	21.9	29.0	31.5	30.6	25.5	16.8	10.5	6.2	5.0
	NORTH	5.3	6.6	11.5	16.8	20.9	24.5	22.0	17.6	12.6	7.9	5.7	4.7

Base Temperature	40	45	50	55	60	65	70	Cooling Degree Days
Heating Degree Days	1827	2477	3267	4189	5247	6433	7747	(Base 65) = 1251

(*Continued*)

TABLE C.1 (*Continued*)

City: Reno, Nevada   Latitude:39.5°
Winter Design Temp.:   Deep Ground Temp.:

Month		JAN	FEB	MAR	APR	MAY	JUN	JUL	AUG	SEP	OCT	NOV	DEC
Average Air	(Day)	38.7	43.3	51.0	54.0	63.0	74.1	83.4	79.8	71.3	58.3	46.3	35.0
Temperature	(Night)	27.7	29.8	34.5	39.2	46.1	56.6	60.3	57.9	49.7	39.0	31.6	28.1
Solar Flux (Horiz.)		15.1	19.6	31.7	45.0	58.3	64.4	63.2	61.9	49.3	30.7	18.5	12.9
V E R T I C A L	SOUTH	26.4	27.7	31.3	32.4	30.2	27.6	29.1	35.2	41.9	38.5	30.3	23.2
	SW/SE	20.2	20.8	26.9	32.5	35.1	34.1	35.5	36.8	38.9	31.4	23.3	17.3
	WEST	10.4	12.4	20.2	28.2	35.3	36.6	37.1	33.8	29.9	19.9	12.5	8.9
	EAST	10.5	14.8	23.5	29.5	36.4	39.5	38.7	38.4	30.7	20.6	12.9	9.6
	NW/NE	4.5	6.3	13.8	20.2	27.2	30.6	29.5	25.2	16.8	9.3	5.4	4.1
	NORTH	4.1	4.8	9.7	13.7	17.6	19.4	18.8	14.0	9.7	6.6	4.6	3.9

Base Temperature	40	45	50	55	60	65	70	Cooling Degree Days
Heating Degree Days	1162	1874	2770	3831	5051	6415	7893	(Base 65) = 949

City: Tonopah, Nevada   Latitude:38.1°
Winter Design Temp.:5, 10   Deep Ground Temp.:51

Month		JAN	FEB	MAR	APR	MAY	JUN	JUL	AUG	SEP	OCT	NOV	DEC
Average Air	(Day)	35.7	43.6	48.5	55.6	65.0	76.9	82.5	80.9	73.4	59.2	46.3	34.8
Temperature	(Night)	24.0	30.7	35.8	39.8	49.1	61.1	66.6	63.1	53.8	41.8	34.5	26.8
Solar Flux (Horiz.)		20.5	20.9	38.1	47.7	59.9	63.3	66.5	62.5	51.1	35.5	22.4	17.8
V E R T I C A L	SOUTH	36.0	28.1	37.5	32.6	29.7	26.4	28.3	34.5	42.1	43.3	37.8	32.6
	SW/SE	27.2	22.1	33.2	31.7	33.4	33.4	33.7	37.3	38.3	34.5	28.2	24.0
	WEST	13.8	13.3	24.1	27.5	33.6	36.5	35.2	35.1	29.8	21.4	14.2	11.6
	EAST	14.2	14.5	24.5	31.9	38.7	38.8	40.6	38.9	32.7	23.5	15.3	12.7
	NW/NE	5.2	6.4	13.6	21.5	28.7	30.6	30.8	25.9	17.7	10.0	5.1	4.7
	NORTH	4.5	4.8	9.6	13.5	17.6	19.7	18.4	14.4	10.0	6.5	4.1	4.2

Base Temperature	40	45	50	55	60	65	70	Cooling Degree Days
Heating Degree Days	1166	1836	2663	3649	4783	6060	7471	(Base 65) = 1061

(*Continued*)

TABLE C.1 *(Continued)*

City: Concord, New Hampshire   Latitude: 43.2°
Winter Design Temp.:-8, -3   Deep Ground Temp.:

Month		JAN	FEB	MAR	APR	MAY	JUN	JUL	AUG	SEP	OCT	NOV	DEC
Average Air	(Day)	23.8	29.3	35.6	51.3	64.1	73.4	77.1	73.5	64.0	54.9	42.2	26.1
Temperature	(Night)	18.1	18.8	27.7	39.1	50.2	58.6	64.2	60.5	53.5	43.6	34.2	20.5
Solar Flux (Horiz.)		13.0	17.0	27.0	38.4	50.0	49.8	50.7	45.2	29.5	21.6	13.0	11.0
V – SOUTH		25.6	25.9	28.5	30.2	30.3	28.1	30.1	31.6	28.3	28.6	22.5	22.1
E SW/SE		19.2	20.7	24.5	29.1	33.1	30.8	33.0	30.8	26.3	23.3	17.4	16.7
R T WEST		9.5	12.2	17.8	24.4	31.7	31.1	32.8	26.8	20.0	14.5	9.0	8.1
I C EAST		9.9	12.3	19.9	25.6	32.0	34.2	33.8	29.9	18.8	15.0	9.1	8.2
A L NW/NE		3.7	5.6	10.9	17.4	23.8	27.0	26.3	20.8	11.9	7.3	4.1	3.5
– NORTH		3.4	4.5	7.3	12.5	16.6	19.2	19.3	14.3	9.2	5.5	3.7	3.3

Base Temperature	40	45	50	55	60	65	70	Cooling Degree Days
Heating Degree Days	2149	2959	3909	4990	6212	7582	9091	(Base 65) = 695

City: Newark, New Jersey   Latitude: 40.7°
Winter Design Temp.: 10, 14   Deep Ground Temp.:

Month		JAN	FEB	MAR	APR	MAY	JUN	JUL	AUG	SEP	OCT	NOV	DEC
Average Air	(Day)	33.8	35.8	43.6	57.0	67.2	77.0	80.2	77.9	70.8	61.1	48.3	37.2
Temperature	(Night)	29.0	30.6	37.4	48.8	57.3	67.5	70.8	69.0	63.2	53.1	44.2	33.9
Solar Flux (Horiz.)		13.5	17.5	30.5	40.5	52.1	50.5	52.1	45.8	34.4	24.2	14.1	12.4
V – SOUTH		24.4	25.1	30.6	30.8	29.9	26.6	28.5	30.5	30.9	30.1	23.1	23.7
E SW/SE		18.7	19.9	27.7	30.9	33.8	30.3	32.4	32.3	29.0	25.4	18.0	17.8
R T WEST		9.6	12.1	20.9	26.8	33.5	31.1	33.2	29.9	22.7	16.7	10.0	8.8
I C EAST		9.6	12.4	20.8	26.9	32.4	31.9	34.2	30.0	21.9	16.5	10.3	9.0
A L NW/NE		4.1	5.6	12.3	18.8	24.5	25.5	26.8	21.7	13.7	7.9	4.7	3.6
– NORTH		3.7	4.5	9.0	13.5	17.4	18.5	19.1	15.4	10.0	5.7	4.1	3.4

Base Temperature	40	45	50	55	60	65	70	Cooling Degree Days
Heating Degree Days	822	1400	2125	2981	3971	5104	6421	(Base 65) = 1107

(Continued)

TABLE C.1 *(Continued)*

City: Albuquerque, New Mexico Latitude: 35.1°
Winter Design Temp.: 12, 16 Deep Ground Temp.:

Month		JAN	FEB	MAR	APR	MAY	JUN	JUL	AUG	SEP	OCT	NOV	DEC
Average Air	(Day)	37.2	43.7	50.7	62.1	71.3	82.6	83.4	80.2	76.3	61.9	48.4	40.5
Temperature	(Night)	30.4	35.2	40.4	50.7	59.3	70.5	71.0	69.5	64.5	51.5	38.8	34.4
Solar Flux (Horiz.)		29.3	30.8	52.7	55.1	69.8	76.0	74.5	65.8	59.8	44.7	32.4	23.0
V E R T I C A L	SOUTH	46.5	37.7	48.1	36.2	34.6	26.9	30.2	36.2	44.6	49.8	49.5	37.3
	SW/SE	35.9	30.3	42.5	37.7	38.0	35.3	35.5	39.7	42.4	42.3	38.1	28.3
	WEST	19.3	19.6	31.9	34.5	39.7	39.3	37.1	37.0	34.5	28.9	20.9	14.8
	EAST	19.4	21.5	34.0	35.7	46.8	44.8	44.8	39.5	37.2	29.2	21.7	15.5
	NW/NE	7.7	10.3	18.5	25.8	36.5	35.3	34.4	28.5	21.6	14.4	8.0	6.8
	NORTH	6.6	7.7	11.9	18.2	23.6	21.1	20.9	18.4	12.5	10.2	6.3	6.1

Base Temperature	40	45	50	55	60	65	70		Cooling Degree Days
Heating Degree Days	635	1127	1703	2500	3523	4597	5844		(Base 65) = 1498

City: Buffalo, New York Latitude: 42.9°
Winter Design Temp.: 2, 6 Deep Ground Temp.:

Month		JAN	FEB	MAR	APR	MAY	JUN	JUL	AUG	SEP	OCT	NOV	DEC
Average Air	(Day)	26.6	27.6	35.3	49.7	58.5	70.8	76.9	73.0	66.3	54.5	41.5	32.1
Temperature	(Night)	24.5	24.2	31.0	42.6	50.2	61.5	66.9	64.5	57.7	48.9	39.0	28.4
Solar Flux (Horiz.)		9.2	11.5	22.9	34.6	49.5	52.0	51.6	45.4	29.4	18.6	9.1	7.4
V E R T I C A L	SOUTH	15.1	15.4	24.3	27.6	30.6	29.1	29.2	31.6	27.6	23.5	13.1	11.2
	SW/SE	11.6	12.6	22.3	27.1	32.1	32.0	34.0	33.1	26.1	19.3	10.6	9.0
	WEST	6.5	8.4	16.5	23.3	30.3	32.0	34.4	29.6	20.7	12.7	6.5	5.3
	EAST	6.9	8.8	15.4	24.2	32.0	34.7	32.4	29.4	19.9	13.4	6.7	5.4
	NW/NE	3.8	5.3	10.1	17.3	23.9	27.4	25.2	20.8	12.9	7.1	4.2	3.5
	NORTH	3.6	4.7	8.3	12.9	17.2	19.7	18.5	14.5	9.8	5.7	4.0	3.4

Base Temperature	40	45	50	55	60	65	70		Cooling Degree Days
Heating Degree Days	1683	2432	3320	4346	5515	6830	8305		(Base 65) = 658

(Continued)

TABLE C.1 (*Continued*)

City: New York, New York   Latitude: 40.8°
Winter Design Temp.: 11, 15   Deep Ground Temp.:

Month		JAN	FEB	MAR	APR	MAY	JUN	JUL	AUG	SEP	OCT	NOV	DEC
Average Air	(Day)	33.7	34.6	41.7	54.5	62.1	71.3	77.1	77.5	69.4	60.6	48.9	39.1
Temperature	(Night)	30.5	29.9	36.6	49.5	56.9	64.2	69.8	71.3	63.4	54.0	45.9	35.0
Solar Flux (Horiz.)		14.5	19.0	31.7	41.0	51.0	48.8	52.6	50.4	35.9	24.6	14.7	12.0
V E R T I C A L	SOUTH	26.3	27.6	32.0	30.2	30.5	27.0	28.1	33.5	32.0	30.6	24.8	22.4
	SW/SE	20.0	21.9	27.6	30.3	33.2	30.7	31.8	35.1	29.9	24.9	18.9	17.3
	WEST	10.1	12.8	19.9	26.4	32.3	31.3	32.4	31.9	23.5	16.1	10.3	8.7
	EAST	10.2	13.1	21.7	27.4	32.8	31.1	33.6	32.1	23.8	16.9	10.9	8.5
	NW/NE	4.4	5.8	12.1	19.1	24.9	25.3	25.9	22.8	14.7	7.9	4.6	3.8
	NORTH	4.1	4.6	8.4	13.4	17.9	19.1	18.3	15.8	10.3	5.7	4.0	3.6

Base Temperature	40	45	50	55	60	65	70	Cooling Degree Days
Heating Degree Days	780	1329	2040	2908	3913	5085	6473	(Base 65) = 830

City: Rochester, New York   Latitude: 43.1°
Winter Design Temp.: 1, 5   Deep Ground Temp.:

Month		JAN	FEB	MAR	APR	MAY	JUN	JUL	AUG	SEP	OCT	NOV	DEC
Average Air	(Day)	23.5	23.5	33.0	46.1	56.0	69.9	72.6	70.4	63.5	53.2	42.4	28.6
Temperature	(Night)	22.5	21.0	31.6	44.2	54.2	66.0	69.3	67.6	61.6	50.1	39.3	27.6
Solar Flux (Horiz.)		11.1	16.5	26.4	38.2	47.5	52.4	56.8	46.8	33.2	19.8	11.8	7.9
V E R T I C A L	SOUTH	19.6	24.6	28.5	29.8	30.4	28.4	31.6	32.4	30.7	25.4	19.7	13.2
	SW/SE	15.9	20.6	26.7	30.3	33.1	33.8	37.7	33.9	30.0	21.9	15.5	10.2
	WEST	8.4	11.9	19.8	26.4	32.1	35.0	38.2	30.4	23.3	14.4	8.3	5.6
	EAST	7.3	10.2	17.3	25.5	31.6	33.5	33.0	29.6	19.8	13.1	8.1	5.9
	NW/NE	3.8	5.1	10.3	17.8	24.0	26.7	25.4	20.8	12.4	7.0	4.1	3.3
	NORTH	3.6	4.4	7.9	13.1	17.8	19.5	19.2	14.8	9.3	5.6	3.9	3.2

Base Temperature	40	45	50	55	60	65	70	Cooling Degree Days
Heating Degree Days	1879	2662	3571	4614	5787	7116	8589	(Base 65) = 740

(*Continued*)

TABLE C.1 *(Continued)*

City: Syracuse, New York   Latitude: 43.1°
Winter Design Temp.: -3, -2   Deep Ground Temp.:

Month		JAN	FEB	MAR	APR	MAY	JUN	JUL	AUG	SEP	OCT	NOV	DEC
Average Air	(Day)	23.1	26.7	34.6	51.9	62.0	71.3	75.8	74.3	67.2	54.1	42.4	31.1
Temperature	(Night)	19.3	21.2	30.5	43.2	53.4	61.6	65.0	64.3	58.1	46.4	39.1	27.9
Solar Flux (Horiz.)		10.6	13.4	23.8	38.7	47.3	50.0	52.2	46.8	30.8	17.3	10.2	8.9
V E R T I C A L	SOUTH	18.7	19.0	25.5	29.7	30.4	27.8	30.2	33.1	29.6	22.0	15.9	15.6
	SW/SE	14.8	15.7	23.6	29.7	31.9	31.8	34.7	35.3	26.5	18.6	13.4	12.1
	WEST	8.0	9.8	17.7	25.5	30.3	32.2	34.8	32.2	20.2	12.6	7.9	6.4
	EAST	7.6	9.5	16.3	26.3	31.2	31.7	32.6	30.7	21.5	12.4	6.8	6.4
	NW/NE	3.8	5.3	10.4	18.1	24.0	25.2	25.5	22.1	13.2	6.9	4.1	3.4
	NORTH	3.6	4.6	8.2	12.5	17.9	18.6	19.0	16.0	9.5	5.7	3.9	3.3

Base Temperature	40	45	50	55	60	65	70		Cooling Degree Days
Heating Degree Days	1894	2640	3512	4512	5660	6903	8418		(Base 65) = 704

City: Ashville, North Carolina   Latitude: 35.4°
Winter Design Temp.: 10, 14   Deep Ground Temp.:

Month		JAN	FEB	MAR	APR	MAY	JUN	JUL	AUG	SEP	OCT	NOV	DEC
Average Air	(Day)	45.3	41.9	47.5	62.0	71.5	75.0	77.7	75.6	68.3	60.4	50.1	43.8
Temperature	(Night)	36.5	32.8	38.7	51.0	57.7	63.1	66.1	65.5	59.0	50.0	39.6	36.7
Solar Flux (Horiz.)		17.3	23.1	40.1	46.7	51.7	52.6	52.2	48.4	40.6	33.1	21.5	17.5
V E R T I C A L	SOUTH	26.4	28.7	35.9	30.0	28.1	26.3	27.5	30.2	32.4	37.5	32.1	28.6
	SW/SE	20.8	23.5	32.8	32.5	32.2	30.8	30.8	32.9	30.6	32.5	26.0	22.6
	WEST	11.9	14.9	25.0	29.8	33.0	33.0	31.7	31.3	24.8	22.0	14.8	12.0
	EAST	11.8	15.3	24.9	28.5	33.9	34.2	35.6	28.7	24.9	20.4	13.6	11.3
	NW/NE	5.5	7.6	14.7	20.4	27.3	28.6	29.3	21.7	16.1	10.4	5.8	5.2
	NORTH	4.9	6.0	10.4	14.1	19.8	21.5	20.9	16.6	11.7	7.8	4.9	4.7

Base Temperature	40	45	50	55	60	65	70		Cooling Degree Days
Heating Degree Days	655	1095	1668	2419	3372	4536	5936		(Base 65) = 863

(Continued)

TABLE C.1 (*Continued*)

City: Greensboro, North Carolina   Latitude: 36.1°
Winter Design Temp.: 14, 18   Deep Ground Temp.:

Month		JAN	FEB	MAR	APR	MAY	JUN	JUL	AUG	SEP	OCT	NOV	DEC
Average Air	(Day)	42.2	43.5	51.9	65.6	71.8	79.5	81.2	80.4	75.1	64.8	55.4	44.3
Temperature	(Night)	33.3	35.4	41.6	53.8	60.9	68.2	70.6	69.8	63.8	52.5	44.5	36.5
Solar Flux (Horiz.)		20.6	21.0	36.1	46.7	48.8	51.2	54.0	48.9	40.5	34.4	19.4	17.7
V E R T I C A L	SOUTH	33.4	26.6	34.6	30.6	26.9	26.1	27.8	29.2	32.4	39.9	29.0	30.6
	SW/SE	25.6	21.9	32.0	32.3	30.7	31.1	32.5	31.7	31.7	33.9	22.3	23.5
	WEST	13.6	14.2	24.1	28.9	31.2	33.5	34.1	30.1	25.9	22.5	12.9	12.2
	EAST	14.0	14.6	22.5	28.7	31.4	33.6	35.1	30.2	24.9	21.7	13.8	12.1
	NW/NE	5.7	7.2	13.7	20.0	25.4	28.0	28.7	22.4	15.9	10.4	6.0	4.9
	NORTH	5.0	5.6	10.5	13.4	18.7	21.2	21.0	15.6	11.2	7.6	5.0	4.4

Base Temperature	40	45	50	55	60	65	70	Cooling Degree Days
Heating Degree Days	514	929	1487	2183	3021	4023	5214	(Base 65) = 1418

City: Bismarck, North Dakota   Latitude: 46.8°
Winter Design Temp.: -23, -19   Deep Ground Temp.:

Month		JAN	FEB	MAR	APR	MAY	JUN	JUL	AUG	SEP	OCT	NOV	DEC
Average Air	(Day)	7.1	19.6	23.7	43.2	59.0	74.5	78.6	78.4	64.3	48.3	29.6	14.5
Temperature	(Night)	3.5	14.1	16.2	35.9	48.4	61.6	64.2	61.8	50.5	39.2	25.6	9.6
Solar Flux (Horiz.)		10.6	17.5	29.0	39.9	49.9	65.5	66.0	58.2	35.2	24.1	11.1	11.2
V E R T I C A L	SOUTH	18.8	27.6	33.3	35.3	37.0	37.4	39.6	42.1	36.4	33.7	18.6	24.4
	SW/SE	15.1	22.2	29.5	32.4	39.4	42.2	43.6	42.5	32.8	26.9	15.2	17.9
	WEST	8.2	13.0	20.9	26.7	37.0	42.0	42.2	36.7	24.4	16.5	8.5	8.1
	EAST	7.5	12.7	19.7	29.4	33.8	42.2	42.5	37.5	24.2	17.6	7.7	8.8
	NW/NE	4.4	6.3	11.5	20.7	27.1	32.3	31.9	24.7	14.3	8.7	4.5	3.7
	NORTH	4.3	5.5	9.1	16.1	22.5	22.9	22.4	15.9	10.4	6.9	4.4	3.7

Base Temperature	40	45	50	55	60	65	70	Cooling Degree Days
Heating Degree Days	3802	4784	5868	7062	8354	9747	11253	(Base 65) = 836

(*Continued*)

TABLE C.1 (*Continued*)

City: Cincinnati, Ohio Latitude: 39.1°
Winter Design Temp.: 1,6 Deep Ground Temp.:

Month	JAN	FEB	MAR	APR	MAY	JUN	JUL	AUG	SEP	OCT	NOV	DEC
Average Air (Day)	29.5	40.4	46.1	59.9	69.1	76.9	81.4	79.6	71.0	56.7	46.2	40.5
Temperature (Night)	26.5	36.4	38.8	51.9	58.9	69.0	71.4	68.7	63.2	49.8	41.2	37.3
Solar Flux (Horiz.)	14.5	16.9	34.9	42.2	53.4	52.5	59.8	55.1	36.0	26.4	17.7	15.4
V E R T I C A L — SOUTH	21.9	20.7	35.2	32.0	34.1	30.8	32.5	35.7	32.6	30.2	26.5	25.6
SW/SE	17.8	17.9	30.7	31.6	36.9	34.0	36.3	38.2	30.7	25.3	21.2	18.7
WEST	10.5	12.4	23.0	28.1	36.3	35.0	37.2	35.6	25.2	17.5	12.2	9.5
EAST	10.1	11.9	24.7	29.4	37.4	36.2	40.2	34.4	25.2	18.3	12.0	11.2
NW/NE	5.9	7.9	15.7	22.2	30.1	30.3	32.1	25.3	18.0	10.6	6.2	5.4
NORTH	5.6	7.1	12.4	17.2	22.8	23.7	23.0	18.3	14.7	8.7	5.7	5.1

Base Temperature	40	45	50	55	60	65	70	Cooling Degree Days
Heating Degree Days	895	1465	2156	2983	3946	5042	6305	(Base 65) = 1275

City: Cleveland, Ohio Latitude: 41.4°
Winter Design Temp.: 1, 5 Deep Ground Temp.:

Month	JAN	FEB	MAR	APR	MAY	JUN	JUL	AUG	SEP	OCT	NOV	DEC
Average Air (Day)	27.1	29.4	36.5	53.2	64.3	68.9	76.4	78.1	67.1	55.2	41.3	28.6
Temperature (Night)	24.8	26.7	31.7	46.0	54.1	61.6	68.2	66.1	59.1	48.3	39.2	27.2
Solar Flux (Horiz.)	11.7	17.4	31.3	42.5	55.5	51.2	54.7	54.0	32.9	22.3	12.7	9.9
V E R T I C A L — SOUTH	17.0	22.9	32.7	32.4	33.3	30.5	33.0	35.8	30.6	26.8	17.8	13.8
SW/SE	14.0	19.7	29.4	33.1	36.0	34.3	36.9	37.7	28.7	22.7	14.2	11.2
WEST	8.4	12.9	22.0	29.0	34.7	34.9	37.0	34.7	23.1	15.5	8.7	6.9
EAST	8.1	11.8	21.3	27.8	36.2	34.1	35.5	35.0	22.9	15.7	9.1	7.2
NW/NE	5.3	7.5	13.2	20.0	27.8	28.2	28.7	24.4	15.8	9.5	5.0	4.9
NORTH	5.1	6.8	10.6	15.0	19.8	22.3	22.4	16.6	12.7	8.2	5.5	4.8

Base Temperature	40	45	50	55	60	65	70	Cooling Degree Days
Heating Degree Days	1618	2356	3201	4178	5303	6578	8006	(Base 65) = 828

(*Continued*)

TABLE C.1 (*Continued*)

City: Oklahoma City, Oklahoma   Latitude: 35.4°
Winter Design Temp.: 9, 13   Deep Ground Temp.:

Month		JAN	FEB	MAR	APR	MAY	JUN	JUL	AUG	SEP	OCT	NOV	DEC
Average Air	(Day)	36.7	41.4	50.4	62.5	69.8	77.6	82.9	81.5	76.7	63.2	51.8	41.7
Temperature	(Night)	32.5	36.5	43.9	57.1	64.6	73.9	77.9	77.7	70.8	59.0	47.7	37.7
Solar Flux (Horiz.)		21.6	23.1	36.4	53.4	53.7	57.2	63.6	55.8	45.7	36.1	24.7	19.9
V E R T I C A L	SOUTH	35.3	29.1	34.1	33.2	27.2	24.9	26.9	30.2	35.1	41.1	38.0	33.5
	SW/SE	27.6	26.0	32.5	35.9	33.2	31.7	35.7	35.1	33.8	36.3	31.2	25.4
	WEST	14.7	17.4	25.6	32.6	34.6	35.0	39.4	34.1	27.6	24.3	17.5	12.8
	EAST	14.1	14.3	24.0	31.6	32.5	33.6	35.9	32.3	27.7	21.2	15.0	13.1
	NW/NE	5.5	7.3	15.1	21.2	25.9	27.6	28.6	23.1	16.8	10.2	6.0	5.2
	NORTH	4.7	5.7	11.2	13.2	18.5	20.1	19.9	14.8	11.0	7.5	5.0	4.7

Base Temperature	40	45	50	55	60	65	70	Cooling Degree Days
Heating Degree Days	675	1096	1637	2306	3129	4105	5231	(Base 65) = 1947

City: Tulsa, Oklahoma   Latitude: 36.2°
Winter Design Temp.: 8,13   Deep Ground Temp.:

Month		JAN	FEB	MAR	APR	MAY	JUN	JUL	AUG	SEP	OCT	NOV	DEC
Average Air	(Day)	39.2	44.9	53.0	66.0	74.4	82.5	88.3	86.9	77.2	70.6	53.8	43.4
Temperature	(Night)	31.0	35.6	43.4	55.3	64.1	72.3	77.2	74.1	67.5	59.4	45.2	35.1
Solar Flux (Horiz.)		18.9	21.7	34.6	42.3	53.3	57.6	60.3	55.9	42.2	30.4	21.0	18.2
V E R T I C A L	SOUTH	31.2	27.8	32.2	29.2	28.7	26.0	27.9	30.8	33.6	34.4	31.8	31.1
	SW/SE	23.6	23.6	28.9	30.8	34.0	33.2	34.7	34.8	32.2	29.3	25.2	23.3
	WEST	12.4	15.2	22.0	28.1	35.2	36.7	37.4	33.2	26.4	19.8	14.3	11.7
	EAST	13.3	13.8	22.7	27.4	34.0	34.1	35.8	33.6	27.1	19.3	14.0	12.5
	NW/NE	5.5	7.0	14.0	20.0	27.0	28.0	28.6	24.0	16.9	9.8	5.7	5.1
	NORTH	4.9	5.7	10.4	14.6	19.6	20.8	20.4	15.1	11.5	7.4	4.7	4.6

Base Temperature	40	45	50	55	60	65	70	Cooling Degree Days
Heating Degree Days	658	1078	1618	2270	3050	3964	5022	(Base 65) = 2184

(*Continued*)

TABLE C.1 (*Continued*)

City: Portland, Oregon   Latitude: 45.6°
Winter Design Temp.: 18,24   Deep Ground Temp.:

Month		JAN	FEB	MAR	APR	MAY	JUN	JUL	AUG	SEP	OCT	NOV	DEC
Average Air	(Day)	36.3	44.2	47.0	53.9	57.1	68.2	75.1	69.3	66.2	58.0	48.8	40.5
Temperature	(Night)	34.3	40.4	40.8	46.9	50.1	57.9	62.2	60.2	56.7	51.2	44.9	37.1
Solar Flux (Horiz.)		8.0	14.3	24.2	35.0	45.3	60.7	69.7	48.7	32.9	19.4	11.0	9.1
V E R T I C A L	SOUTH	10.6	19.7	26.2	31.4	35.4	35.0	37.7	36.4	33.0	24.8	16.5	15.8
	SW/SE	9.2	16.8	24.6	29.8	35.5	40.8	44.9	40.1	32.3	22.6	13.6	12.3
	WEST	6.0	10.7	18.3	25.0	32.8	41.3	45.0	36.1	24.8	15.0	8.1	6.3
	EAST	5.6	9.9	15.7	25.5	32.3	37.5	40.8	29.4	20.0	12.0	7.7	6.5
	NW/NE	4.2	6.0	11.1	19.7	26.5	29.5	30.1	22.1	13.2	7.9	4.0	3.8
	NORTH	4.1	5.4	9.7	16.7	22.9	22.5	20.6	17.8	10.8	7.1	4.6	3.7

Base Temperature	40	45	50	55	60	65	70	Cooling Degree Days
Heating Degree Days	389	841	1554	2520	3747	5201	6806	(Base 65) = 462

City: Philadelphia, Pennsylvania   Latitude: 39.9°
Winter Design Temp.: 10,14   Deep Ground Temp.:

Month		JAN	FEB	MAR	APR	MAY	JUN	JUL	AUG	SEP	OCT	NOV	DEC
Average Air	(Day)	31.7	34.1	43.1	60.2	70.1	77.6	78.2	79.9	71.6	60.2	47.4	34.8
Temperature	(Night)	28.0	30.0	35.5	50.3	59.4	68.4	70.9	69.9	62.0	50.5	41.4	31.9
Solar Flux (Horiz.)		17.1	18.8	37.6	46.9	59.7	54.5	49.1	54.1	41.1	29.3	17.3	15.1
V E R T I C A L	SOUTH	29.0	24.7	37.7	35.1	34.2	31.6	31.3	36.3	37.0	36.5	27.0	25.9
	SW/SE	21.9	20.0	34.3	35.7	39.0	35.9	34.0	38.1	33.8	30.2	20.7	19.8
	WEST	11.9	13.0	25.7	31.6	39.3	37.0	34.0	35.1	26.3	19.8	11.5	10.5
	EAST	13.0	13.9	25.2	31.2	38.0	34.4	34.5	34.7	26.4	20.0	12.5	10.9
	NW/NE	5.9	7.9	15.0	22.4	29.1	28.7	28.8	25.2	16.7	10.2	6.4	5.3
	NORTH	5.4	6.9	11.1	16.6	21.1	23.4	22.9	18.2	12.7	8.0	5.8	5.0

Base Temperature	40	45	50	55	60	65	70	Cooling Degree Days
Heating Degree Days	996	1620	2360	3213	4185	5300	6572	(Base 65) = 1190

(*Continued*)

TABLE C.1 (*Continued*)

City: Pittsburgh, Pennsylvania   Latitude: 40.5°
Winter Design Temp.: 3, 7   Deep Ground Temp.:

Month		JAN	FEB	MAR	APR	MAY	JUN	JUL	AUG	SEP	OCT	NOV	DEC
Average Air	(Day)	26.4	37.1	42.5	56.4	66.4	74.9	76.9	75.9	69.1	53.5	45.0	37.5
Temperature	(Night)	23.8	32.1	35.9	47.6	55.5	65.7	67.1	64.2	60.2	46.1	39.7	33.9
Solar Flux (Horiz.)		13.0	16.8	32.7	42.4	55.5	56.8	59.7	51.8	36.3	25.4	15.9	13.8
V E R T I C A L — SOUTH		18.3	21.1	33.5	32.9	35.1	33.8	35.6	36.0	33.5	29.9	23.5	23.2
SW/SE		15.0	18.3	30.3	32.6	37.4	37.3	39.8	36.8	30.9	25.3	18.7	18.7
WEST		9.4	12.2	22.7	28.7	36.3	37.8	40.4	34.0	24.6	17.4	11.1	10.1
EAST		9.3	11.1	22.5	29.8	37.9	39.0	39.7	36.9	24.9	17.9	11.3	9.3
NW/NE		6.1	7.3	14.5	22.3	29.7	32.5	32.3	27.7	17.2	10.3	6.3	5.2
NORTH		5.9	6.7	11.5	17.5	22.3	25.2	25.0	20.1	14.0	8.4	5.8	5.0

Base Temperature	40	45	50	55	60	65	70	Cooling Degree Days
Heating Degree Days	1214	1887	2668	3593	4657	5870	7246	(Base 65) = 928

City: Charleston, South Carolina   Latitude: 32.9°
Winter Design Temp.: 25, 28   Deep Ground Temp.:

Month		JAN	FEB	MAR	APR	MAY	JUN	JUL	AUG	SEP	OCT	NOV	DEC
Average Air	(Day)	51.0	57.0	65.5	72.0	78.9	80.3	83.4	83.4	77.3	69.4	60.6	50.6
Temperature	(Night)	43.2	47.0	54.3	60.7	67.7	69.3	74.7	74.5	70.5	57.7	48.2	42.6
Solar Flux (Horiz.)		19.2	25.1	37.5	44.4	52.1	51.3	53.7	48.4	40.4	32.1	28.6	21.9
V E R T I C A L — SOUTH		28.0	29.6	33.2	28.6	25.9	25.3	26.7	28.4	31.0	34.4	41.0	34.6
SW/SE		21.5	24.4	30.4	29.3	30.8	30.5	31.6	31.0	29.8	28.8	31.7	27.1
WEST		12.3	15.9	24.2	26.8	32.4	33.5	33.8	30.2	25.3	20.1	17.8	14.6
EAST		13.3	16.4	25.0	28.8	33.8	33.5	35.9	31.4	26.9	21.2	18.5	14.1
NW/NE		5.9	8.3	15.8	20.9	27.3	28.8	30.2	24.6	18.1	11.5	6.9	5.9
NORTH		5.1	6.5	11.9	14.4	19.1	22.4	22.1	17.7	12.9	8.9	5.4	5.2

Base Temperature	40	45	50	55	60	65	70	Cooling Degree Days
Heating Degree Days	148	323	626	1064	1651	2406	3361	(Base 65) = 2038

(*Continued*)

TABLE C.1 (*Continued*)

City: Rapid City, South Dakota Latitude: 44.1º
Winter Design Temp.: -11, -7 Deep Ground Temp.:

Month		JAN	FEB	MAR	APR	MAY	JUN	JUL	AUG	SEP	OCT	NOV	DEC
Average Air	(Day)	27.3	29.4	37.8	48.9	61.8	72.1	78.9	82.3	65.7	55.2	36.7	27.3
Temperature	(Night)	19.4	23.7	27.9	39.1	49.1	57.9	65.6	65.7	51.7	43.6	29.5	22.5
Solar Flux (Horiz.)		10.9	15.9	25.9	39.8	48.7	55.8	59.2	51.1	34.9	23.3	15.1	10.3
V E R T I C A L	SOUTH	20.0	24.5	29.0	32.2	31.3	30.0	31.7	34.7	34.0	32.4	27.8	21.7
	SW/SE	15.2	19.1	24.6	31.1	32.8	32.6	35.5	35.7	30.3	26.4	21.5	15.6
	WEST	7.6	10.8	17.0	25.6	30.9	32.2	35.4	31.6	22.5	16.0	10.8	7.2
	EAST	7.8	11.3	18.2	26.4	33.0	36.0	36.8	32.1	23.8	16.0	10.5	8.2
	NW/NE	3.7	5.1	9.9	17.7	24.8	27.4	27.0	21.5	13.7	7.4	4.3	3.1
	NORTH	3.5	4.3	7.2	12.4	17.8	18.7	18.1	13.9	9.2	5.5	3.8	3.0

Base Temperature	40	45	50	55	60	65	70	Cooling Degree Days
Heating Degree Days	2159	2958	3903	4900	6104	7520	9008	(Base 65) = 867

City: Sioux Falls, South Dakota Latitude: 43.6º
Winter Design Temp.: -15 , -11 Deep Ground Temp.:

Month		JAN	FEB	MAR	APR	MAY	JUN	JUL	AUG	SEP	OCT	NOV	DEC
Average Air	(Day)	16.8	22.9	34.8	51.5	63.3	75.9	79.5	77.7	64.3	57.7	37.2	23.6
Temperature	(Night)	12.2	17.0	26.5	40.6	51.4	63.2	68.0	66.7	54.4	44.6	29.4	19.2
Solar Flux (Horiz.)		10.6	14.9	25.3	38.6	49.3	51.0	56.5	46.9	33.6	24.2	12.8	11.2
V E R T I C A L	SOUTH	19.6	21.9	27.3	30.4	30.0	29.8	32.1	32.8	31.8	33.9	22.6	23.2
	SW/SE	15.6	16.9	23.4	30.4	32.6	34.6	35.8	34.0	29.7	26.7	17.5	17.3
	WEST	8.0	9.7	16.9	26.1	31.2	35.3	35.1	30.3	22.8	15.6	8.8	7.9
	EAST	7.3	10.8	18.5	26.0	31.4	31.5	35.0	30.3	22.0	16.8	8.7	8.2
	NW/NE	3.6	5.2	10.7	17.9	23.2	25.4	26.8	21.0	13.1	7.2	3.9	3.4
	NORTH	3.4	4.4	7.7	12.9	16.4	20.1	19.0	14.4	9.2	5.3	3.6	3.2

Base Temperature	40	45	50	55	60	65	70	Cooling Degree Days
Heating Degree Days	2661	3500	4438	5486	6643	7924	9348	(Base 65) = 955

(*Continued*)

TABLE C.1 (*Continued*)

City: Nashville, Tennessee   Latitude: 36.1°
Winter Design Temp.: 9, 14   Deep Ground Temp.:

Month		JAN	FEB	MAR	APR	MAY	JUN	JUL	AUG	SEP	OCT	NOV	DEC
Average Air	(Day)	44.7	44.2	54.9	65.5	73.6	78.9	82.1	81.9	80.5	64.1	51.1	44.3
Temperature	(Night)	38.3	37.4	46.2	55.0	61.4	66.3	71.5	71.8	70.8	55.4	45.7	40.5
Solar Flux (Horiz.)		18.4	22.9	37.8	48.3	58.4	59.7	58.7	56.8	40.7	28.3	16.9	14.7
V E R T I C A L — SOUTH		27.7	28.4	35.5	33.7	30.8	30.0	29.7	34.1	33.0	30.3	22.1	22.4
SW/SE		22.9	23.9	32.5	35.3	35.3	35.4	34.9	37.1	31.5	26.3	18.5	17.5
WEST		13.6	15.6	25.3	32.2	36.3	38.0	36.8	35.7	26.2	19.3	12.1	10.1
EAST		12.4	14.9	24.8	31.2	38.2	40.2	38.0	36.5	27.3	19.9	11.9	10.5
NW/NE		6.6	8.2	16.1	23.2	30.3	33.7	31.0	26.7	18.8	12.2	7.0	5.6
— NORTH		6.0	7.0	12.8	17.3	21.3	24.6	22.4	18.3	13.9	9.9	6.6	5.3

Base Temperature	40	45	50	55	60	65	70	Cooling Degree Days
Heating Degree Days	461	827	1333	1965	2739	3677	4782	(Base 65) = 1674

City: Brownsville, Texas   Latitude: 25.9°
Winter Design Temp.: 35, 39   Deep Ground Temp.:

Month		JAN	FEB	MAR	APR	MAY	JUN	JUL	AUG	SEP	OCT	NOV	DEC
Average Air	(Day)	66.6	66.6	73.6	79.5	84.5	86.7	86.7	87.6	84.1	79.7	70.2	67.5
Temperature	(Night)	59.3	60.0	65.7	71.4	76.4	77.3	78.6	78.7	77.5	68.9	64.8	59.0
Solar Flux (Horiz.)		25.9	27.7	45.0	48.0	58.7	60.3	58.1	57.0	42.3	44.2	25.4	27.2
V E R T I C A L — SOUTH		30.8	28.0	34.3	28.2	25.1	23.4	26.0	28.6	31.2	40.5	28.4	35.4
SW/SE		25.1	25.4	34.6	32.6	33.4	32.1	33.3	35.2	31.3	36.3	23.3	29.6
WEST		16.4	19.5	29.7	32.7	38.0	38.5	38.2	37.5	28.7	27.8	16.4	18.2
EAST		16.9	18.2	27.4	29.9	35.6	37.2	38.1	37.7	30.2	28.6	18.0	15.9
NW/NE		9.2	12.3	19.1	24.1	30.7	33.5	34.1	30.9	23.0	16.6	10.7	7.9
— NORTH		7.9	10.7	14.6	18.5	23.5	26.9	27.3	21.7	17.6	12.1	9.2	7.0

Base Temperature	40	45	50	55	60	65	70	Cooling Degree Days
Heating Degree Days	1	17	66	169	348	646	1103	(Base 65) = 3877

(*Continued*)

TABLE C.1 (*Continued*)

City: El Paso, Texas Latitude: 31.8°
Winter Design Temp.: 20, 24 Deep Ground Temp.:63

Month		JAN	FEB	MAR	APR	MAY	JUN	JUL	AUG	SEP	OCT	NOV	DEC
Average Air	(Day)	49.3	54.7	67.5	73.0	78.9	85.5	87.9	83.0	78.3	71.6	58.8	44.9
Temperature	(Night)	35.0	43.1	54.1	60.6	65.6	73.9	77.9	72.6	67.8	57.1	47.4	37.2
Solar Flux (Horiz.)		34.6	34.0	50.5	58.8	67.5	66.2	62.4	60.3	54.4	46.5	28.6	26.3
V E R T I C A L	SOUTH	51.8	39.7	42.9	34.7	29.7	24.3	28.8	32.3	38.8	47.4	37.1	40.1
	SW/SE	40.2	32.9	37.9	37.3	37.1	33.4	35.2	35.2	38.4	40.7	30.6	31.6
	WEST	22.1	21.7	29.7	35.6	39.9	38.7	38.5	34.4	32.6	28.4	19.2	17.4
	EAST	22.3	21.9	33.8	38.2	41.5	39.3	38.0	37.6	32.8	28.6	18.5	16.8
	NW/NE	8.6	11.0	20.7	27.7	33.1	32.8	32.0	28.1	20.2	14.4	9.4	7.2
	NORTH	7.0	8.6	14.6	18.1	22.1	22.7	24.3	18.7	12.7	10.1	7.9	6.3

Base Temperature	40	45	50	55	60	65	70	Cooling Degree Days
Heating Degree Days	319	588	964	1463	2098	2880	3845	(Base 65) = 2386

City: Fort Worth, Texas Latitude:32.9°
Winter Design Temp.: 17, 22 Deep Ground Temp.:67

Month		JAN	FEB	MAR	APR	MAY	JUN	JUL	AUG	SEP	OCT	NOV	DEC
Average Air	(Day)	51.6	49.6	56.7	68.0	76.9	85.3	87.8	89.0	80.2	75.0	62.3	52.5
Temperature	(Night)	45.0	43.1	50.5	60.8	68.2	75.2	78.1	79.0	70.0	64.0	52.7	44.5
Solar Flux (Horiz.)		24.6	28.4	40.8	46.5	54.4	60.5	61.9	58.9	49.5	39.5	30.1	22.7
V E R T I C A L	SOUTH	36.1	32.6	35.9	31.5	29.3	27.9	29.7	32.4	37.6	40.5	42.2	34.3
	SW/SE	29.9	28.3	34.7	34.3	34.5	35.9	35.6	36.7	36.7	37.1	33.9	27.6
	WEST	17.7	19.4	28.1	32.1	36.5	40.3	38.6	36.3	31.0	26.5	19.7	15.7
	EAST	15.5	18.1	26.0	28.7	35.8	35.8	41.2	37.2	32.1	23.4	18.7	14.6
	NW/NE	7.5	9.9	18.0	22.5	29.5	30.8	34.4	28.3	20.6	12.6	7.0	7.1
	NORTH	6.6	7.9	14.4	17.8	22.5	24.7	24.8	19.2	13.9	9.1	6.6	6.5

Base Temperature	40	45	50	55	60	65	70	Cooling Degree Days
Heating Degree Days	169	381	722	1194	1808	2555	3458	(Base 65) = 2689

(*Continued*)

TABLE C.1 (*Continued*)

City: Houston, Texas Latitude: 29.7°
Winter Design Temp.: 28, 33 Deep Ground Temp.:

Month		JAN	FEB	MAR	APR	MAY	JUN	JUL	AUG	SEP	OCT	NOV	DEC
Average Air	(Day)	50.8	55.9	65.2	73.5	78.5	83.7	87.4	85.0	83.3	73.6	68.1	56.9
Temperature	(Night)	45.1	48.5	56.0	66.0	71.6	74.0	78.1	77.1	73.1	63.1	59.1	49.6
Solar Flux (Horiz.)		20.3	27.5	40.5	41.8	47.7	59.0	57.7	48.9	46.8	38.6	25.3	20.4
SOUTH		25.6	30.1	34.3	29.0	27.3	25.5	28.6	30.1	34.1	38.4	31.8	27.5
V E R T I C A L — SW/SE		20.6	25.8	34.5	30.6	31.3	32.9	33.7	33.0	33.2	34.4	26.3	23.1
WEST		13.6	18.4	28.9	29.1	33.3	37.7	36.7	33.2	28.9	25.6	17.1	14.5
EAST		14.5	18.3	25.3	28.0	32.1	38.7	40.1	35.1	30.9	24.8	16.6	13.4
NW/NE		8.4	10.7	18.2	22.7	27.9	33.9	34.8	28.9	20.9	14.5	8.7	7.6
NORTH		7.5	9.0	15.0	18.4	23.2	25.9	26.4	21.8	14.5	11.3	7.4	7.0

Base Temperature	40	45	50	55	60	65	70		Cooling Degree Days
Heating Degree Days	85	203	405	724	1171	1772	2552		(Base 65) = 2760

City: Lubbock, Texas Latitude: 33.7°
Winter Design Temp.: 10, 15 Deep Ground Temp.:

Month		JAN	FEB	MAR	APR	MAY	JUN	JUL	AUG	SEP	OCT	NOV	DEC
Average Air	(Day)	43.6	47.1	57.3	70.3	75.2	81.6	83.9	84.3	78.0	67.3	53.3	50.1
Temperature	(Night)	34.3	33.0	43.3	54.0	62.1	68.0	73.2	71.3	66.1	52.8	39.9	36.8
Solar Flux (Horiz.)		26.4	34.9	50.1	58.9	63.1	68.1	64.2	65.3	52.5	44.9	33.7	26.0
SOUTH		38.9	42.6	43.4	36.9	31.0	27.4	30.8	34.4	37.9	49.1	48.7	41.8
V E R T I C A L — SW/SE		30.9	35.7	40.3	39.8	36.0	35.0	37.1	39.9	38.7	41.7	39.1	32.4
WEST		17.6	23.1	31.7	37.2	37.5	39.0	39.8	39.7	32.6	28.0	22.2	17.7
EAST		17.3	22.0	32.2	36.7	40.9	41.4	41.7	40.9	31.3	27.8	20.7	17.6
NW/NE		7.9	10.5	19.6	26.1	32.8	34.3	34.7	29.8	19.5	13.6	8.2	7.4
NORTH		6.8	8.2	13.7	17.7	22.5	23.5	24.9	18.5	12.2	9.7	6.8	6.5

Base Temperature	40	45	50	55	60	65	70		Cooling Degree Days
Heating Degree Days	624	1032	1555	2195	2967	3887	5003		(Base 65) = 1904

(*Continued*)

TABLE C.1 (*Continued*)

City: San Antonio, Texas
Winter Design Temp.: 25, 30
Latitude: 29.5°
Deep Ground Temp.:

Month		JAN	FEB	MAR	APR	MAY	JUN	JUL	AUG	SEP	OCT	NOV	DEC
Average Air	(Day)	53.4	54.1	58.4	73.7	77.4	87.5	87.8	86.3	84.3	76.9	65.7	53.1
Temperature	(Night)	46.4	46.0	50.6	64.1	68.2	77.3	78.5	77.9	72.4	69.1	59.0	46.5
Solar Flux (Horiz.)		22.5	30.9	38.9	46.0	56.6	60.9	61.5	51.4	52.2	33.9	22.8	20.9
V E R T I C A L	SOUTH	28.3	33.6	31.7	29.6	27.4	23.5	25.9	29.5	35.4	32.4	27.2	28.6
	SW/SE	23.2	29.3	32.4	33.1	34.8	32.2	33.9	33.7	35.9	30.4	23.3	22.9
	WEST	15.0	20.1	27.7	32.0	38.1	37.5	38.5	34.3	31.5	23.3	15.6	13.8
	EAST	15.0	18.5	24.2	28.2	33.9	34.7	36.0	31.9	33.1	21.3	14.8	13.8
	NW/NE	8.6	10.2	17.5	22.3	28.7	30.1	30.7	26.2	21.6	14.5	8.7	7.2
	NORTH	7.7	8.4	14.1	17.7	22.6	23.4	23.6	20.5	13.4	12.2	7.5	6.5

Base Temperature	40	45	50	55	60	65	70	Cooling Degree Days
Heating Degree Days	99	247	521	900	1404	2044	2844	(Base 65) = 2903

City: Salt Lake City, Utah
Winter Design Temp.: 3, 8
Latitude: 40.8°
Deep Ground Temp.: 52

Month		JAN	FEB	MAR	APR	MAY	JUN	JUL	AUG	SEP	OCT	NOV	DEC
Average Air	(Day)	33.1	36.9	38.8	54.1	66.1	75.8	84.6	84.0	74.6	59.7	39.0	28.7
Temperature	(Night)	26.6	29.7	31.8	44.9	52.7	61.4	67.9	67.1	58.3	46.1	32.8	23.9
Solar Flux (Horiz.)		11.4	16.6	30.2	40.9	51.4	58.0	64.3	57.0	43.7	26.2	12.4	11.4
V E R T I C A L	SOUTH	19.3	23.2	31.9	30.5	29.8	28.8	31.1	34.9	38.2	33.8	19.4	20.3
	SW/SE	15.6	18.8	26.8	31.1	33.4	33.3	37.3	37.0	35.8	26.7	15.6	16.1
	WEST	8.6	11.6	19.0	27.1	32.8	34.3	38.3	33.4	27.8	16.5	8.8	8.2
	EAST	7.8	11.7	21.3	26.3	33.2	35.8	37.7	34.8	27.8	18.0	8.4	7.6
	NW/NE	4.2	6.0	11.8	18.6	25.4	28.1	28.4	23.3	15.5	8.0	4.5	3.8
	NORTH	3.9	5.0	8.5	13.8	17.8	19.5	18.8	14.0	9.6	5.9	4.1	3.7

Base Temperature	40	45	50	55	60	65	70	Cooling Degree Days
Heating Degree Days	1262	1957	2811	3814	4968	6250	7645	(Base 65) = 1270

(Continued)

TABLE C.1 (*Continued*)

City: Burlington, Vermont   Latitude: 44.5°
Winter Design Temp.: -12, -17   Deep Ground Temp.:45

Month		JAN	FEB	MAR	APR	MAY	JUN	JUL	AUG	SEP	OCT	NOV	DEC
Average Air	(Day)	18.7	22.4	28.4	43.5	56.3	67.8	72.5	69.8	60.8	50.9	39.8	26.1
Temperature	(Night)	16.1	19.3	25.2	37.8	52.0	61.9	67.8	64.8	56.7	47.8	37.6	24.6
Solar Flux (Horiz.)		14.9	18.8	28.6	38.7	51.5	52.3	55.6	47.7	38.1	29.2	15.9	10.9
V E R T I C A L	SOUTH	26.9	27.6	28.9	29.7	30.5	28.6	30.0	31.8	33.4	37.5	26.1	19.4
	SW/SE	20.6	21.0	26.6	29.4	34.0	34.0	32.5	35.1	31.5	30.6	19.9	14.7
	WEST	10.6	12.1	20.1	25.7	33.6	33.4	36.0	32.9	24.5	19.2	10.7	7.7
	EAST	10.5	13.8	19.5	26.6	33.8	34.2	36.5	30.4	24.2	19.7	11.5	8.1
	NW/NE	4.4	5.8	11.9	18.9	26.2	27.7	28.7	21.9	14.4	8.9	4.9	3.8
	NORTH	4.0	4.6	8.8	13.9	18.8	20.4	20.2	15.6	9.7	6.3	4.3	3.6

Base Temperature	40	45	50	55	60	65	70	Cooling Degree Days
Heating Degree Days	1629	2320	3124	4030	5056	6227	7557	(Base 65) = 1108

City: Richmond, Virgina   Latitude: 37.5°
Winter Design Temp.: 14, 17   Deep Ground Temp.:58

Month		JAN	FEB	MAR	APR	MAY	JUN	JUL	AUG	SEP	OCT	NOV	DEC
Average Air	(Day)	39.8	44.1	51.2	64.8	70.9	77.6	82.2	81.6	75.3	63.5	55.2	45.4
Temperature	(Night)	31.6	35.5	42.6	53.0	61.2	66.2	71.9	70.5	63.9	52.6	43.1	36.6
Solar Flux (Horiz.)		16.6	20.1	33.4	45.2	50.5	52.6	52.2	48.4	40.3	27.3	20.0	15.6
V E R T I C A L	SOUTH	27.4	26.8	32.7	31.4	28.7	26.3	28.0	30.0	33.9	32.8	30.7	26.9
	SW/SE	21.5	20.9	30.1	33.1	32.0	30.7	32.4	31.4	31.9	28.6	23.7	19.9
	WEST	11.8	13.0	22.7	30.1	31.8	32.5	33.6	29.5	25.9	19.4	13.3	10.1
	EAST	11.6	14.6	21.8	29.7	32.6	35.0	34.1	32.7	26.9	17.1	13.8	11.1
	NW/NE	5.0	6.9	13.3	20.9	25.8	28.7	27.6	23.9	16.6	8.7	5.9	4.7
	NORTH	4.5	5.4	10.0	14.4	18.7	20.4	20.3	16.0	11.4	7.0	4.9	4.3

Base Temperature	40	45	50	55	60	65	70	Cooling Degree Days
Heating Degree Days	594	1022	1586	2299	3154	4165	5354	(Base 65) = 1466

(*Continued*)

TABLE C.1 (*Continued*)

City: Roanoke, Virginia   Latitude: 37.3°
Winter Design Temp.: 12, 16   Deep Ground Temp.:

Month		JAN	FEB	MAR	APR	MAY	JUN	JUL	AUG	SEP	OCT	NOV	DEC
Average Air	(Day)	38.4	42.8	48.7	61.7	69.7	78.1	80.5	79.3	74.9	61.7	52.1	42.4
Temperature	(Night)	32.6	35.1	40.5	51.1	59.7	66.7	70.0	68.4	64.6	51.6	42.4	35.7
Solar Flux (Horiz.)		16.0	20.2	35.2	44.8	51.6	52.4	54.6	47.8	39.4	30.7	18.4	15.5
V E R T I C A L	SOUTH	26.0	27.0	34.3	31.1	29.3	26.8	28.7	29.3	32.5	36.3	28.2	27.1
	SW/SE	20.6	22.3	32.0	32.5	32.8	31.4	33.1	32.3	30.5	30.4	22.1	21.1
	WEST	11.6	13.9	23.8	28.7	32.6	33.0	34.2	30.7	24.5	19.8	12.6	11.1
	EAST	11.0	13.5	21.7	27.2	32.8	34.5	35.4	31.5	25.4	19.6	12.7	10.7
	NW/NE	4.9	6.5	13.4	19.1	26.0	28.6	28.7	23.4	16.0	9.2	5.6	4.5
	NORTH	4.5	5.0	10.3	13.7	19.0	21.0	20.9	15.7	11.3	6.6	4.8	4.2

Base Temperature	40	45	50	55	60	65	70	Cooling Degree Days
Heating Degree Days	660	1117	1721	2483	3387	4450	5707	(Base 65) = 1268

City: Seattle, Washington   Latitude: 47.5°
Winter Design Temp.: 21, 26   Deep Ground Temp.:52

Month		JAN	FEB	MAR	APR	MAY	JUN	JUL	AUG	SEP	OCT	NOV	DEC
Average Air	(Day)	39.8	43.8	46.1	49.8	57.5	63.2	68.2	67.9	63.3	53.5	47.7	41.2
Temperature	(Night)	38.0	40.7	39.8	43.4	49.4	54.9	57.2	59.0	54.1	48.7	44.8	39.4
Solar Flux (Horiz.)		6.9	10.5	19.4	29.3	44.0	42.0	53.8	47.6	29.3	13.5	6.8	5.6
V E R T I C A L	SOUTH	11.9	15.9	21.5	25.9	30.9	28.7	33.3	35.0	29.4	17.5	10.0	9.8
	SW/SE	9.3	13.0	20.0	24.1	31.5	31.2	37.2	36.7	27.4	15.5	8.0	7.6
	WEST	5.0	7.7	14.4	19.8	28.8	30.3	35.9	31.6	20.0	10.3	5.0	4.0
	EAST	5.0	7.4	12.8	21.3	29.1	27.4	33.4	28.3	18.2	8.9	5.1	4.2
	NW/NE	2.9	4.3	8.2	15.4	21.9	22.3	24.9	18.9	10.7	5.7	3.3	2.5
	NORTH	2.8	3.9	6.6	12.2	16.9	18.8	18.2	13.1	7.8	5.0	3.2	2.5

Base Temperature	40	45	50	55	60	65	70	Cooling Degree Days
Heating Degree Days	284	732	1499	2584	3957	5530	7222	(Base 65) = 243

(*Continued*)

TABLE C.1 (*Continued*)

City: Charleston, West Virginia   Latitude: 38.3°
Winter Design Temp.: 7, 11   Deep Ground Temp.:56

Month		JAN	FEB	MAR	APR	MAY	JUN	JUL	AUG	SEP	OCT	NOV	DEC
Average Air	(Day)	35.8	35.9	48.7	59.1	67.7	77.9	82.5	77.3	72.4	61.2	51.9	42.0
Temperature	(Night)	31.0	31.4	40.3	49.2	55.6	64.5	70.7	66.7	63.0	49.3	43.8	37.1
Solar Flux (Horiz.)		13.2	15.2	28.8	39.6	50.2	52.1	52.8	46.7	34.2	26.4	15.0	11.4
V E R T I C A L	SOUTH	20.8	19.5	28.2	29.4	28.8	27.9	29.2	30.8	29.3	31.5	22.5	18.5
	SW/SE	16.9	16.2	25.7	30.2	32.7	32.3	33.7	34.0	27.9	26.9	18.9	15.3
	WEST	9.7	10.5	19.8	27.0	32.7	33.7	34.5	31.8	22.7	17.6	11.1	8.8
	EAST	8.9	10.5	19.7	26.2	32.0	34.2	33.4	27.0	22.2	16.2	9.4	7.8
	NW/NE	4.7	6.1	12.8	19.5	25.1	28.2	27.2	20.2	15.0	7.9	5.0	4.3
	NORTH	4.4	5.3	10.2	14.9	18.4	21.2	20.6	15.9	11.8	6.2	4.6	4.1

Base Temperature	40	45	50	55	60	65	70	Cooling Degree Days
Heating Degree Days	906	1405	2033	2821	3768	4875	6158	(Base 65) = 1192

City: Madison, Wisconsin   Latitude: 43.1°
Winter Design Temp.: -11, -7   Deep Ground Temp.:

Month		JAN	FEB	MAR	APR	MAY	JUN	JUL	AUG	SEP	OCT	NOV	DEC
Average Air	(Day)	21.3	23.3	36.0	53.5	58.9	70.7	79.5	73.1	63.9	56.0	40.1	28.8
Temperature	(Night)	18.0	16.6	29.9	43.7	49.4	58.1	66.6	60.7	51.3	45.8	34.6	25.5
Solar Flux (Horiz.)		14.2	19.7	27.0	41.7	47.6	55.2	57.0	45.8	38.8	23.6	14.1	10.7
V E R T I C A L	SOUTH	25.3	28.3	28.6	33.6	34.0	32.7	34.4	35.2	36.4	30.2	23.0	18.3
	SW/SE	19.9	23.0	25.0	33.1	35.1	35.7	36.9	34.9	32.8	24.8	18.0	14.8
	WEST	10.3	13.8	18.6	28.5	33.1	35.9	36.8	31.3	25.1	16.0	10.0	8.0
	EAST	9.8	13.8	19.5	28.7	33.4	38.3	39.3	32.7	27.2	16.6	10.2	7.3
	NW/NE	5.0	7.3	13.0	21.0	27.0	30.8	30.7	24.7	16.5	9.2	5.3	4.3
	NORTH	4.7	6.3	10.8	16.4	21.9	23.0	22.7	19.2	11.4	7.7	4.9	4.1

Base Temperature	40	45	50	55	60	65	70	Cooling Degree Days
Heating Degree Days	2128	2952	3888	4961	6173	7523	9032	(Base 65) = 662

(*Continued*)

TABLE C.1 (*Continued*)

City: Casper, Wyoming   Latitude: 42.9°
Winter Design Temp.: -11, -5   Deep Ground Temp.:

Month		JAN	FEB	MAR	APR	MAY	JUN	JUL	AUG	SEP	OCT	NOV	DEC
Average Air	(Day)	26.7	32.3	35.7	44.3	58.7	71.3	80.9	79.1	63.5	53.4	36.6	30.0
Temperature	(Night)	21.6	24.6	26.8	33.2	44.0	54.5	64.2	63.4	49.0	40.6	30.7	25.4
Solar Flux (Horiz.)		13.1	15.9	25.7	34.7	46.6	53.0	58.3	50.2	36.4	23.8	15.1	10.5
SOUTH		25.0	23.6	27.7	28.2	30.3	28.7	30.8	33.8	34.7	31.4	27.2	20.8
SW/SE		17.9	18.7	24.7	27.1	31.7	31.2	32.8	34.6	30.8	26.4	20.9	15.6
WEST		8.6	10.8	18.1	23.3	30.4	31.3	32.1	30.7	23.0	16.7	10.7	7.5
EAST		10.3	10.9	18.5	25.0	33.6	36.7	39.2	32.3	25.0	16.0	10.8	7.8
NW/NE		4.0	5.3	11.1	18.2	26.1	28.8	29.1	22.1	14.3	7.5	4.5	3.3
NORTH		3.7	4.5	8.3	13.8	18.9	19.5	18.2	14.4	9.4	5.6	4.0	3.1

Base Temperature	40	45	50	55	60	65	70	Cooling Degree Days
Heating Degree Days	2111	3003	4045	5212	6495	7892	9404	(Base 65) = 794

City: Cheyenne, Wyoming   Latitude: 41.2°
Winter Design Temp.: -9, -1   Deep Ground Temp.:

Month		JAN	FEB	MAR	APR	MAY	JUN	JUL	AUG	SEP	OCT	NOV	DEC
Average Air	(Day)	29.7	29.5	36.8	49.0	56.3	67.1	76.1	74.3	64.7	54.5	40.0	33.7
Temperature	(Night)	21.7	22.6	28.8	37.3	44.6	54.3	61.7	60.1	51.3	42.0	31.8	27.1
Solar Flux (Horiz.)		13.7	18.6	29.4	39.3	48.4	50.4	55.0	49.0	39.9	24.3	16.8	12.9
SOUTH		24.3	26.5	30.1	30.2	29.6	27.2	29.5	32.6	36.0	31.1	29.8	25.3
SW/SE		18.3	20.5	26.3	29.1	31.0	29.9	31.3	32.8	32.9	25.2	23.5	19.6
WEST		9.2	12.2	19.1	25.1	29.7	30.3	30.9	29.9	25.1	16.1	12.4	9.4
EAST		9.7	13.4	20.5	27.1	32.7	34.9	38.7	33.5	25.4	17.2	11.6	8.8
NW/NE		4.3	6.0	12.0	18.9	25.2	27.8	29.8	23.5	14.8	8.1	4.6	3.7
NORTH		4.0	4.8	8.6	13.8	18.1	19.3	19.3	15.7	10.1	5.9	3.9	3.4

Base Temperature	40	45	50	55	60	65	70	Cooling Degree Days
Heating Degree Days	1858	2683	3678	4820	6119	7572	9140	(Base 65) = 542

(*Continued*)

TABLE C.1 (*Continued*)

City: Rock Springs, Wyoming Latitude: 41.6°
Winter Design Temp.:-9, -3 Deep Ground Temp.:43

Month		JAN	FEB	MAR	APR	MAY	JUN	JUL	AUG	SEP	OCT	NOV	DEC
Average Air (Day)		25.4	25.2	33.0	43.8	56.4	64.9	76.4	73.9	63.1	48.7	34.6	25.2
Temperature (Night)		19.1	19.6	26.0	32.2	43.1	51.9	60.2	58.9	49.1	38.8	26.7	19.1
	Solar Flux (Horiz.)	12.9	14.9	28.4	42.9	52.0	55.4	60.3	51.6	40.7	26.8	16.4	11.5
–	SOUTH	23.5	21.0	30.2	33.1	31.5	29.0	32.1	33.6	37.2	35.4	28.2	22.8
V													
E	SW/SE	18.3	16.6	26.4	31.5	33.0	32.5	35.0	34.0	33.1	29.0	21.0	16.9
R													
T	WEST	9.4	10.2	18.9	26.8	31.5	33.2	34.5	30.5	24.9	17.9	10.7	8.1
I													
C	EAST	9.0	11.0	19.4	30.4	35.8	38.4	39.8	34.8	27.5	17.8	11.8	8.8
A													
L	NW/NE	3.9	5.5	11.2	20.5	27.1	30.4	30.4	23.7	15.5	8.0	4.7	3.5
–	NORTH	3.6	4.5	8.2	14.1	18.6	20.4	20.1	14.7	9.8	5.8	4.1	3.2

Base Temperature	40	45	50	55	60	65	70		Cooling Degree Days
Heating Degree Days	2545	3528	4645	5881	7244	8729	10317		(Base 65) = 492

(*Concluded*)

TABLE C.2 **Weather Data for Canadian Cities**

City: Edmonton, Alberta   Latitude:53.6°
Winter Design Temp. Diff.:53.2   Deep Ground Temp.:1.4

Month	JAN	FEB	MAR	APR	MAY	JUN	JUL	AUG	SEP	OCT	NOV	DEC
Average Air Temp	-16.3	-12.1	-7.3	2.9	9.7	13.3	16.1	14.4	9.7	4.2	-5.6	-12.3
Solar Flux												
VERTICAL SOUTH	11.44	14.32	16.36	14.56	12.13	10.95	11.91	13.33	13.44	13.46	10.91	9.08
EAST	3.93	6.56	9.94	12.63	14.19	14.03	14.34	12.35	9.15	6.27	3.91	2.77
WEST	4.12	7.04	10.56	12.14	13.36	13.32	13.85	12.81	9.37	6.42	4.02	2.90
NORTH	1.93	3.38	5.18	5.17	6.87	7.87	7.36	4.90	3.28	2.24	1.64	1.39

City: Suffield, Alberta   Latitude:49.6°
Winter Design Temp. Diff.:47.1   Deep Ground Temp.:5.4

Month	JAN	FEB	MAR	APR	MAY	JUN	JUL	AUG	SEP	OCT	NOV	DEC
Average Air Temp	-9.4	-5.6	-2.4	5.3	10.9	14.9	18.8	17.6	12.7	7.6	-0.7	-5.5
Solar Flux												
VERTICAL SOUTH	12.69	15.79	17.06	13.39	11.72	10.77	12.27	14.19	15.2	15.55	13.25	11.67
EAST	4.75	7.44	10.63	11.87	14.37	15.10	15.92	14.39	10.77	7.68	4.86	3.92
WEST	4.73	7.53	10.68	11.54	13.32	14.09	15.45	13.74	10.81	7.45	4.97	4.00
NORTH	2.20	3.30	4.47	4.73	6.61	8.19	7.41	5.07	3.38	2.45	1.89	1.69

City: Vancouver, British Columbia   Latitude:49.2°
Winter Design Temp. Diff.:28.2   Deep Ground Temp.:9.8

Month	JAN	FEB	MAR	APR	MAY	JUN	JUL	AUG	SEP	OCT	NOV	DEC
Average Air Temp	2.4	4.4	5.8	8.9	12.4	15.3	17.4	17.1	14.2	10.1	6.1	3.8
Solar Flux												
VERTICAL SOUTH	5.38	8.89	10.44	10.92	11.06	10.16	11.27	11.68	13.10	9.32	6.20	4.94
EAST	2.08	4.01	6.47	9.05	11.49	11.75	13.04	10.68	8.66	4.58	2.41	1.75
WEST	2.21	4.34	7.05	9.94	13.13	13.52	14.54	12.37	9.49	5.22	2.68	1.80
NORTH	1.07	1.79	2.97	4.66	6.53	7.63	6.80	4.97	3.15	2.10	1.21	0.81

(Continued)

TABLE C.2 (*Continued*)

City: Winnipeg, Manitoba   Latitude:49.9⁰
Winter Design Temp. Diff.:52.7   Deep Ground Temp.:2.3

Month	JAN	FEB	MAR	APR	MAY	JUN	JUL	AUG	SEP	OCT	NOV	DEC
Average Air Temp	-18.3	-15.7	-8.1	3.3	10.6	16.5	19.7	18.7	12.6	6.6	-4.4	-13.7

Solar Flux

V E R T I C A L		JAN	FEB	MAR	APR	MAY	JUN	JUL	AUG	SEP	OCT	NOV	DEC
	SOUTH	14.23	17.60	17.98	14.05	11.41	10.45	11.26	12.47	12.91	11.10	9.56	11.52
	EAST	5.22	8.60	11.83	12.52	13.53	14.32	14.50	12.95	9.52	5.77	4.04	4.04
	WEST	5.42	8.66	11.93	11.88	12.92	13.53	14.01	12.48	8.97	5.63	4.01	4.07
	NORTH	2.44	4.02	5.59	5.06	6.31	7.78	7.13	4.91	3.23	2.19	2.02	1.88

City: Fredericton, New Brunswick   Latitude: 45.9⁰
Winter Design Temp. Diff.: 44.3   Deep Ground Temp.:5.5

Month	JAN	FEB	MAR	APR	MAY	JUN	JUL	AUG	SEP	OCT	NOV	DEC
Average Air Temp	-8.8	-8.1	-2.4	4.2	10.6	16.1	19.2	18.1	13.4	7.8	1.7	-6.2

Solar Flux

V E R T I C A L		JAN	FEB	MAR	APR	MAY	JUN	JUL	AUG	SEP	OCT	NOV	DEC
	SOUTH	12.38	14.52	13.41	10.66	8.80	8.98	9.28	10.60	10.82	11.16	9.25	10.05
	EAST	5.01	7.78	9.74	10.05	10.65	11.60	11.28	11.08	8.09	5.99	4.09	3.96
	WEST	4.92	7.45	8.87	9.58	10.20	11.82	11.76	10.81	8.26	5.94	3.73	3.73
	NORTH	2.39	3.67	4.62	4.75	5.65	6.92	6.38	5.15	3.33	2.25	1.71	1.83

City: St. John's, New Brunswick   Latitude: 47.6⁰
Winter Design Temp. Diff.: 34.9   Deep Ground Temp.:9.0

Month	JAN	FEB	MAR	APR	MAY	JUN	JUL	AUG	SEP	OCT	NOV	DEC
Average Air Temp	-4.3	-4.9	-2.9	1.2	5.6	10.3	15.0	15.1	12.0	6.7	2.9	-1.6

Solar Flux

V E R T I C A L		JAN	FEB	MAR	APR	MAY	JUN	JUL	AUG	SEP	OCT	NOV	DEC
	SOUTH	8.23	10.39	10.12	8.84	8.20	8.52	9.31	8.75	9.72	8.00	5.97	5.80
	EAST	3.72	5.84	7.27	7.91	8.73	9.86	10.05	8.22	7.15	4.59	2.77	2.47
	WEST	3.76	5.91	7.48	8.39	9.44	10.82	11.82	9.23	7.76	4.68	2.79	2.60
	NORTH	2.20	3.42	4.44	4.85	5.76	6.76	6.38	4.73	3.51	2.34	1.54	1.49

(*Continued*)

TABLE C.2 *(Continued)*

City: Halifax, Nova Scotia   Latitude: 44.7°
Winter Design Temp. Diff.: 31.6   Deep Ground Temp.:6.9

Month	JAN	FEB	MAR	APR	MAY	JUN	JUL	AUG	SEP	OCT	NOV	DEC
Average Air Temp	-3.8	-4.2	-0.7	4.0	9.0	13.7	17.6	17.8	14.8	10.1	5.2	-0.9

Solar Flux
VERTICAL

		JAN	FEB	MAR	APR	MAY	JUN	JUL	AUG	SEP	OCT	NOV	DEC
	SOUTH	10.77	12.56	12.42	10.03	8.64	8.61	8.30	9.71	10.94	11.22	8.36	8.34
	EAST	4.84	7.19	9.22	9.46	10.20	10.78	9.55	9.90	8.48	6.26	3.89	3.68
	WEST	4.76	7.09	8.86	9.40	10.38	11.50	11.00	10.29	8.72	6.46	3.82	3.53
	NORTH	2.63	3.92	4.71	4.90	5.95	6.77	6.12	4.99	3.75	2.67	1.90	1.99

City: Ottawa, Ontario   Latitude: 45.3°
Winter Design Temp. Diff.: 46.0   Deep Ground Temp.: 5.8

Month	JAN	FEB	MAR	APR	MAY	JUN	JUL	AUG	SEP	OCT	NOV	DEC
Average Air Temp	-10.9	-9.5	-3.1	5.6	12.4	18.2	20.7	19.3	14.6	8.7	1.4	-7.7

Solar Flux
VERTICAL

		JAN	FEB	MAR	APR	MAY	JUN	JUL	AUG	SEP	OCT	NOV	DEC
	SOUTH	12.16	15.00	14.46	11.98	9.21	8.83	9.20	10.43	10.79	10.80	7.56	9.65
	EAST	5.10	7.87	10.12	11.16	11.53	12.09	12.38	11.26	8.31	5.91	3.61	3.92
	WEST	4.99	8.05	10.02	10.89	11.02	11.88	11.87	11.13	8.18	5.74	3.40	3.94
	NORTH	2.56	4.06	4.99	4.53	5.84	6.74	6.32	4.93	3.20	2.24	1.79	2.06

City: Toronto, Ontario   Latitude:43.7°
Winter Design Temp. Diff.:38.2   Deep Ground Temp.:7.5

Month	JAN	FEB	MAR	APR	MAY	JUN	JUL	AUG	SEP	OCT	NOV	DEC
Average Air Temp	-6.3	-5.8	-0.9	6.4	12.2	18.2	20.7	20.0	15.7	9.8	3.4	-3.5

Solar Flux
VERTICAL

		JAN	FEB	MAR	APR	MAY	JUN	JUL	AUG	SEP	OCT	NOV	DEC
	SOUTH	10.04	12.32	12.01	11.40	8.93	8.74	9.28	10.60	11.20	10.50	6.71	7.46
	EAST	4.34	6.59	8.59	11.21	11.28	12.16	12.82	11.78	8.83	5.79	3.40	3.12
	WEST	4.41	6.60	8.51	10.54	11.13	12.03	12.29	11.53	8.95	5.84	3.24	3.15
	NORTH	2.29	3.28	4.04	4.59	5.83	6.81	6.42	4.98	3.30	2.35	1.71	1.69

(Continued)

TABLE C.2 (*Continued*)

City: Montreal, Quebec   Latitude: 45.5°
Winter Design Temp. Diff.: 44.3   Deep Ground Temp.: 6.5

Month	JAN	FEB	MAR	APR	MAY	JUN	JUL	AUG	SEP	OCT	NOV	DEC
Average Air Temp	-9.9	-8.8	-2.3	5.9	12.8	18.5	21.2	19.9	15.3	9.4	2.3	-6.6

Solar Flux

VERTICAL		JAN	FEB	MAR	APR	MAY	JUN	JUL	AUG	SEP	OCT	NOV	DEC
	SOUTH	12.82	15.50	15.27	12.24	9.86	9.39	9.80	10.96	11.65	11.75	8.42	9.93
	EAST	5.35	8.24	10.70	11.34	12.34	12.54	13.02	11.71	9.05	6.50	3.90	4.06
	WEST	5.53	8.50	10.81	11.37	11.63	12.83	12.62	11.75	9.00	6.31	3.90	4.19
	NORTH	2.86	4.33	5.34	4.93	6.30	7.16	6.70	5.22	3.49	2.53	2.03	2.24

City: Saskatoon, Saskatchewan   Latitude: 52.2°
Winter Design Temp. Diff.: 55.0   Deep Ground Temp.: 5.0

Month	JAN	FEB	MAR	APR	MAY	JUN	JUL	AUG	SEP	OCT	NOV	DEC
Average Air Temp	-18.0	-15.0	-7.8	3.9	12.0	15.0	17.0	16.5	11.7	5.0	-5.6	-13.3

Solar Flux

VERTICAL		JAN	FEB	MAR	APR	MAY	JUN	JUL	AUG	SEP	OCT	NOV	DEC
	SOUTH	13.69	17.91	19.21	14.54	12.22	11.08	11.98	13.78	13.99	13.83	11.64	11.42
	EAST	4.64	8.04	11.84	12.63	14.41	14.42	14.97	13.44	9.86	6.63	4.24	3.52
	WEST	4.75	8.10	12.04	12.26	14.09	14.78	15.01	13.74	9.76	6.60	4.37	3.59
	NORTH	2.02	3.59	5.24	4.74	6.49	7.99	7.38	4.90	3.19	2.22	1.79	1.58

City: Swift Current, Saskatchewan   Latitude: 50.3°
Winter Design Temp. Diff.: 52.7   Deep Ground Temp.: 3.3

Month	JAN	FEB	MAR	APR	MAY	JUN	JUL	AUG	SEP	OCT	NOV	DEC
Average Air Temp	-13.6	-11.1	-5.7	3.7	10.3	14.8	18.6	17.6	11.7	6.1	-3.7	-10.0

Solar Flux

VERTICAL		JAN	FEB	MAR	APR	MAY	JUN	JUL	AUG	SEP	OCT	NOV	DEC
	SOUTH	12.94	16.50	17.77	13.69	11.87	10.70	11.78	13.33	14.20	13.91	11.85	11.44
	EAST	4.79	7.99	11.75	12.41	14.44	14.64	15.09	13.40	10.12	6.83	4.49	3.87
	WEST	4.83	8.08	11.39	11.77	13.26	14.03	14.85	13.08	9.90	6.96	4.57	3.88
	NORTH	2.23	3.81	5.36	5.20	6.69	8.05	7.08	4.64	3.13	2.32	1.85	1.66

(*Concluded*)

This appendix includes listings of products and manufacturers. The lists are not complete, but rather are representative of products and materials on the market today. We have attempted to include those items that are typically hard to locate.

ENERGY ANALYSIS COMPUTER SOFTWARE

1. HOTCAN

Described in Chapter 6, this program is a most valuable and easy-to-use tool for the designer or builder of superinsulated houses. In Canada (with Canadian weather data):

Division of Building Research
National Research Council of Canada
Saskatoon, Saskatchewan S7N 0W9

In the U.S. (with U.S. weather data):

Energy Design Associates, Inc.
Box 1709 Ansonia Station
New York, NY 10023
(212) 662 7428

AIR AND VAPOR SEALING PRODUCTS

1. Cross laminated polyethylene:

Tu-Tuf	Rufco 300 and 400
Sto-Cote Products, Inc.	Raven Industries, Inc.
P.O. Box 310	Box 1007
Richmond, IL 60071	Sioux Falls, SD 57117

2. Acoustical sealant for sealing polyethylene air/vapor barriers:

Tremco Acoustical Sealant	10701 Shaker Blvd.
Tremco	Cleveland, OH 44104

3. Spun-bonded polyethylene for air barriers:

Tyvek	Parsec Airtight White
E.I. DuPont, Fibers Dept.	Parsec, Inc.
Centre Road	P.O. Box 38534
Wilmington, DE 19898	Dallas, TX 75238

4. Plastic "polypans" for sealing around electrical boxes:

Solatech	Energy Conservation
7726 Morgan Ave. S.	Equipment
Minneapolis, MN 55423	Box 161
	Worcester, VT 05682
Iberville Products	N.R.G. Saver
100 Longtin	Box 50, Group 32
Saint-Jean-Sur-Richelieu	RR 1B
Quebec, J3B 3G5	Winnipeg, Manitoba R3C 4A3
Canada	Canada

5. Tape for sealing air/vapor barriers and foam sheathing:

Parsec Thermobrite Tape	Contractor Sheathing Tape
Parsec, Inc.	3M Canada
Box 38534	Box 5757
Dallas, TX 75238	London, Ontario
	N6A 4T1 Canada

6. Surface mounted electrical systems:

Gould Electrostrip
George E. Anderson Company
1700 S. Ervay Street
Dallas, TX 75215

INSULATION VENTILATION BAFFLES

ProperVent
Poly Foam Inc.
c/o Residential Products
  Marketers
4901 West 77th Street
Minneapolis, MN 55435

Insul-Tray
Insul-Tray, Inc.
4985 North Cascade Place
Oak Harbor, WA 98277

REFLECTIVE PANELS FOR UNDER-ROOF INSTALLATION

Retroflect Panel
Parsec, Inc.
Box 38534
Dallas, TX 75238

POLYETHYLENE FOAM FOR INSULATING BAND JOISTS

Sill Band Sealer
Sentinel Energy Saving Products
Division of Packaging Industries Group, Inc.
Hyannis, MA 02601

TRUSS SYSTEMS

The Larsen Truss System
Passive Solar Design
  Associates Ltd.
#204 10830 107 Ave.
Edmonton, Alberta T5H 0X3
Canada

SuperTruss
Roki Associates
Box 232
Gorham, Maine 04038

FOUNDATION COATINGS

Conproco
Conproco Corporation
Box 368
Hookset, NH 03106

Dryvit
Dryvit Systems, Inc.
1 Energy Way
Box 1014
West Warwick, RI 02893

Insul/Crete
Insul/Crete Company
4311 Triangle Street
McFarland, WI 53558

Insul-Guard
Trend Products
Box 327
Waupaca, WI 54981

R-Wall
ISPO, Inc.
792 S. Main St.
Mansfield, MA 02048

Surewall
Surewall Producer's Council
Box 241148
Charlotte, NC 28224

Thermaseal
Akona Corporation
1570 Halgren Rd.
Maple Plain, MN 55359

Thoroseal
Thoro Systems Products
7800 NW 38th St.
Miami, FL 33166

BLOWER DOOR MANUFACTURERS

Ener-Corp Management Ltd.
2 Donald Street
Winnipeg, Manitoba R3L 0K5
Canada

The Energy Conservatory
920 West 53rd St.
Minneapolis, MN 55419

Gadzco, Inc.
209 Vetterlein Ave.
Trenton, NJ 08619

Harmax Corp.
6224 Orange Street
Los Angeles, CA 90048

Infiltec
Box 1533
Falls Church, VA 22041

Retrotec Innovations Ltd.
176 Bronson Avenue
Ottawa, Ontario K1R 6H4
Canada

VENTILATING, HEATING AND AIR-CONDITIONING EQUIPMENT

Air-to-Air Heat Exchangers

The following is a partial list of manufacturers of air-to-air heat exchangers at the time of the writing. No claim is made about the completeness of this list.

The Air Changer Co. Ltd.
334 King St. East, Suite 505
Toronto, Ontario, Canada
(416) 947 1105

Air-X-Changer, Inc.
30 Pond Park Rd.
Hingham, MA 02043
(617) 749 8440

Aldes-Riehs
Box 157, Glenfield Road
Sewickley, PA 15143
(412) 741 2659

Automated Controls &
  Systems
ACS-Hoval
935 Lively Road
Wood Dale, IL 60191
(312) 860 6800

Berner International Corp.
216 New Boston St.
Woburn, MA 01801
(617) 933 2180

Blackhawk Industries, Inc.
607 Park St.
Regina, Saskatchewan,
  Canada S4N 5N1
(306) 924 1551

Bossaire
417 Broadway
Minneapolis, MN 55411
(612) 521 7563

Conservation Energy
  Systems, Inc.
Box 8280
Saskatoon, Saskatchewan,
  Canada S7K 6C6
(306) 665 6030

Des Champs Laboratories, Inc.
Box 440
17 Farinella Drive
East Hanover, NJ 07936
(201) 884 1460

EER Products, Inc.
4501 Bruce Ave.
Minneapolis, MN 55424
(612) 926 3999

Ener-Corp Management Ltd.
Two Donald Street
Winnipeg, Manitoba,
  Canada R3L 0K5
(204) 477 1283

Heatex, Inc.
5100 Eden Ave., Suite 101
Minneapolis, MN 55436
(612) 926 3999

Memphremegog Heat
  Exchangers, Inc.
Box 456
Newport, VT 05855
(802) 334 5412

Mountain Energy &
  Resources, Inc.
15800 West Sixth Ave.
Golden, CO 80401
(303) 279 4971

Nutone Housing Group
Scovill Inc.
Madison and Red Bank Roads
Cincinnati, OH 45227
(513) 527 5112

Q-Dot Corp.
701 North First St.
Garland, TX 75040
(214) 487 1130

Star Heat Exchangers
2143 Fraser Ave.
Port Coquitlam, BC
(604) 942 0525

Mitsubishi Electric Sales
  America, Inc.
3030 East Victoria St.
Rancho Cominguez,
  CA 90221
(800) 421 1132

Nutech Energy
  Systems, Inc.
Box 640
Exeter, Ontario,
  Canada N0M 1S0
(519) 235 1440

P.M. Wright Ltd.
1300 Jules Poitras
Montreal, Quebec,
  Canada H4N 1X8
(514) 337 3331

Solartronics, Inc.
Box 534
Fargo, ND 58107
(701) 232 4232

**Dehumidistat for Controlling Air-to-Air
Heat Exchangers**

Ranco J10-809
Ranco
Controls Division
8115 U.S. Route 42 North
Plain City, OH 43064

Direct-Vented Natural Gas Furnaces

The Catalyte
Catalyte Energy Systems
A Division of MTD Products,
  Inc.
P.O. Box 8971
Cleveland, OH 44136

The Lennox Pulse Furnace
Lennox dealers may be found
  in the Yellow Pages.

Suburban Manufacturing
  Company
Box 399
Dayton, TN 37321

Empire Stove Company
918 Freeburg Avenue
Belleville, IL 62222

Locke Stove Company
114 West 11th Street
Kansas City, MO 64105

Williams Furnace Company
225 Acacia Street
Colton, CA 92324

Other sealed combustion furnaces, designed for use in mobile homes, campers, etc. are made by several manufacturers. Contact mobile home heating system suppliers for more information.

Direct-Vented Natural Gas Boilers

Heatmaker HW-series:
BGP Systems, Inc.
141 California St.
Newton, MA 02158

Netaheat:
Ener-quip
99 East Kansas St.
Hackensack, NJ 07601

Hydropulse
Hydrotherm, Inc.
Rockland Ave.
Northvale, NJ 07647

Thermar Powermaster
The Tankless Heater Corporation
Melrose Square
Greenwich, CT 06830

Central Air Conditioners

There is a wide range in the performance of available central air conditioners. Table D.1 lists the most efficient central air conditioners as of mid-1983. The information presented includes brand names and seasonal energy efficiency ratios (SEER); the higher the value of SEER, the more energy conserving it is.

Room Air Conditioners

Table D.2 lists the corresponding information for room air conditioners.

ENERGY-EFFICIENT WATER HEATERS

Heat-Pump Water Heaters

There are numerous manufacturers of heat-pump water heaters for domestic use. The following are the manufacturers of the top-rated integrated units (i.e., not requiring a separate tank) as of July 1984:

1. Therma-Stor
Dairy Equipment Corporation
Available in 52- and 80-gallon models of comparable efficiency.
2. Mor-Flo/American
Available in 50-, 66-, 82-, and 120-gallons models, all of comparable efficiency.

Direct Vented Natural Gas Water Heaters

The only direct-vented storage gas water heater (i.e., with storage tank) on the market early in 1984 is the Turbo Super Saver by State Industries. It comes in 30 and 40 gallon sizes. A. O. Smith is scheduled to introduce, in mid-1984, a new high-efficiency line of gas water heaters called the PGCS series. Both the Turbo Super Saver and the PGCS series are significantly more efficient than conventional gas water heaters.

A direct-vented *tankless* water heater called the Thermar is available from the Tankless Heater Corporation, Melrose, CT 06830.

On the horizon is a sealed-combustion gas water heater with power burner being developed at Advanced

Mechanical Technology, Inc. of Newton, Massachusetts. This unit is expected to be more efficient than other storage-type gas water heaters.

Low-Flow Shower Heads There are many low-flow shower heads commonly available. The very-low-flow compressed air-driven shower, MINUSE, is available from:

Water and Power Conservation International (MINUSE)
P.O. Box 310
Mokelumne Hill, CA 95425

ENERGY-EFFICIENT APPLIANCES

Tables D.3 through D.6 list the most efficient refrigerators, freezers, clothes washers, and dishwashers sold in the United States. This information, together with the most efficient air conditioners listed in tables D.1 and D.2, ir reprinted with permission from *The Most Energy Efficient Appliances, Spring 84,* compiled by the American Council for an Energy-Efficient Economy (ACEEE). ACEEE expects to update these lists twice a year. Contact: ACEEE, 1001 Connecticut Ave., Suite 530, Washington, DC 20036.

Refrigerators

The most efficient refrigerators as of Spring, 1984 are listed in Table D.3 by capacity and defrost characteristics. We have listed the units by capacity without model numbers because model numbers change frequently. Since many manufacturers produce several models with equal capacity but different efficiency, care should be taken to select the most efficient unit.

The annual electricity consumption (kWh per year) of the models are also listed in Table D.3. To find out the energy consumption of a model from the yellow "Energyguide" label posted on the appliance, simply divide the dollar figure printed in large letters on the label by the assumed price of electricity printed on the label. In 1983, this was 7.63 cents per kWh. For instance if a 17.1 cubic foot automatic-defrost refrigerator has an Energyguide label reading $67 and the electricity price is 7.63 cents per kWh, then it is expected to consume 67/0.0763 or 880 kWh/yr.

Freezers

Table D.4 lists the brand names, capacity, defrost characteristics and estimated annual energy use of freezers. The above comments on refrigerators also apply to the choice of freezers.

Clothes Washers and Dishwashers

Tables D.5 and D.6 list the brand names and estimated annual energy use and energy cost of clothes washers and dishwashers. The tables assume that hot water is provided by electricity.

TABLE D.1 Most Efficient Central Air Conditioners

Capacity Range: 22,000 to 28,000 Btu/hr	
Brand	SEER
Coleman (T.H.E. Series)	13.3, 12.9
Bryant (Super efficient)	13.2
Day & Night (Super efficient)	13.2
Payne (Super efficient)	13.2
Lennox (Landmark III/IV)	13.15, 13.0
Trane	12.4
Rheem/Rund	12.3

Capacity Range: 28,000 to 34,000 Btu/hr	
Brand	SEER
Coleman (T.H.E. Series)	13.2, 12.8
Lennox (Landmark III)	12.5
Bryant (Super efficient)	12.1
Day & Night (Super efficient)	12.1
Payne (Super efficient)	12.1

Capacity Range: 34,000 to 40,000 Btu/hr	
Brand	SEER
Lennox (Landmark III/IV)	14.0, 12.7
Coleman (T.H.E. Series)	12.4
Bryant (Super efficient)	12.1

TABLE D.1 (*Continued*)

Day & Night (Super efficient)	12.1
Payne (Super efficient)	12.1
Rheem/Ruud	12.1

Capacity: Greater Than 40,000 Btu/hr	
Brand	SEER
Lennox	12.0–12.65

TABLE D.2 Most Efficient Room Air Conditioners

Capacity Range: 5,000 to 6,999 Btu/hr	
Brand	EER
Emerson	9.5
Kenmore	9.4
Airtemp	9.0
Amana	9.0
Carrier	9.0
Climatrol	9.0
Fedders	9.0
Friedrich	9.0
Montgomery Ward	9.0

TABLE D.2 (*Continued*)

Sanyo	9.0
White-Westinghouse	9.0

Capacity range: 7,000 to 8,999 Btu/hr

Brand	EER
Friedrich	10.1, 9.8
Citation	9.6
Gibson	9.6
Kelvinator	9.6
Kenmore	9.6
Tempmaster	9.6

Capacity Range: 9,000 to 10,999 Btu/hr

Brand	EER
Friedrich	11.5
Carrier	11.0
General Electric	10.9, 10.3
Friedrich	10.3

Capacity Range: 11,000 to 12,999 Btu/hr

Brand	EER
Sanyo	9.6
Carrier	9.5
Climatrol	9.0
Fedders	9.0
Frigidaire	9.0
General Electric	9.0
Montgomery Ward	9.0
White-Westinghouse	9.0

Capacity Range: 13,000 to 14,999 Btu/hr

Brand	EER
Kenmore	9.9
Whirlpool	9.9
Friedrich	9.6
Kenmore	9.6
Climatrol	9.2
Airtemp	9.2
Fedders	9.2

Capacity Range: 15,000 to 16,999 Btu/hr

Brand	EER
Comfort-aire (230 volt)	9.1
General Electric (230V)	8.7
Hotpoint (230 volt)	8.7
Panasonic (230 volt)	8.7
Kelvinator (230 volt)	8.7
General Electric (115V)	8.5
Hotpoint (115 volt)	8.5

Capacity Range: 17,000 to 19,999 Btu/hr

Brand (All 230 volts)	EER
Friedrich	9.3
Climatrol	9.3
Fedders	9.3
Emerson	9.3
Frigidaire	9.0
Montgomery Ward	9.0
White Westinghouse	9.0

TABLE D.3 Most Efficient Refrigerators

Single Door, Manual Defrost, 10 to 13 Cu. Ft.

Brand	Cu. Ft.	kWh/yr	$/yr
Absocold	10.3	390	30
Kenmore	11.0	430	33
Sanyo	11.0	430	33

Top Freezer, Partial Automatic Defrost, 12 to 15 Cu. Ft.

Brand	Cu. Ft.	kWh/yr	$/yr
Amana	14.2	640	49
Kenmore	12.0	760	58
Whirlpool	12.4	790	60

Top Freezer, Automatic Defrost, 14 to 16.4 Cu. Ft.

Brand	Cu. Ft.	kWh/yr	$/yr
Amana	14.2	920	70
Caloric	16.0	940	72
Coronado	16.0	940	72
Frigidaire	16.0	940	72
Gibson	16.0	940	72
Kelvinator	16.0	940	72
Kenmore	16.0	940	72
Tempmaster	16.0	940	72
White-Westinghouse	16.0	940	72

Top Freezer, Automatic Defrost, 16.5 to 18.4 Cu. Ft.

Brand	Cu. Ft.	kWh/yr	$/yr
Kenmore	17.1	880	67
Whirlpool	17.2	880	67
Amana	17.7–17.8	965	74
Kenmore	18.0	980	75
Whirlpool	18.0	980	75

Top Freezer, Automatic Defrost, 18.5 to 20.4 Cu. Ft.

Brand	Cu. Ft.	kWh/yr	$/yr
Amana	19.7–19.9	1020	78
Kenmore	19.6	1090	83
Whirlpool	19.5	1090	83
Gibson	19.0	1110	85
White-Westinghouse	19.0	1110	85

Top Freezer, Automatic Defrost, 20.5 to 22.4 Cu. Ft.

Brand	Cu. Ft.	kWh/yr	$/yr
Crosley	21.0	1075	82
Whirlpool	22.2	1180	90

Side-By-Side Freezer, Automatic Defrost, 18.5 to 20 Cu. Ft.

Brand	Cu. Ft.	kWh/yr	$/yr
Kenmore	19.1	1320	101
Whirlpool	19.1	1320	101

Side-by-Side Freezer, Automatic Defrost, 20 to 25 Cu. Ft.

Brand	Cu. Ft.	kWh/yr	$/yr
Kelvinator	22.0	1300	99
Philco	22.0	1300	99
White-Westinghouse	22.0	1300	99
Frigidaire	24.0	1300	99
Gibson	24.0	1300	99
Marquette	24.0	1300	99

TABLE D.4 Most Efficient Freezers

Upright, Manual Defrost, 14 to 17 Cu. Ft.

Brand	Cu. Ft.	kWh/yr	$/yr
Kenmore	15.1	730, 770	56, 59
Whirlpool	15.1	770	59

Upright, Manual Defrost, 18 to 21 Cu. Ft.

Brand	Cu. Ft.	kWh/yr	$/yr
Kenmore	20.0	810, 880	62, 67
Whirlpool	20.0	810	62

Upright, Automatic Defrost, 14 to 17 Cu. Ft.

Brand	Cu. Ft.	kWh/yr	$/yr
Whirlpool	15.2	1010	77
Amana	14.1	1110	85
Amana	16.2	1270	97

Upright, Automatic Defrost, 18 to 21 Cu. Ft.

Brand	Cu. Ft.	kWh/yr	$/yr
Kenmore	19.6	1245	95
Whirlpool	19.6	1245	95

Chest, Manual Defrost, 14 to 17 Cu. Ft.

Brand	Cu. Ft.	kWh/yr	$/yr
W.C. Wood Co.	14.8	500	38
Amana	15.0	710	54
Kenmore	15.1	710	54
Whirlpool	15.2	710	54

Chest, Manual Defrost, 17.5 to 21 Cu. Ft.

Brand	Cu. Ft.	kWh/yr	$/yr
W.C. Wood Co.	20.3	525	40
W.C. Wood Co.	17.7	550	42
Gensave	19.5	575	44
HPC	19.5	575	44

TABLE D.5 Most Efficient Clothes Washers

Style: Compact
(Less Than 16 Gallons Capacity)

Brand	kWh/yr*	$/yr
Philco	360	27
General Electric	623	48
J.C. Penney	623	48
Kelvinator	623	48
Warranty Central	623	48
White-Westinghouse	623	48

Style: Standard
(Greater Than 16 Gallons Capacity)

Brand	kw/yr*	$/yr
Gibson	486	37
White-Westinghouse	486	37
Philco	506	39
Montgomery Ward	594	45
White-Westinghouse	594	45

* Based on electric resistance water heating

TABLE D.6 Most Efficient Dishwashers

Brand	kWh/yr*	$/yr
Gaffers and Sattler	643	49
Kenmore	643	49
Frigidaire	712	54
White-Westinghouse	712	54
Gibson	714	54
Kelvinator	714	54
Montgomery Ward	714	54

* Based on electric resistance water heating

In this appendix we list books, reports, periodicals, and organizations that provide additional information and services of potential interest to designers, builders, and owners of superinsulated houses.

BOOKS

1. *Superinsulated and Double-envelope Houses,* by William A. Shurcliff. Brick House Publishing Co., 1981.

    The first book on superinsulated houses.

2. *Thermal Shutters and Shades,* by William A. Shurcliff. Brick House Publishing Co., 1980.

    More than you may ever want to know about the subject. Very thorough and complete discussion on all kinds of ways of reducing window heat loss at night.

3. *Air-to-Air Heat Exchangers for Houses,* by William A. Shurcliff. Brick House Publishing Co., 1982.

    This is the first book on the subject. The operating principles of heat exchangers are explained carefully and in detail. Also includes a comparison of the various models of heat exchangers then available.

4. *Super-Solar Houses,* by William A. Shurcliff. Brick House Publishing Co., 1984.

    Describes the principles of operation of Norman Saunders's cleverly designed solar houses, which require no auxiliary heat, even in Massachusetts.

5. *Earth Sheltered Residential Design Manual,* by the University of Minnesota, Underground Space Center. Van Nostrand Reinhold Company, 1982.

    Although written about underground homes, this book provides exceptionally good information about below grade heat loss and insulation, much of which can be applied to superinsulation foundation insulation design.

6. *Sun/Earth Buffering and Superinsulation,* by Don Booth. Community Builders, 1983.

    A good presentation of low-energy design principles, incorporating passive solar and superinsulation.

7. *Superhouse,* by Don Metz. Garden Way Publishing, 1981.

    Conceptual design approach, incorporating passive solar, superinsulation, earth-sheltering, and double envelope principles.

8. *Builders' Guide to Energy Efficiency in New Housing,* by the Housing & Urban Development Association of Canada, 1980.

    Many design details and economic analyses for several types of low-energy house designs.

9. *New House Planning & Idea Book,* by Alberta Agriculture. Brick House Publishing Company, 1983.

    A basic book on energy-efficient house design.

10. *The Superinsulated Retrofit Book,* by Brian Marshall and Robert Argue. Published by Renewable Energy in Canada, Toronto, 1981. Superinsulation for existing houses.

11. *Indoor Air Pollution: Characterization, Prediction, and Control,* by Richard A. Wadden and Peter A. Scheff. John Wiley & Sons, Inc. Publishers, 1983.

    This scholarly work will be of particular interest to the technically oriented reader interested in finding out more about air pollutants, their health effects, and techniques for measuring them. The chapter on indoor air-quality control, though useful, does not contain some of the recently developed techniques for air pollution control in houses. Masses of data in tables and figures make this book a useful reference.

12. *Indoor Air Quality Handbook,* by Environmental Studies, Anachem Inc. and the Environmental Research Division of Sandia National Laboratories. Sandia Report SAND 82-1773. Available from:
National Technical Information Service
U.S. Department of Commerce
5285 Port Royal Road
Springfield, VA 22161

This 180-page handbook is intended for "designers, builders, and users of energy-efficient residences." It is easy to read and well illustrated. The Handbook sections on techniques for measurement and control of individual indoor air contaminants would be useful to designers and builders who are interested in looking further into the subject of indoor air quality. This book was the source of much of the information on indoor air pollutants presented in Chapter 4.

13. *Air Vapor Barriers,* by D. Eyre and D. Jennings, Saskatchewan Research Council, 1981.

This is the first book detailing the construction of superinsulated houses based on research and the experience of builders in Saskatchewan. Many of their design details have been adapted in this book. Available from Energy, Mines, and Resources Canada, Energy Conservation & Oil Substitution Branch, 580 Booth St., Ottawa Ontario, K1A OE4.

REPORTS

1. *Heat Recovery Ventilation for Housing: Air-to-Air Heat Exchangers,* by Robert J. Corbett and Barbara A. Miller of the National Center for Appropriate Technology (NCAT), Butte, MT, 1984.

A very well-written booklet. The authors were kind enough to let us excerpt significant portions of this booklet in our Chapter 12. The booklet discusses principles of operation, but focuses on practical aspects of choosing, sizing, and installing air-to-air heat exchangers.

2. *Moisture and Home Energy Conservation: How to Detect, Solve, and Avoid Related Problems,* by Toby T. Benson and Barbara A. Miller, National Center for Appropriate Technology (NCAT), Butte, Montana, 1983. Report No. DOE/CE/15095-4, available from U.S. Govt. Printing Office, Washington, DC 20402.

A good general introduction to understanding moisture flow in houses.

PERIODICALS

Many of the popular scientific and housing magazines often contain articles relevant to superinsulation construction. In addition, the following newsletters are particularly useful.

1. *Energy Design Update*
Cahners Publishing Company
221 Columbus Avenue
Boston, MA 02116
(617) 536 7780
Edited by J. D. Ned Nisson, co-author of this book, EDU provides the latest "nuts-and-bolts" information about superinsulation design and construction. Published monthly.

2. *Superinsulated Building Newsletter*
56 John F. Kennedy St., Suite 7
Cambridge, MA 02138
Less technical than *Energy Design Update,* this newsletter is generally limited to policy news and commentary.

3. *Energy and Housing Report*
Tri-State Associates
951 Pershing Drive
Silver Spring, MD 20910
This newsletter deals mostly with national news on residential energy conservation.

ORGANIZATIONS

1. Division of Building Research
National Research Council of Canada
Saskatoon, Saskatchewan S7N 0W9
(306) 665 5248

One of the most important centers for superinsulation research in North America. Together with the Saskatchewan Research Council, the Canadian NRC in Saskatoon was responsible for the design and construction of the Saskatchewan Conservation Home.

2. Applied Science Division
Lawrence Berkeley Laboratory
University of California, Berkeley
Berkeley, CA 94720

3. Center for Building Technology
National Bureau of Standards
U.S. Department of Commerce
Washington, DC 20234

The above two listings are major centers of government-sponsored research on energy efficiency in housing. Other research centers include various universities, private research organizations, and manufacturers, but these are too numerous to list here.

4. The National Center for Appropriate Technology (NCAT)
   Box 3838
   Butte, MT 59702

   This organization produces numerous booklets and audio-visual materials about superinsulation and other energy-related topics.

5. Superinsulation Designs:
   Corbett/Hansen & Associates
   Box 3706
   Butte, MT 59702

   This private group sells house plans and provides consultation and design services for superinsulated houses. Their house plans are considered the best available.

6. Rochester Area Vocational Technical Institute
   1926 Second Street S.E.
   Rochester, MN 55904

   This school sponsors the national conferences on superinsulation and produces educational materials on superinsulation.

7. Center for Energy and Environmental Studies
   Princeton University
   Princeton, NJ 08544

   This group developed the Princeton Scorekeeping Method (Chapter 14) and performs other re-search in the field of home energy conservation. For information, contact Dr. Margaret Fels.

8. National Indoor Environmental Institute
   5200 Butler Pike,
   Plymouth Meeting, PA 19462

   The National Indoor Environmental Institute provides measurement, analytical, investigation, certification, and educational services in the field of indoor air quality. NIEI has prepared a publication entitled *Indoor Air Pollution: A Serious Health Hazard*. We have excerpted portions of this well-written booklet (with their permission) in Chapter 4 of this book.

9. Princeton Energy Partners
   P.O. Box 1221
   Princeton, NJ 08542.

   This company provides training in the use of infrared thermography combined with house pressurization for testing houses.

10. Energy Design Associates, Inc.
    P.O. Box 1709 Anconia Station
    New York, NY 10023
    (212) 662 7428

    A private design organization offering a wide variety of information services about energy-efficient design and construction, including design consultation, training, and preparation of instructional materials.

Appendix F
S.I. units, conversion factors, and energy content of fuels

This book is written in Imperial units, which are commonly used in the United States. Practically all other countries have adopted the International System of Units (S.I.). In this appendix, we first introduce the basic S.I. units and some of the derived units relevant to the design of energy-efficient houses (Table F.1). We then list some of the more useful conversion factors (Table F.2). Finally, we list the energy content of various fuels (Table F.3).

TABLE F.1

Basic S.I. Units of Measurement

Quantity	Name	Symbol
length	meter	m
mass	kilogram	kg
time	second	s
electric current	ampere	A
temperature	kelvin	K

Derived S.I. Units

area	square meter	m^2
conductivity, thermal, k	watt millimeter per square meter degree Celsius	$W\,mm/m^2.°C$
density	kilogram per cubic meter	kg/m^3
energy	joule	J
force	newton	N
frequency	hertz	Hz
potential, electric	volt	V
power, radiant flux	watt	W
pressure	pascal	Pa
volume	cubic meter	m^3

TABLE F.2   Conversion Factors

The conversion factors presented below are for converting quantities in Imperial units to S.I. units. For a reverse conversion, the appropriate conversion factor is merely the reciprocal of the number listed below. For instance, to convert an R-value into the S.I. units, called RSI, we would multiply by 0.176. Thus an R-30 wall becomes an RSI-5.28 wall. To convert from RSI to R, we would divide by 0.176. Thus an RSI-9 ceiling becomes an R-51.1 ceiling.

Multiply	By	To Obtain
Btu	1.055	kJ
Btu/ft^3	37.3	kJ/m^3, J/l
Btu/gal (US)	0.279	kJ/l
Btu-in/ft^2-hr-°F (k, thermal conductivity)	144	$W.mm/m^2.°C$
Btu/hr	0.293	W
Btu/ft^2	11.4	kJ/m^2
Btu/hr-ft^2	3.15	W/m^2
Btu/ft^2-hr-°F (U, overall heat transfer coefficient)	5.68	$W/m^2.°C$
Btu/lb	2.33	kJ/kg
Btu/lb-°F (specific heat)	4.19	kJ/kg.°C
cents per gallon	0.264	cents/l
cents per gallon (no. 2 fuel oil)	0.0677	$/GJ
cents per gallon (no. 6 fuel oil)	0.0632	$/GJ
cents per gallon (propane)	0.112	$/GJ
cents per kWh	2.78	$/GJ
cents per therm	0.0948	$/GJ
cost, $ per square foot	10.8	$/m^2$
cost, $ per pound	2.205	$/kg

(Continued)

TABLE F.2 (*Continued*)

Multiply	By	To Obtain
ft	0.3048	m
ft^2	0.0929	m^2
ft^3	28.3	1
ft^3	0.0283	m^3
ft/min	0.00508	m/s
ft/s	0.3048	m/s
ft^3/hr	7.87	ml/s
ft^3/min (cfm)	0.472	l/s
ft^3/s	28.3	l/s
ft^2-hr-°F/Btu (R, thermal resistance)	0.176	m^2.°C/W
gallon (U.S.)	3.79	l
gallon (U.S.)	0.00379	m^3
gpm (U.S.)	0.0631	l/s
grain (1/7000 lb)	0.0648	g
horsepower	0.746	kW
inch	25.4	mm
in of mercury	3.38	kPa
in of water	249	Pa
in^2 (area)	645	mm^2
in^3 (volume)	16.4	ml
kWh	3.60	MJ
litre	0.001	m^3
mile	1.61	km
mph	1.61	km/h
mph	0.447	m/s

TABLE F.2 (*Continued*)

Multiply	By	To Obtain
perm (permeance)	57.4	10^{-6}g/kPa.s.m^2
perm inch (permeability)	1460	10^{-6}g.mm/kPa.s.m^2
pint (liquid)	473	ml
pound mass (lb)	0.454	kg
pound mass	454	g
lb/ft^3 (density)	16.0	kg/m^3
ppm	1.00	mg/kg
psi	6.89	kPa
R-value	0.176	RSI value
therm	106	MJ
watt per square foot	10.8	W/m^2

TABLE F.3   Energy Content of Various Fuels

Natural gas	1025 Btu/cubic ft	38.2 kJ/l
Fuel oil		
#2	138,000 Btu/gal	38.5 MJ/l
#6	153,000 Btu/gal	42.7 MJ/l
Propane	92,000 Btu/gal	25.7 MJ/l
Electricity	3413 Btu/kWh	3.6 MJ/kWh

Index